Education and Troubled Times

"Progressive educators have always been better at critique than at possibility. This book promises not to ignore critique, but to favor possibility. It is most rare and greatly welcomed."

Richard Quantz, Miami University

"The editor argues that in a material world, depicted by consumerism, spiritual nihilism and conspicuous consumption, there is need to offer a new vision and direction in education that would promote a more harmonious, holistic, values-oriented schooling that transforms persons into moral beings, who care for others. ... In terms of innovative ideas and approaches to pedagogy and theorizing about schooling, this volume is at the top of pedagogical discourses and thinking."

Joseph Zajda, Australian Catholic University (Melbourne Campus)

Education and Hope in Troubled Times brings together a group of the best and most creative educational thinkers to reflect on the purpose and future of public education. These original essays by leading social and educational commentators in North America attempt to articulate a new vision for education, especially public education, and begin to set an alternative direction. This is a time of crisis, but also of renewed possibility—one that offers the opportunity to radically reconsider what is the meaning of education for a generation that will bear the brunt of grappling with the extraordinary dangers and challenges we confront today. At its core, this volume questions what it will mean to be an educated human being in the twenty-first century, compelled to confront and address so much that threatens the very basis of a decent and hopeful human existence. Carrying forward a project of redefining and reshaping public discourse on education in the U.S., it is a critical catalyst and focus for rethinking public policy on education.

H. Svi Shapiro is Professor in the Department of Educational Leadership and Cultural Foundations, University of North Carolina at Greensboro. His professional interests include critical and liberatory pedagogies; the moral and spiritual dimensions of education; education and social policy as these relate to social justice, huma   ial change and peace education; and qualitativ

Sociocultural, Political, and Historical Studies in Education

Joel Spring, Editor

Shapiro (Ed.) • *Education and Hope in Troubled Times: Visions of Change for Our Children's World*

Spring • *Globalization of Education: An Introduction*

Benham (Ed.) • *Indigenous Educational Models for Contemporary Practice: In Our Mother's Voice, Second Edition*

Shaker/Heilman • *Reclaiming Education for Democracy: Thinking Beyond No Child Left Behind*

Ogbu (Ed.) • *Minority Status, Oppositional Culture, and Schooling*

Spring • *Wheels in the Head: Educational Philosophies of Authority, Freedom, and Culture from Confucianism to Human Rights, Third Edition*

Spring • *The Intersection of Cultures: Global Multicultural Education, Fourth Edition*

Gabbard (Ed.) • *Knowledge and Power in the Global Economy: The Effects of School Reform in a Neoliberal/Neoconservative Age, Second Edition*

Spring • *A New Paradigm for Global School Systems: Education for a Long and Happy Life*

Books (Ed.) • *Invisible Children in the Society and Its Schools, Third Edition*

Spring • *Pedagogies of Globalization: The Rise of the Educational Security State*

Spring • *Political Agendas for Education: From the Religious Right to the Green Party, Third Edition*

Sidhu • *Universities and Globalization: To Market, To Market*

Bowers/Apffel-Marglin (Eds.) • *Rethinking Freire: Globalization and the Environmental Crisis*

Reagan • *Non-Western Educational Traditions: Indigenous Approaches to Educational Thought and Practice, Third Edition*

Books • *Poverty and Schooling in the U.S.: Contexts and Consequences*

Shapiro/Purpel (Eds.) • *Critical Social Issues in American Education: Democracy and Meaning in a Globalizing World, Third Edition*

Spring • *How Educational Ideologies are Shaping Global Society: Intergovernmental Organizations, NGOs, and the Decline of the Nation-State*

Lakes/Carter (Eds.) • *Global Education for Work: Comparative Perspectives on Gender and the New Economy*

Heck • *Studying Educational and Social Policy: Theoretical Concepts and Research Methods*

Peshkin • *Places of Memory: Whiteman's Schools and Native American Communities*

Hemmings • *Coming of Age in U.S. High Schools: Economic, Kinship, Religious, and Political Crosscurrents*

Spring • *Educating the Consumer-Citizen: A History of the Marriage of Schools, Advertising, and Media*

Ogbu • *Black American Students in an Affluent Suburb: A Study of Academic Disengagement*

Benham/Stein (Eds.) • *The Renaissance of American Indian Higher Education: Capturing the Dream*

Hones (Ed.) • *American Dreams, Global Visions: Dialogic Teacher Research with Refugee and Immigrant Families*

McCarty • *A Place to Be Navajo: Rough Rock and the Struggle for Self-Determination in Indigenous Schooling*

Spring • *Globalization and Educational Rights: An Intercivilizational Analysis*

Grant/Lei (Eds.) • *Global Constructions of Multicultural Education: Theories and Realities*

Luke • *Globalization and Women in Academics: North/West–South/East*

Meyer/Boyd (Eds.) • *Education Between State, Markets, and Civil Society: Comparative Perspectives*

Roberts • *Remaining and Becoming: Cultural Crosscurrents in an Hispano School*

Borman/Stringfield/Slavin (Eds.) • *Title I: Compensatory Education at the Crossroads*

DeCarvalho • *Rethinking Family–School Relations: A Critique of Parental Involvement in Schooling*

Peshkin • *Permissible Advantage?: The Moral Consequences of Elite Schooling*

Spring • *The Universal Right to Education: Justification, Definition, and Guidelines*

Nieto (Ed.) • *Puerto Rican Students in U.S. Schools*

Glander • *Origins of Mass Communications Research During the American Cold War: Educational Effects and Contemporary Implications*

Pugach • *On the Border of Opportunity: Education, Community, and Language at the U.S.–Mexico Line*

Spring • *Education and the Rise of the Global Economy*

Benham/Heck • *Culture and Educational Policy in Hawai'i: The Silencing of Native Voices*

Lipka/Mohatt/The Ciulistet Group • *Transforming the Culture of Schools: Yu'pik Eskimo Examples*

Weinberg • *Asian-American Education: Historical Background and Current Realities*

Nespor • *Tangled Up in School: Politics, Space, Bodies, and Signs in the Educational Process*

Peshkin • *Places of Memory: Whiteman's Schools and Native American Communities*

Spring • *The Cultural Transformation of a Native American Family and Its Tribe 1763–1995*

For additional information on titles in the Sociocultural, Political, and Historical Studies in Education series visit www.routledgeeducation.com

Education and Hope in Troubled Times

Visions of Change for Our Children's World

Edited by

H. Svi Shapiro

Routledge
Taylor & Francis Group

NEW YORK AND LONDON

First published 2009
by Routledge
270 Madison Ave, New York, NY 10016

Simultaneously published in the UK
by Routledge
2 Park Square, Milton Park, Abingdon, Oxon OX14 4RN

Routledge is an imprint of the Taylor & Francis Group, an informa business

© 2009 Taylor and Francis

Typeset in Minion by
Book Now Ltd, London
Printed and bound in the United States of America on
acid-free paper by Edwards Brothers, Inc.

Library of Congress Cataloging in Publication Data
Education and hope in troubled times: visions of change for our children's
world/edited by H. Svi Shapiro.
        p. cm. — (Sociocultural, political, and historical studies in education)
Includes bibliographical references.
1. Critical pedagogy. 2. Educational sociology. I. Shapiro, H. Svi.
LC196.E383 2008
370.11′5—dc22   2008036284

ISBN10: 0–415–99425–X (hbk)
ISBN10: 0–415–99426–8 (pbk)
ISBN10: 0–203–88185–0 (ebk)

ISBN13: 978–0–415–99425–5 (hbk)
ISBN13: 978–0–415–99426–2 (pbk)
ISBN13: 978–0–203–88185–9 (ebk)

For all those who imagine an education that invigorates a deep democracy, nurtures peace, sustains the earth and nourishes the quest for a compassionate and just world

Contents

Preface

This volume brings together a number of the most important educational and social thinkers and visionaries each of whom was invited to envisage the possibilities of educational change and reform in the United States. They include pioneers in the field of critical pedagogy such as Henry A. Giroux and Peter McLaren; seminal analysts of educational policy, politics and culture such as Michael W. Apple, Jean Anyon, Richard A. Brosio, Joel Westheimer and Sue Books; individuals such as David E. Purpel, Ron Miller and Nel Noddings who have provided powerful insights into the moral and spiritual dimensions of schooling; Rick Reitzug, Steve Gross and Joan Shapiro, who have sought to redefine the field of educational leadership so that it becomes one grounded in ethical critique and possibility; others such as Don Johnson, Mara Sapon-Shevin and Sherry B. Shapiro, whose work has provided extraordinary new openings towards seeing the embodied nature of human existence and learning; Hephzibah Roskelly and AnaLouise Keating, who provide powerful alternative visions of the connections between the way knowledge is constructed and transmitted and how human consciousness is formed; and the groundbreaking insights of Rianne Eisler, who has helped us to reconceptualize social and economic relations away from the "dominator" model which has held sway during so much of human history towards a "partnership" model that rests on the values of social justice, compassion and cooperation.

This book comes to completion during a time in the United States when there is a deep and increasing yearning for change in our social and political life. Each day seems to make visible new crises in our society: the financial "meltdown" on Wall Street—the worst since the Great Depression, a global credit crisis, loss of jobs, housing foreclosures, environmental destruction, energy costs and shortages, the duration and consequences of a seemingly endless war, corporate and government corruption, and the debacle of health care insurance. At the same time there are remarkable new constellations of political mobilizations around the unprecedented presidential nomination campaigns of female and African-American candidates within the Democratic Party, and the extraordinary triumph of Barack Obama as the first Black President of the United States. With this comes the possibility for an impressive agenda of progressive change after eight years of conservative rule. Yet it is a great disappointment that this agenda still offers no radical departure from the orthodoxy that has prevailed around educational matters over recent decades. While there is now some public criticism of No Child Left Behind and its preoccupation with standardized tests and the "one-size-fits-all" approach to measuring learning, the underlying emphases of American educational policy and practice remain intact. It should be noted that serious questions are now being raised about the failure of the reform to make any real changes to the racial gap in educational achievements, the domination of schooling with mindless and repetitive forms of testing, and the narrowing of the curriculum. And there are continuing issues about the unfairness of the tests in regard to those without adequate English language proficiency and in relationship to special needs children. Yet education remains firmly within the grip of narrowly defined behaviorist approaches to accountability; competitive-individualism characterizes the moral ambience of schools and classrooms; business and corporate priorities rather than civic and democratic concerns shape educational goals; and schools continue to mirror the severe inequities of race and class in the United States with all of its consequences for classroom resources, quality of teaching, and educational and economic opportunity.

So there is much work to be done in not only challenging the prevailing orthodoxies of education in this country but offering new visions of change and possibility during these times. And this is what I have sought to do in this volume by inviting this group of outstanding scholars and teachers to respond to the challenges we face, both as a nation and as a global community. Their collective response represents a remarkable statement not just of criticism concerning present priorities and goals but of possibilities and visions for rethinking and reimagining what it means to educate our children for the world they will live in and experience. It is a response that speaks to questions of war and peace, the search for moral and cultural identity, social justice in a world of growing poverty and inequity, participation and empowerment, and environmental sanity and sustainability.

Most of all it speaks to the quest for an education that offers meaning, purpose and dignity to those coming of age in a world that cries out for a radical shift in the content and character of human relationships. It is my fervent hope that this collective statement will be a catalyst for a deep process of reflection concerning how we envisage, and what we hope for in, our children's education. And the vision of education we hold is, in the end, nothing less than a metaphor for the kind of world we hope our children will inherit.

Svi Shapiro, *Raleigh, North Carolina*

They shall beat their swords into plowshares, And their spears into pruning hooks. Nation shall not lift sword against nation, and they shall not again experience war.

Micah 4: 3–4

Each of us should be encouraged to accept his own diversity, to see his identity as the sum of all his various affiliations, instead of as only one of them raised to the status of the most important, made into an instrument of exclusion and sometimes into a weapon of war.

Amin Maalouf

The bourgeoisie … has resolved personal worth into exchange value and … has set up that single unconscionable freedom—Free Trade. In one word, for exploitation, veiled by religious and political illusions, it has substituted naked, shameless, direct, brutal exploitation.

Karl Marx

A concern for the critical and the imaginative, for the opening of new ways of "looking at things," is wholly at odds with the technicist and behaviorist emphases we still find in American schools. It represents a challenge, not yet met, to the hollow formulations, the mystifications so characteristic of our time.

Maxine Greene

Contributors

Jean Anyon is Professor of Social and Educational Policy at the Graduate Center of the City University of New York.

Michael W. Apple is John Bascom Professor of Curriculum and Instruction and Educational Policy Studies at the University of Wisconsin, Madison.

Sue Books is Professor of Secondary Education at SUNY at New Palz.

Richard A. Brosio is Lecturer at the University of Wisconsin, Milwaukee, and Emeritus Professor at Ball State University.

Jenifer Crawford is a Ph.D candidate at the UCLA Graduate School of Education and Information Studies.

Riane Eisler is President of the Center for Partnership Studies at Pacific Grove, California.

Henry A. Giroux is Global TV Network Professor of Cultural Studies at McMaster University in Hamilton, Ontario.

Steven Jay Gross is Associate Professor of Educational Administration at Temple University.

Nana Gyamfi is an Attorney with the Human Rights Advocacy Project in Los Angeles.

Don Hanlon Johnson is Professor of Somatics at the California Institute of Integral Studies.

AnaLouise Keating is Professor of Women's Studies at the Texas Woman's University.

Peter McLaren is Professor of Education and Cultural Studies at the UCLA Graduate School of Education and Information Studies.

Ron Miller is editor of *Education Revolution* and adjunct faculty member at Champlain College, Vermont.

Nel Noddings is Lee Jacks Professor Emerita at Stanford University.

David E. Purpel is Professor Emeritus at the University of North Carolina at Greensboro.

Ulrich C. Reitzug is Professor of Educational Leadership at the University of North Carolina at Greensboro.

Hephzibah Roskelly is Linda Arnold Carlisle Distinguished Professor of Women's and Gender Studies at the University of North Carolina at Greensboro.

Mara Sapon-Shevin is Professor of Inclusive Education at Syracuse University.

H. Svi Shapiro is Professor of Education and Cultural Studies at the University of North Carolina at Greensboro.

Joan Poliner Shapiro is Professor of Educational Administration at Temple University.

Sherry B. Shapiro is Professor and Director of Women's Studies at Meredith College in Raleigh, North Carolina.

Deborah L. West is a doctoral student in the ED.D program at the University of North Carolina at Greensboro.

Joel Westheimer is University Research Chair and Professor of Education at the University of Ottawa.

1
Introduction
Education and Hope in Troubled Times

H. Svi Shapiro

In my letter of invitation to the contributors in this book I wrote that *Education and Hope in Troubled Times: Visions of Change for Our Children's World* would be a collection of essays by a number of the leading social and educational thinkers and commentators in this country. Its motivation, put succinctly, was to help articulate a new vision and purpose—and begin to set an alternative direction—for our children's education at a time when, as I believe, there is an increasing delegitimation of the prevailing assumptions and orthodoxies that have shaped our public life over the past few years. There was, in addition, a deep hunger for the articulation of what Michael Lerner[1] has called a *new bottom line* for education—one that focuses on the lives of our children as human beings who will assume the ethical, political and social responsibilities of our shared national and global communities.

I do not think (my original letter continued) I am being overly optimistic to believe that we are now witnessing the implosion of the neo-conservative "revolution" in the United States. All signs point to our being in a transitional period in which the assumptions that have governed political life for the past six years are in grave crisis. At the core of these assumptions has been the belief that the United States had a free and unopposed hand to make and reorganize the world according to the interests and inclinations of our governing elites. We can now see quite clearly that this arrogance of power has hit a resistant wall. The world cannot be remade through our military muscle and economic power quite as easily as some may have wished. The lies and deceit that have brought us to this catastrophic moment have been laid bare. The belief that this country could act unilaterally on the world stage without much broader international support has produced unparalleled anger and distrust towards the U.S. Many now see that terrorism is only one of a number of serious threats that confront us: global warming, lethal epidemics, poverty, violence and war, nuclear proliferation, racism and ethnic hatred. All are part of the increasingly pressing agenda for action in the world. And the severity and complexity of human problems will demand from us, and especially from our children, inclinations, dispositions and knowledge quite different from those which have shaped, and continue to shape, our social identities and ideological outlooks, moral preferences and attitudinal priorities. *This is a time of crisis, but also of renewed possibility—one that offers us the opportunity to reconsider radically what is the meaning of education for a generation that will bear the brunt of grappling with*

1

these extraordinary challenges and dangers. What will it mean to be an educated human being in the 21st century, compelled to confront and address so much that threatens the very basis of a decent and hopeful human existence?

The unraveling of the "neo-con" consensus is likely to bring in its train many questions about our public policy priorities. Already there is a growing populist resentment towards the increasing concentration of wealth in the U.S. There is growing disillusionment with the effects of free trade agreements on the lives and economic security of working- and middle-class Americans which includes the anxiety felt by many towards the influx of migrants from these free trade areas. For many Americans there is an inability to meet the basics of a decent existence through the absence of affordable health care or dependable retirement income. Katrina exposed us to the harsh realities of poverty and racism that continue to disfigure American life. Catastrophic weather patterns have ignited concerns about humanly influenced climate change. Continuing war is resulting in escalating disillusionment with government's failure to respond to our dependence on oil and the development of alternative energy sources. At the same time the authoritarian Christianity of the "theo-cons" has led the nation down a path of intolerance, discrimination and religious chauvinism. Its constricted moral rage has been blind to questions of poverty, social injustice and environmental degradation. Meanwhile there is an increasingly pervasive sense that there is a crisis of meaning and values in America—one that leads to a debasement of human relationships, accelerating materialism and greed, and misplaced fixation on celebrity and glamor. *In this context there is a compelling need to articulate a new bottom line for education—one that offers a different vision for educating our children that directly and cogently speaks to human purpose and meaning in the world that that they will inherit.* Taken together, the essays in this volume, I believe, provide just such a powerful and cogent response to this need.

The No Child Left Behind Debacle

Of course any such attempt will need to start with the failure that is No Child Left Behind. I do not think I need to spell out here the deleterious effect of this legislation on schools in this country. These have been noted by a host of researchers and other observers. They include the failure significantly to reduce the racial achievement gap; the penalizing of immigrant children and special students; increased drop-out rates; the narrowing of the curriculum and the shallow reductionist form of learning; the increased stress and anxiety among students resulting from the obsessive focus on standardized tests; the diversion of public funds to private tutoring sources and other for-profit outfits; and the deskilling of teachers' work and the reliance on "programmed" learning. One could go on. All of this points to a bankruptcy in what has been the paramount public policy in education. And as the failures and unpopularity of NCLB gather steam there are increasing calls to tether education even more closely to the human capital demands of big business, as well to intensify the measurements of accountability in public schools (and in higher education). Little is heard in the public discourse about education's responsibility to nurture the knowledge, attitudes and dispositions of a democratic polity. Short shrift is given to the value of developing the imagination and creative aptitudes of the young. There is little attention afforded to the capacity of education to enhance the ability of young people to critically interrogate popular media or the sources of public information. Intellectual and creative activity as a joyful human act, not simply a vehicle for instrumental advantage, comes to be regarded as frivolous waste. And it is taken as axiomatic that the moral context of the classroom and school is one that emphasizes individual achievement, competitive advantage, and willingness to subordinate authentic interests and passions to the compulsive quest for college and career success. It is fully understandable that parents are concerned about the capacity of their children to achieve basic literacy and numeracy. These skills are, after all, fundamental to the ability to negotiate the modern world. Yet the emphasis on these to the exclusion of all else produces a sadly limited form of education devoid of any larger human vision—one that speaks to the quest for lives of meaning and purpose. Separated from the latter and focusing only on the transmission of skills and technical competencies, the classroom quickly becomes a site of boredom, stifled curiosity and joyless learning.

Yet, as I have suggested above, the growing political crisis holds out the possibility of change and hope. The Republican Party has exhausted its armory of chauvinistic aggression and its agenda of hateful moralism and demonization. The Democrats have failed, so far, to articulate a courageous path of political, ethical and social renewal for our national community. This is a moment of uncertainty but also of opportunity—one in which I have invited the contributions of those in this volume to the reshaping of the public language of education. This is an opportunity to participate in the articulation of a shared vision of what it should mean to educate a new generation who will have to contend with increasingly perilous social circumstances, but also extraordinary possibilities for transforming our world into one that is socially just, compassionate and environmentally responsible. In many ways, as my long-time colleague and collaborator David Purpel[2] has argued, there are no educational problems, only social issues that get played out on the terrain of education. So my invitation has been to address simultaneously both the crisis of education and the broader challenges that confront us as part of the larger community of humankind. My hope was that these essays would be written in a language that is both inviting and accessible to a broad public audience, and that each should provide a strong, imaginative and persuasive message of change and possibility in regard to what should be the overarching meaning, purpose and vision of education for the coming generation of young people. The magnitude of the human and ecological crisis we confront demands more than the often arcane and ego-inflating exegesis of academic discourse. Can we really doubt that our situation today calls for a language and vision that is bold, courageous and resonant to the fears, concerns and hopes of the broad majority of human beings?

Education and the Crisis of Democracy

In my own writings[3] I have tried to describe the contours of such a vision and the educational agenda that can be drawn from it. There is surely little doubt that we face a deep crisis of meaningful citizenship in this country. And in this regard education has abdicated its responsibilities. Indeed schooling contributes in important ways to the evisceration of civic culture and the erosion of identities that are capable of seriously enacting democratic citizenship. Meaningful citizenship—what Stuart Ewen[4] refers to as a "democracy of expression"—is more and more replaced by what he calls a "democracy of consumption." For many people—young people especially—choice, power and freedom are increasingly reduced to one's capacity to buy. The marketplace defines "democratic" action more than the polling booth or public engagement and advocacy. The credit card defines one's eligibility as a citizen. That critical aspect of democracy—the capacity to exert power over one's circumstances—is reduced to the ability to shop from the ever-expanding, dizzying array of available products. Advertisers have appropriated the language of democratic life so that change, innovation, renewal, and the energy of public life are concentrated and distilled into the excitement of fashion, automobile ownership, the latest upgrade in the technology of communication, or the promise of optimal experiences offered through travel, drink or sex. The question of how much fulfillment or meaning is ultimately available from this culture of consumption and its preoccupation with glamor, fame and money is certainly something to which we must return below. What is clear is how far this focus is from Ewen's democracy of expression. If democracy is about a shared search for a better society, then consuming is all about what *I have acquired or experienced*. If democracy is about improving our common wellbeing, then consumption relentlessly offers the prospect of "getting an edge" and being one up on our neighbor in looks, acquisitions, opportunities and style. A possessive and competitive individualism is at its motivational core. In sharp contrast to this, a democracy of expression concerns the capacity to name and articulate the circumstances that enable or limit a full and satisfying human existence, not just for oneself but for all of us who are members of our shared polity.

Yet it is a rarity when schooling offers students the opportunity to develop that capacity for expression that enhances democratic life and citizenship. School for most students is primarily about the process of domestication and conformity, as they learn the grammar and syntax of test-taking skills and become adept at the search for the single correct answer on the test sheet. Creative thought, critical questioning, the articulation of ideas and insights about students' lives and concerns have little place in the classrooms of most young people. The suffocating regime of NCLB and its state equivalents squeezes out any possibility of educating young people so that they develop genuine curiosity about their world, a passion to pursue and understand life's purpose, and the will to challenge accepted truths and conventions. Most of all, schools now develop accountants of test scores and grade point averages, and adept manipulators of college résumés through the accumulation of curricular and extra-curricular experiences. Little here can contribute to a mind that is alert and awake to the challenges we face as a human community, nor one that is imbued with the desire to question deeply and boldly those social, moral and epistemological assumptions and categories that shape our dangerously divisive, wasteful and materialistic world. After Abu Ghraib and the abuses of Guantánamo and elsewhere, we must be concerned again with the propensity towards an unthinking conformity—a readiness to do or say whatever is deemed necessary in order to oblige those in authority. As we know so well, the path towards what Hannah Arendt called so aptly the "banality of evil" starts in school with the message about doing what one is told to do without question or reflection. When success in school comes to mean rote memorization, the search for the single right answer, and intellectual conformity or timidity, then we have created the conditions in which human beings learn that it is right to abdicate their capacity for moral autonomy and "wide-awake" thoughtfulness and decision-making.

The shrinking ability to see knowledge as having any transformative power other than as the crass instrument of individual advantage is also the consequence of the world of spin that engulfs political and corporate life in the United States. This is a point well made by Bernard Cooperman,[5] for whom our culture is one that induces cynical, disbelieving attitudes towards any claims about truth or judgment. Whether it is about the deleterious effects of tobacco or the crisis around climate change, someone can always be found (backed up of course by powerful vested interests) to refute whatever claims are made. People are taught, first and foremost, to see themselves as consumers who choose sides as a matter of temporary and shifting taste or convenience. Intellectual conviction and ethical commitment are replaced by cant, spin and short-term interests. And this, says Cooperman, is reflected in our classrooms, where students have lost the ability to think critically about the world because they do not believe in knowledge itself. These difficulties, however, should, of course, only strengthen our conviction as to the need to understand education's crucial role in revitalizing a democratic culture. In the face of the extraordinary and intensifying power of elites—corporate, political, military—to structure the language and set the limits of public debate in this country, any significant new educational vision must be one that includes the prospect of a critically reflective, boldly questioning and imaginatively creative citizenry.

Education and the Struggle for Community

The crisis of democratic citizenship is also the crisis of community. The withering of what Cornel West[6] refers to as *parrhesia*—the capacity for bold and courageous thinking—is also the erosion of social cohesion and communal interdependence. And in each case schools are an important (though certainly not the sole) factor in this decline. School is after all that place where children first learn the "culture of separated desks." It is the place where they are first formally introduced to a worldview in which life's rewards—material and symbolic—are seen as the product of an endless struggle with one's neighbors. The mentality of the bell-curve instructs them that scarcity of affirmation, recognition and reward is part of the very DNA of human existence. It is a social imperative, they learn, to acquire those skills, manners, dispositions and knowledge that give them an advantage over the next individual. Whatever is said about friendship, sharing and caring in our schools and classrooms, the real effect of the curriculum is to teach the centrality of competition and individualism in our social relations. In this world, children learn that not everyone can be someone; some of us are inevitably destined for failure and invisibility. To be "somebody" rests on the capacity to classify another as being "nobody." It is a lesson relentlessly emphasized through schools' constant attention to the markers of success and failure, validation and rejection. It is a message that deeply penetrates students' understanding of human existence. The world is a predatory place. The fear of failure hangs over all of us, and with it a distrust and suspicion towards those who appear to have acquired something more than we have. It is a world in which envy, dissatisfaction, and an incessant drive towards invidious comparison permeate our lives. From the gold stars of kindergarten to the status hierarchy of college selection, schooling is an insistent socialization into the world of hierarchy, status and human separation. We are, through this process, driven apart, not together; led to see ourselves as working against one another rather than acting cooperatively; and primed for an aggressive egoism rather than an open-hearted generosity.

Those who would argue that fear is the root emotion of our competitively driven, aggressively self-oriented culture make a convincing argument. There is the anxiety that what we have must constantly be protected from those who jealously desire to take it from us, resent our hard-won gains, or wish to diminish our success in some way. Such pervasive *ressentiment* produces what Barbara Ehrenreich[7] refers to as the constant "fear of falling"—the sense that in a ferociously competitive world someone is always just behind you on the ladder waiting for you to slip (and hoping that you will do so). The encircling arms of young children as they protect their assignment from the eyes of other children so aptly embodies the world-view of a fearful and suspicious individualism. Their answers dare not be shared with other children, for that would diminish their special claim to success and recognition. For those whose arms and hands are used to hide what they know produce an inadequate response; the body language manifests the shame and vulnerability of failure in that painful world in which worth is always contingent on success and achievement.

In this landscape of human fragmentation and separation the hunger for connection, genuine friendship, closeness and camaraderie finds expression—but often in ways that still bear the marks of a hostile and fearful environment. Our preoccupation with the flag speaks to a desperate desire for some unifying focus of a shared community. Sadly, such a focus invariably becomes a fetish that carries the insistence on patriotic conformity. It comes quickly to stand for that nationalistic sense of togetherness which leaves little room for dissent. It is a community in which the price of membership is an unquestioning allegiance to governmental authority or the belief in the perennial rightness of one's cause. Not surprisingly, such patriotic belonging is underpinned by triumphalism and an uncritical celebration of always being on the right side of history. This sense of connection with others is marked too by a Manichean view of the world in which the ties that bind us to some situate others as our inveterate enemies. We are locked into a constant struggle between ourselves—the forces of light—and others who represent the side of evil. It is hardly surprising that this kind of patriotism seems always to find, or construct, a threatening force in the world which we are required to oppose with a uniformity of ideological and political support. The construction of community here is rooted in a zero-sum world of enemies; connection among us is predicated by our hostility towards, and fear of, those who appear to threaten our way of life. It is easy to see how young people are socialized into this kind of world-view. The school pep rally and varsity athletics rivalry inculcate a frenzied support for one's own team. Pride and loyalty towards one's "own" side come together with a demonizing of the opposition. The celebration of our shared identity is always one side of a coin whose other face is fierce competition and the will to superiority or dominance. The poison of a community constructed through invidious comparison with others who are viewed as inferior, immoral or bent on our destruction has very deep roots in our culture. We do not have to look far to see a politics built around the contrast between those of "us" who inhabit the normal, safe and hygienic world of heterosexuality and those who appear to threaten its acceptance. Our world is riven by religious claims as to who speaks with the one and only true voice of God and those who are heretical pretenders. Migrants from other countries seeking a better life for themselves and their families are made to appear as a dangerous threat to the national culture and language. Modernity with its drive towards unceasing change, dislocation and uncertainty produces a world of extraordinary alienation and anxiety. Unprecedented movements of people across borders, disruption of settled ways of life through the cultural "invasion" of TV, movies and the internet, and economic upheavals caused by rapid technological innovation and global movements of capital and finance all add to the transitoriness and flux of everyday life. It can hardly be surprising that such conditions are a catalyst for attempts to forge stable identities around what Zygmunt Bauman[8] calls "neo-tribalism." Such identities are often ones that are turned in on themselves—absolutist in their thinking, resistant to any outside influences, and rigidly hierarchical (usually aggressively patriarchal). These communities of resistance to the destabilizing effects of modernity and globalized capitalism provide a sense of connection and meaning in an atomized and disrupted world.

Fierce assertion of communal identity reflects also a spiritual and physical resistance by those whose ethnicity, gender, religious traditions and national identity have been degraded, repressed and submerged. These allegiances are formed from the pain and humiliation dealt to oppressed groups. Such communities are both political and therapeutic, attempting to assuage the wounds of humiliation, invisibility and marginality while demanding redress for the social injustices they have constantly had to endure. Such communities frequently demand schools of their own where the pride of heritage and identity can be transmitted to a younger generation. We see this in schools that emphasize an Afrocentric curriculum, in Jewish day schools, in schools for Indian and other indigenous groups, in Muslim schools, in the gender-specific education of women, and in some kinds of Christian schools. There is an understandable wish among communities whose history has been one of exclusion and oppression to provide for their young an education that reverses the pattern of marginality, humiliation and invisibility. Such educational goals are integral to a vision of a culturally diverse democracy. Yet there is a tension here that should not be ignored between democracy's promise of the affirmation of plural cultural, ethnic and religious communities and the need to ensure a *universal* human ethic and a global civic culture.

The enormous challenge in the 21st century is to allow and facilitate the genuine recognition and flourishing of all those communities that have hitherto been made invisible by the exercise of hegemonic cultures and, at the same time, to ensure that fierce allegiance within these communities does not preclude a sense of wider human connection and interdependence. *It is, I believe, the task of education both to facilitate the former while also encouraging the latter.* This means that education has a double role around the issue of community. Schools need to provide the space in which particularistic identities can be nurtured. They need also to build and encourage communities of a much wider span in which a universal human ethic and consciousness flourishes. It is surely necessary to assert as never before the connectedness of the human species (and of course the interdependence on earth of all life). We face as a human community threats to our very existence as a species, from pollution, climate change, water shortages, nuclear armaments, the spread of disease across national borders, and violence that makes no distinction between combatants and innocent civilians. Education will have to be a part of a process that asserts and supports identities that are a complex weave of the particular and the universal, the local and the global, the partial and the whole. We know enough now about the meaning of identity to understand the importance of rootedness and place to human wellbeing. But we also are increasingly aware of the malignant and dangerous consequences to others when such identity refuses to acknowledge the bonds that connect all of our species as social, ethical and spiritual beings. Citizenship education today must be one that is concerned with our plural identities *and* the social cohesion stemming from our common concerns and needs as human beings.[9]

Schooling and Global Justice

Of course it is impossible to address the pressing question of community in our lives if we do not acknowledge its inseparability from issues of social justice. Community is, after all, that mode of being in which each of us is visible and recognized within the circle of human presence. Each of us takes our place within this circle as a presence of inestimable value, equally empowered and responsible for what is collectively undertaken, and fully supported and secure in the care of one's neighbors. The evidence points to a deep hunger for community among human beings, yet the practices and reality of our daily lives constantly contradict its possibility. We are, in school and elsewhere, constantly subjected to a process that creates a world of winners and losers—a hierarchy of worth and recognition in which, as John Holt once noted, a few learn to get what they like, and many learn to like what they get. School is, in the words of educational historian Joel Spring, first and foremost a "sorting machine" that socializes the young into a world of inequality. The primary and most insidious lesson of education is the legitimacy of unequal treatment and differential human value. School is nothing if it is not a vehicle for the transmission of hierarchical distinctions of respect, worth, ability and economic expectations. It is the seeding ground for a society in which we accept astonishing inequalities in the circumstances of our lives—access to health care, decent housing, availability of food, opportunities for rest and recreation, security of employment, dignity and respect in the community and on the job. Of course such hierarchical ordering stands in sharp contrast to our vision and desire for a community that is something more than the clichés of a Hallmark card. The classroom itself, as we have already noted, is a place in which the ethic of mutual caring and support is undone by the relentless process of competitive individualism in which students learn and are urged "to get ahead" of one another. And talk of a national community is mocked by the extraordinary differences in children's lives consequent upon differences of race, wealth and gender. All talk of "no child left behind" is pure obfuscation in a society where social and economic inequalities bear down heavily on children's lives, hopelessly blighting the possibilities for success or achievement among so many. And talk of a shared national interest is much of the time a cover for glaring and increasing inequalities in the lives of citizens. Hurricane Katrina provided a window onto the horrifying world of racial and class discrimination in the United States, where the lives of thousands of poor and working-class citizens were subjected to a callous disregard by their government in an hour of overwhelming need.

In the wider world the new global economic order has been a prescription for increasing inequalities in the shape of people's lives. Nearly 3 billion people on the planet live on less than 2 dollars a day; 850 million people go hungry and, according to UN estimates, 20,000 to 30,000 children die every day of starvation or preventable diseases related to malnutrition. More and more power accrues to gigantic transnational businesses that undermine any notion of a democratic polity where ordinary people have a real say about the kind of world in which they live. Talk of community when such extraordinary disparities exist in the distribution of wealth and in the exercise of power becomes emptied of any real meaning. In a world in which elites have such a disproportionate capacity to influence our culture, our economic wellbeing, social policy around matters such as education and health care, and how we deal with our environment, the general interest of the many is supplanted by the greed and self-aggrandizement of the few. When community is understood as one of shared social and economic concerns, mutual human respect, and the pursuit of our common wellbeing, then the present course of national and international development belies any such vision. Our nation and our world are suffused with the images of environmental toxicity and degradation that fall hardest on the poorest among us. The security of working people is undercut by the callous and indiscriminate search for more profits. The underdeveloped places of our planet are ruthlessly plundered and exploited by those with political and military power. Millions die from the lack of medicines withheld because of the greed of the drug industry. And thousands of young women are the exploited commodities of sexual "tourism." An education that is to nurture the sense of human connectedness both within our nation and within the larger global human family is an imperative of our time. It is the only alternative to a world of increasing and unnecessary suffering, more cataclysmic war and violence, and lives blighted by a dehumanized existence in which people are treated as throwaway and expendable items of little enduring value.

To educate towards the now pressing vision of human community cannot be separated from the need to move human consciousness away from the impulse to sort, select and rank, and to find and to legitimate winners and losers. In our schools this will be no easy task, since education is almost unimaginable today when not about such a process. Yet we need to be reminded that, despite the power and influence of such ideas, other ethical, political and spiritual visions persist. These visions speak to the continuing possibility of a world in which all are affirmed in their worth, respect and autonomy; in which all deserve to live with decency and security; and in which meaning is found through the sharing of our earthly resources. Such a vision must surely infuse what Raymond Williams once referred to as the long revolution that we are called upon to make both in our schools and throughout our social institutions.

Towards a Pedagogy of Peace

All of this rests on the belief in a universal human ethic. It is an ethic rooted in the concept of the infinite value and preciousness of each and every human life. Its central imperative is to refuse violence against others. We cannot separate a vision of education centered on the quest for democracy, community and social justice from the need for an education that negates the violence that pervades our culture. The third great responsibility of education today is to cultivate a culture of peace. But in the end this goal cannot be separated from the need to cultivate the bonds of universal human community and a culture of democracy. The first challenge of educating for peace is overcoming the dualistic and Manichean thinking that shapes so much of human consciousness in our world. At every turn we learn to understand our world as one constructed from rigid and binary categories: black vs. white, male vs. female, gay vs. straight, disabled vs. able, native vs. alien, Europe vs. Africa, our country vs. their country, and so on. We learn to view all things through a prism that separates and opposes one side from another. And to this separation we add the qualities that give "our" side its supposed superiority. This is a way of constructing reality that ensures not just a world of immovable divisions but one in which we come to see our attributes, allegiances and preferences as the stuff that makes us better, more deserving, more enlightened than, or even genetically superior to, all others. This polarized us/them world is the recipe of inevitable and certain prejudice and hatred. Fear and anger corrode all relationships. Resentment of mistreatment and the ache of dehumanization fill the lives of those distinguished by their supposed failings and pathologies. And fear of the encroachment of the other shapes the psychology and politics of those who hold themselves as superior. If we don't act with force to restrain and contain the other, it is held, we might succumb to their influence. In this view, security comes through the domination and suppression of others.

Educating for peace works within what appears to be a paradoxical world-view. It asserts on the one hand the ancient spiritual wisdom that all human life is of inestimable value. In this view all people have unconditional or infinite worth. It asserts that all our distinctions and separations obfuscate the fundamental oneness of existence and the endless recycling and regeneration of our common origins within the elemental stardust of the universe. From this perspective education means to emphasize the precious value and meaning of all life. It shifts our focus from the qualities that separate us, and polarize us, to those that connect us and speak to our similarities. Security in this view depends not on our capacity to dominate or exclude, but on our willingness to show generosity and open-heartedness towards others. Our wellbeing, as Michael Lerner suggests,[10] depends on the wellbeing of everyone on our planet.

While educating for peace requires that we see the essential humanity of all people, it also requires that we fully recognize the way in which our lives have been conditioned and shaped through the particularity of our language, history, gender, culture and class. What has the experience of living meant for this person and those who share that particular experience? It has been said that one's enemy is someone whose story you have not heard. Peace education certainly demands the possibility of dialogue in which one's life can be shared with others. It means cultivating a hermeneutical approach to "truth" in which the emphasis is less on whose view is right than simply on hearing what it means to grow up and deal with a particular set of circumstances. It is a process that emphasizes sympathetic listening rather than the impulse to quick judgment. It means to struggle with one's own immediate assumptions and prejudices in order truly to hear the challenges and obstacles in the life of the other. Such dialogue breaks down or deconstructs—the simplistic and damaging binary view of identities. In its place emerges a more complex and fluid understanding of one's neighbor: someone who is different in some respects from oneself yet so similar in others; a person whose being is not defined solely through a single characteristic of religion, race, nationality, disability, etc., and a person who is not fully formed and complete but one whose life is evolving and changing.

Of course the sharing and naming of experience can be only a part of what it means to educate for peace. There must also be exploration of the culture of violence—the social conditions that predispose us towards the harming of others on the macro-scale we now witness. We have to look at what Zygmunt Bauman has termed *adiaphorization*[11]—the tendency, so pronounced in our world, to become desensitized to the pain and humiliation of others. We have to look here at the way in which violence becomes entertainment; the way wars are depicted through the mass media as video games; and the overall consequence of the barrage of violent images and themes on our sensibilities as human beings. We have to consider how poverty and unemployment sap human beings of hope for a better future and open the door to a nihilistic rage, or the way in which domination—cultural, economic and political—humiliates and dehumanizes people and can become a catalyst for suicidal revenge. And we must recognize that so much of the violence in the world is overwhelmingly perpetrated by men. Here we have to consider the way masculinity is constructed around the axis of power and dominance. Vulnerability, dependence and the desire for nurturance are regarded as signs of human weakness (read femininity) that evoke hostility and disgust and are an incitement to violent suppression, whether in oneself or in others.

Without this kind of critical social reflection we run the risk of approaching the issue of violence as simply a manifestation of individual or even collective pathology.

The mass murders in our schools are approached only as a matter of psychopathology requiring more efficient mental-health systems. Suicidal bombings by Muslims are disconnected from the history of colonialism, the trauma of Palestine, or current Western domination of much of the Arab world. Rape and brutality directed against women, or homophobic violence, are not seen within the context of aggressive and authoritarian forms of male identity. And war is somehow disconnected from the multibillion-dollar economic interests that enthusiastically encourage militaristic resolutions of social conflicts.

***

A fuller and more radical expression of democracy, a culture of peace that teaches us to practice non-violent means of resolving human conflicts, and relationships between people that celebrate and affirm the bonds of community and interdependence among us are some of the great challenges before us in this century. Their failure to be seriously addressed confronts us with threats to the very possibility of a desirable human future. And all these challenges will require efforts and interventions in a multiplicity of ways both within our individual lives and across the landscape of our public institutions. There can be no doubt of the extraordinary importance of education to making these changes. Education is after all that sphere where reason, reflection, imagination, and the capacity to act with thoughtfulness and creativity are stirred and nurtured. Yet it is clear that this is far from where the present discourse of education has taken us. Schools, as is so well documented here in this book and elsewhere, have become instruments of conformity and passivity. They are in thrall to the language of management and controlled outcomes, measured by their usefulness to the state as the means to supply trained workers, and, for parents, schools mirror all of the fears and uncertainties of an unsafe and rapidly changing world. For the latter, education can, perhaps, provide their kids with an edge, or at least the minimum set of skills and aptitudes that will enable them to survive in an increasingly competitive society. Yet even within a culture so dominated by fear there is still hope. Out of the frozen ground we see shoots of possibility. There are moments of recognition by parents and citizens that our children's education should be a joyful, creative and thought-provoking experience, not the dull grind of endless tests. Teachers are becoming more vocal about their frustrations as to the lack of opportunities for dialogue, critical reflection and meaningful learning in the classroom. Members of the community are voicing their concerns that schooling seems to provide little that prepares young people for active and thoughtful participation as citizens of a democracy. Among students there is increasing criticism of the "drill and test" variety of education, with its resulting boredom and alienation. More students are demanding a curriculum that is relevant to their lives and to what is happening in the world. Still it might be that, in the end, the awesome and terrifying events that now confront us as a species will provide the powerful catalyst for change in how we view the task of education. More and more we see that the fate of the earth itself is now in the balance. We will have to confront the fundamental challenges to the way we have constructed our social world or face the dangerous consequences of inaction. We will need to teach our children to think deeply and critically about the costs of a consumer culture and how human wants are manipulated into an endless desire for more, with all of its devastating consequences for our resources and the flow of pollutants into our environment. We will need to teach our children to think in ways that are holistic—understanding that human life and nature do not stand opposed to each other but are seamlessly connected in an interdependent web. We must be stewards, not violators, of our natural world. We will need to teach so that our children see themselves not as isolated and self-contained beings, but as members of an interdependent community with common needs and shared responsibilities. And we will need to emphasize that a sense of social justice must be present in all of our human actions so that the privileged lives of some do not depend on a callous disregard for the lives or fate of others.

In this time of great danger and also extraordinary possibility, educators are called towards a prophetic role. They must insist that, in the conditions that now confront us, the present educational agenda only reinforces and even compounds our problems. To educate today must instead be an act that helps transform human consciousness and conscience. The vision that animates our work as educators must be rooted in the ancient quest for *Tikkun Olam*—the effort to repair and heal our world as a place of generous and loving community, in which there is a just sharing of rewards and obligations, where human differences are mediated by respect and recognition, where there is ecological sanity and responsibility, and where there is the widest diffusion of opportunities for human beings to participate in shaping the world in which they live. No matter how far-fetched or unrealistic such a vision may appear to be in relation to the present concerns of schooling, this is no time for timidity. The immense dangers and the extraordinary suffering within which we are now engulfed demand from us the kind of bold, daring and imaginative thinking found among the contributors to this volume. Anything less is an irresponsible negation of our obligations to coming generations.

Notes

1. Lerner, Michael (2006) *The Left Hand of God*. San Francisco: Harper.
2. Purpel, David (2004) *Reflections on the Moral and Spiritual Crisis in Education*. New York: Peter Lang.
3. See, for example, Shapiro, H. Svi (2006) *Losing Heart: The Moral and Spiritual Miseducation of America's Children*. Mahwah, NJ: Lawrence Erlbaum.
4. Ewen, Stuart (1988) *All Consuming Images*. New York: Basic Books.
5. Cooperman, Bernard (2007) letter in *Newsweek,* September 3.
6. West, Cornel (2004) *Democracy Matters*. New York: Penguin.
7. Ehrenreich, Barbara (1990) *Fear of Falling*. New York: Harper Perennial.
8. Bauman, Zygmunt (1997) *Postmodernity and its Discontents*. New York: New York University Press.
9. Maalouf, Amin (2000) *In the Name of Identity*. New York: Penguin.
10. Lerner, *The Left Hand of God*.
11. Bauman, *Postmodernity and Its Discontents*.

2

Education and Schooling in the 21st Century

The Role of the Profession

David E. Purpel

Preface and Assumptions

The focus of my contribution to this collection will be on what role the educational profession should play in helping to influence the direction of the future of educational policies and practices. Before going on to explore this topic, I want to lay out a number of assumptions relevant to my analysis and orientation, particularly as they relate to the matter of vision. First, and at the risk of committing the sin of essentialism, I would assert that there are a number of basic beliefs that should *not* be changed and instead ought to be reaffirmed. I speak here of a vision of what constitutes the basic dimensions of a life of meaning and goodness. It is this basic vision that presumably should guide the development of an educational vision that resonates with and facilitates the fulfillment of the aspirations and hopes contained in our larger dreams.

The questions surrounding determining ultimate goals and moral visions are surely extraordinarily complex and deeply contentious, not only because of the incredibly knotty inherent philosophical difficulties, but more importantly because of their supreme significance to the challenge of delineating what it means to be human. Nothing is more important and nothing is more daunting.

I believe very strongly that we ought to be wary of underestimating the difficulty of these challenges even as we accept the necessity of addressing them. By the same token we must also not be paralyzed or overwhelmed by the magnitude of the task for, in spite of its complexity and contentiousness, I believe it is possible to lay out a general, necessarily tentative vision that has a high enough degree of consensus to enable us to move forward. This is not the place to provide the specifics of such a vision, but I offer a brief and broad outline of what I have in mind.

Part of that vision should certainly be the affirmation of the principles of the inherent dignity of each person, reverence for life, and concern for the welfare of our brothers and sisters. This certainly involves the acceptance of individual and communal responsibility for the creation of a society rooted in a commitment to justice, peace, love and joy for all. For me this means, more specifically, that everyone is entitled to basic necessities such as having enough to eat, decent housing, good medical care and meaningful work. I believe that such notions are deeply embedded in our cultural consciousness as reflected in a near consensual admiration of many of the teachings of religious as well as secular personages and texts. I have in mind such people as the biblical prophets, Gandhi, and Martin Luther King, and such texts as the Sermon on the Mount and the UN Declaration of Universal Human Rights.

This is, at best, a cursory sketch of a vision, but I hope and expect it resonates with the much larger and richer sense of the moral impulses that move us to pursue continuously and assiduously the search for a good and meaningful life for all. It goes without saying that we need to subject such attempts at articulating any moral vision, however attractive it may be, to continuous analysis and probing in order further to sharpen and clarify what should be a never ending but determined quest for wisdom. My point here is a limited one, namely that we as a people have already done an amazing amount of extraordinarily profound work on charting a course of meaning and purpose that provides us with enormously important direction and momentum. Let us be thankful for this and acknowledge what has been achieved as we strive to consolidate and extend our accomplishments.

More specifically, we are asked in this book to address the issue of how formal education has or has not facilitated our dreams for a life of meaning and purpose. At this point, I believe it important to remind us all of the critical distinction between schools and education, a distinction that is as obvious as it is so often ignored. There is, of course, a difference between the general concept of education as the process by which information and ideas are transmitted in any number of ways and places—word of mouth, peer relationships, the workplace, family, etc.— and the existence of particular institutions (schools, universities, academies, etc.) dedicated centrally to that process. The two terms are often conflated, and, to add to the confusion, many people use the term "education" and/or "schools" when they really mean the public school system. The general concept of education can become somewhat solipsistic when we say that a culture and a society per se is education, in the sense that societies and cultures are basically in the business of conveying beliefs and values and do so inevitably and incessantly. Indeed, in order to put some limits and coherence to the constant flow of information and viewpoints, societies develop institutions to bring order to the collection and dissemination of beliefs and values. Hence, the most basic issues of educational institutions deal, first, with the principles of ordering the immense amount of knowledge and, second, with notions of the conditions under which the knowledge is to be taught. All this is to say the obvious—we have had to create and have created theories of education as well as theories of schooling.

I want to focus here on one dimension of such theories, namely ideas on how both education and the schools connect to the project of realizing the social and moral vision similar to the one I've just sketched out. Some educators posit that an educational system is vital to and indeed inseparable from the quest for a just and loving world, while others see a more limited role for public schools, such as meeting the dominant social and cultural requirements of the time. Implicit in this disagreement is the larger issue of whether there need to be major changes in our basic social, political and economic structures. Educational theories also differ on the degree of significant departure from current practice required to make a vision real and on where the changes need to be made. Some say that we can and should work for incremental change within the existing educational system, either because that is all that is possible or because that is all that is necessary, even if it is not sufficient. Others say that the achievement of the vision we have suggested is one that requires much more fundamental changes in our social, cultural, political and economic structures, and indeed that public schools are not the path to such changes but a major obstacle to them. In other words, do we and can we work within the educational system as presently constituted as one of the major ways to fulfill our highest aspirations or do we give up on the redemptive possibilities of public education? One can logically say that an *educational* process is perforce required to facilitate our vision but that the dominant educational model as reflected in the policies and practices of the *public schools* cannot be, or does not aspire to be, the major instrument in that process.

My experience is that neither our political, social and cultural leaders nor the public typically distinguish between education and school and that most of the public discourse focuses on the intimate relationship between social and educational (read schools) policy. Curiously the same pattern seems to describe those voices that speak out for major social and cultural change. Both conservatives and liberals are wont to believe that their political and social agendas can be advanced through existing educational structures, albeit with varying approaches. The incessant call is for educational reform, and when the reformers specify what they have in mind they usually press for changes within the existing system of public schools and/or higher education.

My own broad position on these matters is twofold. First, I believe that it is highly improbable that the schools are or can be a powerful vehicle for the fulfillment of our dreams of a community permeated with love, justice and freedom for all. It is very clear to me that, if we want real fundamental changes in our social-economic-political structures, we cannot engage in that struggle by relying on institutions that are the embodiments of the very structures that need changing. Given this assumption, my very strong suggestion is that educational theorists should revisit the concept of "alternative education," since the current application of that concept has been distorted and coopted into one that really means "alternative schooling" and proposes only modest rearrangements of the dominant schooling model that serve, paradoxically enough, to distract us from considering changes in the model itself.

Second, I believe that we should also be mindful of the responsibility to provide constructive criticism of present educational policies and practices for schools as well as to offer imaginative and practical recommendations for change. If we are truly serious about achieving significant success in improving the quality of public schools, I believe it imperative that we explore the reasons why there has been so much resistance over the years to a plethora of new ideas, many of them imaginative and doable. This resistance is surely a reflection of an essentially conservative society, but we must also confront the issue of how the profession is implicated in the fierce rigidity of the system.

The Role of the Profession: The Problems

In this section I want to explore the particular responsibilities of our profession involved in developing and implementing educational policies and practices for the 21st century. My own impression of the record of the profession in the 20th century is that it is simultaneously impressive and disheartening. Among some of the more remarkable achievements are the establishment of professional standards in various fields; the creation of a vast number of professional specialties and organizations; the steady rise in minimum qualifications for entrance into the profession; and the tremendous production of a very large amount and variety of research, much of it of high quality. One could also list a number of other areas with mixed results, but I want to focus on what to me has been the most disappointing effort, namely, the profession's failure to become an authoritative and persuasive participant in the public dialogue regarding the development of educational policy. More particularly, I believe that the profession has been remiss in its responsibility to enrich the dialogue by providing a discourse that is both accessible and sophisticated, one that reflects the complexity, breadth and depth of the issues and problems.

Critical to a vital democracy is an informed public willing and able to engage in meaningful debate of what is in the common interest. Furthermore, in an increasingly complex society in which power and influence is ever more concentrated in smaller and smaller circles, it is even more critical that the public, in its commitment to participatory democracy, be able not only to resist the onslaughts of spin and partisanship but also to have the knowledge and skills to be proactive in public dialogue. Unfortunately, the quality of public discourse on educational policy and practice is appallingly superficial; it is amazingly devoid of careful analysis, is full of clichés and bromides, and refuses to address the paradoxical and contradictory nature of educational goals. This is rooted, in my view, in three realities: 1) in the emotionally charged veneration of traditional schools; 2) in differing views of child-rearing; and 3) in the resistance to any fundamental cultural change that might pose a threat to stability and order. All the more reason for a more reasoned and reflective inquiry into educational matters and all the more reason for the profession, whose members presumably know better, to engage vigorously in the practice of elevating the quality of public discourse on education.

I used to believe that we could change public opinion by simply revealing the existence and content of the hidden curriculum, but I now see that hope as naïve and oversimplified. I now believe that the public has a rough but ready sense of what's really going on. Without necessarily knowing the jargon of the educational discourse of the relationships among issues of class, race and gender and schooling, I believe there is considerable understanding of the broad dimensions of these dynamics. Surely, most parents know the score and have brushed aside all the disingenuous rhetoric about raising educational standards and recognize that it is really all about the intense struggle for economic and social advantage, if not survival. It is also clear to me that many parents are distressed over the testing madness and all the nonsense that comes with it—the obsession with homework, the cramming and the anxiety, as well as the neglect of the educational program not deemed important enough to be tested, for example, the arts and physical education. The tragedy is that so many parents feel powerless to deal with their contradictory responsibilities—on one hand, to ensure that their children can compete in the struggle for a good life and, on the other hand, to help their kids to have a meaningful and joyous childhood.

The reality is a harsh one—it is not only that our society is such that the race goes to those who achieve (e.g., in grades and test scores) but, even more cruelly, it goes to those who have the resources to enhance ability (e.g., through tutoring and coaching). Many parents have become convinced (with a great deal of justification) that the quality and nature of formal education plays a vital, if not defining, role in determining what the quality of our children's lives will be. Hence, the intense anxiety involved in dealing with the treacherous obstacle course that is the stuff of our current school regimen—getting good grades and high scores, choosing the right extra-curricular activities, struggling with writing an exemplary essay for college admissions, paying for college, getting into the right college and professional school, paying off educational loans, and all the rest that creates an ordeal that is as unavoidable as it is painful.

Regrettably, our political leaders have for the most part exploited these fears and anxieties rather than offering imaginative and bold alternatives to the current disaster that is institutionalized education. In a context of contentious politics, it is quite remarkable how similar is the political rhetoric on education—each politician exclaiming their passionate devotion to "raising standards," their unabated outrage at the lack of "accountability," all the time relying on the availability of the schools to serve as a convenient scapegoat for basic social and cultural problems. Moreover, many politicians who ought to know better have persisted in discussing education simplistically and superficially, thereby prompting the suspicion that they have chosen either not to pay attention to serious educational research and analysis or to ignore it.

The public deserves a much more sophisticated and nuanced discourse than the current mélange of strident and mock outrage at low standards and mediocre teachers that masks a reluctance to address the complexities of creating a sensible educational policy. I believe that there exists within the profession any number of ideas, concepts and formulations that could significantly add to the richness and vitality of public discourse on education but, for whatever reason, have not yet seen the public light of day. This knowledge gap is especially painful because it exists in spite of the valiant efforts of many of our colleagues to reach a wider audience. This is certainly not to say that the profession has a silver bullet that will solve all our educational problems, but only to point out that the public is being deprived of many of the rich ideas contained in any number of professional debates and disputes.

There are at least two hard sells involved in the process of enriching the quality of public educational discourse, namely the struggle to gain access to the general public and the struggle to change consciousness. It is true that there are many stories and features in the media concerning education, but most of them are superficial, misleading at best and distorted at worst. One often sees, for example, features on so-called innovative techniques or practices that seem to have stimulated some interest, such as a six-day school week or a requirement that students wear uniforms. There is a feel-good quality to these stories because the people involved seem to be highly energized and very optimistic about the efficacy of these "innovations." We typically do not get any theoretical or empirical justification for these ideas, and it is seldom that we get to see or read follow-ups to these stories. Another frequent story in the media will focus on the introduction of a different kind of administrative structure borrowed from the corporate world or on the appointment of an administrator from outside the field, such as a former general or a corporate executive. Often we are led to believe that this new kind of leadership will be much more focused and relentless in eliminating inefficiency and increasing productivity than the listless and flaccid leadership of the past. Again these stories typically miss the opportunity to present insights into the historical, political and economic dimensions of school problems. By focusing on colorful personalities and isolated and unique success stories, the media offer a sense of false optimism that there are simple (and inexpensive) solutions to the complex and perplexing problems of public education.

Not only will it likely continue to be very difficult for professionals to influence the media to report on education in more depth and with greater discernment, it will be even harder to move public opinion in this area. As indicated above, a great deal of the public have very clear and focused notions on the function and role of schools as they literally involve issues of life and death, so that attempts at radical changes are likely to seem threatening and risky. Hence the public is more likely to be interested in reforms that could improve the existing system, but with higher degrees of enthusiasm for less costly changes, such as those in homework policy and block scheduling, and less enthusiastic for more costly changes, such as decrease in class size or more course offerings (very expensive). However, although the public is deeply committed to the existing system for reasons mentioned above it is not without serious concerns and reservations. There is a lot of pain involved in our current educational system, much of it on the backs of students, but enough to add to the tensions and travails of child-rearing for parents.

Parents in particular need assistance in wrestling with the dilemma of helping their children to participate in the rat race or working to shield them from its toxic effects. Obviously, what is basically required are significant changes in the socio-economic system, but that is of little solace to parents who have to deal every night with homework-hating kids and every ten weeks with parsing report cards. They need some language and concepts to help them make some sense of this tortuous process of selecting the winners and losers of tomorrow, but more importantly they need the leadership and support of an authoritative, influential and articulate profession that is as vocal as it is respected. As of now, parents have to rely on the shibboleths and slogans of cowed and overworked school officials, a determinedly uninformed media, self-righteous politicians, and the self-serving and pompous declamations of commissions sponsored by corporate America.

Let me offer, as an example of the day-to-day struggles parents face, the constant demand from our leaders that parents and teachers work closely and in harmony with each other in order to improve student performance. This is, on the surface, a perfectly reasonable proposition, since communication, cooperation and success are all good things. Sometimes, however, parents encounter situations in which their children are suffering from certain schools practices, for example, excessive homework, questionable assignments and intense pressure, that lead the parents to sympathize with their kids' complaints.

In such situations, cooperation seems more like cooptation and supporting the schools could amount to betraying their kids. How on earth can we justify lots of children crying in fear and lots of parents pulling out their hair in frustration? Surely we cannot justify this pain in the name of affirming loyalty to a system unable to act on its own beliefs and unwilling to express outrage at being forced to do so. What a travesty it is that the educational process comes to be a matter of fear and loathing rather than a source of enlightenment and joy and when the major task of students is to find a way to endure school and get through it rather than to savor the opportunity to learn and have fun.

This crisis in the meaning of education does not speak well of a culture unable to provide an educational system that we can embrace with affection and gratitude. And it speaks even less well of a profession responsible for providing the reasons and wisdom to do so. My own conclusion is that the extraordinary project over the past century or so to develop a profession of education that can speak with intellectual and moral authority such that it can enrich our nation has so far been much more of a failure than a success. Here, I am speaking not of a form of radical education that is concerned with cultural transformation but in the more limited area of developing more meaningful educational experiences within the existing system. This is certainly not to deny the reality of a great number of hard-working, talented and dedicated people who continue and will continue to direct their energy towards the improvement of the system. It is only to state the obvious—that in spite of these efforts we have a school system that is, in the minds of many of us, at very serious odds with the profession's aspirations and hopes. We must address the question of the nature and degree of our responsibility for this state of affairs— just how is it that we don't have a system that most of us can be proud of or one that is not a model for the world?

The Role of the Profession: What are the Options?

I believe what is needed is for the profession to undergo an "agonizing reappraisal," to borrow an expression from the 1950s—that is to say, that we as a profession need to look candidly at our history by confronting our disappointments and the reasons we have not been able to be as successful as we could have been. I want to examine this notion through two lenses—one from the point of view of those (like me) who have stressed that the schools can change only to the extent that the society and culture changes. The other perspective is one that takes the position that significant social and cultural change can emerge from appropriate changes in the educational system. These two positions can be summed up as either "you can change the society by changing the schools" or "if you want to change the schools you've got to change the social and social structure first." Obviously, these positions are not mutually exclusive and there is plenty of room in the middle, but I believe that focusing on the opposite ends of the continuum can be a useful analytic tool in gaining insight into the issues.

I would guess that a great many of us entered the field in the belief that we could change the world for the better by working for significant changes in the educational system. There is a powerful logic to this hope since education, by definition, is the process of transmitting values and beliefs, and the principal and most influential locus for that function is presumably the public schools. I, for one, bought into the concept and became convinced that, although it would be a long and arduous struggle, the schools could be transformed in such a way that they could significantly transform the larger community. That is, until I began to take seriously the research on the hidden curriculum, which began my journey to the edge of despair, a journey greatly accelerated by the political events of the last two decades. Given a highly conservative culture that is deeply committed to preserving hierarchy and privilege, a society tightly controlled by corporate and military interests, and a weak, demoralized and impoverished educational system, it seems to me that the schools are about the last place to look to in order to form the advanced guard of a movement directed at structural transformation.

The whole thrust of setting up the tax-supported, politically controlled public school system was and continues to be directed primarily at providing for stability, continuity and preservation, a powerful mode of distributing privilege and for providing a reliable and skilled workforce. Indeed, it has served those functions very well and, moreover, has done it on the cheap. This should come as no surprise, since we do not have a robust and vital tradition of a broad struggle for radical social change.

Yet, in spite of all these tremendous obstacles, we absolutely need to continue the struggle for a more just and loving world. However, it seems to me that to see the schools as playing anything but a very modest and peripheral role in this is to reveal a very high level of denial and naïveté. I say it is time to give up the fantasy of believing that cultural transformation can come through changing the hearts and minds of educators and their constituents. In this regard, it is important to confront one especially difficult issue for the profession, and that involves the matter of solidarity and unity: that is, do we consider ourselves to be one profession, albeit with many subdivisions, with the expectation that we will be largely supportive of each other and that we will try to avoid airing our disputes in public?

This is a particularly sensitive issue difference between those who are school practitioners and those who define themselves primarily as researchers/theorists. Understandingly enough, teachers and administrators, who are typically under great public pressure and who are often embattled, do not appreciate additional criticism from their professional colleagues. In fact, many practitioners partially define "being professional" as avoiding being critical of colleagues or policies in public and instead as presenting a common front. Working in the trenches can be very taxing, even overwhelming, and we must not only have compassion for our dedicated and hardworking colleagues in the field but also strive to improve the conditions under which they teach. These people are not only our friends and colleagues, but more importantly they are human beings deserving of respect and dignity.

One has to acknowledge the dilemma of wanting to express solidarity and compassion with one's colleagues while at the same time exercising the responsibility to examine educational policies and practices critically and fairly. In a field as wide and diverse as ours, there will inevitably be sharp differences of opinion, and in an area as controversial and fundamental as education there will be very passionate feelings and deep commitments. Having said that, it must also be said that there is wide consensus that the field is in dreadful shape, which perforce means that the responsibility for this must to a large extent involve the profession itself. Even as we are aware of the enormous pressures and major obstacles that face the profession, and even as we empathize and sympathize with our brothers and sisters, we have to continue our commitment to being honest and candid with each other. In that spirit, I want to focus on a number of basic orientations that are quite dear to many theorists and practitioners, and indeed to me, but that I now find to have been unwise and which have, instead, become counter-productive.

I have already suggested that we give up one very powerful idea, one that is so much a part of all of us, namely the notion that we can substantially improve our society by way of the public schools. It is not only a highly unlikely possibility, it serves to distract us from what we can and should do as well as raising false hopes and unrealistic expectations. I believe that the reasons so many of us have held on to this fantasy are related to a generally overly optimistic and romantic view of the world, in which people of good will can come together for the common good and work out their differences through rational persuasion. Although there is an enormous amount of evidence that this is not the case, I, for one, still maintain that we are better off acting as if that premise were true till it is proven dead wrong. Yet, there are some less global flirtations that have developed into romances that we should be prepared to give up since they, like many flings, have clouded our vision and messed with our better judgment. There are two in particular I want to mention—one a romantic view of teachers and the other a romantic view of students.

Most of us have been teachers and are aware, at least to some extent, of the difficult if not impossible conditions under which many teachers work, and hence we admire and sympathize with them. We are upset when they are unfairly blamed for the failures of the schools, failures that probably ought to be attributed to deeper social, political and economic issues. At the same time, it must be said that, given these very difficult conditions, some teachers do better than others in overcoming them and, indeed, there are many gifted and dedicated teachers who are able to transcend serious obstacles and do extraordinary work. It must also be said that there are a great many mediocre teachers and surely a number of truly bad ones. It should not be particularly surprising that, in a workforce of over 2 million, one would find a wide range of abilities and talents and a correspondingly wide range of effectiveness. My point is only to demythologize, to move us away from the temptation to blame the ills of public education on shallow administrators, self-serving politicians and a cruel society. We have all probably experienced one way or another the damage and pain that can be and has been inflicted by callous, dim-witted and rigid teachers, and it is not any more helpful for making public policy to be tolerant of such teachers than it is to be obsessed by them. By the same token, many have benefited from experiencing talented, caring and inspiring teachers. I don't know if the distribution of talent among teachers is substantially different from what it is in other professional groups of comparable size, but we need to ward off the tendency to romanticize teachers as primarily helpless victims of an oppressive school regime dedicated to stifling creativity and individuality.

The basic message here is that those who are serious about making significant positive changes in the schools must include the issue of teacher quality in their agenda. This means that we must take on the hugely complex and controversial matter of teacher accountability head on and participate in efforts to develop fair and sensible modes of evaluating teachers. At minimum, we must find a way to protect our children from incompetent and cruel teachers. There is no question that there are bad teachers out there, and there is simply no justification knowingly to allow that to continue. I find it hard to believe that we cannot devise sensitive and imaginative ways to do this without threatening the academic and human rights of all teachers.

There is a parallel and related issue in attitudes that many of us hold towards students, who are often depicted as vulnerable and innocent cherubs tossed into a hostile and relentless system of imposed and arbitrary demands. This is a highly persuasive and compelling narrative, one to which I am particularly drawn, and it is truthful—but perhaps only to a point. Again we must confront the numbers, and in the instance of students we are talking of tens of millions of them—surely a magnitude that does not allow for easy generalizations. Lest I be misunderstood, I want to say as strongly as I can that my fundamental conviction is that *every* child should be treated with utmost respect and afforded full dignity and that the public is obligated to provide a fully meaningful education for *all* children. It is clear to me that, as a society, we have yet to provide sufficient resources to make this possible and, as a profession, we have not been successful in reaching out to all of our children and in developing appropriate learning experiences for them.

Many of our children come to school with serious problems and afflictions: some are ill or disabled, some are suffering emotionally, some are struggling with very distressing family situations, some are angry, some are terrified, some are hostile, and all come in the hope that their pain can be eased. Frankly, it is an open question as to whether our society is willing to provide the enormous resources required to meet the needs of all of our children. Nonetheless, it is the profession's responsibility to provide leadership and direction in formulating sensitive and sensible policies and practices for *all* children. As we accept and embrace this task we are also required to acknowledge the profound difficulties involved in facing this issue—not only the anguish and pain of the children and their families but the anguish and guilt that comes from our inability to know what to do.

One subset of children are those who are hostile, angry, even violent, and who act out their frustrations in school, causing further anguish and frustration among school staff. This phenomenon is particularly disheartening for those of us who are likely to take a progressive and gentle approach to matters of order. We abhor the use of harsh discipline and stern measures to deal with difficult children as much as we recoil from writing these children off as hopeless. The sad reality, however, is that there are many unruly and hostile children who can and do act out, often violently, in spite of friendly and supportive teachers. This is a matter where we need to be to be more sympathetic to teachers who complain about unmanageable kids rather than chiding them for not being more understanding and compassionate. There is no contradiction in believing that classroom misbehavior has its roots in poverty, dysfunctional families, emotional disorders and inequality and accepting the bleak reality that some kids can make teachers' lives miserable. Hollywood feeds romantic notions of what can happen when inspired teachers respond to the needs and interests of children with love, patience and faith. There is a constant stream of heartwarming movies depicting remarkable teachers who, in spite of heavy-duty student hostility, parental apathy and school torpor, are able to perform miraculous turnarounds in achievement and behavior. The cruel reality is that many caring and thoughtful teachers have had their hearts broken in the process of trying to reach out to some of these children. I certainly believe that teachers ought to be patient and imaginative and that they should involve students in learning, and I also believe that there are indeed remarkable teachers capable of having extraordinary success in very difficult situations.

At the same time, I believe that it behooves us to accept a reality in which we have yet to find a way to cope with a great many difficult classroom situations and that there are lots and lots of kids who successfully resist efforts to engage them in the educational process. I join those who tend to accept the notion of the inherent goodness and educability of all people, but I also believe we would be better off by dealing honestly with the very strong contrary empirical evidence. For example, as much as I find the practice of requiring uniforms or of offering military cadet type schools disquieting, I have to consider the high probability that there are kids who would likely benefit from such practices by encountering structure and developing self-confidence and self-esteem. Single-sex schools do not register with my notions of how teenagers should learn about gender differences, but there seems to be anecdotal evidence that it is appropriate in many situations. I believe we need to come to grips with the fundamental significance of individual differences and recognize the familiar but oft forgotten truism that people learn in different ways, including ways that disappoint us.

Recommendations

I have already made clear what I believe to be the most important way that our profession can contribute to the wellbeing of children of the 21st century, namely by providing the public with the conceptual tools necessary for a deeper, more sophisticated and far-ranging discourse on educational policies and practices. This means not only sharing and communicating the accumulated wisdom and insight of our research and analyses in all its complexities, paradoxes and uncertainties, but also in providing vigorous leadership and meaningful direction. This is our mandate, and it is our responsibility to do so with integrity and competence. By doing so we honor our commitment to support and nourish the ideals of the democratic vision.

Within this broad recommendation, I want to suggest a few more specific ones as they relate to two differing orientations I have discussed, one seeing the schools as being a critical force for social and cultural transformation, and the other that believes that, although the schools are not constituted to play that role, there is a continuous opportunity for incremental improvements within the existing model. I have already given my overarching response to this issue by urging us to give up as a lost cause on the notion that *the schools* can play a critical role in the quest for a much more just and loving community. However, I strongly reaffirm the belief that the *education* of children is an inevitable element of any process for fundamental socio-political-economic change. I also want to reaffirm the obvious, namely that the schools are an extremely important and influential institution and that we need to do everything we can to enrich the lives of students and teachers who spend so much of their lives there.

Having said that, I believe we must take steps to blunt the momentum towards further cementing the current schooling model, with its obsession with high-stakes testing, its increasingly narrow curriculum, and its steady march towards uniformity. I believe instead that educational theorists should work towards reenergizing and reconceptualizing the concept of alternative schools. The alternative schools movement in its early stages offered the possibility of stimulating the development of bold and imaginative educational models within the existing school system, and many such programs did emerge—as seen, for example, in the proliferation of magnet and charter schools.

We particularly need ideas on the boundaries of alternative schools—what elements are needed and which are not acceptable. In other words, we need to wrestle with the question of what should be the constitutive elements of a meaningful program of diverse education that emerges from the mix of imagination and daring with basic pedagogical and moral principles. I referred earlier, for example, to the military academy model as an alternative that has been used with some enthusiasm. I, for one, am not clear if this is entirely appropriate, and would appreciate some insights and considerations that could help us judge the appropriateness of this particular alternative, as well as others that have been proposed.

For starters, I would urge that such a framework should include the requirement that any alternative approach commits itself to treating all those involved (students, staff, parents, community) with utmost respect and dignity, that it should incorporate modes of strengthening a democratic consciousness in its program, that it should commit itself to working for the preservation of the environment, that it should provide opportunities for children to develop intellectually, morally, physically and emotionally, and that it should focus on stimulating critical and imaginative thinking as well as creativity and play. Moreover, in order to gain the absolutely critical support of the community in accepting the concept of a truly diverse educational program, we will need to pay due regard to community expectations and to what realistically can be achieved. Many parents will want to know what impact the proposed program will have on the prospects for college admissions, some parents will wonder if the program has sufficient structure and order, while others might have issues about the provision of particular offerings (e.g., athletics, music, foreign languages, etc.). Staff members will want to know if there are sufficient resources available and if there is a reasonable fit between the concept of the program and the particularities of the community and school.

Most importantly, the profession needs to provide the public with a framework of alternative schooling itself—why it's needed, what are its advantages and disadvantages, and how it fits into our social and cultural framework. As for myself, I believe there is a need for alternative schooling because of the reality of vast individual differences among children in their capacities and interests. At the same time, alternatives by themselves are not a good or a bad thing: what we want is better, more imaginative and effective alternatives and the availability of criteria to judge which are worth pursuing. I do not believe that we have come anywhere near fulfilling the possibilities inherent in the idea of the schools accommodating and promoting curricular and instructional diversity or that we have developed a sufficiently sophisticated conceptual framework that can guide such efforts. It seems to me that most alternatives stress different instructional approaches towards conventional goals rather than providing genuinely different notions of what constitutes a good education. However, when we get to this point we are very likely to come up against the question of the degree to which the dominant community and the school establishment are willing to make truly, perhaps scary significant changes.

Alternatives to Schooling

In addition to assisting the public to come up with alternatives to the existing and dominant schooling model, we have the further responsibility to encourage and nurture dialogue on alternative *education*. As I have said, it is clear to me that the public schools as presently constituted are not nearly compatible with the ideals of a truly democratic society dedicated to providing liberty, justice, meaning and joy for all. Indeed, part of the reason the public is bereft of ideas of an education that is consonant with these ideals is that we have contributed to the perpetuation of the fantasy that what happens in schools is education rather than the reality of thoroughgoing acculturation and socialization. If the schools are that good, why do poverty, hunger and homelessness persist? To what degree are schools accountable, not for reading levels and test scores but for corporate greed, political arrogance and hate crimes? Have the schools played any part in the enormous gap between the rich and the poor?' Are they connected in any way to the scandal of our health system? Are they not implicated at least somewhat in the horrific phenomenon of school shootings? If the schools are not having an impact on such critical issues, then why bother with them at all? Where then is the locus of responsibility for a society that somewhere along the way has been educated, at best, to tolerate our failings as a society and, at worst, to further them?

If it is possible at all to develop and implement a set of educational programs and principles that are truly compatible with the quest for a more just and loving society, it will have to happen primarily in venues other than the public schools and in radically different forms. As I have said, I believe that educational changes are more likely to follow social and cultural changes than vice versa, but that doesn't mean that education and schooling cannot contribute in a synergistic way to promoting significant change.

I believe that the hope for major educational change does not lie in the barren and sterile wasteland that is the school but in the latent possibilities of other educational modes and institutions. There are existing examples of imaginatively bold and doable educational enterprises outside the system, as shown, for example, in the variety of educational programs available for adults interested not in getting a degree but in enrichment. We as a profession ought to be engaged with the public in a dialogue about the distinction between schools and education and on ways we can diversify not only our schooling programs but our educational ones as well. We need to take very seriously what we already know, that people can have and have had, very positive educational experiences outside the conventional confines of formal educational institutions.

We do have a powerful instance of one area that has been able to break the iron grip of conventional and stultifying thinking in a vital part of our society, and here I speak of what has happened in the past generation in the discourse on medical care. We have seen an incredible increase in public awareness of alternative approaches to good health, and with it has come significant changes in the thinking of the medical profession. At the very least, there is a lively debate going on that involves a much better informed public and a much more responsive profession that has fundamentally altered the discourse on medical policies and practices. We need a public debate of parallel depth and daring for both education and schooling.

There is vast panoply of educational institutions and settings, whether they be formal or informal, already identified or potential, plus a rich lore of educational experience out there to be utilized. We already know the immense potential of the internet, of work experiences, of camp, of service programs, of internships, of intensive programs in any number of areas—in the arts, in the martial arts, in meditation, in science and technology, etc., etc. Once we add the power of imagination, the list becomes infinite. Once we open the gate to possibility there are no limits. Even more alternatives to this vast array of existing and putative approaches become apparent when we consider the almost limitless number of possible combinations and permutations that could be devised. Perhaps we can imagine the development of a new profession of personal educational advisers who could sit down with families and help plan and coordinate a program of educational experiences (including schools) with periodic and timely opportunities for reassessment. The particular combination of experiences would vary, of course, from student to student, but here again we would need dialogue on what should constitute a common core of concerns, as mentioned above in my discussion of alternative schools.

Talking about alternative *education* is, of course, not primarily about instructional techniques, curricular innovations or modes of funding, but at bottom it is about discussing alternative ways of being in the world. It has been a while since we have conjoined debate about what would constitute a truly more just, loving and sustainable world with a debate on an educational process commensurate with that vision. It is clear to me, to paraphrase Audre Lorde, that we cannot create the new world we all so desperately ache for with the tools that forged the increasingly dangerous and dying world in which we now live. The hope I have that the 21st century will be a time for extraordinarily creative thinking about education is based on the principle of plain old necessity, for we face the prospect of calamity if we do not make serious changes in the ways we live with each other and dwell within ourselves. The material threats to us are familiar and clear—war, hunger, poverty, environmental degradation—as are the spiritual dangers—alienation, cynicism, nihilism and despair. As a people, we have to confront these daunting challenges in the context of a realty in which we can no longer rely on incremental change, patience and endurance to help us muddle through from crisis to crisis. As educators, we can and must participate in what is sure to be perhaps the most exciting and important educational experience of all time, namely how to learn to overcome stupidity with wisdom, greed with generosity, and hatred with love before we finish our rush towards self-destruction.

3

Is There a Place for Education in Social Transformation?

Michael W. Apple

Introduction

I began writing this chapter soon after my return from giving an address at an international conference in Cuba. As many of you will know, it is not easy for U.S. citizens to go to Cuba. Special licenses are required. Permission is only given if the person has a "legitimate" purpose for going. And in the case of academic lectures at conferences, permission is only given if the conference is not sponsored by the Cuban government.

During the time I was in Havana, the United States tightened these regulations even more to make it even harder for Cuban Americans to send money to, or even to visit, relatives living in Cuba. This was on top of over forty years of economic and cultural/political blockade.

I am decidedly not in favor of these policies, which seem to me and many others to be deeply flawed. However, my interest here is not in such policies, but in my address at the conference itself. I began with a statement of political and educational solidarity with the people in the audience—most of whom were educators—and with the large number of countries they represented. I distanced myself from a number of the international economic and cultural policies advocated by the United States. I then critically discussed in much greater detail the problems with two major emphases in education internationally: 1) neo-liberal educational reforms, such as the immense pressure towards marketization and privatization exemplified by vouchers and the growth of for-profit schools; and 2) neo-conservative policies involving the push for ever-increasing national standards, national curricula and (increasingly high-stakes) national testing. Finally, I stated that these were not only dangerous tendencies (see, for example, Apple 2006; Apple et al. 2003) but very simplistic ones. There were alternatives to the policies and practices of what I called "conservative modernization." I pointed to the schools represented in *Democratic Schools* (Apple and Beane 2007), in the work of educators associated with the progressive educational journal *Rethinking Schools*, and in the Citizen School and participatory budgeting movements in Porto Alegre, Brazil (Apple et al. 2003), successful models of critical education to which I shall return later in this chapter.

As with any speaker, I was heartened by the fact that the large international audience greeted my address with applause. I looked forward to some serious discussions with the participants over the course of the conference. This did occur. But so did something else.

Immediately after my address, a person came up to me. He was visibly agitated and literally stuck his nose into my face and yelled at me. "Dr. Apple, you are a creep and a disgrace to the American flag!" He was an official from a school system in Florida, someone who saw my arguments and criticisms as unpatriotic. Perhaps he was also personally threatened by my public worries about the move towards vouchers in his own state, about the move towards conservative definitions of "common culture" in the curriculum and the growing overemphasis on reductive forms of testing, about the concerns I had about the increasing influence of ultra-conservative religious movements on schooling in the United States organized around people who believe that God only speaks to them, and about my argument that educators in our country have much to learn from some of the educational successes of nations in the "South." But whatever his motivations, his attack says something about the ways in which some "Americans" equate a lack of substantive criticism as patriotic and define critical sensibilities in general as outside the boundaries of legitimate expression.[1]

Yet in my mind, when a nation and its government and major institutions do not deliver on their promises and on the sets of values they officially profess in education and elsewhere, then substantive criticism is the ultimate act of patriotism. Such criticism says that "We are not just passing through. This is our country and our institutions as well, built by the labor of millions of people such as ourselves. We take the values in our founding documents seriously and demand that you do so too."

Of course, the arguments I've been making in this chapter are quite political. But that is the point. Over the past three decades, many committed and critical educators have argued that education must be seen as a political act. They have suggested that, in order to do this, we need to think *relationally*. That is, understanding education requires that we situate it back into both the unequal relations of power in the larger society and into the relations of dominance and subordination—and the conflicts to change these things—that are generated by these relations. Thus, rather than simply asking whether students have mastered a particular subject matter and have done well on our all too common tests, we should ask a different set of questions: Whose knowledge is this? How did it become "official"? What is the relationship between this knowledge and who has cultural, social, and economic capital in this society? Who benefits from these definitions of legitimate knowledge and who does not? What can we do as critical educators and activists to change existing educational and social inequalities and to create curricula and teaching that are more socially just (Apple 2000, 1996; Apple and Beane 2007)?

These are complicated questions and they often require complicated answers. However, there is now a long tradition of asking and answering these kinds of critical challenges to the ways education is currently being carried on, a tradition that has grown considerably since the time when I first raised these issues in *Ideology and Curriculum* (Apple 1979; see also the more recent 3rd edition, Apple 2004). Perhaps the best way of documenting why we need to keep these political issues at the forefront of our vision of what schools now do and what they should do is to focus on the life of a student, someone I knew very well. I hope that you will forgive me if at times throughout this chapter I use personal narratives to make larger points. But it seems to me that sometimes such a writing style can bring home points in ways that more abstract ways of presenting things cannot. Such a style also makes the politics of education not something "out there" in some abstract universe very far away, but something "right here" in terms of our personal choices inside and outside of education.

Remembering Real Schools and Real Children

Joseph sobbed at my desk. He was a tough kid, a hard case, someone who often made life difficult for his teachers. He was all of nine years old and here he was sobbing, holding on to me in public. He had been in my fourth-grade class all year, a classroom situated in a decaying building in an east coast city that was among the most impoverished in the nation. There were times when I wondered, seriously, whether I would make it through that year. There were many Josephs in that classroom and I was constantly drained by the demands, the bureaucratic rules, the daily lessons that bounced off of the kids' armor. Yet somehow it was satisfying, compelling and important, even though the prescribed curriculum and the textbooks that were meant to teach it were often beside the point. They were boring to the kids and boring to me.

I should have realized the first day what it would be like when I opened that city's "Getting Started" suggested lessons for the first few days and it began with the suggestion that, "as a new teacher," I should circle the students' desks and have them introduce each other and tell something about themselves. It's not that I was against this activity; it's just that I didn't have enough unbroken desks (or even chairs) for all of the students. A number of the kids had nowhere to sit. This was my first lesson—but certainly not my last—in understanding that the curriculum and those who planned it lived in an unreal world, a world *fundamentally* disconnected from my life with those children in that inner-city classroom.

But here's Joseph. He's still crying. I've worked extremely hard with him all year long. We've eaten lunch together; we've read stories; we've gotten to know each other. There are times when he drives me to despair and other times when I find him to be among the most sensitive children in my class. I just can't give up on this kid. He's just received his report card and it says that he is to repeat fourth grade. The school system has a policy that states that failure in any two subjects (including the "behavior" side of the report card) requires that the student be left back. Joseph was failing "gym" and arithmetic. Even though he had shown improvement, he had trouble keeping awake during arithmetic, had done poorly on the mandatory city-wide tests, and hated gym. One of his parents worked a late shift and Joseph would often stay up, hoping to spend some time with her. And the things that students were asked to do in gym were, to him, "lame."

The thing is, he had made real progress during the year. But I was instructed to keep him back. I knew that things would be worse next year. There would still not be enough desks. The poverty in that community would still be horrible; and health care and sufficient funding for job training and other services would be diminished. I knew that the jobs that were available in this former mill town paid deplorable wages and that, even with both of his parents working for pay, Joseph's family income was simply insufficient. I also knew that, given all that I already had to do each day in that classroom and each night at home in preparation for the next day, it would be nearly impossible for me to work any harder than I had already done with Joseph. And there were another five children in that class whom I was supposed to leave back.

So Joseph sobbed. Both he and I understood what this meant. There would be no additional help for me—or for children such as Joseph—next year. The promises would remain simply rhetorical. Words would be thrown at the problems. Teachers and parents and children would be blamed. But the school system would look like it believed in and enforced higher standards. The structuring of economic and political power in that community and that state would again go on as "business as usual."

The next year Joseph basically stopped trying. The last time I heard anything about him was that he was in prison.

This story is not apocryphal. While the incident took place a while ago, the conditions in that community and that school are much worse today. And the intense pressure that teachers, administrators and local communities are under is also considerably worse (Kozol 1991; Lipman 2004). It reminds me of why large numbers of thoughtful educators and activists mistrust the incessant focus on standards, increased testing, marketization and vouchers, and other kinds of educational "reforms" which may sound good in the abstract, but which often work in exactly the opposite ways when they reach the level of the classroom (see Apple 2006; Valenzuela 2005; Lipman 2004; McNeil 2000). It is exactly this sensibility of the contradictions between proposals for reform and the realities and complexities of education on the ground that provides one of the major reasons so many of us are asking the questions surrounding how education can make a more serious contribution to social justice. I want to say more about this in the next section of this chapter.

The Politics of Educational Reform

Critical educators have long demonstrated that policies often have strikingly unforeseen consequences. Reforms that are instituted with good intentions may have hidden effects that are more than a little problematic. We have shown for instance that the effects of some of the favorite reforms of neo-liberals and neo-conservatives—voucher plans, national or state-wide curricula, and national or state-wide testing can serve as examples—quite often reproduce or even worsen inequalities. Thus, we should be very cautious about accepting what may seem to be meritorious intentions at face value. Intentions are too often contradicted by how reforms may function in practice. This is true not only for large-scale transformations of educational policies and governance, but also about moves to change the ways curriculum and teaching go on in schools.

The framework that politically and educationally progressive educators have employed to understand this is grounded in what in cultural theory is called the act of repositioning. It in essence says that the best way to understand what any set of institutions, policies and practices does is to see it from the standpoint of those who have the least power. Speaking personally, growing up poor myself made this almost a "natural" perspective for me to take. That is, every institution, policy and practice— and especially those that now dominate education and the larger society—establishes relations of power in which some voices are heard and some are not. While it is not preordained that those voices that will be heard most clearly are also those who have the most economic, cultural and social capital, it is most likely that this will be the case. After all, we do not exist on a level playing field. Many economic, social and educational policies, when actually put in place, tend to benefit those who already have advantages.

These points may seem overly rhetorical and too abstract, but unfortunately there is no small amount of truth in them. For example, at a time when all too much of the discourse around educational reform is focused on vouchers and choice plans, on the one hand, and on proposals for national or state curricula, standards and testing, on the other, as I have shown in a number of volumes (Apple 1995, 1996, 2000, 2006; Apple et al. 2003), there is a good deal of international evidence now that such policies may actually reproduce or even worsen class, gender and race inequalities. Thus, existing structures of economic and cultural power often lead to a situation in which what may have started out, in some educators' or legislators' minds, as an attempt to make things better, in the end is all too usually transformed into another set of mechanisms for social stratification.

While much of this is due to the ways in which race, gender, class and "ability" act as structural realities in this society and to how we fund (and don't fund) schools, some of it is related to the hesitancy of policy-makers to take seriously enough the complicated ways in which education is itself a political act. These very politics and the structurally generated inequalities that stand behind them provide much of the substance underpinning the organizational principles of critical work.

A key word in my discussion above is *reform*. This concept is what might be called a "sliding signifier." That is, it has no essential meaning and, like a glass, can be filled with multiple things. As Wittgenstein (1953) reminded us, it is always wise not to accept the meaning of a concept at face value. Instead, one must contextualize it. The meaning is in its *use*. Let us look at this in a bit more detail.

The language of educational reform is always interesting. It consistently paints a picture that what is going in schools now needs fixing, is outmoded, inefficient or simply "bad." Reforms will fix it. They will make things "better." Over the past decades certain language systems in particular have been mobilized. Not only will specific reforms make things better, they will make schools more democratic. Of course, the word "democracy" is one of the best examples of a sliding signifier. It carries with it an entire history of conflicts over its very meaning (Foner 1997). Like reform, democracy doesn't carry an essential meaning emblazoned on its head, so to speak. Instead it is one of the most contested words in the English language. Indeed, one of the major tactics of dominant groups historically and currently is to cement particular meanings of democracy into public discourse. Thus, under current neo-liberal policies in education and elsewhere, there are consistent attempts to redefine democracy as simply consumer choice. Here democracy is not a collective project of building and rebuilding our public institutions. It becomes simply a matter of placing everything that was once public onto a market. Collective justice will somehow take care of itself as the market works its wonders.

As Mary Lee Smith and her colleagues have recently demonstrated in their powerful analysis of a number of educational reforms, the nice-sounding and "democratic" language used to promote reforms is often totally at odds with the actual functioning of these reforms in real schools in real communities (Smith et al. 2004). A significant number of things that were advertised (and that is often the appropriate word) as making schools more responsive and "better" (increased testing and parental choice through marketization may serve as examples) may have exacerbated problems of inequality. (Think of Joseph and what happened to him in an earlier round of increased testing and "raising standards.")

One of the reasons this is the case is because the formation of a good deal of educational policy is actually a form of "symbolic politics," basically a kind of theater (Smith et al. 2004). This is not to claim that policy-makers are acting in bad faith. Rather, because of the distribution (or not) of resources, tragic levels of impoverishment, the ways policies are implemented (or not), and the cleverness of economically and culturally dominant groups in using reforms for their own advantage, the patterns of benefits are not anywhere near the supposedly democratic ends envisioned by some of their well-meaning proponents. (Some reforms as well may simply be the result of cynical manipulation of the public for electoral advantage; but that's a topic for another essay.)

Understanding Conservative Social Movements in Education

The arguments I made above are related to a particular claim that it is important to make. Many of us have spent a good deal of time showing that it is social movements, *not* educators, which are the real engines of educational transformations (Anyon 2005; Apple 2006). And the social movements that are the most powerful now are more than a little conservative. I want to argue in fact that, unless we think very tactically about what the Right has been able to accomplish and what the balance of forces now are, all too many of our attempts at putting in place more critically democratic reforms may be less powerful than we would like.

Over the past decade, a good deal of concerted effort has been devoted to analyzing the reasons behind the rightist resurgence—what I have called "conservative modernization"—in education and to try to find spaces for interrupting it (see Apple 2006; Apple and Buras 2006). My own aim has not simply been to castigate the Right, although there is a bit of fun in doing so. Rather, I have also sought to illuminate the dangers, and the elements of good sense, not only bad sense, that are found within what is an identifiable and powerful new "hegemonic bloc" (that is, a powerful set of groups that provides overall leadership to and pressure on what the basic goals and policies of a society are). This new rightist alliance is made up of various factions—neo-liberals, neo-conservatives, authoritarian populist religious conservatives, and some members of the professional and managerial new middle class. These are complicated groups, but let me describe them briefly.

This power bloc combines multiple fractions of capital who are committed to neo-liberal marketized solutions to educational problems, neo-conservative intellectuals who want a "return" to higher standards and a "common culture," authoritarian populist religious fundamentalists who are deeply worried about secularity and the preservation of their own traditions, and particular fractions of the professionally oriented new middle class who are committed to the ideology and techniques of accountability, measurement and "management." While there are clear tensions and conflicts within this alliance, in general its overall aims are in providing the educational conditions believed necessary both for increasing international competitiveness, profit and discipline and for returning us to a romanticized past of the "ideal" home, family and school (Apple 2006, 1996).

I have had a number of reasons for focusing on the alliance behind conservative modernization. First, these groups are indeed powerful, as any honest analysis of what is happening in education and the larger society clearly indicates. Second, they are quite talented in connecting to people who might ordinarily disagree with them. For this reason, I have shown in a number of places that people who find certain elements of conservative modernization relevant to their lives are not puppets. They are not dupes who have little understanding of the "real" relations of this society. This smacks of earlier reductive analyses within the critical tradition that were based in ideas of "false consciousness."

My position is very different. I maintain that the reason that some of the arguments coming from the various factions of this new hegemonic bloc are listened to is because they *are* connected to aspects of the realities that people experience (Apple 1996; Apple and Pedroni 2005). The tense alliance of neo-liberals, neo-conservatives, authoritarian populist religious activists, and the professional and managerial new middle class only works because there has been a very creative articulation of themes that resonate deeply with the experiences, fears, hopes and dreams of people as they go about their daily lives. The Right has often been more than a little manipulative in its articulation of these themes. It has integrated them within racist nativist discourses, within economically dominant forms of understanding, and within a problematic sense of "tradition." But, this integration could only occur if they were organized around people's understanding of their real material and cultural lives.

The second reason I have stressed the tension between good and bad sense and the ability of dominant groups to connect to people's real understandings of their lives—aside from my profound respect for Antonio Gramsci's writings about this (Gramsci 1968, 1971)—has to do with my belief that we have witnessed a major educational accomplishment over the past three decades in many countries. All too often, we assume that educational and cultural struggles are epiphenomenal. The real battles occur in the paid workplace—the "economy." Not only is this a strikingly reductive sense of what the economy is (its focus on paid, not unpaid, work; its neglect of the fact that, say, cultural institutions such as schools are also places where paid work goes on, etc.) (Apple 1986), it also ignores what the Right has actually done.

Conservative modernization has radically reshaped the commonsense of society. It has worked in every sphere—the economic, the political and the cultural—to alter the basic categories we use to evaluate our institutions and our public and private lives. It has established new identities. It has recognized that to win in the state, you must win in civil society. That is, you need to work at the level of people's daily experiences, not only in government policies. The accomplishment of such a vast educational project has many implications. It shows how important cultural struggles are. And, oddly enough, it gives reason for hope. It forces us to ask a number of significant questions. *What can we learn from the Right about how to build movements for social transformation? If the Right can do this, why can't we?*

I do not mean these as rhetorical questions. As I have argued repeatedly in my own work, the Right has shown how powerful the struggle over meaning and identity—and hence, schools, curricula, teaching and evaluation—can be. While we should not want to emulate their often cynical and manipulative processes, the fact that they have had such success in pulling people under their ideological umbrella has much to teach us. Granted there are real differences in money and power between the forces of conservative modernization and those whose lives are being tragically altered by the policies and practices coming from the alliance. But, the Right wasn't as powerful thirty years ago as it is now. It collectively organized. It created a decentered unity, one where each element sacrificed some of its particular agenda to push forward on those areas that bound them together. Can't we do the same?

I believe that we can, but only if we face up to the realities and dynamics of power in unromantic ways—and think tactically about what can be done now even under conditions that we may not always control. And this means not only critically analyzing the rightist agendas and the effects of their increasingly mistaken and arrogant policies, but engaging in some serious criticism of some elements within the progressive and critical educational communities as well. Thus, as I argue in *Educating the "Right" Way* (Apple 2006), the romantic possibilitarian rhetoric of some of the writers on critical pedagogy is not sufficiently based on a tactical or strategic analysis of the current situation, nor is it sufficiently grounded in its understanding of the reconstructions of discourse and movements that are occurring in all too many places. Here I follow Cameron McCarthy, who wisely reminds us, "We must think possibility within constraint; that is the condition of our time" (McCarthy 2000).

We need to remember that cultural and educational struggles are not epiphenomenal. They *count*, and they count in institutions throughout society. In order for dominant groups to exercise leadership, large numbers of people must be convinced that the maps of reality circulated by those with the most economic, political and cultural power are indeed wiser than other alternatives. Dominant groups do this by attaching these maps to the elements of good sense that people have and by changing the very meaning of the key concepts and their accompanying structures of feeling that provide the centers of gravity for our hopes, fears and dreams about this society. The Right has been much more successful in doing this than progressive groups and movements, in part because it has been able to craft—through hard and lengthy economic, political and cultural efforts—a tense but still successful alliance that has shifted the major debates over education and economic and social policy onto its own terrain. And the sometimes mostly rhetorical material of critical pedagogy simply is unable to cope with this. Only when it is linked much more to concrete issues of educational policy and practice—and to the daily lives of educators, students and community members—can it succeed. This, of course, is why journals such as *Rethinking Schools* and books such as *Democratic Schools* (Apple and Beane 2007), that connect critical educational theories and approaches to the actual ways in which they can be and are present in real classrooms, become so important. Thus, while we should support the principles of critical theory and critical pedagogy in the United States, we also need to act as internal critics when the latter has forgotten what it is meant to do and has sometimes become simply an academic specialization at universities.

Working Strategically

The story of how the book I mentioned above, *Democratic Schools* (Apple and Beane 1995, 2007), came about may be a good way of showing what I mean here. Along with many other people, including many of the contributors to this book, I've argued that it is essential that critical educators should not ignore the question of practice. That is, we must find ways of speaking to (and learning from) people who now labor every day in schools in worsening conditions, which are made even worse by the merciless attacks from the Right. This means that, rather than ignore "mainstream" organizations and publications, it's important to occupy the spaces provided by existing "mainstream" publication outlets to publish books during a conservative era that provide *critical* answers to teachers' questions such as "What do I do on Monday?" As I hinted at earlier, this space has too long been ignored by many theorists of critical pedagogy.

This is where *Democratic Schools* enters as an important success. One very large "professional" organization in the United States—the Association for Supervision and Curriculum Development (ASCD)—publishes books that are distributed each year to its more than 150,000 members, most of whom are teachers or administrators in elementary, middle or secondary schools. ASCD has not been a very progressive organization, preferring to publish largely technicist and overtly depoliticized material. Yet it has been concerned that its publications have not sufficiently represented socially and culturally critical educators. It, thus, has been looking for ways to increase its legitimacy among a wider range of educators. Because of this legitimacy problem, and because of its large membership, ASCD approached me to write a book about what critical educational theory had to say to practitioners. Paradoxically, this invitation happened at exactly the time it had become clearer to me that it was important to convince major organizations and publishers to publish and widely circulate material that would demonstrate the actual practical *successes* of critical models of curriculum, teaching and evaluation in solving real problems in schools and communities, especially with working-class and poor children and children of color.

At first I emphatically said "No"—not because I was against such a project, but because I believed quite strongly that the best people to do such a book would be those practicing critical teachers and administrators who were now engaged in doing what needed to be done "on Monday." In essence, I felt that I should be their secretary, putting together a book based on their words, struggles and accomplishments. If ASCD was willing for me to play the role of secretary, then I would do it. But I had one caveat. It had to be a truly honest book, one in which these critical educators could tell it as it really was.

After intense negotiations that guaranteed an absence of censorship (in which ASCD did try to engage when the manuscript was in fact completed), I asked Jim Beane, one of the leaders of the progressive education movement in the United States, to work with me on *Democratic Schools*. Both of us were committed to doing a book that provided clear practical examples of the power of Freirian and similar critical approaches at work in classrooms and communities. *Democratic Schools* was not only distributed to most of the 150,000 members of the organization, but it has gone on to sell at least an additional 100,000 copies. Thus, nearly 250,000 copies of a volume that tells the practical stories of the largely successful struggles of critically oriented educators in real schools are now in the hands of educators who daily face similar problems. The new and expanded second edition of the book promises to keep these stories alive.

This is an important intervention. While there is no guarantee that teachers will always be progressive (nor is there any guarantee that those who are progressive around class and union issues will be equally progressive around issues of gender, sexuality and race), many teachers do have socially and pedagogically critical intuitions. However, they often do not have ways of putting these intuitions into practice because they cannot picture them in action in daily situations. On account of this, critical theoretical and political insights, then, have nowhere to go in terms of their embodiment in concrete pedagogical situations where the politics of curriculum and teaching must be *enacted*. For both Jim and me, and for the authors included in this book, this is a tragic absence and strategically filling it is absolutely essential. Thus, we need to use and expand the spaces in which critical pedagogical "stories" are made available so that these positions do not remain only on the theoretical or rhetorical level. The publication and widespread distribution of *Democratic Schools* provides one instance of a crucial set of tactics, using and expanding such spaces in ways that make critical educational positions seem actually doable in "ordinary" institutions such as schools and local communities.

Learning from Others

Our understanding of these political and educational issues, of the dangers we now face, and of what can and must be done to deal with them is not only grounded in our ongoing political and educational experiences, in the gritty realities of working with children such as Joseph, in the research we've carried out on what schools do and do not do in this society, or in, say, the work that many of us do with practicing educators on building more critical and democratic curricula and teaching strategies. For me, it also has been profoundly affected by the extensive international work in which I have been fortunate to engage in Latin America, Asia, Africa and elsewhere. For example, beginning in the mid-1980s, I began to go to Brazil to work with the

Ministry of Education in the southern city of Porto Alegre and to give both academic and more popular lectures at universities and to teacher union groups. Most of my books had been translated there. Because of this, and because of similar theoretical and political tendencies in my own work and that coming out of Brazil, I developed close relationships with many politically active educators there.

This also meant not only that I developed an ongoing relationship with activist educators and researchers in the Workers Party throughout Brazil, but, just as importantly, an even closer relationship with the great Brazilian critical educator Paulo Freire grew as well (see, for example, Freire 1972; Apple in press). But what I have learned through my experiences in Brazil has been crucial. One of the most important lessons is this. Critical educators in the United States must also look outside our borders for lessons on what is possible and how to achieve it. The best example of this can be found in the city of Porto Alegre.

In Porto Alegre, a set of policies has been instituted that has had what seem to be extensive and long-lasting effects. Influenced by Paulo Freire's work, this has occurred in large part because the policies are coherently linked to larger dynamics of social transformation and to a coherent strategy that aims to change the mechanisms of the government and the rules of participation in the formation of state policies. The policies of the "Popular Administration" in Porto Alegre involving the "Citizen School" and participatory budgeting are explicitly designed to change radically both the municipal schools and the relationship between communities, the state and education. This set of polices and the accompanying processes of implementation are constitutive parts of a clear and explicit project aimed at constructing not only a better school for the least advantaged members of society but also a larger project of radical and thick democracy. In essence, they have recaptured from the Right the meaning of democracy.

The reforms being built in Porto Alegre are still in formation, but they have crucial implications for how we might think about the politics of education policy and its role in social transformation. The city's experiences have considerable importance not only for Brazil, but for all of us who are deeply concerned about the effects of the neo-liberal and neo-conservative restructuring of education and of the public sphere in general. The principles of how specifically one can build a curriculum based on the lived culture of oppressed peoples, of how thick democracy can actually be made to work among the poor and disenfranchised (and among all citizens), of how the bureaucratic nature of educational governance can be reformed in genuinely democratic ways—all of these are issues that are faced daily in the educational realities of the United States. And these are exactly the foci of Porto Alegre's ongoing experiences. Given this, there is much to learn from the successful struggles there. Reversing teacher and taught in international educational relations, so that the "South" becomes the teacher of the "North," is a good place to start.

Can Education Change Society?

Of course, the examples to which I pointed both of critically democratic schools and of what is happening in Porto Alegre raise a significant question. Can schools actually contribute to a more just society? Paulo Freire and many others who were more specifically rooted in the history of critical educational and cultural work in the United States, such as George Counts, Harold Rugg, Miles Horton, W. E. B. DuBois, Carter Woodson, and others, have been guided by an abiding concern not just with the role of education in reproducing dominance, but also in its role in challenging dominance. As for these people, one of the major questions that has served as an unacknowledged backdrop for the work of the authors in this volume is simple to state but very difficult to answer: "Can education change society?" I need to say something more about this here.

Let me begin by pointing out that this way of wording the question has some serious conceptual, empirical and political problems. First, it is important to realize that education *is* a part of society. It is not something alien, something that stands outside. Indeed, it is a key set of institutions and a key set of social and personal relations. It is just as central to a society as shops, businesses, factories, farms, health-care institutions, law firms, unpaid domestic labor in the home, and so many other places in which people and power interact.

But there are other things that make it decidedly not an "outside" institution. Even if one holds to the orthodox belief that only economic institutions are the core of a society, and that before we can change the schools we need to change the economy, schools are places where people *work*. Building maintenance people, teachers, administrators, nurses, social workers, clerical workers, psychologists, counselors, cooks, crossing guards, teacher aides—all of these groups of people engage in paid labor in and around the places we call schools. Each of these kinds of position has a set of labor relations and class distinctions attached to it. And each is stratified not only by class, but by race and gender as well.

Thus, teaching is often seen as women's paid work, as are the jobs of school nurses and the people who usually serve the food in the school cafeteria. In many areas these same women who serve the food are women of color, as are teacher aides in many urban areas. The labor of building maintenance is usually done by men. School secretaries are most often women. Not only is the labor process of each different (although there is a significant dynamic of proletarianization and intensification of teachers' work (Apple 1986, 1995)—indeed the best description of teaching I've ever heard is from my neighbor, a secondary-school teacher who said "Once again I didn't have time to even go to the bathroom today!")—but there are significant differences in pay and prestige socially attached to each. Thus, it would be very wrong to see schools as other than "society."

As paid workplaces, they are *integral parts* of the economy. As differentiated workplaces, they reconstitute (and sometimes challenge) class, gender and race hierarchies. And as institutions that have historically served as engines of working-class mobility in terms of employing upwardly mobile college graduates from groups who have often been seen as "not quite worthy," or even as "despised others" such as people of color, they have played a large role as arenas in the struggle over class, gender, and race economic advancement. My own history of being born very poor, and then going from poor schools, to night school to become a teacher, to graduate work at Columbia University, documents parts of this struggle. It is the result of *both* cooptation (giving poor and working-class children a chance to make it as individuals, but not radically changing the structures that create impoverishment in the first place) and successful struggle.

But it is not just as workplaces that schools are part of the economy. They are also places that are increasingly being put on a market through such things as voucher plans. The children inside them are increasingly being bought and sold as "captive audiences" for advertising in "reforms" such as Channel One. Interrupting the selling of schools and children *is* a form of action that challenges the economy. And this is one of the reasons many of us have worked with others in an alliance with community activists throughout the country to get Channel One out of schools (Apple 2006, 2000; Molnar 1996).

So far, I have focused upon the ways in which educational institutions are very much part of the economy, not upon things that exist somehow apart from it. But, as I mentioned earlier, this ignores the ways in which cultural struggles are crucial and, while they are deeply connected to them, cannot be reduced to economic issues without doing damage to the complexity of real life (Apple et al. 2003; Apple and Buras 2006).

Take the history of African American struggles against a deeply racist society. Schools have played central roles in the creation of movements for justice in general, but have been central to the building of larger scale social mobilizations within communities of color. In essence, rather than being peripheral reflections of larger battles and dynamics, struggles over schooling—over what should be taught, over the relationship between schools and local communities, over the very ends and means of the institution itself—have provided a crucible for the *formation* of larger social movements towards equality (Hogan 1983; Apple et al. 2003; Anyon 2005; Ladson-Billings in press). These collective movements have transformed our definitions of rights, of who should have them, and of the role of the government in guaranteeing these rights. Absent organized, community-wide mobilizations, these transformations would not have occurred (Fraser 1997; Giugni et al. 1999). In cases such as this, education has been and is a truly powerful arena for building coalitions and movements, one whose social effects can echo throughout the society.

But this is not all. Education clearly plays a key social role in the formation of identities (Apple and Buras 2006). That is, children spend a very large part of their lives inside the buildings we call schools. They come to grips with authority relations, with the emotional labor of managing their presentation of self and of being with others who are both the same and different. Transformations in the content and structure of this key organization have lasting effects on the dispositions and values that we do and do not act upon, on who we think we are and on who we think we can become. Here too this is not only an intellectual and political position, but one based on very intense personal experiences. I, for instance, have too many memories of the way my son Paul was treated differently throughout his school career simply because he is African American—and the truly damaging effects this had both on his sense of self and on his understanding of what it was possible for him to become.

Yet, schools also are part of the cultural apparatus of society in other ways than building (positive or negative) identities. They are key mechanisms in determining what is socially valued as "legitimate knowledge" and what is seen as merely "popular." In their role in defining a large part of what is considered to be legitimate knowledge, they also participate in the process through which particular groups are granted status and other groups remain unrecognized or minimized. Thus, here too schools are at the center of struggles over a politics of recognition over race/ethnicity, class, gender, sexuality, ability, religion, and other important dynamics of power (Fraser 1997; Binder 2002). These too are spaces for political and educational action.

Taking Risks

In the last paragraph of the previous section, I made a number of arguments about the importance of seeing schools as places for action. Yet, having said this, I want to be honest about some of the implications of this argument. Engaging in political/ educational action in and through schools is *risky*. I mean this in two ways. It can lead to arrogance: "I've got *the* correct answer, the correct ethical and political stance, and don't have to listen to you." This is a very real danger, one that has surfaced more than once within the critical educational community. Political commitment must be countered by humility and an equal commitment to listen carefully to criticism.

But there's a second danger. Actually acting on one's deeply held ethical, political, and educational commitments to building an education that responds to all of us, one that embodies a vision of the common good that says that it needs constant criticism and revision to keep it alive, can be threatening to people with power. Let me return to a personal story that documents this in my own life, but at the same time shows that victories can still be won (Apple 1999).

In the last few years of my public school teaching career—after I had spent some time teaching children such as Joseph in inner-city schools and well before I ever dreamed of becoming a "critical scholar" and had joined with many others to help develop the more organized ways of making the arguments about schools and social transformation found in the previous section—I was an elementary-school teacher in a small and strikingly conservative town in a rural area of a northeastern state. While there was a middle-class population, most of the town was certainly considerably less affluent. My own classroom was filled with children who were relatively poor or working class and also had a number of children whose parents were migrant laborers who worked on local farms picking crops for extremely low pay and under conditions that can only be described as inhuman and exploitative. The curriculum and the textbooks (they were one and the same) were not only completely out of touch with these children's cultures, histories and daily lives, but they were simply *boring*, both for me and for the students in that class.

To try to overcome this, we reorganized the curriculum. We wrote and performed plays. We studied local histories, the relations between food production and the conditions of farm labor, and the hidden histories of the people who were invisible in their texts but who had lived in the area. (For example, the town at one time had a small black farming community near it that had been a stop on the Underground Railroad, where escaped slaves had been safely housed as they made their way to the industrial cities in the northern part of the state.) We interviewed parents, grandparents and others about their lives and histories there and elsewhere. These were written up into narratives. The texts of these people's lives became the texts of historical study and led to our going to the local archives to connect the lived versions of historical events with the "official news" that was published. Histories of racial tensions and racial subjugation were uncovered. Histories of racial segregation in the local area (which supposedly never happened in such northern states) were bared. Stories of the uncommon courage of people (black, Chicano/a and white), where people collectively and individually stood up to racist movements and policies, surfaced as well. The students put out an informal "newspaper" to tell what they had learned.

Much of this was—how can I put this kindly?—"unsettling" to some people. The local chamber of commerce felt that these kinds of topics were "not appropriate for young minds" (the students in my class were twelve and thirteen years old), but also that the kinds of things being publicly brought up would put the town "in a bad light." This could be "bad for business." A local fundamentalist minister who believed that the Bible clearly showed that "God had made the white race superior" led a small but very vocal group that added to the criticism of what they felt were "radical" and "unchristian" methods. (It may be that the later work I did on the growing influence of conservative evangelical movements in education had their roots here—See Apple 2006, 1996). Either I was to stop doing this or pressure would be put on the school board to ensure that my contract would not be renewed.

Like many teachers, I suppose, I was initially shocked by the hostility of these groups to what seemed to me and the students to be simply an attempt to create the conditions for a *serious* education. But after the initial shock had worn off, I decided that I could not let these attacks go unchallenged. I spoke at meetings about the racism being exhibited. I publicly demonstrated the quality of the reading and writing that the students were doing and the open-mindedness with which they approached their historical research. I showed that the scores the students had achieved on the standardized tests (yeah, we all have to compromise, don't we?) were actually higher than before. (Is it so odd that, when students are actually engaged in educational work that seems socially and personally serious to them, they tend to do better at it?)

The students themselves, and their parents, were not silent about these attacks. They spoke out as well to members of the school board and to other members of the community, often more than a little eloquently. Colleagues of mine—even those who were more politically and educationally conservative than I was—lent support. They too knew that what was at stake was the loss of autonomy in creating curricula and teaching that were in any way critical. Soon, considerable counterpressure arose. The conservative ideologues had to back down. But for years teachers, administrators and students looked over their shoulders whenever methods or content got a bit more "creative" than the norm.

I look back on this time with both joy and distress. The students, the parents, and my colleagues and I had gained—at least temporarily—some important educational space. We had collectively demonstrated that it *was* possible to engage in educational practices that were personally meaningful, that asked critical questions, that were grounded in a sense of critical literacy, and that connected the school to a wider community in serious ways. Yet the fact that it continues to be both professionally and personally risky to engage in this kind of pedagogic action—and in fact, because of the power of the current conservative restoration, may be even more risky at times now (even at universities, not only at elementary, middle and secondary schools)—is not something that is the stuff of joy. But it does remind me constantly of what I think a significant portion of our work must be about. And it reminds me again of why books such as *Democratic Schools* and journals such as *Rethinking Schools* are important to all of us to provide an ongoing sense that it *is* still possible to make a difference, even under the circumstances we face today.

But let us be honest. The personal vignette I've just told could be retold by a significant number of politically active educators at all levels of our school system. And sometimes the stories do not have such positive endings. I do not want to minimize the nature of what can happen to educators in a time of conservative attacks that are even worse now than what I experienced as a teacher in that little town. Nor do I want to speak for others. Let's face it; it's much easier for me to say these things when I'm now a holder of a "distinguished professorship" at a major and politically progressive university. People must make their own lives and must make their own decisions based on how much they can risk.

But let us also be honest about something else. We live in a society where every day millions of people are denied what should be their rights to respectful employment at a respectful wage, health care, decent housing, schools that are well funded and respectful both to the teachers and students who go to them and to the communities in which they are based, a respectful treatment of their histories and cultures, and a government that doesn't lie—and here I must stop myself because the list gets larger and larger and my anger increases. The risks that millions of people who live in the United States (and elsewhere) must take every day to survive, the dangers they confront when they struggle against the oppressive conditions they and their children face—these risks are real and cannot simply be dealt with rhetorically.

Conclusion

Much more could be said about the structural inequalities of this society, just as much more could be added about the crucial role that schools can play both as an arena of reproducing inequalities and as an arena for critical understanding and action in changing these inequalities. I could, for example, point to ways in which religious sentiment and motivations need not always be connected to conservative positions on education, the government and the economy (Purpel 2004; Shapiro 2005), as all too much of these sentiments are today. This is a crucial issue that shows how hybrid alliances can be built across ideological divides, and is one that a number of us have tried to deal with at greater length elsewhere (see, e.g., Wallis 2005; Apple 2006). Other areas cry out for further discussion as well, of course.

The point of the combination of "academic" discussion and personal storytelling that I've undertaken in this chapter is to remind us why the continuing struggle over schooling—over what is and is not taught, over how it is taught and evaluated, over how students with different characteristics are treated, over how teachers and other school employees are respectfully dealt with, over how the relationship between schools and their communities can be democratized, and so much more—is absolutely crucial to the pursuit of social justice.

I've occasionally employed elements of my biography to reflect on these issues. What stories could you add to my own? In this regard, we can relearn something from the forces of "conservative modernization." As they constantly have demonstrated, education is an arena that is more than a little important in transforming society. Struggling in the school *is* struggling in society. Thus, the question I noted earlier comes forward again. If they can do it, why can't we? Let the struggle for social justice continue, even in the face of our being labeled as "creeps."

Note

1. I have purposely put the word "Americans" in quotation marks for a specific reason. Perhaps because I have spent a good deal of time working on democratizing educational policy and practice throughout Central and South America, it is clear to me these too are "America." There is something arrogant about the fact that the word "American" has been taken over by one nation out of the many more that actually exist in the Americas.

References

Anyon, Jean (2005) *Radical Possibilities.* New York: Routledge.

Apple, Michael W. (1979) *Ideology and Curriculum.* Boston: Routledge & Kegan Paul.

Apple, Michael W. (1986) *Teachers and Texts.* New York: Routledge.

Apple, Michael W. (1995) *Education and Power* (2nd ed.). New York: Routledge.

Apple, Michael W. (1996) *Cultural Politics and Education.* New York: Teachers College Press.

Apple, Michael W. (1999) *Power, Meaning, and Personal Identity.* New York: Peter Lang.

Apple, Michael W. (2000) *Official Knowledge* (2nd ed.). New York: Routledge.

Apple, Michael W. (2004) *Ideology and Curriculum* (25th anniversary 3rd ed.). New York: RoutledgeFalmer.

Apple, Michael W. (2006) *Educating the "Right" Way: Markets, Standards, God, and Inequality* (2nd ed.). New York: Routledge.

Apple, Michael W. (in press) The tasks of the critical scholar/activist in education. In Rachelle Winkle-Wagner, Debora Henderliter Ortloff & Cheryl Hunter (Eds.), *Methods at the Margins.* New York: Palgrave.

Apple, Michael W., & Beane, James A. (Eds.) (1995) *Democratic Schools.* Alexandria, VA: Association for Supervision and Curriculum Development.

Apple, Michael W., & Beane, James A. (2007) *Democratic Schools: Lessons in Powerful Education* (2nd ed.). Portsmouth, NH: Heinemann.

Apple, Michael W., & Buras, Kristen L. (Eds.) (2006) *The Subaltern Speak: Curriculum, Power, and Educational Struggles.* New York: Routledge.

Apple, Michael W., & Pedroni, Tom (2005) Conservative alliance building and African American support of voucher reform. *Teacher College Record*, 107: 2068–105.

Apple, Michael W., et al. (2003) *The State and the Politics of Knowledge.* New York: RoutledgeFalmer.

Binder, Amy (2002) *Contested Curricula*. Princeton, NJ: Princeton University Press.

Foner, Eric (1997) *The Story of American Freedom*. New York: Norton.

Fraser, Nancy (1997) *Justice Interruptus*. New York: Routledge.

Freire, Paulo (1972) *Pedagogy of the Oppressed*. New York: Herder & Herder.

Giugni, Marco, McAdam, Doug, & Tilly, Charles (Eds.) (1999) *How Social Movements Matter*. Minneapolis: University of Minnesota Press.

Gramsci, Antonio (1968) *The Modern Prince and Other Writings*. New York: International Publishers.

Gramsci, Antonio (1971) *Selections from the Prison Notebooks*. New York: International Publishers.

Hogan, David (1983) Education and class formation. In Michael W. Apple (Ed.), *Cultural and Economic Reproduction in Education*. Boston: Routledge & Kegan Paul.

Kozol, Jonathan (1991) *Savage Inequalities*. New York: Crown.

Ladson-Billings, Gloria (in press) Race still matters: Critical race theory in education. In Michael W. Apple, Wayne Au & Luis Armando Gandin (Eds.), *Routledge International Handbook of Critical Education*. New York: Routledge.

Lipman, P. (2004) *High Stakes Education*. New York: RoutledgeFalmer.

McCarthy, C. (2000) Lecture given at the International Sociology of Education Conference, University of Sheffield, England, January.

McNeil, Linda (2000) *The Contradictions of School Reform*. New York: Routledge.

Molnar, Alex (1996) *Giving Kids the Business*. Boulder, CO: Westview Press.

Purpel, David (2004) *Reflections on the Moral and Spiritual Crisis in Education*. New York: Peter Lang.

Shapiro, Svi (2005) *Losing Heart*. Hillsdale, NJ: Lawrence Erlbaum.

Smith, Mary Lee, et al. (2004) *Political Spectacle and the Fate of American Schools*. New York: RoutledgeFalmer.

Valenzuela, Angela (Ed.) (2005) *Leaving Children Behind*. Albany, NY: State University of New York Press.

Wallis, James (2005) *God's Politics*. San Francisco: HarperCollins.

Wittgenstein, Ludwig (1953) *Philosophical Investigations*. New York: Macmillan.

4

What is to be Done? Toward a Rationale for Social Movement Building

JEAN ANYON

The introduction to this volume describes the many dangers that beset the United States, its working people, and its education system. This chapter argues that what is needed in order to realize the radical possibilities that also inhere in these moments of danger is a social movement for the economic and educational rights of working people and people of color.

As I argued in *Radical Possibilities* (2005), U.S. history demonstrates that social movements from the political Left have typically led to passage of progressive social policies. In fact, just about every U.S. government policy that has increased equity for working people, women and minorities has followed periods of concerted protest, demonstration and struggle by progressive forces. These struggles have typically been organized as social movements (e.g., the Populist Movement of the late 1800s, the Socialist Movement of the early 1900s, the 1930s Labor Movement, the Civil Rights Movement, and both women's movements of the 20th century). All of these social movements led to important policy accommodations on the part of governments.

Social movements have changed education, too. Although in some fundamental ways education remains much the same as in 1900 (e.g., organizationally), there have been other, profound progressive changes. These improvements have come from policies that are typically prompted by social struggle, often in the form of social movements: immigrants' struggles for education in the early 1900s yielded adult worker education and Catholic schools for children; the Civil Rights Movement led to national Head Start programs as well as increased educational opportunities; Latino struggles produced bilingual education; the 1970s women's movement yielded curricular change as well as increased entitlements; disabilities organizing prompted federal protections and entitlements. The struggles continue: queer students' activism, ongoing; urban youth of color in high schools working for college prep and immigrants' education rights, ongoing; low-income parents in urban neighborhoods organizing for better schools, ongoing.

Quiescence on the Left during the 1980s and early 1990s, and a gathering of social forces of the political Right (in corporate board rooms, think tanks, political meetings and legislatures, and the media) have, in the last two decades, regressed education policy into NCLB and conservative accountability measures. The progressive forces in this country are now faced with the enormous challenge of wresting education from powerful conservatives. How do we do that?

Can we learn from history? I will argue that an important lesson history teaches is that, no matter what *other* methods we use to promote equitable economic and education policies (e.g., research and scholarship, or collaboration with unions, community groups, principals, districts and state legislatures), we must involve, support, and ultimately depend on persistent grassroots organizing—and the power that social movements so developed bring to bear.

Interest in social movements has grown as the limits of prevailing school reform efforts have been intimated during five decades of work to transform low-income schools and districts into successfully high achieving institutions. Despite a half century of effort, there is not one large U.S. city in which the majority of low-income students achieve at high levels. Increasingly, scholars and reformers have recognized the need to address inequalities of opportunity that lie beyond those in schools and districts but that nevertheless have substantial impact on education. More attention is being paid to the ways in which political and economic institutions affect—and, in low-income minority areas, constrain—educational opportunities.

The chapter defines social movements, then shows how progressive movements develop and what they can accomplish. It describes the contributions of social movements to educational equity from the mid-19th century to the current time, and considers the challenges of social movement-building in a technologically sophisticated and global economy.

Social Movements

A social movement connects what may feel like personal, individual exclusion or subordination to social structure and political causes. Social movements also provide a way of connecting with other individuals and groups across neighborhoods, cities, regions and states to forge collective solutions to social problems. They offer a forum for working together to develop community power, and to collaborate with others in making fundamental shifts in the political and social arrangements that have caused inequities, exclusions and subordination. Thus, social movements are not symptoms of a "dysfunctional" political system, as some earlier scholars argued (e.g., Neil Smelser 1962). Rather, in a healthy democracy, social movements are part and parcel of the process of change.

The concept of a social movement does not apply just to workers in the struggle for unions and higher wages. The concept applies to all people and groups struggling for what political philosopher Nancy Fraser (2000) calls recognition or redistribution— for racial rights, economic justice, women's reproductive freedom, or educational opportunities. Social movements can also strive for negative goals such as ending unpopular wars or seemingly unwarranted invasions of other countries.

There have of course been movements on the political Right (e.g., the "Right to Life" movement). But this chapter concerns progressive social movements, and what those involved in school reform and public engagement can learn from them (to garner lessons from the Right, see Apple 2001).

A comprehensive definition of social movements, summarizing several decades of sociological research, is as follows: we have a social movement in process when individuals and organizations are involved in "collective conflictual relations with clearly identified opponents" (Della Porta and Diani 2006, 20). The conflict involves "an oppositional relationship between actors who seek control of the same stake—be it political, economic or cultural power—and in the process make ... claims on each other which, if realized, would damage the interests of the other actors" (Tilly 1978, in ibid., 21). Thus, the conflict can be cultural and/or political-economic. The conflict has as a goal to promote (or, in the case of most conservative movements, to oppose) social change. In a social movement, the actors engaged in the collective action are linked by dense informal networks of organizations and individuals. They share a collective identity or sense of mission. The networks and interactions between groups and members yield social and cultural capital, which are important to bridging locales, groups and opportunities, and provide the skills involved in planning, mobilizing, and executing actions and campaigns. People involved in a social movement typically feel a collective identity. They feel connected by a common purpose and share commitment to a cause; they feel linked or at least compatible with a broader collective mobilization (Touraine 1981; Della Porta and Diani 2006).

It is important to note that one organization, no matter how large, does not make a movement. The dense and sometimes overlapping networks that constitute a social movement are made up of multiple organizations, all of whom are in pursuit of a common goal (Della Porta and Diani 2006; see also Tilly 2004 and Touraine 1981). Nor are social movements isolated protest events or short-lived temporary coalitions that form around an issue. They involve episodes of action that are perceived as components of longer-lasting measures, over time—typically multiple years of effort. Social movements use various forms of protest against the specified targets and may also involve cultural expressions of belief, as in group singing and the production of art and music that contain a social message. In sum, when people feel excluded or subordinated; when people face governments or other groups whose actions they believe are unjust; and when they belong to networks or organizations that share goals and collaborate over long periods of time to attempt to increase equity through protest and sustained political and social contention against the targeted groups, they are engaged in a progressive social movement, or social movement-building.

Most successful social movements are national in scope. As the U.S. Civil Rights Movement and the Labor Movement suggest, full-blown social movements engage the whole nation. This national scope and agenda are part of what gives the movements power to demand fundamental political or economic change. One of the important aspects sociologists identify in national movements is the existence of umbrella organizations (e.g., Morris 1984). Umbrella groups provide coherence and organization to the many smaller groups agitating for change. Morris argues, for example, that, without such groups as the Southern Christian Leadership Conference (SCLC) in the South, the Civil Rights Movement might have been rent by disagreements over agenda and strategy.

Social movements differ from other forms of public advocacy such as community organizing or creating networks and alliances in that, when movements form and grow, they usually emerge from and build upon these other forms of activity. The Civil Rights Movement again provides an example. As black churches in the South began publicly to confront Jim Crow segregation, the networks among women and families in congregations became vital links between communities; these networks allowed news of activities to spread and encouraged participation in protest. Similarly, the alliances that arose between the Student Nonviolent Coordinating Committee, the SCLC, the Congress of Racial Equality, and other civil rights organizations were important spurs to the growth of regional and then national planning.

Accomplishments of Social Movements

Progressive social movements have not always been successful (as the aborted immigrants' rights movement of the early 21st century attests) but, throughout U.S. history, social movements from the political Left have often had profound results. They have led to the passage of a number of social policies that have increased the rights of working people, women and minorities and also to important policy accommodations on the part of governments and social institutions. Indeed, when social movements successfully apply national pressure, they often result in legal or constitutional changes that increase the pool of persons who can participate in U.S. democratic institutions.

The twenty-year-long women's movement that culminated in 1920 in the right of women to vote is a case in point. This movement produced national pressure that concluded in the 19th Amendment to the Constitution, ratified on August 18, 1920.

The Civil Rights Movement, of course, produced the Voting Rights Act of 1965, which applied a nationwide prohibition against the denial or abridgment of the right to vote based on the use of literacy tests common in the South. Enforced, this act allowed black citizens to vote across the U.S.—most for the first time.

The Labor Movement as well produced legislation in the 1930s that made deep changes to the U.S. economic system; these transformations limited business owners' power over workers and provided rights to employees that were new—including the legal right of unions to organize and bargain, an eight-hour limit to the legal work day, social security, and unemployment insurance, among others. It is doubtful that the political and economic elites who governed would have passed such legislation limiting business owners' rights over workers without the pressure of the social movements of the 1930s.

Social movements can sometimes change education as well—as I will later describe in detail. Although in many ways education remains the same as in 1900, there have been significant progressive changes wrought by the concerted protest of social movements. Low-income parents in urban neighborhoods are today organizing for better schools and, if their efforts continue and coalesce, they could potentially build a social movement for educational civil rights. Groups such as ACORN and the IAF are in the forefront of this struggle. I will describe these groups later in this chapter.

There are many groups organizing for educational justice today (in New York City, over 100 grassroots groups are active). For the most part, however, each group operates independently of the others; there is little if any cross-state or national collaboration. An important lesson history teaches is that, no matter how active single actors or groups are in their struggle against injustice, and no matter what other methods we use to promote equitable education policies, it typically occurs that efforts are strengthened if we make the long-term alliances and build the power of a social movement.

The Development of Social Movements

How do social movements form, and what catapults them to national attention at certain historical moments? Community and other grassroots organizers work to transform subordinated or excluded people's fear into anger, moral indignation, and action directed at the system. Organizers therefore provide information that demonstrates ways the system contributes to personal difficulties. For people to take action against political or social oppression, they must see systematic causes of their subordination. To develop systemic analyses of subordination that accounts for people's oppression, organizers discuss local issues by connecting personal and neighborhood problems to regional, national, and sometimes global processes and powerful groups (Della Porta and Diani 2006).

Moreover, in order for people to take action, they typically must believe that they have the power to bring about change (Piven and Cloward 1977). To build this confidence, movement organizers work to provide fledging groups with small "wins." In order to attract members, organizers may also demonstrate to recruits that participation in social movement organizations exhibits some of the deepest pleasures of life—a sense of community and connectedness and also meaning (Jasper 1997).

Participation in movements is facilitated by a variety of personal and social resources—sufficient income and time to attend meetings and protests, available organizations and alliances to join, ties to these networks, and effective leadership, among other resources (McAdam 1982; Diani and McAdam 2003).

The prevailing cultural context may also influence participation in movements. If critical public discourses in the media, or artistic works such as novels, on the topic of concern are available—or if there is critical scholarship that reaches people in communities—then ideas in support of change may circulate in discussion and facilitate dissent and participation.

The political environment sometimes affects whether people join movements, and may contribute to the form and intensity of collective action. For example, electoral instability in a country may encourage dissent and protest. Political opportunities such as the availability of influential allies, the tolerance for protest among elites, and the openness of the political system may also facilitate social movement-building (see McAdam 1982; Tarrow 1998; and McAdam et al. 2001). In sum, sympathetic scholarly observers often see the "Zeitgeist" as important to whether and when movements build and grow.

However, as I argued in a recent book (Anyon 2005), a typically *un*acknowledged factor influencing the ascendance of social movements is the decades of prior preparation, or what Civil Rights Movement activist Ella Baker called "spadework." For example, blacks in the South had been resisting, demonstrating, and working the courts for five decades before the movement gained national notice in the 1950s. The development over the years of activist networks, organizations, and sympathetic legal decisions laid the foundation for the success of the nationally catalyzing Montgomery Bus Boycott in 1955.

Moreover, an open political system, an acceptance of protest by political elites, is not always necessary for movements to build or "erupt." Movements sometimes grow rapidly and come to flower during decades of political conservatism and extreme repression. The decade in which the American Civil Rights Movement burst onto the national scene in the Montgomery Bus Boycott was a decade of virulent McCarthyism and conservative dominance in politics. Moreover, the five previous decades of organizing and building by community and labor organizers in the South took place in an exceedingly repressive environment regarding racial rights (see Kelly 1990).

Of importance to public engagement efforts today may be that the political conservatism and federal attitude towards dissent in the 1950s was not terribly different from the Zeitgeist of the current era, as the Patriot and Homeland Security Acts and the resulting abrogation of civil liberties to fight a "war on terror" suggest. But there may be reason for optimism: the last quarter century of community organizing for school reform may have prepared the ground for substantial change. And the year 2000 brought with it twenty-five years of legal battles at the state level to remove urban educational inequities. Over 70 percent of these court cases have been successful, and many new state mandates have been written by the courts; more than a few await the public political pressure that might force full funding. These cases, and the years of education organizing that are behind us and that continue, may provide the legitimation and leverage needed for national movement-building.

With collaboration, a joint vision and a fortuitous catalyst, public engagement efforts such as education organizing and alliance-building could develop into a national social movement. What would facilitate this growth is that education reformers engage with the public conversations and actions that have emerged in low-income communities around issues that are intimately related to education achievement but have not been part of most education reform efforts to date— struggles for living wages, decent jobs, health care and housing, and immigrant rights (see Anyon 2005 for suggestions). If education activists were to collaborate with groups already working in these social and economic arenas, we could conceivably think of our activity as social movement-building: the development of a social movement for educational and economic justice.

Social Movements and Educational Equity

Although not the only source of equity—upper-class reformers, business groups, and politicians have at times advocated successfully for new educational resources or opportunities—progressive social movements have made substantial gains in increasing educational equity in America. Although we do not usually think of social movements as characterizing U.S. educational history in the early or mid-19th century, one can document substantial pressure from below that contributed to important educational change during those years.

The 19th Century

Horace Mann and his colleagues were not the only force pressing for the establishment of common schools in America in the 19th century. Historian Joel Spring points out that

> [t]raditional labor history ... stresses the key role of working men's parties in the late 1820s and 30s in fighting for common school reforms. This interpretation places the American worker at the forefront of the battle for common schools. Of particular importance ... is the opposition of workers to the ... charity schools, which they felt reinforced social-class distinctions. (2008, 100)

Active in the northeastern states of the U.S., the Workingmen's Parties believed that, "kept in ignorance, workers could be deprived of their rights, cheated in their daily business, and 'gulled and deceived' by ... 'parasitic politicians,' 'greedy bank directors,' and 'heartless manufacturers'" (Russell 1981, in Spring 2008, 100). These early union members believed that knowledge was power: knowledge, to be acquired in schools available to everyone, was essential to protect workers' rights in the economic system.

Irish Catholics also fought against the public schools they faced. Between 1850 and 1900, Irish church officials and Catholic parishioners fought tenaciously against the public schools created by upper-class reformers. Catholics rebelled against the Protestantism and anti-Catholic sentiment expressed in reading materials and personnel of the public schools, and by 1900 they had established a wide network of Catholic schools for their children (Ravitch 2000; Spring 2008). In addition to providing opportunities for Irish families around the turn of the 20th century, the establishment of a system of Catholic schools in America provided opportunities later for children of color in cities as an alternative to public schools deemed deficient by parents. The existence of a system of religious schools had ramifications as well on federal education policy that continue to this day.

Foreshadowing later civil rights struggles, the 1820s Boston's African American community, led by black abolitionist David Walker, began a thirty-year fight against segregated public schools in that city. Their contestation ultimately led to a formal decision by the Massachusetts governor to end legal segregation in the state. In September of 1855, the Boston public schools were legally integrated "without any violent hostilities" (Spring 2008, 121). As we are aware, there would be more struggle for civil rights necessary in the next century.

The 20th Century

During the Progressive Era, labor organizations, settlement house reformers, and immigrant families all put pressure on public school administrators to respond to the needs of the immigrant working-class population. While there was a substantial effort in the reforms of that era to "Americanize" newcomers, the schools were also responding to the pressures of the working-class majority in cities such as New York. Schools as *social centers* with services enjoyed by many thousands of students and immigrant adults were the result; the school as a social center soon developed throughout the country at the turn of the 20th century.

The movement to establish teachers' unions radically changed the politics of U.S. public education and increased equity for the teaching force. The unionization of teachers raised their salaries and removed the most egregious forms of administrative control over their employment. Most teachers' associations in the early part of the 20th century were politically conservative. But teacher organizations in those years in New York and Chicago had a radical ideology and developed out of the Labor Movement (in the case of Chicago there were close ties to the early women's movement as well). The teacher federations in both cities fought openly with conservative business interests and school administrators (Spring 2008). Out of these struggles— and in concert with less radical pressures exerted by the more cautious teachers' organizations—policies regulating the teaching force were instituted that made salaries and working conditions considerably more equitable than they had been.

The 20th-century Civil Rights Movement, of course, achieved many educational victories for minorities. Although the *Brown* decisions in the 1950s did not initially bring about education integration in the South, they did renew and strengthen activist organizing towards that end, and ultimately the decision delegitimated separate but equal accommodations in the civil sphere. As a consequence of the national social movement for political rights of black Americans, this decision and others following it produced vastly increased opportunities in education for people of color—in educational admissions, the availability of administrative positions, K–16 curriculum offerings, expanded programs for students of color in public school, and federal, state and local policies and programs that supported these and other advances.

The Head Start program, for instance, was a product of pressure from the Civil Rights Movement. Black and white civil rights workers, most of whom were involved in the 1960s in building Freedom Schools and the 1964 "Freedom Summer" (when scores of Northern college students went south to assist in voter registration drives), developed a program in rural Mississippi that provided education and services for poor children. Funded with War on Poverty money, the centers were staffed by civil rights activists and local people. After two years, in 1966, Southern white politicians in Congress succeeded in defunding these early Head Start centers in Mississippi. With money from wealthy Northern supporters, local activists and families took two busloads of preschool children to Washington in protest.

> There, with their teachers and teacher's aides, they would show what Head Start in Mississippi was all about. "A romper lobby from Mississippi petitioned Congress today for a redress of grievances," was the New York Times' lead in its February 12 story on what others were calling "the children's crusade." Forty-eight black children and their teachers turned the hearing room of the House Education and Labor Committee into a kindergarten, complete with pictures and children dragging "quacking Donald Ducks across the floor." (Dittmer 1994, 374–5)

Two weeks later the Office of Economic Opportunity awarded the group a grant to continue operations. Head Start moved to center stage in the Johnson administration's efforts to support the education of low-income minorities, and has remained a major source of opportunity for the education of young low-income children.

The women's movement of the 1960s and 1970s also was responsible for increased opportunities in education, specifically for female students. A confluence of civil rights and feminist organizing during these decades yielded laws and programs to protect and support women. What follows is from a 1997 report by Bernice Sandler, whose activism was central to the passage of Title IX, which outlaws and provides penalties for discrimination against women in educational institutions from elementary through university settings.

> The year was 1969. I had been teaching part-time at the University of Maryland for several years during the time I worked on my doctorate and shortly after I finished it. There were seven openings in the department and I had just asked a faculty member, a friend of mine, why I was not even considered for any of the openings. It was not my qualifications; they were excellent. "But let's face it," he said, "You come on too strong for a woman."

> Was this really a question of my being "too strong?" After all there were many strong men in the department. In the next few months I had two more similar rejections. A research executive who interviewed me for a position spent nearly an hour explaining to me why he wouldn't hire women because they stayed at home when their children were sick. (That my children were in high school was deemed irrelevant.) Then an employment agency counselor looked at my resume and told me that I was "not really a professional" but "just a housewife who went back to school."[1]

> But this was 1969. Although sex discrimination was indeed illegal in certain circumstances, I quickly discovered that none of the laws prohibiting discrimination covered sex discrimination in education.

> I began to do research on the status of women and the law, and read a report of the U.S. Commission on Civil Rights which examined the impact of anti-discrimination laws on race discrimination. The report described a presidential Executive Order prohibiting federal contractors from discrimination in employment on the basis of race, color, religion and national origin. There was a footnote and, being an academic, I quickly turned to the back of the report to read it. It stated that Executive Order 11246 had been amended by President Johnson, effective October 13, 1968, to include discrimination based on sex. This is just what [the women's movement] needed! (Sandler 1997, 1–2)

Sandler then describes the research and organizing in which she and women around the country took part in order to build the case and advocate for a law that would eliminate sex discrimination in educational institutions. Several years later, they succeeded in arranging seven days of Congressional hearings.

> On June 23, 1972, ... two years after the hearings, Title IX of the Education Amendments of 1972 was passed by Congress on July 1, and was signed into law by President Richard Nixon.

The historic passage of Title IX was hardly noticed [by the press]. I remember only one or two sentences in the Washing papers. (Ibid.)

But Title IX would have a huge impact on education. It protects students, faculty and staff in federally funded education programs at all levels. Title IX also applies to programs and activities affiliated with schools that receive federal funds (such as internships or School-to-Work programs) and to federally funded education programs run by other entities such as correctional facilities, health-care entities, unions and businesses. The act covers admissions, recruitment, educational programs and activities, course offerings and access, counseling, financial aid, employment assistance, facilities and housing, health and insurance benefits and services, scholarships and athletics. It also protects from discrimination against marital and parental status. Both male and female students are protected from harassment, regardless of who is committing the harassing behavior.

A further example of increases in opportunities and resources resulting from social movement pressure is the right to learn and be taught in one's native language. Federal legislation creating bilingual programs was implemented in most parts of the nation originally as a result of organizing by Puerto Ricans in New York City and Chinese residents of San Francisco (San Miguel 2004). Tony DeJesús and Madeline Pérez (in press) describe the first legal decree that resulted in bilingual education programs. During the late 1950s and 1960s in New York City, Puerto Ricans, aided by sympathetic African Americans and whites, continually protested at the Board of Education, met with and petitioned the board, for the establishment of programs to support the education of what were, by the 1960s, 80,000 Puerto Rican students in New York City schools. Frustrated, ASPIRA (in conjunction with United Bronx Parents, PRLDEF, and other Puerto Rican organizations) in 1972 sued the board for bilingual education programs. ASPIRA activists wrote that:

> [We] chose to pursue the goal of establishing bilingual education for several reasons, among them the need for the Puerto Rican community to demonstrate that it was capable of defining policy solutions for the needs of its children. Luis Nieves, director of ASPIRA during the time of the lawsuit, described the organization's decision to pursue bilingual education services not necessarily as a sound philosophy of teaching but "rather as a tool for political organization; as a means of preserving community identity, maintaining children in neighborhood schools, and reinforcing language and culture; and a route for Puerto Ricans to access jobs and the benefits of the education system." While these political goals were clear, [activist] Isaura Santiago identified three structural and instructional goals that ASPIRA also sought to obtain through the lawsuit. These included the provision of special education programs for Limited English Proficient (LEP) students, compensatory services for bilingual students as opposed to "sink or swim" teaching practices, and a guarantee that Puerto Rican parents could choose maintenance bilingual education for their children. (DeJesús and Pérez in press)

DeJesús and Pérez point out that:

> The result of the case was a court-monitored consent decree, a binding legal agreement between ASPIRA and the Board of Education that established a transitional bilingual education program in New York City's schools. ... [T]he Consent decree became a model nationwide and ... the case was significant because it involved the largest school system in the country as well as the largest plaintiff group at the time (over 80,000 Puerto Rican students were potentially affected). (Ibid.)

Two years before the ASPIRA suit, the Supreme Court had held—in a case brought by Chinese families in San Francisco—that the failure to have instruction in one's native language was a violation of the right to an equal education. "The *Lau v. Nichols* case was a major victory for bilingual education nationally, upholding bilingual cases throughout the country. It provided leverage for the plaintiffs in *ASPIRA v. Board of Education* to enter into a Consent decree with New York City as its corporation council realized that a new legal precedent had been established recognizing the language rights of English language learners" (ibid.).

These examples demonstrate that pressure from below has been a force for educational equity in the U.S. for a long period of time. The struggles continue.

Recent Organizing for Educational Equity

The last fifteen years have witnessed the appearance and rapid growth across the nation of community organizing specifically for school reform or education organizing. This type of advocacy involves the actions of parents and other community residents to change neighborhood schools through an "intentional building of power" (Mediratta et al. 2002). Education organizing aims to create social capital in communities and to encourage parents and other residents to utilize their collective strength to force system change. It attempts to build leadership in parents by providing skill training, mentoring, and opportunity for public actions. Parents conduct community and school surveys, speak at rallies, mobilize other parents and community residents, and plan and enact campaigns aimed at school and district personnel and practices.

Because education organizing gives parents a base outside of school—typically in alliance with other community groups—parents are not dependent on school personnel for approval or legitimacy. When successful, parent organizing in poor communities yields the clout that parents create among themselves in affluent suburbs—where, with their skills and economic and political influence, they closely monitor the actions of district educators and politicians.

Several studies of parent organizing groups in low-income neighborhoods around the country document their rapid increase in number and influence, especially since the early 1990s (Mediratta et al. 2002). Moreover, 80 percent of sixty-six parent organizing groups studied by the Collaborative Communications Group are working not only in local neighborhoods, but in regional or state coalitions formed to improve district or state education policy. One such group is Mississippi-based Southern Echo, which has grassroots community organizations in Tennessee, Arkansas, Louisiana, South Carolina, Kentucky, Florida, North Carolina and West Virginia. Southern Echo is an exemplar in several ways: it is regional, multi-generational, and led by former civil rights and labor union activists. The group describes itself as a "leadership development, education and training organization working to develop new, grassroots leadership in African American communities in Mississippi and the surrounding region". Until 1992, their work focused on jobs, affordable housing, and rebuilding community organizations. When they shifted their attention to education in the early 1990s, they began to organize around minority rights.

Southern Echo worked to create a force that could put pressure on state education officials. They provided training and technical assistance to help community groups carry out local campaigns and created residential training schools that lasted two days or more; they published training manuals and delivered hundreds of workshops in communities. One result of the work of Southern Echo and an affiliate, the Mississippi Education Working Group (MEWG), is that on October 23, 2002, the Mississippi State Board of Education agreed to comply fully with federal requirements for providing services to special education students—for the first time in thirty-five years. Echo leaders report that this was "the first time the community came together to force legislators, the state board of education, superintendents, special education administrators and curriculum coordinators to sit down together."

A particularly impressive education organizing group in the North is the Logan Square Neighborhood Association (LSNA) in Chicago, founded in the 1960s to work with the variety of problems local residents faced in their community. In 1988, when the Chicago School Reform Law created local schools councils, LSNA began to assist parents and community members work to improve their schools (Mediratta et al. 2002, 27). Among the accomplishments of the LSNA and parents are the construction of seven new school buildings, evening community learning centers in six schools, mortgage lender programs to offer incentives for educators to buy housing in the area, parent training as reading tutors and cultural mentors of classroom teachers, the establishment of bilingual lending libraries for parents, a new bilingual teacher-training program for neighborhood parents interested in becoming teachers, and collaboration with Chicago State University to offer courses at the neighborhood school at no cost to participants (ibid., 28). Mediratta, Fruchter and Lewis report that the extensive parent engagement and other initiatives by the LSNA "have contributed to achievement gains at its member schools. In its six core schools, the percent of students reading at or above the national average in 1990 ranged from 10.9 percent to 22.5 percent. By 2000, the percent of students reading at or above national average ranged from 25.4 to 35.9 percent" (ibid.).

The final example of education organizing comes from South Bronx, New York. This group, Community Collaborative for District 9 (CC9), provides an important instance of coalition-building—between parents, community-based organizations (CBOs), the teachers' union, and a university partner (Mediratta et al. 2002, 29).

Organizational members are ACORN (which has been organizing parents in Districts 7, 9 and 12 for a decade); the New York City American Federation of Teachers (AFT); the Citizens Advice Bureau (a local CBO providing educational services to residents for thirty years); High Bridge Community Life Center (a CBO providing job training and educational services since 1979); the Mid-Bronx Senior Citizens Council (one of the largest CBOs in the South Bronx); parents from New Settlement Apartments; the Northwest Bronx Community and Clergy Coalition (which unites ten neighborhood housing reform groups); and the Institute for Education and Social Policy (which conducts research and evaluation and provides other technical assistance to community organizing groups).

The CC9 coalition researched educational best practice to determine what reform they were going to pursue. They decided that stabilizing the teaching force was critical, and that increased staff development and lead teachers at every grade level in the schools would give teachers skills to be more successful with their students and thus encourage them to remain in district classrooms. The coalition then organized residents, petitioned, demonstrated, and engaged in other direct action campaigns to obtain New York City Department of Education funding to pay for the reforms. At every step, neighborhood parents were in the forefront. In April, 2004, New York City provided $1.6 million for lead teachers and staff development throughout the ten-school district. Since that time, CC9 has expanded to include collaborations across the city and has been engaged in efforts to improve middle-school education system wide.

Challenges of Social Movement-Building in a Global Age

Some scholars argue that a major impact of globalization on social movement-building is that advanced technology such as cell phones, email and the world wide web make social movement-building faster, easier, and capable of reaching larger numbers of people more quickly than in previous times. This connectivity, they argue, increases the success of mass movements. Technology analyst Howard Rheingold, for example, in *Smart Mobs* (2002), argues that, because the masses of people who protest are typically now connected by text messaging and other forms of communicative technology, they are replacing older forms of dense local networks and organizations in building social movements. He describes as evidence for the success of new, international social movement-building the following three cases.

In November 1999 autonomous but connected groups of demonstrators protested the World Trade Organization meeting and utilized "swarming" strategies involving cell phones, websites and laptop computers to prevail in the "Battle of Seattle." In September 2000 thousands of British citizens used cell phones, email from laptop computers, and taxi CB radios to coordinate a national protest against sharp increases in gas prices; the technology allowed them to coordinate dispersed groups to block fuel delivery in various strategic areas. In the 1990s "Critical Mass Moving Demonstrations" in San Francisco began (and have since spread to other cities) in which members would alert each other to directional strategies by email and cell phones (Rheingold 2002, 158).

Sociologist Charles Tilly comments on Rheingold's argument, pointing out that, indeed, as compared with traditional forms of protest, "internationally organized networks of activists, international nongovernmental organizations, and internationally visible financial institutions all figure more prominently in recent social movements, especially in the richer and better connected parts of the world" (2004, 98). In this global picture, public engagement in the form of social movement organizing has indeed taken new directions, increasing the possibilities for international collaborations.

Yet, as Tilly also notes, international technology-based movements have not replaced the local, regional and national forms of protest and organization that prevailed during the 20th century (2004, 98). Moreover, he argues, the advent of communicative technologies can make the world more *un*equal:

> To the extent that internationally coordinated social movements rely on electronic communications, they will have a much easier time of it in rich countries than in poor ones. Second, electronic communications connect social movement activists selectively both across countries and within countries. Anyone whom a Norwegian organizer can reach electronically in, say, India or Kazakhstan already belongs to a very small communications elite. ... [T]his important aspect of globalization is making the world more unequal. (2004, 104)

Late 20th- and 21st-century globalization has indeed made the problems that public engagement efforts seek to solve no longer purely local. The causes of neighborhood problems such as poorly funded education or lack of jobs often lie outside of the neighborhood and city in regional, state, and often national and global developments and policies. But while the problems people face may not be local, Tilly points out that most organizing *is* still local. The vast majority, he notes, still takes place in communities rather than on the global stage.

It may be that the important challenge of globalization for social movement-building efforts in education (and economic) justice is that our organizing campaigns need to *transcend neighborhoods*. By this I mean to suggest that the issues around which education reform groups develop campaigns need to be those that affect people in most or all of the neighborhoods of a city, and in most or all of the cities of the state and nation. And the analysis that informs public advocacy needs to make the link to global causes. In this regard, analyses ought to transcend local power sources as causes and be supplemented by the identification of national and global developments and policies that affect neighborhoods. For instance, a local campaign against an underfunded urban school or district might connect the lack of public monies available for education to twenty-five years of diminished state and federal tax rates on corporations, or to the huge federal spending on foreign wars. And, as I have suggested above, we could expect synergy if we connected this local effort for increased education funding to alliances across sectors and indeed across the nation, in this case by joining education funding struggles to national anti-war and other alliances.

Note

1. In the Preface to the 2000 edition of *The Great School Wars*, Diane Ravitch relates what—in 1972—a celebrated historian at Columbia University told her when she sought advice about applying to the history department for a doctorate. He "told me not to waste my time and theirs because I had three strikes against me: First, I was too old (I was 34); second, I was a woman (yes, he did say that); and third, I was interested in education, and historians did not study education" (p. xiv).

References

Anyon, Jean (2005). *Radical possibilities: Public policy, urban education, and a new social movement*. New York: Routledge.

Apple, Michael (2001) *Educating the "right" way: Markets, standards, God, and inequality*. New York: Routledge.

DeJesús, Anthony, & Pérez, Madeline (in press) From community control to consent decree: Puerto Ricans organizing for education and language rights in New York City. In Matos-Rodriguez, Felix, & Totti, Xavier (Eds.), *Puerto Ricans in America: 30 years of activism and change*. New York: Palgrave.

Della Porta, Donatella, & Diani, Mario (2006) *Social movements: An introduction*. Oxford, UK: Blackwell.

Diani, Mario, & McAdam, Doug (2003) *Social movements and networks*. New York: Oxford University Press.

Dittmer, John (1994) *Local people: The struggle for civil rights in Mississippi*. Urbana: University of Illinois Press.

Fraser, Nancy (2000) Rethinking recognition. *New Left Review,* May/June: 107–20.

Jasper, James (1997) *The art of moral protest: Culture, biography, and creativity in social movements*. Chicago: University of Chicago Press.

Kelly, Robin (1990) *Hammer and hoe: Alabama communists during the great depression*. Chapel Hill: University of North Carolina Press.

McAdam, Doug (1982) *Political process and the development of black insurgency, 1930–1970*. Chicago: University of Chicago Press.

McAdam, Doug, Tarrow, Sidney, & Tilly, Charles (2001) *Dynamics of Contention*. Cambridge, UK: Cambridge University Press.

Mediratta, Kavitha, Fruchter, Norm, & Lewis, Anne (2002) *Organizing for school reform: How communities are finding their voices and reclaiming their public schools*. New York: Annenberg Institute for School Reform.

Morris, Aldon (1984) *The origins of the civil rights movement*. New York: Free Press.

Piven, Frances, & Cloward, Richard (1977) *Poor people's movements: Why they succeed, how they fail*. New York: Pantheon.

Ravitch, Diane (2000) *The great school wars: A history of the New York City public schools*. Baltimore, MD: Johns Hopkins University Press.

Rheingold, Howard (2002) *Smart mobs: The next social revolution*. Cambridge, MA: Perseus.

Russell, William (1981) *Education and the working class: The expansion of public education during the transition to capitalism*. Ph.D dissertation, University of Cincinnati.

San Miguel Jr., G. (2004) *Contested policy: The rise and fall of federal bilingual education in the United States, 1960–2001*. Denton: University of North Texas Press.

Sandler, Bernice (1997) "Too strong for a woman"—the five words that created title IX. In *About Women on Campus* [The former newsletter of the National Association for Women in Education], Spring.

Smelser, Neil (1962) *Theory of collective behavior.* New York: The Free Press.

Spring, Joel (2008) *The American school* (7th ed.). Boston: McGraw-Hill.

Tarrow, Sidney (1998) *Power in movement.* Cambridge, UK: Cambridge University Press.

Tilly, Charles (1978) *From mobilization to revolution.* Reading, MA: Addison-Wesley.

Tilly, Charles (2004) *Social movements, 1768–2004.* Boulder, CO: Paradigm.

Touraine, Alain (1981) *The voice and the eye: An analysis of social movements.* Cambridge, UK: Cambridge University Press.

5
Mechanics of Unfairness
How We Undercut Poor Children's Educational Opportunity

SUE BOOKS

> We were taught under the old ethic that man's business on this earth was to look out for himself. That was the ethic of the jungle; the ethic of the wild beast. Take care of yourself, no matter what may become of your fellow man. Thousands of years ago the question was asked: "Am I my brother's keeper?" That question has never yet been answered in a way that is satisfactory to civilized society. Yes, I am my brother's keeper. I am under moral obligation to him that is inspired, not by any maudlin sentimentality but by the higher duty I owe myself. What would you think of me if I were capable of seating myself at a table and gorging myself with food and saw about me the children of my fellow beings starving to death?
>
> (Eugene Debs, 1908)

Although few children in the United States are literally starving to death, many are sitting before the educational equivalent of an empty plate while others, not far away, are enjoying full meals with all the trimmings. As Jonathan Kozol has said repeatedly, school funding is one of the few places where we tell children exactly what we think they are worth (see Hayden & Cauthen 1998; Kozol 1991, 2006). Per-pupil spending numbers suggest starkly different evaluations of children in affluent families, disproportionately white, and children growing up in poverty, disproportionately black and Latino.

Kozol's observation, really an accusation, is troubling because it suggests not only that poor children suffer from the moral judgments institutionalized in our educational policies and practices, but also that adults, even those far removed from poor children's personal lives, contribute to the suffering. In this chapter, I support Kozol's charge with documentation of disparities in school funding and of the economic, racial and ethnic segregation that results from school districting. I also look at what happens before and after: the child-care crisis that shapes many poor children's preschool years, and the college competition that favors those who can pay and those groomed to meet narrow standards of qualification. Finally, I share my thoughts on Kozol's challenge and its implications for teacher educators like myself. Let me start, however, with some general observations about poverty and education.

Poverty Matters

Poverty matters in schooling, but not in the ways that many commentators and political leaders presume it matters. Poverty does not doom children to school failure. Many young people thrive educationally despite growing up in families chronically stressed by not having enough money to meet basic needs. Poverty also does not "brand" children educationally. Poor children need good teaching, not a special "pedagogy of poverty" consisting of excessive regimentation, drill of the basics, and harsh discipline (Haberman 1991).

At the same time, it is important to recognize that children growing up in poverty, as a group, do bear the brunt of a whole range of social injustices: a scarcity of doctors and dentists willing to care for families without health insurance (U.S. Department of Health and Human Services 2000); exposure to lead and other environmental toxins, which are concentrated in the poorest neighborhoods (Books 2000), and underfunded, sub-par schooling (see Kozol 1991, 2006, among many others). These injustices affect the educational wellbeing of children and youth significantly, and are far too important to be brushed aside with a "no excuses" rhetoric that puts unfounded faith in "raising expectations." As Paul Houston, executive director of the American Association of School Administrators, puts it, "I don't think there's an educator who wouldn't stand up and say, 'Poor kids have more problems when they come to school than kids who come from homes where they are not poor'" (quoted in Hayden & Cauthen 1998). Poor children's educational needs must be met, not ignored through what amounts to a "poverty-blind" discourse. Sadly, the numbers tell a different story: from early child-care arrangements, where poor children vie for far too few slots in public centers, to college, where admissions policies favor the best prepared, poor children and youth get less.

Child Care

Because public child-care programs are so underfunded and private care costs so much—$4,000 to $10,000 a year and sometimes even more—the child-care crisis in the United States hits hardest those children in the poorest families. Long wait lists for public programs exist in more than twenty states, and only one in every seven children eligible for a child-care subsidy based on family income actually receives one (Children's Defense Fund 2005). In New York City 38,000 children were on wait lists for subsidized care in 2004 (Carlson & Scharf 2004).

Implementation of the 1996 welfare "reform" legislation pushed millions of poor single mothers into the low-wage labor market, including those with infants as young as twelve weeks. Caseloads dropped by half nationwide between 1996 and 2000 and continued to decline thereafter, although more slowly (Urban Institute 2006). Millions more mothers working outside the home created an enormous need for child care. Affordable, quality care, however, has not been provided for poor children on anywhere near the scale required.

Low-income mothers spend an average of more than 18 percent of their total income on child care, and some spend as much as 25 percent, compared to an average of 6 percent by mothers in upper-income households (Boushey & Wright 2004).

The federal Head Start program, chronically underfunded, serves only half the four-year-olds nationwide who meet the income guidelines, and most programs do not provide "wraparound care" for working parents (Polakow 2007). Given this squeeze—a seller's market on one hand and a woefully inadequate public safety net on the other—the result is predictable: our poorest children end up in unregulated patchwork arrangements that range from adequate to terrible (ibid.).

Consequently, far too many poor children start school without the kind of enriching preschool experience children in wealthier families enjoy, and then continue to be shortchanged. As Russlyn Ali (2006), director of the Education Trust-West, told the Commission on No Child Left Behind, "Instead of structuring our schools to ameliorate the challenges outside of school, we do the opposite—we take the kids who have the least outside of school, and we give them less inside of school, too."

Public Schooling

Funding

Funding for public schools in the U.S. comes from three primary sources: state revenues, local property taxes, and federal funds. The federal share is small: now less than 9 percent. The size of the state and local shares vary considerably, but on average account for about 45 percent each of the total pie. Disparities exist at every level—among states, among districts within states, and among schools within districts. In 2003–4, the ten highest-spending states spent an average of more than 50 percent more per pupil than the ten lowest-spending states, which are clustered in the South, Southwest and West and serve a disproportionate share of the nation's poorest children. Per-pupil funding (state and local revenues) in 2003–4 ranged from a high of $9,425 in Vermont to a low of $4,857 in Utah (Liu 2006).

Because property values differ so significantly from one school district to another, local revenues do too. Low-poverty districts can and do raise more, and often much more, than their poorer counterparts, even when, as is often the case, they have lower tax rates. Heavy reliance on local property taxes as a source of school funding means parents who can afford to buy million-dollar homes essentially can afford to buy top-shelf (but publicly subsidized) schooling for their children as well. Although state funds theoretically could be used to offset these disparities, gaps remain. In 2005 low-poverty school districts (the 25 percent of districts nationwide with the least poverty) received $938 *more* in state and local funds than high-poverty districts (the 25 percent with the most poverty) (Arroyo 2008).

Gaps in funding among districts are especially significant between large, predominantly minority city districts and nearby, predominantly white suburban districts. For example, Illinois Board of Education data for 2003 show per-pupil spending of $8,482 in Chicago (87 percent minority), but $17,291 in nearby suburban Highland Park (10 percent minority). This pattern holds in large metropolitan areas across the nation. As in the Chicago area, so too in the Philadelphia, Detroit, Milwaukee, Boston and New York City areas (Kozol 2006).

Recent research has uncovered "hidden disparities" among buildings within single school districts. Nationwide, teachers in high-poverty schools are paid less, and often significantly less, than their colleagues in low-poverty schools (Clotfelter et al. 2006; Roza 2006). However, these disparities do not usually show up in district-wide budget reports, which generally report the distribution of staff positions, not teacher salary costs.

Federal funds, the third source for public schools, come primarily through Title I of the Elementary and Secondary Education Act, reauthorized most recently as the No Child Left Behind Act. Title I funds are supposed to benefit poor children and to supplement state and local revenues. However, because federal regulations direct more money to states that spend relatively generously on education, and because these states tend to be low-poverty states, the federal funding actually makes matters worse. For example, whereas Arizona, a low-spending state with considerable child poverty, received $881 for each poor child in the state in 2003–4, Wyoming, a high-spending state with much less child poverty, got $2,957 per poor child (Liu 2006).

This way of funding public schools results in children in the poorest schools in the poorest districts in the poorest states receiving far, far less than they should, based on any notion either of fundamental fairness or of educational need. Even funding for basic infrastructure goes disproportionately to schools in wealthier communities. Despite record-level spending for the period 1995–2004, the most disadvantaged students received only about half as much per pupil as their wealthier counterparts. The poorer schools had to spend most of the money they did get on basic safety provisions, such as roof repairs and asbestos removal, rather than things such as science labs and computer rooms, which the wealthier schools bought (Filardo et al. 2006).

Outside the formal structure of public school funding, private donations from parents, alumni and corporations increase the disparities. These donations, on the rise in recent years, have been used to fund a wide range of needs and wants for the target schools: equipment, supplies, artists-in-residence, and so on. Many schools, of course, have no significant donors. Concerned about the unfairness of this situation, school administrators in Greenwich, Connecticut, ten years ago capped the amount a single school could receive: about $64,600 per elementary school and $104,500 per middle school. However, school officials often then waived the caps when large donations were offered. An analysis in 2005 by the local school board showed "continuing inequities," especially among elementary schools: $17,000 for one school compared to more than $50,000 each for eight others (Cowan 2007).

To try to spread the wealth more equitably, eighteen school districts in Westchester and Putnam counties in New York State joined together in the late 1990s to create the nonprofit Learning Foundation. The regional organization faltered a few years later, however, when "some of the well-heeled participants expressed interest in creating foundations that catered exclusively to their schools" (Cowan 2007).

Although the question of whether "money really matters" continues to arise in school funding lawsuits, decades of litigation attests to broad agreement that it does.[1] Significant disparities in funding mean that students in property-rich districts typically attend classes in well-maintained buildings, with well-qualified and adequately compensated teachers and abundant opportunities to participate in art, music and sports programs. Students in property-poor districts, however, all too often face years of schooling in buildings in varying states of disrepair, with outdated textbooks that must be shared, with few extracurricular activities, and with teachers lacking credentials (or even full-time positions). With more money at their disposal, wealthier school districts can and do lure the "better teachers," which means that children in higher-poverty districts—disproportionately children of color—end up with the newest teachers, teachers with the weakest credentials, and teachers who have been "pushed out" of other schools (Kozol 1991, 2006; Clotfelter et al. 2006; Peske & Haycock 2003; Roza 2006). As Thurgood Marshall wrote thirty-five years ago in his passionate dissent in the landmark school funding case *San Antonio v. Rodriguez*, "It is an inescapable fact that if one district has more funds available per pupil than another district, the former will have greater choice in educational planning than will the latter."

School Districting

Poor children are shortchanged not only by our failure to fund public schools fairly, but also by the way we draw school districts—an arena, in my view, that has been vastly understudied and critiqued. We create school districts that divide children on the basis of race, ethnicity and family income, whether intentionally or not, then use these boundaries to rationalize the inequities cited above.

Consider three school district configurations near my home in upstate New York—first, the Roosevelt Union Free School District, a municipal jurisdiction in Nassau County on Long Island. This tiny, 1.5 square-mile district with 2,801 students exists only as a school district, not as a town or village. Nine out of every ten of the students are eligible for free or reduced-price lunch and only 0.5 percent (fourteen) are white (New York State Education Department 2005).[2] Although Roosevelt's property tax rate is among the highest in New York State, its spending is the lowest in Nassau County because its property values are so low.

When the State Commissioner of Education and the New York Board of Regents considered dissolving the Roosevelt district a few years ago and dispersing its students to surrounding schools, parents in the neighboring districts protested loudly. A flyer campaign in the predominantly white district of East Meadow urged residents to "keep Roosevelt students out" and warned that, if the plan went through, "We will have no choice except to remove our children from the East Meadow schools and move away. But who will buy our homes? People with a lot less money, for much lower prices. Our property values will drop dramatically" (cited in Kozol 2006, 158). The campaign seemingly succeeded, as the proposal was dropped shortly thereafter. As Kozol notes, "If ever there had been an opportunity to end the educational apartheid of a small community of children, this had been it. The tiny population of the Roosevelt schools could, physically at least, have been absorbed with ease into surrounding districts" (ibid., 159).

Consider next the Spackenkill community, another jurisdiction that exists only as a school district. Throughout the 1960s and early 1970s the Spackenkill Board of Education battled with the New York State Education Department over its plan to merge the 6 mile-wide Spackenkill Union Free School District, centered around an IBM plant in the town (but not the city) of Poughkeepsie, with the neighboring Poughkeepsie City Schools. With help from its friends in the State Legislature and strong community support, the Spackenkill school board defied the state's directive, built its own high school, initially without state funding, and thereby created a K–12 district that enabled it to pull the Spackenkill students out of Poughkeepsie High School (Books 2006).

Lilli Zimet, a Poughkeepsie resident who lived through the struggle, recalled in 2005:

> The feeling was that [Spackenkill going its own way] was detrimental to the rest. The fear was that it would split off, well, a "well-off" group. Real estate was higher there. The fear was it would deprive the Poughkeepsie district, which would become more imbalanced, financially and in terms of [academic] standards. And, of course, that's what did happen. Poughkeepsie [High] became an inner-city school. (Books 2006)

Today, 1,801 students attend Spackenkill schools; 81 percent are white or Asian and 10 percent are eligible for subsidized lunch. Next door, 4,660 students attend the Poughkeepsie City Schools, where only 18 percent are white and 81 percent are eligible for subsidized lunch (New York State Education Department 2008).

Finally, consider public schooling in Westchester County, a 433 square-mile county just north of New York City that contains forty school districts. Although Westchester had the eighth highest per capita income in the nation in 2004, it also has significant pockets of poverty. One consequently would expect to find significant economic integration in the schools. State data reveals instead a picture of economic segregation. Table 5.1 shows demographic data for two neighboring school districts in the county, Port Chester-Rye, with very few white students and considerable poverty, and Rye Central, predominantly white with very little poverty.

JFK Magnet Elementary in the Port Chester-Rye district, where 82 percent of the students are eligible for the federally subsidized lunch program and only 5 percent are white, is *2 miles away* from Midland Elementary in the Rye Central district, where 2 percent of the students are eligible for the lunch program and almost all (87 percent) are white. Merging these districts would require neither massive bussing nor loss of a concept of neighborhood schools. It would mean, however, that poor children, largely children of color, would go to school with much wealthier and largely white children.

As in these districts in New York, so too in schools across the nation: *de facto* segregation along racial lines means segregation along economic lines as well. The National Center for Education Statistics (2006) found that, in 2005, almost half of all black and Latino students (48 percent and 49 percent, respectively) attended schools in which three-quarters or more of the students were eligible for subsidized lunch. In their study of public schools in North Carolina, Clotfelter et al. (2006) found that the rich–poor gap among schools is actually increasing. High-poverty schools have become poorer over the last decade, both absolutely and relative to low-poverty schools.

TABLE 5.1 Demographic Data for Elementary Schools in Adjoining School Districts in Westchester County, New York, 2005–6

	Port Chester-Rye Union Free School District			
	JFK Magnet Elementary	*King St. Elementary*	*Park Ave. Elementary*	*Thomas Edison*
% eligible for subsidized lunch	82%	34%	39%	67%
% white	5%	41%	30%	6%

	Rye Central School District		
	Midland Elementary	*Milton Elementary*	*Osborn Elementary*
% eligible for subsidized lunch	2%	1%	2%
% white	87%	88%	83%

Source: New York State Education Department, school and district report cards for school year 2005–6.

A euphemistic discourse of "neighborhood schools" distorts the reality of public schooling in the United States. We've carved the nation into 14,000 separate school districts in ways that, on the surface, seem quite illogical—no consistency in size or shape and sometimes no correspondence with other natural boundaries. In fact, though, the gerrymandering serves a social purpose: it keeps poor students, disproportionately students of color, away from others. And the separation matters, if for no other reason than because poor children consistently get less—less qualified teachers (Clotfelter et al. 2006; Peske & Haycock 2003), a less rigorous curriculum, fewer extracurricular opportunities, and buildings that are often are bleak, if not hazardous (Kozol 1991, 2006).

Higher Education

Poor children who do make it through high school, despite the many resource-based challenges (created in part by the way school districts are drawn), face daunting odds if they try to continue their education. A "preparation gap" compounded through years of schooling in sub-par conditions shows up as a "qualifications gap" when it comes time to apply for college. Low-income high-school graduates in the top academic quartile attend college at approximately the same rate as high-income graduates in *the bottom academic quartile* (Advisory Committee on Student Financial Assistance 2001). The probability of then graduating from college also differs significantly by income. Whereas 81 percent of high-income students who are college qualified complete a bachelor's degree within eight years,[3] only 36 percent of low-income students do so (Adelman 2006, cited in Long & Riley 2007). Looking at this pattern from a different angle, Haveman and Wilson (2005) found in their analysis of Michigan data that only 7 percent of all college graduates come from the 25 percent of families with the least income and greatest financial need, and less than 3 percent come from the 10 percent of families with the least income.

A significant shift over the last decade towards merit-based aid versus need-based aid has placed college out of the reach of many low-income students (Long & Riley 2007). Unpreparedness is systematically produced in high-poverty schools, then "discovered" in the competition for college aid, which increasingly is based more on test-derived assessments of merit than on financial need. Even if low-income students were not hurt by a very large college-preparation gap, "a quarter century of tuitions rising much faster than family incomes, family incomes becoming more unequal, huge disparities of wealth and savings by class and race, and a dramatic shrinkage in the proportion of college costs funded by need-based student aid" still would put higher education beyond the reach of many students (Orfield 2004, xi). Pell Grants, the primary federal need-based aid program, covered 52 percent of the average cost (tuition, fees, room and board) of a four-year public college in 1986–7, but only 32 percent in 2004–5 (Baum & Steele 2007). Whereas need-based grant aid almost doubled over the last decade, spending on non-need-based grant aid grew by almost 350 percent (National Association of State Student Grant and Aid Programs 2006).

As tuition costs at public colleges and universities continue to rise—in part because state support for public higher education continues to fall—and as the most prestigious schools become more and more selective, those pushed out all too often are the poorest students who are least likely to attend an academically competitive high school, to score exceptionally well on the SAT, or to be regarded as probable donors down the road (Fischer 2006). Although many institutions have continued to increase their spending on financial aid, "in fact they are just compensating for becoming more expensive and are not necessarily providing greater assistance to low-income and middle-income students" (Wilkinson 2005). By the early 2000s, students with family incomes of $160,000 and up were qualifying for need-based grants at some of the most expensive colleges. "An old joke that Harvard's idea of diversity is putting a rich kid from California in the same room as a rich kid from New York is truer today than ever" (Leonhardt 2005).

What Can and Should We Do?

A discussion such as this cries out for something more: a "solution" or way forward. What should we do? What can we do? The numbers are consistent: poor children are systematically shortchanged by our education systems almost from day one. At every turn, it seems, they get less. Relegated to the worst child-care situations, then assigned to the worst public schools, where they are ill-prepared to compete for college aid that increasingly rewards narrowly defined achievement rather than supporting financial need, young people who grew up in poverty, not surprisingly, attend college in distressingly small numbers. And the broader society condones this shameful state of affairs.

In one sense, steps in the right direction could be taken fairly easily. We could choose to fund public schools in the way that almost all other industrialized nations do: primarily through our national wealth. This would break the link between the value of local property and the educational needs of children. And we could stop trying to justify this illogical connection between property and education through a euphemistic discourse of "neighborhood schools." Neighborhoods are made and can be remade and enlarged. We could choose to draw school district lines in ways that would reduce, if not eliminate, economic as well as racial and ethnic segregation—not because there is anything magic about a black child sitting next to a white child or a poor child next to a wealthy classmate, but because segregation reflects and invites jockeying for advantage and callousness towards the plight of others.

In Alaska, New Jersey and Maryland, students in the poorest 25 percent of districts now receive considerably more funding per pupil in state and local revenues ($1,000 or more) than students in the wealthiest 25 percent of districts (Arroyo 2008). Other states could follow suit. Recognizing the toll that concentrated poverty takes on school achievement, the LaCrosse district in Wisconsin implemented a school assignment plan fifteen years ago to ensure that poor children are not clustered together in a few schools. About forty other districts have now followed its lead and implemented similar plans as a way to increase student achievement districtwide, largely with good results (Rimer 2003). More districts could try this.

The United Nations Human Rights Committee has expressed concern about the continuing "discrepancies between the racial and ethnic composition of large urban districts and their surrounding suburbs, and the manner in which school districts are created, funded and regulated" in the United States. We could take this embarrassing critique to heart and do as the U.N. commission suggests: "respect and ensure that all persons are guaranteed effective protection against practices that have either the purpose or the effect of discrimination on a racial basis, … conduct in-depth investigations into … de facto segregation … and take remedial steps, in consultation with affected communities" (United Nations Human Rights Committee 2006).

That said, I believe the fundamental challenge is not primarily one of policy-making, but rather one of moral and ethical sensibility. Our system of public schooling reflects a spirit of competitiveness and selfishness that seeks not the best for all, but the best for oneself and one's own. We've lost and need urgently to regain a sense of the common good. Who are we, as Kozol charges, who put price tags on individual children, however indirectly and with whatever rationalizations? By "the common good" I mean a feeling that the whole matters, each and every child, and that we cannot take pride in the fruits of our collective labor until we know it is shared by all.

I think of a scene in a beautiful film, *Etre et avoir* ("To Be and to Have"), about a one-room schoolhouse in rural France. It's pouring rain one afternoon when the school bell rings, so the teacher takes the children two by two under an umbrella to their bus. One child runs ahead, and the teacher can't cover both, so the other child gets wet—a simple metaphor for a profound truth. In calling for a stronger sense of the common good, I am appealing not to obligation, but rather to a sense of family or community that is incompatible with exclusion, scorn, or leaving behind in a race to be first.

We had opportunities to come together in grief as a people after the 9/11 terrorist attack in 2001 and especially after the predictable (and predicted) disaster of Hurricanes Katrina and Rita in 2005. Sadly, we squandered both. First responders with a host of lung problems after 9/11 are now mired in lawsuits over health insurance claims (DePalma 2006), and victims of the hurricanes, many still homeless (Herbert 2006), have been shortchanged by almost everyone—including and especially apathetic federal officials and insurance companies looking for legal loopholes to let themselves off the hook. In its "third anniversary" edition of the *New Orleans Index* the Brookings Institution reported that "many recovery trends [had] slowed or stagnated … as tens of thousands of blighted properties, lack of affordable housing for essential service and construction workers, and thin public services continue[d] to plague the city and region" (Liu & Plyler 2008, 1). Two years after the hurricane, "Basic services—including schools, libraries, public transportation, and childcare—remain at less than half of the original capacity in New Orleans, and only two-thirds of all licensed hospitals are open in the region. Further, lack of repairs to pubic facilities is undermining police effectiveness" (ibid.).

Nevertheless, there were moments after both tragedies when it seemed possible to rise above narrow interests to reach out to others in a spirit of generosity and compassion. We need to remember those moments and learn from them. The wisdom of the Dalai Lama comes to mind. Education, he once said, "is much more than a matter of imparting the knowledge and skills by which narrow goals are achieved. It is also about opening the child's eyes to the needs and rights of others." Similarly, I would say that educators—those of us who see teaching as part of our responsibility as adults, whether or not we are paid to do this work—need to do much more than help others figure out how to work the system in their own favor. Rather, we need to encourage broad reflection on the needs and rights of others and on the flip side of this coin—namely, our responsibility to foster a sense of the common good as the foundation of a lasting community. I believe a strong moral and ethical discourse that invites such reflection would resonate with many, many people. Knowing that structures that benefit one's own children harm others is not a satisfying way to live.

More specifically, I believe that teacher educators, including myself, need to consider the relevance of a teacher-education curriculum that encourages prospective teachers to learn to "differentiate instruction," but rarely to consider the deep injustices and differentiations that take such a harsh toll on children. A better understanding of the educational experience of poor children will not make any one child's life less difficult, but it could provide the foundation for a broad public conversation about the responsibility of the adult generation to provide, at a minimum, a viable path for all young people to a fulfilling life unconstrained by poverty. We could do this and we should, if for no other reason than because we can. Widespread reflection on the needs and rights of poor children could provide an ethical anchor—a way to set priorities, to make decisions, and to remind ourselves that the children who suffer from so many of the social policies and practices we rationalize and sustain are in fact our greatest responsibility.

Notes

1. As of 2006, forty-five states had been sued over their school funding procedures, and plaintiffs had prevailed in almost two-thirds of the cases (National Access Network 2007).
2. Eligibility for free or reduced-price lunch is a commonly used proxy for poverty. A family income below 130 percent of the federal poverty level qualifies children for free school lunches and a family income below 185 percent of the poverty level for reduced-price lunches.
3. The definition of "college qualified" is from Berkner & Chavez (1997). Students were regarded as college qualified if they met any of these five criteria, which would place them among the top 75 percent of four-year college students for that criteria: 46th percentile class rank, GPA of 2.7, SAT score of 820, ACT score of 10, or NELS-88 test score of the 56th percentile.

References

Adelman, C. (2006) *Internal analysis*. Washington, DC: U.S. Department of Education, Office of Vocational and Adult Education, August.

Advisory Committee on Student Financial Assistance (2001) *Access denied: Restoring the nation's commitment to equal educational opportunity*. Washington, DC: U.S. Department of Education.

Ali, R. (2006) *Testimony of Russlyn Ali, Director, Education Trust-West, before the Commission on No Child Left Behind*, April 11. Retrieved from http://www2.edtrust.org.

Arroyo, C. G. (2008) *The funding gap*. Washington, DC: Education Trust. Retrieved from http://www2.edtrust.org.

Baun, S., & Steele, P. (2007) *Trends in student aid*. Washington, DC: College Board. Retrieved from http://www.collegeboard.com/prod_downloads/about/news_info/trends/trends aid_07.pdf.

Berkner, L., & Chavez, L. (1997) *Access to postsecondary education for the 1992 high school graduates*. Washington, DC: National Center for Education Statistics.

Books, S. (2000) Poverty and environmentally induced damage to children. In V. Polakow (Ed.), *The public assault on America's children: Poverty, violence, and juvenile injustice* (pp. 42–58). New York: Teachers College Press.

Books, S. (2006) The politics of school districting: A case study in upstate New York. *Educational Foundations*, *20*, 3–4, 15–33.

Boushey, H., & Wright, J. (2004) *Working moms and child care*. Data Brief No. 3, May 5. Washington, DC: Center for Economic and Policy Research. Retrieved from http://65.181.187.63/documents/publications/child_care_2004.pdf.

Carlson, B. C., & Scharf, R. L. (2004) *Lost in the maze: Reforming New York City's fragmented child care subsidy system*. New York: Welfare Law Center. Retrieved from http://www.nclej.org/pdf/LostInTheMaze.pdf.

Children's Defense Fund (2005) *Child care basics*. Retrieved from www.childrensdefense.org.

Clotfelter, C., Ladd, H. F., Vigdor, J., & Wheeler, J. (2006) *High-poverty schools and the distribution of teachers and principals*. National Center for Analysis of Longitudinal Data in Education Research (CALDER) working paper, December 7. Retrieved from http://www.caldercenter.org/PDF/1001057_High_Poverty.pdf.

Cowan, A. (2007) Schools' deep-pocketed partners. *New York Times*, June 3. Retrieved from www.nytimes.com.

DePalma, A. (2006) Officials slow to hear claims of 9–11 illnesses. *New York Times*, September 5. Retrieved from www.nytimes.com.

Filardo, M. W., Vincent, J. M., Sung, P., & Stein, T. (2006) *Growth and disparity: A decade of U.S. public school construction 1995–2004*. Washington, DC: BEST (Building Educational Success Together).

Fischer, K. (2006) Elite colleges lag in serving the needy. *Chronicle of Higher Education*, May 12, A1, A12–A17.

Haberman, M. (1991) Pedagogy of poverty v. good teaching. *Phi Delta Kappan, 73*, 290–4.

Haveman, R., & Wilson, K. (2005) *Economic inequality in college access, matriculation, and graduation*. Working Paper No. 2005-032. LaFollette School of Public Affairs, University of Wisconsin-Madison. Retrieved from www.lafollette.wisc.edu/publications/working papers/haveman2005-032.pdf.

Hayden, J., & Cauthen, K. (Producers) (1998) "Children in America's schools." Film. Columbia, SC: South Carolina ETV.

Herbert, B. (2006) The Ninth Ward revisited. *New York Times*, December 25. Retrieved from www.nytimes.com.

Kozol, J. (1991) *Savage inequalities: Children in America's schools*. New York: HarperCollins.

Kozol, J. (2006) *The shame of the nation: The restoration of apartheid schooling in America*. New York: Crown.

Leonhardt, D. (2005) The college dropout boom. *New York Times*, May 24. Retrieved from www.nytimes.org.

Liu, G. (2006) How the federal government makes rich states richer. *Funding gaps 2006* (pp. 2–4). Retrieved from www2.edtrust.org.

Liu, A., & Plyer, A. (2008) *The New Orleans index anniversary edition: Three years after Katrina*. Washington, DC: Brookings Institution Metropolitan Policy Program & Greater New Orleans Community. Retrieved from http://www.brookings.edu/reports/2007/08neworleansindex/aspx.

Long, Bridget T., & Riley, E. (2007) Financial aid: A broken bridge to college access? *Harvard Educational Review, 77*, 1, 39–47.

National Access Network (2007) *Litigation*. Teachers College, Columbia University. Retrieved from http://www.schoolfunding.info/litigation/litigation.php3.

National Association of State Student Grant and Aid Programs (2006) *Thirty-sixth annual survey report on state sponsored student financial aid: 2004–05 academic year*. Washington, DC: Author.

National Center for Education Statistics (2006) Elementary/secondary education: Concentration of enrollment by race/ethnicity and poverty. In *The Condition of Education 2006* (p. 33). NCES, Institute of Education Sciences. Retrieved from http://nces.ed.gov/pubs2006/2006071.pdf.

New York State Education Department (2005) *New York State district comprehensive report, Comprehensive information report, 2004–2005*. Retrieved from http://www.emsc.nysed.gov/irts/reportcard/.

New York State Education Department (2006) *New York State report card database*. Retrieved from https://www.nystart.gov/publicweb/DatabaseDownload.do.

New York State Education Department (2008) *NY Start: New York State Accountability Reporting Tool*. Retrieved from https://www.nystart.gov/publicweb/County.do?year=2007acounty-Dutchess.

Orfield, G. (2004, October 14). Forword. In D. Heller & P. Marin (Eds.), *State merit scholarship programs and racial inequality*. The Civil Rights Project, Harvard University. Retrieved from www.civilrightsproject.ucla.edu/research/meritaid/fullreport/04.php.

Peske, H. G., & Haycock, K. (2003) *Teaching inequality: How poor and minority students are shortchanged on teacher quality*. Washington, DC: Education Trust. Retrieved from http://www2.edtrust.org/NR/rdonlyres/010DBDgF-CED8-4D2B-9EOD-91B446746ED3/0/TQReportJune2006.pdf.

Polakow, V. (2007) *Who cares for our children? The child care crisis in the other America*. New York: Teachers College Press.

Rimer, S. (2003) Cambridge schools try integration by income. *New York Times*, May 8. Retrieved from http://www.nytimes.com.

Roza, M. (2006) How districts shortchange low-income and minority students. *Funding gaps 2006* (pp. 9–12). Retrieved from www2.edtrust.org.

United Nations Human Rights Committee (2006) *Consideration of reports submitted by states parties under Article 40 of the Covenant: Concluding observations of the Human Rights Committee, United States of America*. Retrieved from http://www.unhchr.ch/tbs/doc.nsf/0/0d83f7fe89d83ed6c12571fb00411eb5/$FILE/G0644318.pdf.

Urban Institute (2006, June) *A decade of welfare reform: Facts and figures*. Fact Sheet. Washington, DC: Office of Public Affairs. Retrieved from http://www.urban.org/UploadedPDF/900980_welfarereform.pdf.

U.S. Department of Health and Human Services (2000) *Oral health in America: A report of the surgeon general*. Rockville, MD: U.S. Department of Health and Human Services, National Institute of Dental and Craniofacial Research, National Institutes of Health.

Wilkinson, R. (2005) What colleges must do to help needy students. *Chronicle of Higher Education*, October 7. Retrieved from http://chronicle.com/weekly/v52/i07/07b00701.htm.

Zimet, Lilli (2005) Telephone conversation with the author, January 10.

6

The Moral and Spiritual Poverty of Educational "Leadership" … and a Hope for the Future

ULRICH C. REITZUG AND DEBORAH L. WEST

A Personal Reflection

Seven years after American soldiers entered Nazi concentration camps at Buchenwald, Dachau and other locations, I was born in Bad Rothenfelde, Germany, the fourth child of my German parents. My father was a pilot in the German Luftwaffe. He was shot down behind Russian lines, but survived the war. My mother had to flee across the frozen Baltic Sea to escape the advance of Russian troops. She survived the flight, but many others did not. Among the many lives lost in World War II were those of 6 million Jews, exterminated by Hitler, the Nazis, the complicity of ordinary Germans, and the complacency of the United States and much of the rest of the world (Berenbaum 2006). My parents were not Jewish—they were German Catholics. When I ask them about the Holocaust, they answer that there were many rumors during the war, but that the rumors were so awful that they did not believe that they could possibly be true.

Recently I had the opportunity to visit the United States Holocaust Memorial Museum in Washington, DC. I was not prepared for the power of the experience. I had just finished touring the National Air and Space Museum, and the Holocaust Museum was simply intended to be the next stop on my whirlwind tour of DC museums. As I stepped off the elevator that takes visitors to the fourth floor of the Holocaust Museum—the beginning of the exhibit—I was brought to an abrupt halt in front of the first photograph. I was not prepared to stand frozen, gripped by a profound sadness, as I stared at the life-sized, black-and-white image in front of me, a photograph of corpses scattered across the railroad tracks of one of the concentration camps. Later, as I slowly worked my way through the exhibit, I was not prepared for the way it sucked me into my ancestral heritage … and into the horrors of our inhumanity to each other. I was not prepared, as I came to the exhibit of a concentration camp bunk house where human bodies had lain—side by side, starving, freezing and frightened—for my hand to reach out involuntarily in solidarity to touch gently the rough wood of the bunk house. I was not prepared, hours later, as I exited the darkness of the exhibits and entered the Chapel of Remembrance, for the tears that formed in my eyes as the sunlight came streaming through the narrow windows that lined the chapel walls.

I live in Greensboro, North Carolina. Greensboro, where, in 1960, four young men sat at a lunch counter and refused to leave until they were served—a lunch counter at which they were prohibited from eating because they were "colored." Greensboro, where, as recently as 1979, five civil rights protesters were gunned down and killed by Klan and Nazi sympathizers while the police looked the other way. I live in a country that elected for a second term a president who deceived the American people in order to start a war—a war that has claimed hundreds of thousands of lives and destroyed a country. I live in a world where, century after century, highly educated, intelligent people still cannot figure out a better way of resolving differences than using guns and bombs and starting wars.

As an educator, I reflect on my roots, on the national and global scripts that have been and continue to be written, and on the policies and practices that prevail in public education. There are times when, after spending more than thirty years trying to influence our world positively through my work as an educator, I am tempted to resign myself to the way things are, to spend my energy contemplating happy retirement thoughts of travel—winters on a beach in a warm, sunny climate, and summers in the mountains close to nature. But I cannot turn my back on the future any more than I can ignore the present or forget about the past. When I reflect on the events that are part of my history, my community and my world, I see the many ways that education and humanity have fallen short and I wonder: What does it mean to be educated? What does it mean to be human? What are our responsibilities to others? How can we live together in peace, harmony and fulfillment? Unless questions such as these serve as the context for all that occurs in schools, our schools will simply educate students who are able to create better buildings, develop better bombs, identify better ways of acquiring more, and engage in better ways of killing each other. I cannot help but conclude that education and schooling need to be about much more than facts, figures, skills and tests.

The notion of leaving no child behind in our schools and our society is a noble one. No child should be left behind from the opportunity to learn things that are interesting and meaningful and that enrich a life. No child should be left behind from the opportunity to learn about, and grow to cherish, our common humanity. No child should be left behind from the opportunity to learn about the things that are unique and different about us and that make life so precious and wondrous. No child should be left behind from the opportunity to develop the habits of mind and heart that will enable them to participate in making our world a better place. All children should have these opportunities. However, taking the notion of not leaving any child behind and attaching it to legislation called No Child Left Behind (NCLB), and translating that legislation into a program of testing that wrings the life, meaning and humanity out of education, is manipulative and, indeed, sacrilegious.

For the past twenty years I have been a professor of educational leadership. A big chunk of my work—and my commitment—has been preparing people to be school principals, a position I once held myself. For twenty years I have been committed to preparing principals who are moral leaders (Sergiovanni 1996) rather than simply school managers or administrative bureaucrats. Prior to the passage and implementation of No Child Left Behind, informal discussions with prospective and practicing principals covered a wide gamut of issues, often revolving around what needed to happen in schools with students in order for them to impact the world positively. Since No Child Left Behind, conversations with principals and prospective principals cannot typically continue for more than a few minutes without testing and the whole lexicon of test-related terms and acronyms dominating the discussion. Have principals thrown out the idealism and moral vision that many of them once held? Are principals serving as moral leaders in their schools? Or are they simply functionaries promulgating government-developed education policy?

Talking with Principals

My co-author and I recently had the opportunity to conduct interviews with currently practicing principals. We talked with twenty individuals from all levels of schooling and with varying degrees of experience as principals. We were interested in hearing how they talked about their work, their leadership, instruction, and their vision for their schools. The opening prompt that was given to each was simply, "Tell me about your work as a principal." Follow-up questions were based primarily on the direction established by the principal in her or his response. What follows is what they told us and our reflections on their words. We have divided our discussion of what they told us into several themes.

Theme: Aligning Curriculum, Instruction, Assessment and Testing

> The goal that I have for this school … is to make sure that there's a tight alignment between the written, formal curriculum documents, the delivered instruction, and then the assessed instruction … We periodically benchmark and assess what we taught. Once we benchmark, we have the discussion about what worked, what didn't work, and we look back, and we reteach what the students didn't master. It's a continuous cycle. (Principal #4)

The quote above reflects what we heard on a regular basis from our principals. Virtually all of our twenty interviewees talked at some point during their exchanges about their efforts to align testing and the state-based curriculum document with instructional processes. As noted by the principals, alignment processes consist of the following:

- using the state-provided curriculum document as the foundation (the assumption being that it is aligned with the standardized tests taken by students);
- developing pacing guides by taking the formal curriculum document, segmenting it into chunks, and attaching a target by which time each chunk of the curriculum is to be mastered;
- delivering instruction consistent with the pacing guide;
- administering criterion-referenced, "benchmark" tests at regular intervals to assess whether a chunk of the curriculum has been mastered;
- reteaching as needed, based on benchmark testing results.

The linear, alignment-focused approach to curriculum and instruction is problematic in a number of respects. For starters, principal discourse was about aligning curriculum, but seldom was there talk of aligning students' interests, needs and learning styles with instruction. Additionally, the linear approach is grounded in the assumption that the state-approved curriculum reflects what is most worth knowing. Rigid adherence results in a static curriculum that leaves little room for being impacted by students' lives. The absence of curricular connections to the daily lives of students essentially renders them voiceless. The message to students is that their lives and their experiences are not important, or certainly less important than those bestowed with significance by adults in faraway comfortable offices who write curriculum documents. Should it thus be any surprise to us when students are disengaged from schooling and conduct themselves in ways that give voice to their alienation?

At issue also is how a state-prescribed curriculum that is vigorously implemented by principals connects with events that occur daily in our country and world—events that demand deep inquiry and thoughtful discourse by students if we are to prepare them for meaningful, intelligent and humane participation in a democracy. Unfortunately, as one principal noted, "No matter what happens, the curriculum is written, it's stamped 'approved for the year,' and that's what it is we're going to be tested on. So curriculum doesn't really change." This principal did go on to note that, in the aftermath of Hurricane Katrina, many of the social studies teachers in the high school did temporarily take a curricular detour to address "American culture, American response to tragedy, disasters in previous history." One wonders, however, whether they engaged students in exploring questions such as those cited by historian Michael Eric Dyson in his book on Katrina:

> Why did the Black and the poor get left behind? What took the government so long to get to the Gulf Coast, especially to New Orleans? What do politicians sold on the idea of limited governance offer to folk who need, and deserve, the government to come to their aid? Why is it that the poor of New Orleans, and, really, the poor of the nation, are hidden from us, made invisible by our disinterest in their lives? … Has the [Bush] administration's hostility to science matters like global warming made us even more vulnerable to natural disaster? Has the war in Iraq diverted critical social attention from pressing domestic issues and depleted our emergency resources? … Can we really afford to proceed as a nation without addressing how race, poverty, and class gang up on too many of our citizens and snatch from them their futures? (Dyson 2006, xi–xii)

Whose interests are served by a state-approved curriculum? Whose interests do principals serve when they give blind allegiance to this curriculum? Whose interests does it serve when their schools achieve high test scores? Who really benefits from a curriculum focused on teaching to the test: principals who are able to keep their jobs when their schools achieve high test scores, or students who are subjected to a curriculum from which all the things that make school exciting and motivating have been removed?

SUB-THEME: ALIGNING INSTRUCTION WITH CURRICULUM

> Curriculum obviously is developed by the state. Our county takes it and breaks it into chunks and really gives us a format for how to pace our curriculum. We have pacing guides ... which I think is a great thing because it tells everybody what pace they need to be moving and how many days they need to be spending on that. So a lot of that curriculum and pacing is done for us, which I appreciate. (Principal #7)

Pacing guides are a second problematic aspect of a linear, alignment-focused approach to curriculum and instruction.[1] The use of pacing guides and curriculum maps appear to take individual student needs out of the learning equation and negate the progress made in previous years by our increased understanding of the constructivist nature of learning. Rather than commencing instruction based on student needs, pacing guides require starting ... where the pacing guide and its developer dictate. To assume that a teacher can productively move forward at a learning pace established by someone in a district office or elsewhere is a regression to a past less-informed era. Clearly all students do not move forward at the same pace, nor will all classes move forward at the "ideal" pace established by an "all-knowing" person in a remote location who developed the pacing guide without knowledge of *any* of the students who will be subject to it. Although some principals talked of using benchmark data in combination with the pacing guides and then reteaching as necessary, this would appear to be in direct opposition to the principles of such a guide. Clearly, taking the time to reteach slows down the pace of instruction and renders the specifications of the pacing guide moot.

SUB-THEME: AN EMPHASIS ON ROTE INSTRUCTION

> I started investigating what programs are working in other schools. How did School X make AYP [Adequate Yearly Progress] with their disparate group? What did they attribute their success to? ... Several of the schools said, "Well, SRA Corrective Reading." ... It's a very scripted program that I'm not usually for, but if it works, and they've got research to show that it has worked ... so I'm going "Okay, we're going to try it. If it's not good for children, I don't want to do it." ... So, we got that program into place, got the funding for that. And then I bought the program SuccessMaker. I've been saving for three years ... We got it installed finally in October. (Principal #3)

A number of other principals also mentioned the SRA and SuccessMaker pre-packaged commercial programs, which are very prescriptive and drill-and-practice oriented. The implication was that instruction that was intended to yield high test scores should be linear and embrace rote processes. Indeed, the principal cited above went so far as uncritically to equate high test scores with "what's good for children." One wonders, is it good for students to be subjected to mind-numbing, contextless rote instruction that results in their tuning out, turning off and disengaging? Rather than involving discussions focused on better ways of teaching students, or on trying to "understand kids" in order to be able to teach them better, the emphasis of school improvement appears to have shifted to "installing" context-free programs that take students, who they are, and what they need (other than high test scores) completely out of the equation.

The assumption that rote processes and teaching to the test result in higher test scores is, perhaps, the most influential assumption guiding instructional practice in schools in the high-stakes testing era of No Child Left Behind. That there has been such wholesale and uncritical acceptance of this assumption is truly an educational and societal tragedy when one considers that there is significant research evidence, from both quantitative and qualitative studies, that shows that standardized test scores are higher in schools where more authentic instruction occurs (e.g., Newmann & Wehlage 1995; Newmann & Associates 1996; Marks & Printy 2003; Marks et al. 1996).[2] Not only does authentic instruction result in higher test scores, but the achievement gap between high and low socio-economic students is also smaller in schools that restructured in ways that permitted more authentic instruction. Why then is there a continued slavish adherence by many principals to the erroneous assumption regarding the relationship between rote instructional processes and higher test scores?

Beyond research-based arguments for authentic instruction, there are also moral arguments in its favor. Indeed, authentic instruction could be argued to be a democratic form of pedagogy. One of its key components, instruction that is designed to permit individual student "construction of knowledge," is grounded in assumptions that each student will bring a different foundation of knowledge and experience to each lesson, and thus will construct knowledge pertaining to that lesson differently. The objective is not for each student to learn the exact same thing; the objective is for each student to learn what is of value for them at that point in their intellectual and social development. In essence, this aspect of authentic instruction serves to honor and give voice to who the student is and what they bring to their learning at each point in time. It honors student difference, recognizes that students bring varying experiences to the classroom, and views student difference as intrinsic, natural, and to be valued, rather than as a deficit that needs to be corrected (O' Hair et al. 2000). Additionally, authentic instruction requires the inclusion of "disciplined inquiry." As Dewey (1916) argues, in a democracy there must be widespread participation in all aspects of public life, decisions should be made by engaging in discourse in which differences are resolved not by power but through inquiry, and the grounds for decision-making should be balancing individual needs and the common good. Engaging in disciplined inquiry appears a good match for preparing students for democratic citizenship; prescriptive and rote learning processes do not.

Theme: Using Data to Make Decisions

You've got to be a statistician to be a principal now. Three different spreadsheets this week. A new Scantron achievement series website that takes your benchmark, orderly data and it does it by item, and it does it by student, and it does it by grade-level, and by teacher, and you sort the percentages attained, and then you meet with your grade-level and decide what your action plan's going to be for the next nine weeks. Learning how to manipulate all of that data and the websites so that's it's meaningful. Three new programs this year like that. (Principal #3)

Almost all of the principals we interviewed talked about the use of data to make decisions. As a professor who almost a decade ago developed a course entitled "Schools as Centers of Inquiry," a course which focused on the collection and analysis of data as a way of studying and developing thoughtful, informed responses to school issues, I should be heartened by the principals frequently citing the use of data as a key part of their work. However, in analyzing how they talk about the use of data, several things become clear:

- they discuss data almost exclusively in terms of using them to "drive instruction";
- they discuss, almost exclusively, only test and test-related data;
- they mention only quantitative data and never qualitative data.

While there is nothing intrinsically wrong with having instructional practice informed by quantitative testing data, this is only a slice of what should inform instructional decisions, and is a very narrow approach to making such decisions. An understanding of the ways students, teachers, parents and others are experiencing various aspects of schooling is more likely to be found in qualitative data. How do students believe they learn best? What facilitates their engagement in academic work? What are teachers struggling with in their teaching? What are parents' understandings of how they might assist in their child's education?

One could argue that the seemingly heavy reliance on quantitative testing data is actually a step (or two) backwards when it comes to making informed decisions. Prior to the proliferation of testing and the hyper-analysis of test data, instructional decisions were made considering all the information and data that were available to teachers and principals. Some of this may have come from test score reports, but other data came from the informal daily observation of teachers in their classrooms as they watched students work and learn and talked with them about their work and their lives. Although these qualitative data may not have been systematically collected and analyzed, they were legitimate, reality-based, first-hand and, often, rich data. Based on what the principals we interviewed said, it appears that this personal knowing is either no longer considered or, at least, has lost a significant amount of cachet. In its place, the data that are now being used are impersonal and reflect a student's performance on a narrow slice of learning at one moment in time. The resulting depersonalization that has occurred is reflected in the following words of one principal.

> Graduation rate, ABCs, AYP, teacher attendance, student attendance—there's a multitude of pieces of data. Everything has a number to it. That's important, so I have to make sure all those numbers are increasing ... Once that's taken care of, *then* what's important to me is making sure again that every single individual student in this school has what they need to be successful, that they can move to the next level ... (Principal #9)

Principals regularly used the language of "students first" and "doing what's good for students," but are principals and schools really acting consistently with that sentiment when their focus is so heavily on test scores? Wouldn't a "student first" perspective start with concentrating on creating a learning environment that is engaging for students? Isn't this a more humane approach than focusing on high test scores—whose collateral damage is often boredom, disengagement and, perhaps, even alienation? From a utilitarian perspective, who is likely to achieve higher test scores (and learn more): students who are engaged in their learning or students who are disengaged?

Theme: Principals as Vessels of the State—the Abandonment of Moral Leadership

> There's a curriculum guide that tells you "teach this" and at the end there's going to be a test that reflects that. It's not too hard. It's kind of a no-brainer system that we have in [this state]. Now, if teachers think they're more creative than that and would like to teach outside of that ... they're getting the students in trouble with that ... If you don't teach what the state says is important, the students aren't going to do very well on the test ... What's important to me—and I probably shouldn't start here but I will—is what's important to Washington County schools because they're going to decide whether I stay or don't stay. So first I have to take care of those things before I can do anything else. (Principal #9)

Based on what the principals said, it appeared that, in many cases, they have ceded the leadership rights for their school to the district, to the state, and to federal education policy. Are principals really leading their schools if they are simply developing ways to comply effectively with the wishes outsiders have for the school? Can we really call principals leaders if they are merely following the drumbeat of those who are leading them down the low road of striving, first and foremost, for higher test scores? Is taking and stimulating actions on behalf of someone else's goals really leadership?

Collaboratively developing a vision for a school and leading others in the pursuit of that vision has long been recognized as a hallmark of an effective principal. However, in the case of most of our principals, it appeared that individual school vision has been coopted by No Child Left Behind and the state and local influentials who promote it. Although there is no legal requirement for achieving high test scores to be the *de jure* vision for schools, it has, in fact, become the *de facto* vision for many. Instead of viewing test scores as an inevitable byproduct of a meaningful and humane curriculum and engaging high quality instruction, high test scores have become the vision and the goal—with side effects that are harmful to the intellectual and psychic health of students.

Caveats and Hope

While we have shared the prevailing sentiment of what principals said, several caveats must be acknowledged. First, we are convinced that all of the principals we interviewed have only the best of intentions for students and teachers in their schools. While we have issues with their focus and often with how they carry out their work, we also have the luxury of observing their work from afar. Which brings us to our second caveat: all of the principals labor under tremendous stress and pressure—stress and pressure which push some of them close to the breaking point. The extent of the pressure under which they labor was an unexpected dimension of our interviews and was a story worth telling in its own right (see West & Reitzug 2007). Thus, as somewhat distant observers, we do not know how we would respond under similar circumstances and certainly do not wish to judge our principals. Nonetheless, it is part of our responsibility as educational researchers and educational leaders to critique practice and propose alternative visions of what might be. Finally, it should be noted that the prevailing sentiments of our principals were not universal sentiments. There were some countervailing perspectives. However, these were merely glimmers of hope, rather than more comprehensive alternative perspectives of what schooling and the role of a principal might be. One principal, however, did offer a radically different vision.

Principal as Prophet: A Prophetic Vision for Schooling[3]

> I think administrators should be *prophets*. One of the major things they do is say things in new ways to empower people. A *prophet* pulls everyone in together with a purpose. The "people" have to be called into another vision, into another more just "possibility" for action/existence. [A prophet] needs to nudge the individual and collective consciousness and consciences of a people so that there is always a discomfort with the status quo. (Principal #18/Rachel)

The metaphor that this principal (Rachel; a pseudonym) explicitly uses to describe her practice as a principal is "prophet." Throughout her interview, she described what might be termed a prophetic vision of schooling and the principalship. As she described her work, she provided examples of how she nudged "the individual and collective consciousness and consciences" of her staff, pulled them "in together with a purpose," and *called* them "into another vision" (i.e., a vision other than the politically expedient one).

In order to provide a contrast between Rachel's narrative and the narratives of the principals discussed in the previous sections of this essay, what follows are excerpts from Rachel's interview that speak to each of the previously discussed themes.

On Curriculum, Instruction, Assessment and Testing

> Administrators need to teach teachers a different way of thinking and they need to try to support them in that sort of talk and thinking, and give them opportunities for those kinds of discussions. I like to say, "Forget the curriculum, and tell me what you think third graders need to know. What do they really need to know? Make a list for me. Hash it out. Then look at the state

curriculum. Where can you put it in? What's left? What are the odds they really need to know that?" I think you end up with a much better year for kids. And the teachers are happier, they feel more connected, and they feel empowered, because they have made decisions in the same way they've been taught to do … "Who better to do that than you? You know!" Teachers are not often told that they really know … Top down accountability is saying to them that they don't really know and there is a watchdog that is not from within them telling them what they're supposed to do and they feel powerless …

On Using "Data" to Make Decisions

We started having meetings where everybody had a chance to speak before anyone had a chance to speak again … It was a matter of putting in a somewhat democratic process … It's about everyone having a voice and people listening to everyone's voice … We had to start talking about what we believed in … what it meant to work with a team of people and with parents, and kids, and have a learning community. And how do you promote community and … what is it that's right to be learned—and not just the state curriculum? … We started talking about, "Is this good for kids, and in what ways? Is this curriculum good? Is this book good? Is this method good? Will this strategy work? Will it make kids feel more connected? Will it create peaceful relationships among kids and teachers? Will this make for a more positive school climate?" Those were the issues and the questions that we initially started talking about … I want to know what people think and that they are learners and thinkers … I am learning at the same time that I'm trying to teach and I would like for them to do the same thing.

On Principal Moral Leadership

So there was a day when I said, "Let me tell you who I am." And then I just talked to them about my philosophy of schooling and life, and spiritual and political alienation, and having a great passion for seeing lives changed, and education being peaceful, and building learning communities, and all that sort of talk … From then on things started moving in a different sort of direction … Near the end I could even talk about spiritual connections to various things. Before that I could say, "Is this a positive connection to the self? Is this a positive connection to the community? Will this help influence kids to get along better? Does this promote the type of learning that we know we want to do that's over and above what the state requires?" It was a given that we did the state curriculum. What over and above do we do that promotes what we want in the school? … And even in our discipline policy … we tried to make everything we did a learning kind of situation that could build community and make kids connected to and value what we were doing in school … We talked a lot about the dignity of children. That was a term that I could use that was very powerful.

... I don't think ... [testing] should be the main focus of schools. Quite frankly, I'm opposed to it. But I do work for that system and I do want to do my work, so I think you give Caesar what's due Caesar and you do what you know is right ... I'd much rather people [i.e., teachers] ... be stressed out ... over making sure kids learn what they know is the right thing to learn, rather than being stressed out over test scores ... If we could ever get to where we just operated on that, all the other things would take care of themselves. But that's not the system ... a lot of negative energy goes to the other ...

Grounding Prophetic Leadership

The grounding for a prophetic vision of schooling is the theological literature on the prophetic tradition. Having its origins in the biblical prophets, this literature explores the meaning of the prophets' lives for our lives today. David Purpel, in his seminal work *The Moral and Spiritual Crisis in Education*, notes,

> The prophets did not specialize in predicting the future, for they were not endowed with extraordinary powers of clairvoyance. Rather, they were keenly aware of what were understood to be divine imperatives and very much aware of human responses to them ... *Prophets were passionate social critics who applied sacred criteria to human conduct*, and when they found violations of these criteria they cried out in anguish and outrage. (1989, 80; emphasis added)

Elsewhere, Purpel notes that prophets

> are not to be seen as seers, sorcerers, or crystal ball readers but as *shrewd and sensitive social and cultural critics*. Their task is to interpret the degree to which a community has been true to its commitments and to speak openly ... (1999, 125; emphasis added)

In a similar vein, Brueggeman notes that the role of a "prophetic ministry" is to "nurture, nourish, and evoke a consciousness, and perception alternative to the dominant culture" (1978, 13). Cornell West adds that to act in the prophetic tradition means to "engage in relentless criticism and self criticism, and project visions, analyses, and practices of social freedom" (1988, 38). Heschel (1962) summarizes, "Above all, the prophets remind us of the moral state of a people".

Educators acting in the prophetic tradition are not only likely to function as "social critics" when they speak to issues such as justice, oppression, inequity and poverty (Purpel 1989), but also to perform in this capacity when they challenge the appropriateness of state and federal government mandates for education, and other external influences on schools. Purpel notes,

> Our work as educators has little to do with increasing productivity, patriotism, and pride, but much more with meeting our responsibilities to create a compassionate consciousness ... An education that speaks in a prophetic

voice responds not to the possibility of becoming rich and famous, but to the possibility of becoming loving and just. Its reference point is not the erosion of America's economic and military might but humanity's erosion of its vision of universal harmony, peace, and fulfillment. (1999, 129–30)

Rachel serves as a social critic—a prophet—in her school through the questions she asks and the discussions she initiates and facilitates. These questions and discussions help the school identify and articulate its purpose and vision and cause teachers to consider issues of teaching, learning and education that go beyond simply raising test scores—thus challenging the prevailing political winds. The discussions empower teachers by teaching them "a different way of thinking" and supporting them in "that sort of talk and thinking." They ultimately result in "pull[ing] everyone in together with a purpose" via the consideration of the educative purposes of schooling—purposes that go beyond test scores and focus more on our "sacred" commitments as educators (Purpel 1989, 80).

What does a prophetic vision of leadership mean for principals? In his various writings on prophetic education, Purpel uses the terms "re-search" (1989, 105), "re-mind" (1989, 105; 1999, 125), "re-new" (1999, 125) and "re-form" (1999, 125). Applying these concepts to prophetic leadership has the following implications for principals. Principals who are prophetic leaders engage teachers and the broader the school community in:

- re-searching their commitments as individuals and as a community;
- re-minding themselves about their initial and organically evolving reasons for becoming educators;
- re-newing their allegiance to their commitments;
- re-searching the extent to which commitments are being upheld in the school's practice;
- re-forming current policies and practices that are incongruent with their rediscovered commitments.

Conclusion

I wrote at the beginning of this essay about the attempted extermination of the Jewish race by the Nazis. I wrote about the killing in my current hometown of civil rights workers—massacred by gun-toting Klansman while the local police looked the other way. I wrote about a United States president who misled our country into war but whom we still reelected. Although, seemingly, these are extreme cases, the daily lives of all of us are filled with opportunities to be complicit or to resist, to accept at face value or to inquire more deeply, to discuss or to be silent, to lead or to follow, to care and to feel or to be cold and unfeeling, to serve or to expect to be served. These are the daily choices of being human. How does the education we receive in schools prepare us to make these choices? What is the relationship between these choices and achieving AYP on the No Child Left Behind-inspired tests?

Clearly, an education in which state curriculum is tightly aligned with instruction and standardized testing has little in common with these choices. The knowledge that tests can measure may be necessary, but by itself that knowledge is neither significant nor worthwhile. Knowledge and skills by themselves are, at best, meaningless and, at worst, dangerous—if they are put to non-humanitarian uses. Education must be not only of the mind, but also of the heart.

With the exception of the prophetic vision of leadership and a few other isolated examples, the silence in the words of our principals was the absence of a moral or spiritual discourse. Certainly we did not expect the interviewed principals to become deeply philosophical with us, but, other than attaining high test scores, they did not hint at any vision for the types of human beings they want their students to be and to become. It could be argued that the Holocaust was evidence of the failure to provide a moral education for a nation. Similarly, it could be argued that the results of the presidential election discussed in this essay are evidence of a failure of U.S. schools adequately to prepare students for informed and critical democratic citizenship. We are left to ponder: What is the purpose of schools? What are the curricular and pedagogical implications for schools who wish to prepare students to work for a world that is more humane and peaceful? Will higher test scores prepare students to create a better world?

Notes

1. The discussion of pacing guides is taken from our work *Conceptualizing Instructional Leadership: The Voices of Principals* (Reitzug, West & Angel, 2008).
2. Authentic instruction was defined in these studies as instruction that incorporates disciplined inquiry, requires students to construct knowledge, and has some "value beyond school" (Newmann & Wehlage 1995, 9).
3. The discussion of a prophetic vision of schooling is adapted from our previous work. See Reitzug, West & Angel (2008).

References

Berenbaum, M. (2006) *The world must know: The history of the Holocaust as told in the United States Holocaust Museum* (2nd ed.). Baltimore, MD: Johns Hopkins University Press.

Brueggeman, W. (1978) *The prophetic imagination*. Philadelphia: Fortress Press.

Dewey, J. (1916) *Democracy and education*. New York: Free Press.

Dyson, M. E. (2006) *Come hell or high water: Hurricane Katrina and the color of disaster*. New York: Basic Civitas.

Heschel, A. J. (1962) *The prophets*. New York: Harper & Row.

Marks, H. M. & Printy, S. M. (2003) Principal leadership and school performance: An integration of transformational and instructional leadership. *Educational Administration Quarterly, 39,* 370–97.

Marks, H. M., Newmann, F. M., & Gamoran, A. (1996) Does authentic pedagogy increase student achievement? In F. M. Newman & Associates, *Authentic Achievement: Restructuring schools for intellectual quality*. San Francisco: Jossey-Bass.

Newmann, F. M. & Associates (1996) *Authentic achievement: Restructuring schools for intellectual quality*. San Francisco: Jossey-Bass.

Newmann, F. M. & Wehlage, G. G. (1995) *Successful school restructuring.* Alexandria, VA: Association for Supervision and Curriculum Development.

O'Hair, M. J., McLaughlin, H. J., & Reitzug, U. C. (2000) *Foundations of democratic education.* Belmont, CA: Wadsworth.

Purpel, D. E. (1989) *The moral and spiritual crisis in education.* New York: Bergin & Garvey.

Purpel, D. E. (1999) *Moral outrage in education.* New York: Peter Lang.

Reitzug, U. C., West, D. L., & Angel, R. (2008) Conceptualizing instructional leadership: the voices of Principals. *Education and Urban Society, 40*, 6, 694–714.

Sergiovanni, T. J. (1996) *Moral leadership: Getting to the heart of school improvement.* San Francisco: Jossey-Bass.

West, C. (1988) *Prophetic fragments.* Grand Rapids, MI: Africa World Press.

West, D. L., & Reitzug, U. C. (2007) Psychological toxic trauma of the principalship. Paper presented at the University Council for Educational Administration conference, Washington, DC, November.

7

Fear versus Possibility

Why We Need a New DEEL for Our Children's Future

Steven Jay Gross and Joan Poliner Shapiro

In the face of repressive accountability regimes in education that echo similar neo-conservative policies in other fields, colleagues around the world joined committed practitioners to take action. We call this movement the New DEEL (Democratic Ethical Educational Leadership). Our group was born in the academic year 2004–5, when faculty members from six universities, practitioners from various educational organizations, and the executive director of the University Council of Educational Administration (UCEA) joined forces. Since then, we have grown to include colleagues from over twenty universities as well as numerous school districts in the U.S., Canada, the U.K., Australia and Taiwan.

The New DEEL's mission is to create an action-oriented partnership, dedicated to inquiry into the nature and practice of democratic, ethical educational leadership through sustained processes of open dialogue, right to voice, community inclusion, and responsible participation towards the common good. We define leadership broadly to include faculty, students, staff, parents and community members, as well as educational administrators, because we believe that each of these groups is needed to create democratic ethical communities. Beyond the challenge of working to reverse legal excesses, such as No Child Left Behind (NCLB) in the U.S., the New DEEL seeks to expand the concept of educational leadership to include community leadership in the pursuit of social justice and social responsibility. To this end, the movement is currently focusing on six strands: research, publication, curriculum development, an ethical code, funding and technology. While the concepts of democracy and ethics are in contention, the promise of a just future for the next generation is worthy of our struggle. Therefore, our contribution to *Education and Hope in Troubled Times: Visions of Change for our Children's World* will highlight the New DEEL as a movement in a turbulent and frequently fearful world on the threshold of possibilities.

Clarifying and Contextualizing Democracy and Ethics for Our Movement

What do we mean by democracy? What do we mean by ethics? Clarification is more than merely in order as a matter of good form; it is critical. Otherwise, we are simply trapped into mindless sloganeering or, worse, coopted by others who would manipulate these words for opposite ends. In this chapter we explore democracy and ethics in greater detail. First, we will reframe the question of democracy by asking what we in the New DEEL mean by democracy *as it relates to social justice*. In parallel fashion, we will next consider the meaning of ethics in the New DEEL *as it relates to social responsibility*. Finally, we will reconnect democracy with ethics to illustrate the transformational profile we envision for New DEEL leaders.

Fear versus Possibility, Take One

Qualities of the Educational Leader[1] Pursuing Democracy and Social Justice

If educational leaders are to side with democracy and social justice, we believe that two critical choices need to be made. First, educators must choose between seeing learners as individual consumers or contributing members of an organic community. Second, we must choose between building schools as narrow training grounds or a place to learn about democracy through action. Below, we will briefly explore each of these propositions.

ARE LEARNERS CONSUMERS OR COMMUNITY MEMBERS?

How we conceptualize learners is foundational to the notion of democracy in our work. On one hand, there is pressure to see students as merely one more group of consumers/workers stuck in the role of passive users of preordained services. This is a pattern found in many facets of post-industrial societies entrenched in conservative economic projects.

Harvey (2005) describes the process of reducing human beings to objects. As objects, even those who feel themselves to be successful are hoodwinked by a false sense of security. Commenting on this fallacy from an African American perspective in the aftermath of Hurricane Katrina, Dyson (2005) states, "Narrow career interests and risk aversion define our number. Too many of us are 'safe Negroes' who don't realize that we can never really be safe until all Black people are safe."

Perhaps the most graphic and startling example of this citizen-as-passive consumer came in the days immediately following September 11th, 2001. While the American public hungered for a chance to sacrifice in the spirit of national solidarity, President Bush admonished the country to express its willingness to help by heading to the malls and go on a shopping spree. We were left with the depressing realization that our once dynamic citizenship had atrophied to the point being mistaken for sheepishness in the eyes of the commander-in-chief.

Gross, Shaw and Shapiro (2003) found a market-forces style of consumerism to be one of the major ways that journalists described accountability in education. In this model, children and their families enter into fragile contracts with education providers in much the same way that they enter a store at the local shopping mall. The for-profit school movement is one obvious manifestation of this trend. The experience is transactional and transitory, leading to the illusion of choice and empowerment but really being typified by conformity and isolation. Duignan takes the idea a step further:

The steady growth in self-centered modes of living can diminish us as moral agents in the pursuit of the common good. In fact, it is likely that there is a connection between these contemporary individualistic tendencies and a growing indifference to communitarian justice and equality. (2006, 7)

The connection between economic forces and the fraying of the social fabric leading to an atomized and alienated individualism has clear historic roots. Commenting on Dewey's analysis of the impact of industrialism in the early 20th century, Ryan explains: "Dewey's response was to insist that democracy must be committed to re-creating in an industrial society the mutual comprehension and appreciation that we experience in 'face-to-face' communities" (1995, 219).[2] Following Dewey's vision, there is a different possibility, one that views all of us as the creators and sustainers of community, not as an afterthought but as an integral element of our humanity. Archbishop Desmond Tutu uses the traditional concept of *ubuntu*, which captures the spirit of a new perspective on society and illustrates the potential of community in a democratic-ethical educational context: "In the end, our purpose is social and communal harmony and well-being. Ubuntu does not say, 'I think, therefore I am.' It says rather, 'I am human because I belong. I participate. I share" (2004, 27).

Allied with Desmond Tutu's perspective, and taking the notion of community to the school itself, is the work of Gail Furman (2002, 2004). According to Furman's ethic of the community, the concept itself is transformed from an entity to *community as processes*. Similarly, Greene connects an organic, engaging democratic life to the socially just community: "democracy, or what has been called 'a community always in the making,' cannot be attained by the passive, careless, or the thoughtless" (1988, 223).

This vision is in stark contrast to the self-oriented individual-as-consumer model. It is more robust, more oriented to engaged citizenship, aware of lives of others, and, therefore, more appropriate for an educational plan that values democracy and social justice.

Are Schools for Training or Democratic Living?

If we opt for engaged community life for learners instead of an atrophied existence as consumers, we must pose the next question: How broadly will we define the mission of this learning community? Since this is the site of community action, our answer is of pivotal importance.

Allied with the consumer/lone individual role for learners is the equally narrow and, we hold, equally undemocratic concept of the school as the location for narrow training where students continually prepare for some future, always receding in the distance. Dewey put the point succinctly:

Who can reckon up the loss of moral power that arises from the constant impression that nothing is worth doing in itself, but only as a preparation for something else, which in turn is only a getting ready for some genuinely serious end beyond? (Dewey 1909, 25–6, cited in (Kliebard 1986, 122).

The broader concept of the school is a place to learn about democratic life through experience. In an era when we are attempting to emerge from the intellectual and emotional shackles of a zealous accountability regime, one might wonder how we dare assert such a possibility. Again, history and precedent are illustrative.

Counts (1932) wrote *Dare the Schools Build a New Social Order?* as a call to greater purpose in the midst of the devastating economic collapse of the Great Depression. Simply put, Counts urged educators to take leadership in reforming their profession and the world around them. Urban (1978) advises us not to dismiss this work as an artifact of another era when he states that it "is as directly related to the educational and social problems of our time as it was to those of the 1930's" (1978, xiii–xiv). Several years earlier, Harold Rugg (1926), Counts's colleague, shared much the same spirit. Both placed heavy responsibilities on the school to become a place for democratic possibility.

In a recent call for a renewed progressive vision for education, Svi Shapiro remarked:

> Our concern for a vibrant democracy surely requires a younger generation educated in the skills, knowledge and dispositions that ensure democratic ideas are much more than abstract words on the pages of a civics textbook. They will need to infuse the classrooms, hallways, and assemblies of our schools. (2008, 19)

Freire illustrates the difference between life in a democratic classroom with that of a training regime in his famous critique of the banking method of instruction.

> For the anti-dialogical banking educator, the question of content simply concerns the programme about which he will discourse to his students; and he answers his own question, by organizing his own programme. For the dialogical, problem-posing teacher-student, the programme content of education is neither a gift nor an imposition. (1970, 65–6)

We hold that our current accountability movement, like its predecessors, is fully bent on an anti-dialogical banking approach to schooling. As Freire makes clear, the products of such an imposition are the defeat of democracy, the dismissal of learner interests, and a linear rigidity in instruction.

Beyond the classroom, the democratic school is organized in remarkably different ways than is the training institution. Ella Flagg Young, the first woman to run a major American city school system, and a close colleague of John Dewey, also was a pioneer in shared governance with her invention of teacher councils. Classroom teachers were empowered to conduct investigations and help to design policy for the public schools of Chicago (Webb & McCarthy 1998).

We in the New DEEL believe that the top priority for the education is the complex task of raising the next generation of citizens ready to sustain and broaden a democratic society. This means learning the meaning of democratic life through constant practice for all members of the school community, students, teachers, staff, administrators, parents, and community members. Gross (2004) found sophisticated examples of shared governance systems including all of these groups at schools dedicated to serious innovation. He further found that these democratic structures were credited with sustaining those innovations, especially during turbulent times. No one is alien to this enterprise and, as such, its purposes are connected to everyone in the community writ large.

We further contend that the creation of such a robust democratic community not only has strong historic roots, it is an essential part of initiating and sustaining serious educational innovation. The recent literature is filled with examples of adaptive, creative and socially just forms of organizations (Aiken 2002; Begley 1999; Begley & Zaretsky 2004; Boyd 2000; Gross 2006, 2004; Mitra 2001; Reitzug & O'Hair 2002; Sernak 1998; Shapiro & Purpel 2004; Shapiro & Stefkovich 2005; Starratt 2004; Young et al. 2002). A working understanding of democratic practice is the best way to stand our students in good stead for the dynamic future we foresee because it teaches deep flexibility, interdependence and responsibility.

Recalling Counts's critique of early 20th-century progressive schools as failing to assert a coherent social vision, we come to the question of overarching purpose. If, as we argue, learners should not be merely consumers but rather members of a dynamic democratic community, and if schools should dismiss the role of mechanical trainer in favor of becoming the center of democratic life, then we can logically turn to the question of project. What are worthy goals for these democratic community members learning in a school that sees its mission as broad-based social engagement?

If the idealism and vision of education stop squarely at the schoolhouse doors or university gates, never daring to challenge the appalling inequalities of the wider world, they remain micro-democracies, little more than limited experiments. To promote democracy and social justice in a vacuum supports neither. Of course, our focus is upon the school and the university, but only as a center of first action, not the bounded world of all possible activity. Reasonable equality, shared governance, mutual support, and common commitment to deep learning may start at the school but must also transcend it if there is a possibility for the school, the community, and the wider world to see these visions realized.

But to what level of democratic life should we aspire? Philip Woods summarizes models of democracy. His range of four levels consists of the most constrained type, referred to as *liberal minimalism*, to the most robust, called *developmental democracy*. It is the latter that we believe most deserves our support because it calls for "extensive political participation, enhancement of individuals' human capacities through political participation and collective state action, social justice and democratisation of civil society" (2005, 5).

In the wake of Hurricane Katrina, Dyson quoted Martin Luther King Jr.'s reflections on the biblical account of the good Samaritan: "True compassion is more than flinging a coin to a beggar; it is not haphazard and superficial. It comes to see that an edifice which produces beggars needs restructuring" (2005, 152).

While the birth of a completely fair and free society may be beyond the reach of this generation, or even the next, it would not be asking too much if we were to organize our school leaders at every level to work with community members and families in order to respond to such devastating problems as the lack of health care, decent housing, maternity and paternity leave, neighborhood safety, and employment opportunities.

Clearly, there are critical choices as we consider the meaning of democracy and social justice in the New DEEL. In the context of our work, we envision a pre-K–20 education system with a robust sense of mission and a high level of engagement. We see our vision in stark contrast to the dreary one projected by an aging and increasingly ossified accountability movement. On one side, there is the lonely consumer, trained for jobs that may not exist in the future, serving an increasingly divided economic order (Pink 2005; Zhao 2007). On the other side, there is membership in a dynamic community, supported by a school committed to the practice of democratic life aimed at cooperative work towards a fairer social condition around the world.

Fear versus Possibility, Take Two

Qualities of the Educational Leader Pursuing Ethics and Social Responsibility

If educational leaders are to emphasize ethics and social responsibility, we believe that two critical choices need to be made. First, educators must determine whether they want to accept social responsibility rather than accountability. Second, they must decide if they want to turn to other ethics and not just the ethic of justice.

SHOULD WE USE THE TERM SOCIAL RESPONSIBILITY OR ACCOUNTABILITY?

The African proverb *It takes a whole village to raise a child* indicates the importance of social responsibility not only in raising a child, but in educating one. Returning to this wise saying is essential if we are to consider new visions for educating a child for this century.

Social responsibility is an ethical term. As defined by John Stuart Mill, this term is at the heart of the New DEEL. Mill wrote: "Everyone who receives the protection of society owes a return for the benefit, and the fact of living in society renders it indispensable that each should be bound to observe a certain line of conduct toward the rest" (1978, 23). Social responsibility can easily apply to the education of our children. However, all too frequently, it is the term "accountability" that is used in regard to education. In the New DEEL, we want to move away from the accountant's ledger, which is the focal point of accountability, towards placing the best interests of children at the center (Shapiro & Stefkovich 2001, 2005; Stefkovich 2006).

Purpel explains well what has been happening in U.S. public schools of late. He writes:

> Schools have been captured by the concept of "accountability," which has been transformed from a notion that schools need to be responsive and responsible to community concerns to one in which numbers are used to demonstrate that schools have met their minimal requirement—a reductionism which has given higher priority to the need to control than to educational considerations. (Purpel 1989, 48)

To understand how accountability has gained in importance, it is important to look at it in historical perspective. "Accountability—a contagious disease?" (Shapiro 1979) was a paper focusing on a taxpayer's revolt that began in California with Proposition 13. In 1978, voters rejected local school district support of public education. Concurrently, Michigan introduced "blanket" testing for teachers, and the test results were utilized for dismissals and promotions of teachers. In the area of teacher training, at that time, performance-based standards were required in seventeen states. And "back to basics" was the slogan used for curriculum development.

In the 1970s, accountability gained prominence and attention for two major reasons. Bowles and Gintis (1976) described the public's increasing disdain for the American dream in which the majority of the young people in the country could graduate from college and find excellent jobs. They also mentioned the instability of the social reforms and progressive education that occurred in the 1960s. Control, through accountability and through a back to basics curriculum, was thought to be the panacea.

The accountant's ledger was becoming the bottom line in education. This movement was seen as a way to put educators in their place by making them produce measurable results through testing. Underlying accountability, at that time, was attribution theory (Martinko 1995) or blaming.

In the U.S. *A Nation at Risk* (National Commission on Excellence in Education 1983), *America 2000* (1991), *Goals 2000* (1993) and *No Child Left Behind* (2002) were documents that continued developing the concept of accountability in education. These reports made it clear that holding educators accountable for learning outcomes was essential. Deconstructing *America 2000*, for example, Sewell et al. discovered that the term "accountability" was mentioned twenty-three times—the same number of pages as the report (1998, 317).

Although discussed in general terms initially, accountability has proven to be a far more complicated concept. For example, Darling-Hammond and Snyder (1992) discovered five types of accountability—*political, legal, bureaucratic, professional* and *market*. Later on, Gross et al. (2003) added four other forms of accountability that they uncovered in deconstructing articles from scholarly journals, practitioner journals and newspapers. They were *parent, fiscal, student* and *personal*. Gold and Simon (2004) contributed a tenth type, *public* accountability, to the list.

Accountability could be classified as a disease that has metastasized over time. In fact, Leithwood (2001) calls this era the "accountability age," while Normore, when discussing the plight of school administrators today, refers to the current situation as "the edge of chaos" (2004, 55). Attribution theory remains part of accountability today.

The term "social responsibility," instead of blaming individuals or groups, places the onus to care for and educate the next generation of children on all of us (Gross & Shapiro 2002; Shapiro & Gross 2008). Since responsibility comes from within, blaming others is not its focus. Thus, in the New DEEL, we urge educators to reconsider the word "accountability" and substitute the term "social responsibility" in its place. But, beyond this, the New DEEL asks all of us to play an active part in educating the next generation. It does indeed take a town, a state, a nation and a global village to raise a child.

WHY EMPHASIZE THE ETHIC OF JUSTICE AND NOT THE ETHICS OF CRITIQUE, CARE, THE PROFESSION AND COMMUNITY?

Litigation is commonplace in societies that are focused on accountability. When faced with this fear, frequently educators turn to the ethic of justice. The ethic of justice deals with laws, rights and policies and is part of a liberal democratic tradition that, according to Delgado, "is characterized by incrementalism, faith in the legal system, and hope for progress" (1995, 1). Present-day philosophers and writers, coming from a justice perspective, frequently have dealt with issues such as rights and impartiality that are very much a part of distributive justice. In fact, Rawls (1971) defined justice as fairness.

When faced with an ethical decision, an educator might ask in regards to the ethic of justice: Is there a law, right or policy that relates to a particular case? If there is a law, right or policy, should it be enforced? And if there is not a law, right or policy, should there be one?

However, the ethic of justice is not the only paradigm to turn to when making an ethical decision. Frequently, the ethic of critique opposes or highlights problems inherent in the ethic of justice. Many writers and activists (e.g., Apple et al. 2003; Bakhtin 1981; Foucault 1983; Freire 1970; Giroux 2003; Greene 1988; Larson & Murtadha 2002; Shapiro & Purpel 1998; Shapiro 2006; Shapiro 1999) are not convinced by the analytic and rational approach of the justice paradigm.

An educator turning to the ethic of critique might ask: Who makes the laws, rules and policies? Who benefits from them? Who has the power? Who are silenced?

Some scholars (e.g., Beck 1994; Gilligan 1982; Ginsberg et al. 2004; Goldberger et al. 1996; Grogan 1996; Marshall 1995; Noddings 1992, 2003; Sernak 1998) have made the ethic of care more central to moral decision-making and to society in general.

Although the ethic of care most recently has been associated with feminists, men and women alike attest to its importance and relevancy. Male ethicists and educators, including Buber (1965) and Sergiovanni (1992), have helped to develop this paradigm. These scholars have sought to make education a "human enterprise" (Starratt 1991, 195). This ethic asks educators to consider questions such as: Who will benefit from what I decide? Who will be hurt by my actions? What are the consequences of a decision I make today? What are the unintended consequences of a decision? And, if I am helped by someone now, what should I do in the future about giving back to this individual or to society in general?

Shapiro and Stefkovich (2001, 2005) gave considerable attention to the ethic of the profession in their writings. This ethic can include one's personal and professional codes; the professional codes of appropriate organizations; the ethic of the community; and the standards of the profession. Shapiro and Stefkovich placed the best interests of students at the center of this ethic.

The development of professional ethics is far from a clear process and often presents pitfalls. In fact, Shapiro and Stefkovich (1998, 2005) identified four possible clashes that affected the creation of one's own professional ethical codes.[3] First, there may be clashes between an individual's personal and professional codes of ethics. Second, there may be clashes within the professional code itself. Third, there may be clashes of professional codes among educational leaders; what one administrator sees as ethical, another may not. Fourth, there may be clashes between a leader's personal and professional code of ethics and customs and practices set forth by a community. For example, behavior that may be considered unethical in one community might, in even a neighboring community, be seen merely as a matter of personal preference.

Questions that may arise from the ethics of the profession include: What is in the best interests of the student? Are there any ethical codes from my profession that are appropriate? And how does a decision dovetail with my own ethical personal and professional beliefs and those of the community?

Furman (Furman-Brown 2002; Furman 2004) expanded on what she characterized as a separate ethic of the community. In her writings, she challenged educational leaders to move away from heroic (solo) managerial decisions and turn towards community involvement in the decision-making process.

In the New DEEL, it is hoped that educational leaders will not immediately accept resolutions from the ethic of justice when faced with a challenging ethical dilemma. Instead, if they broaden their quest for solutions by considering other ethics, their decisions might be better. In addition, in so doing, they will lean towards transformational rather than transactional leadership.

Moving Beyond Fear towards a Democratic Ethical Model of Educational Leadership

We believe that the New DEEL offers educational leaders at all levels a series of critical choices that will shape not only their profession, but the lives of the children they work with and the state of the society beyond the schools. In each case, we argue for a transformational leadership dedicated to dynamic democratic life tied to social action that flows from a deep sense of ethical responsibility. Table 7.1 depicts some of the differences between the leadership that we advocate and that of the traditional model.

Conclusion

The purpose of this chapter was to explore the foundational questions of democracy and ethics as they relate to the New DEEL, and we have, therefore, devoted ourselves to the theoretical and philosophical aspects of our work. Before closing, it is worth remarking that we have also joined our words with deeds. Progress has been made in each of the six projects mentioned in the introduction of this chapter. We have held two conferences for scholars and practitioners at Temple University, where thoughtful educators from around the world have gathered to debate, share ideas,

TABLE 7.1 Transformational vs. Transactional Leadership

New DEEL vision for leaders	*Behaviour of traditional school leaders*
Transformational	*Transactional*
1. Guided by inner sense of responsibility to students, families, the community and social development on a world scale.	1. Driven by an exterior pressure of accountability to those above in the organizational/political hierarchy.
2. Leads from an expansive community-building perspective. A democratic actor who understands when and how to *shield* the school from turbulence and when and how to *use* turbulence to facilitate change.	2. Bound by the system and the physical building. A small part of a monolithic, more corporate structure.
3. Integrates the concepts of democracy, social justice and school reform through scholarship, dialogue and action.	3. Separates democracy and social justice from guiding vision and accepts school improvement (a subset of school reform) as the dominant perspective.
4. Operates from a deep understanding of ethical decision-making in the context of a dynamic, inclusive, democratic vision.	4. Operates largely from the perspective of the ethic of justice, wherein obedience to authority and current regulations is largely unquestioned despite their own misgivings.
5. Sees their career as a calling and has a well-developed sense of mission towards democratic social improvement that cuts across political, national, class, gender, racial, ethnic and religious boundaries.	5. Sees their career in terms of specific job titles, with an aim to move to ever greater positions of perceived power within the current system's structure.

and build a sense of community. We have designed and launched the first New DEEL graduate courses and have initiated significant new research endeavors, the first of which centers on high-school student engagement.

But beyond these concrete manifestations of movement, there is an emerging spirit and a spontaneous interest in the New DEEL. Some of us are motivated by a generative feeling because we want to pass along an invigorated profession. Others, early in their careers, want to build a robust, democratic ethical profession in which to practice and conduct scholarship. All of us are energized by the sense of duty we have to this generation and succeeding generations of the world's children. In the face of fear we are standing squarely for democratic ethical leadership dedicated to social justice and social responsibility.

Notes

1. It is critical to understand that the term "leader" for the New DEEL is broadly defined to include teachers, students parents, staff and community members as well as school and

district administrators. See Gross & Shapiro (2005) Our new era requires a New DEEL: Towards democratic-ethical educational leadership. *UCEA Review, 47*, 3, 1–4.

2. Growing up in Vermont, Dewey experienced such face-to-face institutions as town meetings directly. See Rockefeller (1991, 32).

3. In subsequent writings, Shapiro and Gross have combined the latter's turbulence theory with multiple ethical paradigms to deal with both rational decision-making and the need to help educators determine the relative intensity of ethical dilemmas. See Shapiro & Gross (2008).

References

Aiken, J. (2002) The socialization of new principals: Another perspective on principal retention. *Educational Leadership Review, 3*, 32–40.

America 2000: An education strategy (1991) Washington, DC: U.S. Government Printing Office.

Apple, M. W., et al. (2003) *The state and the politics of knowledge.* New York: Routledge Falmer.

Bakhtin, M. (1981) *The dialogic imagination.* Austin: University of Texas Press.

Beck, L. G. (1994) *Reclaiming educational administration as a caring profession.* New York: Teachers College Press.

Begley, P. T. (Ed.) (1999) *Values and educational leadership.* Albany: State University of New York Press.

Begley, P. T., & Zaretsky, L. (2004) Democratic school leadership in Canada's public school systems: Professional value and social ethic. *Journal of Educational Administration, 42*, 6.

Bowles, S., & Gintis, H. (1976) *Democracy and capitalism.* New York: Basic Books.

Boyd, W. L. (2000) The R's of school reform and the politics of reforming or replacing public schools. *Journal of Educational Change, 1*, 225–52.

Buber, M. (1965) Education. In M. Buber (Ed.), *Between man and man* (pp. 83–103). New York: Macmillan.

Counts, G. (1932) *Dare the schools build a new social order?* New York: John Day.

Darling-Hammond, L., & Snyder, J. (1992) Reframing accountability: Creating learner-centered schools. In A. Lieberman (Ed.), *The changing contexts of teaching: Ninety-first Yearbook of the National Society for the Study of Education* (Pt. 1, pp. 11–35). Chicago: National Society for the Study of Education.

Delgado, R. (1995) *Critical race theory: The cutting edge.* Philadelphia: Temple University Press.

Dewey, J. (1909) *Moral principles in education.* Boston: Houghton Mifflin.

Duignan, P. (2006) *Educational leadership: Key challenges and ethical tensions.* Cambridge, UK: Cambridge University Press.

Dyson, M. E. (2005) *Come hell or high water: Hurricane Katrina and the color of disaster.* New York: Basic Civitas.

Foucault, M. (1983) On the genealogy of ethics: An overview of work in progress. In H. L. Dreyfus & P. Rabinow (Eds.), *Michel Foucault: Beyond structuralism and hermeneutics* (2nd ed., pp. 229–52). Chicago: University of Chicago Press.

Freire, P. (1970) *Pedagogy of the oppressed* (trans. M. B. Ramos). New York: Continuum.

Furman, G. C. (2004) The ethic of community. *Journal of Educational Administration, 42*, 215–35.

Furman-Brown, G. (Ed.) (2002) *School as community: From promise to practice.* Albany: State University of New York Press.

Gilligan, C. (1982) *In a different voice.* Cambridge, MA: Harvard University Press.

Ginsberg, A. E., Shapiro, J. P., & Brown, S. P. (2004) *Gender in urban education: Strategies for student achievement.* Portsmouth, NH: Heinemann.

Giroux, H. A. (2003) *The abandoned generation: Democracy beyond the culture of fear.* New York: Palgrave Macmillan.

Goals 2000: Educate America Act (1993) Washington, DC: U.S. Government Printing Office.

Gold, E., & Simon, E. (2004) Public accountability: School improvement efforts need the active involvement of communities to succeed. *Education Week, 23,* January 14.

Goldberger, N., Tarule, J., Clinchy, B., & Belenky, M. (Eds.) (1996) *Knowledge, difference and power.* New York: Basic Books.

Greene, M. (1988) *The dialectic of freedom.* New York: Teachers College Press.

Grogan, M. (1996) *Voices of women aspiring to the superintendency.* Albany: State University of New York Press.

Gross, S. J. (2004) *Promises kept: Sustaining school and district innovation in a turbulent era.* Alexandria, VA: Association for Supervision and Curriculum Development.

Gross, S. J. (2006) (Re)constructing a movement for social justice in our profession. *International Electronic Journal for Learning in Leadership, 10,* 30.

Gross, S. J., & Shapiro, J. P. (2002) Towards ethically responsible leadership in a new era of high stakes accountability. In G. Perreault & F. Lunenburg (Eds.), *The changing world of school administration* (pp. 56–66). Lanham, MD: Scarecrow Press.

Gross, S. J., Shaw, K., & Shapiro, J. P. (2003) Deconstructing accountability through the lens of democratic philosophies: Toward a new analytic framework. *Journal of Research for Educational Leadership, 1,* 3, 5–27.

Harvey, D. (2005) *A brief history of neo-liberalism.* Oxford, UK: Oxford University Press.

Kliebard, H. M. (1986) *The struggle for the American curriculum, 1893–1958.* New York: Routledge.

Larson, C., & Murtadha, K. (2002) Leadership for social justice. In J. Murphy (Ed.), *The educational leadership challenge: Redefining leadership for the 21st century.* NSSE Yearbook. Chicago: University of Chicago Press.

Leithwood, K. (2001) School leadership in the context of accountability policies. *International Journal of Leadership in Education, 4,* 217–36.

Marshall, C. (1995) Imagining leadership. *Educational Administration Quarterly, 31,* 484–92.

Martinko, M. J. (Ed.) (1995) *Attribution theory: An organizational perspective.* Delray Beach, FL: St. Lucie Press.

Mill, J. S. (1978) *On liberty.* Portland, OR: Hackett.

Mitra, D. (2001) Opening the Floodgates: Giving Students a Voice in School Reform. *Forum, 43,* 2, 91–4.

National Commission on Excellence in Education (1983) *A nation at risk: The imperative for educational reform.* Washington, DC: U.S. Government Printing Office.

No Child Left Behind Act of 2001 (2002) Pub.L. No. 107–110, 115 Stat. 1425 (codified as amended at 20 U.S.C. 6301 et. seq.

Noddings, N. (1992) *The challenge to care in schools: An alternative approach to education.* New York: Teachers College Press.

Noddings, N. (2003) *Caring: A feminine approach to ethics and moral education* (2nd ed.). Berkeley: University of California Press.

Normore, A. H. (2004) The edge of chaos: School administrators and accountability. *Journal of Educational Administration, 42,* 4, 55–77.

Pink, D. H. (2005) *A whole new mind*. New York: Riverhead Books.

Purpel, D. E. (1989) *The moral and spiritual crisis in education: A curriculum for justice and compassion in education*. New York: Bergin & Garvey.

Rawls, J. (1971) *A theory of justice*. Cambridge, MA: Harvard University Press.

Reitzug, U. C., & O'Hair, M. J. (2002) From conventional school to democratic school community: The dilemmas of teaching and leading. In G. Furman-Brown (Ed.), *School as community: From promise to practice*. Albany: State University of New York Press.

Rockefeller, S. C. (1991) *John Dewey: Religious faith and democratic humanism*. New York: Columbia University Press.

Rugg, H. (1926) *The twenty-sixth yearbook of the National Society for the Study of Education: The foundations and technique of curriculum-construction*. Bloomington, IL: Public School Publishing Co.

Ryan, A. (1995) *John Dewey and the high tide of American Liberalism*. New York: W. W. Norton.

Sergiovanni, T. J. (1992) *Moral leadership: Getting to the heart of school improvement*. San Francisco: Jossey-Bass.

Sernak, K. (1998) School leadership—balancing power with caring. New York: Teachers College Press.

Sewell, T. E., DuCette, J. P., & Shapiro, J. P. (1998) Educational assessment and diversity. In N. M. Lambert & B. L. McCombs (Eds.), *How students learn: Reforming schools through learner-centered education* (pp. 311–38). Washington, DC: American Psychological Association.

Shapiro, H. S., & Purpel, D. E. (Eds.) (1998) *Social issues in American education: Transformation in a postmodern world*. Mahwah, NJ: Lawrence Erlbaum Associates.

Shapiro, H. S., & Purpel, D. E. (Eds.) (2004) *Critical social issues in American education: Democracy and meaning in a globalizing world* (3rd ed.). Mahwah, NJ: Lawrence Erlbaum Associates.

Shapiro, J. P. (1979) Accountability—a contagious disease? *Forum: For the Discussion of New Trends in Education, 22*, 16–18.

Shapiro, J. P. (2006) Ethical decision making in turbulent times: Bridging theory with practice to prepare authentic educational leaders. *Values and Ethics in Educational Administration, 4, 2*, 1–8.

Shapiro, J. P., & Gross, S. J. (2008) *Ethical educational leadership in turbulent times: (Re)solving moral dilemmas*. New York: Lawrence Erlbaum Associates.

Shapiro, J. P., & Stefkovich, J. A. (1998) Dealing with dilemmas in a morally polarized era: The conflicting ethical codes of educational leaders. *Journal for a Just and Caring Education, 4*, 117–41.

Shapiro, J. P., & Stefkovich, J. A. (2001) *Ethical leadership and decision making in education: Applying theoretical perspectives to complex dilemmas*. Mahwah, NJ: Lawrence Erlbaum Associates.

Shapiro, J. P., & Stefkovich, J. A. (2005) *Ethical leadership and decision making in education: Applying theoretical perspectives to complex dilemmas* (2nd ed.). Mahwah, NJ: Lawrence Erlbaum Associates.

Shapiro, S. (1999) *Pedagogy and the politics of the body*. New York: Garland.

Shapiro, S. (2008) It's time for a progressive vision of education! *Tikkun, 23*, 17–19, 70–72.

Starratt, R. J. (1991) Building an ethical school: A theory for practice in educational leadership. *Educational Administration Quarterly, 27*, 185–202.

Starratt, R. J. (1994) *Building an ethical school*. London: Falmer Press.

Starratt, R. J. (2004) *Ethical leadership*. San Franscisco: Jossey-Bass.

Stefkovich, J. A. (2006) *Applying ethical constructs to legal cases: The best interests of the student.* Mahwah, NJ: Lawrence Erlbaum Associates.

Tutu, D. (2004) *God has a dream.* New York: Doubleday.

Urban, W. (1978) Preface. In G. Counts, *Dare the schools build a new social order?* Carbondale: Southern Illinois University Press.

Webb, L., & McCarthy, M. C. (1998) Ella Flagg Young: Pioneer of democratic school administration. *Educational Administration Quarterly, 34*, 223–42.

Woods, P. (2005) *Democratic leadership in education.* London: Paul Chapman.

Young, M. D., Petersen, G. J., & Short, P. M. (2002) The complexity of substantive reform: A call for interdependence among key stakeholders. *Educational Administration Quarterly, 38*, 136–75.

Zhao, Y. (2007) Education in the Flat World: Implications of Globalization on Education. *Edge* [a publication of Phi Delta Kappa international], *2*, 4, 3–19.

8

Capitalism's Continuing Attempts to Dominate Civil Society, Culture and Schools

What Should Be Done?

RICHARD A. BROSIO

Background

The latest accumulation crisis (the inability to increase profit margins enough) within the global capitalist system has been an important determinant of what has occurred since the late 1960s within political, social, cultural schooling/education, as well as many other sites, institutions and processes. Granted that causes and effects are very complex, but this does not mean that a series of determinants and consequences, when based on rigorous inquiries, are impossible to understand. The U.S. hegemon and its principal assistant, the U.K., provided the leadership in making the world economy open to unprecedented advantages for capital. The results have been dramatic: good for some, although a relatively small minority, and not so good and/or disastrous for the majority of the world's people. Richard Sennett provides a succinct portrayal:

> The breakdown [in 1973] of the Bretton Woods currency [Conference, 1944] agreements [which tied the American dollar to gold] ... meant national con-straints on investing weakened; in turn ... corporations reconfigured them-selves to meet a new international clientele of investors ... more intent on short-term profits in share prices than on long-term profits in dividends. Jobs began similarly ... to cross borders. So did consumption and commu-nications. By the 1990s, thanks to micro processing advances in electronics, the dream/nightmare of automation became a reality in both manual and bureaucratic labor: at last it would be cheaper to invest in machines than to pay people to work. (Sennett 2006, 6–7)

Sennett's claim may be made clearer when placed within the historical tradition of civil society literature. Civil society has been defined as a safety zone between citizens and a potential authoritarian government. Most Western writers have insisted that a healthy civil society must include a market economy as well as a liberal political system. Others have argued that capitalism and authentic democracy are incompatible, and that capitalism has become a total system. Adam Seligman focuses on one of the most important problems within civil society argu-ments, namely the disagreement between the liberal-individualist and socialist views. This tension is based on the private and public realities of our social lives. The liberals have stressed liberty, whereas the socialists have championed equality. Were individual liberty to become dominant, in a totally laissez-faire market economy, social equality would become impossible. Conversely, if equality dominated, it would require the state's regulation of the capitalist market—as well as its participants' "freedoms" (Seligman 1992, 115–16). Seligman argues that we are still wrestling with the problem of reconciling the problem of abstract rights for the individual of liberal construction and the demands for concrete entitlements and "mutual welfare." According to Seligman, the addition of socio-economic rights to civil and political ones represents an important extension, and even a universalization, of citizenship. Moreover, it served to oppose the extreme individualism of liberal 19th-century political theory and practice.

From Communities to Border Crossing—Flexibility and the Bosses' New Clothes

Various critical theorists have questioned what liberals and conservatives—and others who believe capitalism and democracy are compatible—have done, as the latter refuse to consider contemporary capitalism as a total system. The former contend that this refusal allows their opponents to portray capitalism as merely another component of a more complex and diversified civil society. Of course such a refusal presents a serious threat to the notion that socialism is capitalism's greatest nemesis! Democratic Marxists consider civil society in the West as a place and institution that has been, from its very beginnings in modern times, a historical construction by the victorious bourgeoisie for their own regime of capitalism. Contemporary civil society in the U.S. is saturated by the complex power of consumer capitalism (Brosio 2004, 2). Among the many effects of this saturation are the decline of communities that did—to some extent—include places where various kinds of people could and did interact meaningfully on a daily basis. This is not to claim this as a golden age of perfect democratic space.

Large corporations are obviously central to capitalism; however, Sennett names the erosion of community as part of the dismantling of many large corporations within which "ordinary" people could find some security, camaraderie and "narrative" that helped make sense of their lives. Rather than villages, among them urban ones—that once included nearby places of work—the neo-liberal onslaught on security and solidarity results in places that resemble "train stations." Many writers in the postmodern world—a place or concept that is integral to today's capitalism and empire—write honorifically about "border crossers"; however, this movement is enjoyed only by a minority. Most "crossers" are people whose places and kinds of work have been marginalized and/or destroyed by the most recent "gales of creative destruction."

The global movement of poor people seeking work in industrial countries has become a flood. Sennett tells of a CEO who admitted aggressively that past service counts for little or nothing—it does not guarantee a place in the organization. He continues: only a "peculiar" kind of personality or character could or would discount the experiences that they had as worker and person. "This trait of personality resembles ... the consumer ever avid for new things, discarding old if perfectly serviceable goods" (Sennett 2006, 5). The postmodern "cultural ideal" that best serves this phase of capitalism and its colonization of the everyday, including the workplace, damages many persons who must succumb to this expectation in various ways.

The most recent phase of historical capitalism was voted for neither by large constituencies who were well informed, nor in fair "elections." As usual, in "thin" democracies many people accept structural changes with resignation as though they are inevitable. The proponents of and propagandists for the current capitalist order claimed those who accepted the somewhat new rules with regard to work, talent and consumption would experience freedom in what has been called "liquid modernity." This alleged liquidity/fluidity/flexibility, or claims to erase former impossibilities to overcome class differences, has been made popular by Thomas Friedman's term—"a flat world" (2005). Some would call it a level playing field. Sennett's rejoinder is that the new order has failed to set the majority of people on the planet free. Mountains of inequality persist. He urges people to examine rigorously what the "facts" are when placed next to the promises and the ongoing propaganda used by those who labor in the service of their "betters" and bosses. There is no inevitability in what has occurred. There are alternatives that can serve all of us better—if not the superlative best!

One might call what has been articulated above a form of the bosses' new clothes. The practiced arts of deception have been brought to bear upon ordinary people around the world. Many practitioners have learned their propagandist skills within the advertising world—one that has flourished first and foremost in the U.S. I continue to use Sennett's work to arrive at descriptions of character(s) that are, arguably, most representative of certain historical periods—ones that are influenced greatly by the continuous need for the agents of capitalism to address the accumulation crises.

> Perhaps the most confusing aspect of flexibility [today's capitalist work relations and expectations] is its impact on personal character. ... It is the ethical value we place on our own desires and on our relations to others. ... [For example] character ... depends on one's connections to the world. In this sense, "character" is a more encompassing term than its more modern offspring "personality," which concerns desires and sentiments which may fester within, witnessed by no one else. (Sennett 1998, 10)

Flexibility, as defined by the bosses and experienced mostly by their employees, gives contemporary meaning to Marx's recognition that capitalist dynamism causes so much of what seemed solid to melt into air, especially for those who are "unprepared" during this episode of historical capitalism. Those who trumpet the liberating powers of capitalism and some of their right-wing "family values" allies seem not to understand that flexibility—an apparent honorific term—all too often causes conflicts for those who want to do well economically, including for their families, but end up recognizing that the job's demands interfere with the family goal. Sadly, many people think that the "market" requires this because of the demand for immediate and constantly higher profits from the roiling power of capital shooting around the world at manic speed. People ascribe a deity-like identity and power to the market without realizing that this process is controlled by certain powerful—not omnipotent—people who use the mechanism for their own advantage.

Economics in American schools is rarely presented to students as a field of study that should be approached within the complexities of the civil society to which it is attached. This is a grave error in so-called democracies that should offer critical and holistic civic education to all students. There are reasons why this is not done, as many historians of education have explained. The schools are set into the very fabric of society and culture; therefore, one might ask how long-term purposes and projects can coexist within a society that is constantly faced with adjustments to economic-driven "new innovations." The recent insistence on privatizing elementary and secondary schools in the U.S. is typical of these changes, ones that usually turn out to be gimmicks rather than profound progressive changes. The No Child Left Behind legislation is a dramatic example of strategies employed by those who rarely realize that schooling crises are in fact societal phenomena that are transferred to our schools.

However, this legislation's weaknesses, if not bad intentions, are being exposed to those who have been aware of the origins, implementations and results. There is plenty of evidence to suggest that the intense demand for privatization of schooling is part of the neo-liberal/neo-conservative insistence to privatize just about everything. The public islands within our society that remained unconquered in the late 20th century were hit with economist Milton Friedman's total vision, translated into action. William Greider accused Friedman of championing "an ethic of unrelenting, unapologetic self interest that effectively pushed aside human sympathy" (Greider 2006, 6). Friedman recommended that Medicare, welfare, the U.S. postal system, and the K–12 public schools be privatized!

Aggressive Capitalism and the "Superculture"

As has been noted above, neo-liberalism demands that privatization must be accomplished everywhere, totally, and at the expense of the public islands (including schools) that remained unconquered during the 20th century. Character-types are importantly formed and changed by past and continuing capitalist efforts to solve accumulation crises as they arise. Our world is very complicated, therefore ruling out mono-causality; however, some phenomena are more causal than others.

The following provides examples of what occurs in an economy that causes important results in how people relate to the ever-changing capitalist political economy. Since the 1970s more and more women have become engaged in paid labor—at least among working-class Caucasians. African American women have been engaged in various forms of (low) paid labor since 1865. For Caucasian women, the reasons were many. Some were attracted to paid labor and others were forced into work in order to keep their families somewhat affluent during a time when working people's wages and salaries were beginning to stagnate. As more and more people where sucked into the vortex of capitalism's "gales of creative destruction" as workers, there occurred a related expansion of the consumer market. However, all too many Americans were either unable to find work or did not earn enough pay from their labor to become more active as consumers. This helps explain the increasing indebtedness among many people in the U.S.

Taking into consideration social class, race, ethnicity, gender, religious affiliations, and other differences, some contend that people have been overwhelmed by the developing "superculture" of the last forty years. Alvin Toffler's "best seller" *Future Shock* (1970) introduced this term. In his glib celebration of the technical and corporate destruction of communities and other institutions and practices of the working classes in the U.S., Toffler ridicules those who seek "diplomatic immunity" from change. He seems to approve of rootless corporate bosses and technicians who are mobile rather than the "not so super" majority. He writes approvingly of the emerging "fad" economy that competes with the older ordinary product one. They are commodities all the same, but represent a different phase of capitalism. He is a cheerleader for temporary products, methods and needs. Turnover has become more frenetic as throwaway commodities—and perhaps easily discarded customs, habits and practices—prevail.

One need not be a cultural conservative, such as Robert Nisbet (for example, in his *The Quest for Community*, 1953), to see the imposition of power upon those with little or no resources to resist effectively. Paul Goodman's *New Reformation: Notes of a Neolithic Conservative* (1970) refered to his concern about what Toffler and others were championing. Goodman argued that young people were too mesmerized by seeming inevitabilities and no longer recognized what was worth defending, let alone fighting enemies who cloaked themselves in "inevitability" claims. The absence of an authentic Left—grounded in economics and its role in the whole of our society and communities—made it easy for the capitalist new "gales of creative destruction" to succeed. The paradox of coupling "creative" with "destruction" epitomizes the chaos that capitalism has brought upon us.

Whatever various moorings existed that helped us make sense of our lives, what John Dewey called the conversion of "raw occurrence into composed tales of meaning" (Brosio 1972, 31), their weakening does not bode well for the existence and further development of empowered worker-citizens in democratic societies. Young people in the U.S. and elsewhere have been more powerfully influenced by the corporate media, the consumer market itself, their peers, and the "superculture" than could have been imagined before this began—as the radical 1960s morphed into rightist reaction that aimed at placing the market over all. Daniel Bell's *The Cultural Contradictions of Capitalism* (1976) helps us understand that American capitalism led the way to this demand: one must be "straight"—a loyal hard worker—during one's shift, but a "swinger" who is consumer driven, partly, by one's emotions that are related to overt or hidden advertisement persuaders.

Although it is difficult to explain precisely and definitively all, or even some, of the symptoms and causalities as the American federal, state, and even local governments moved steadily to the Right—beginning with the first Nixon administration—I continue to keep my focus on the economy. However, my analysis of capitalism goes beyond the economic features, because certain alliances that may seem paradoxical were and are still being made, for example, economic elitists with conservatives of a different kind than neo-liberal leaders. Neo-liberalism is an attempt to allow the capitalist market to work its magic, allegedly without the participation of "big" government. Thomas Frank's *What's the Matter with Kansas? How Conservatives Won the Heart of America* (2004) helps explain why one of the poorest counties in America, in Kansas, voted 80 percent for George W. Bush in 2000. Frank explains the Republican strategy since 1968:

> The hallmark of a "backlash conservative" is that he or she approaches politics not as a defender of the existing order or as a genteel aristocrat, but as an average working person offended by the arrogance of the "liberal" upper class. The sensibility was perfectly caught … [by] "Joe Six-pack" who does not understand why the world and his culture are changing and why he doesn't have a say in it. These are powerful words, the sort of phrase that could have once have been a slogan of the egalitarian left. Today, though, it was conservatives who claimed to be fighting for the little guy, assailing the powerful, and shrieking in outrage at the direction in which the world is irresistibly sliding. (Frank 2005, 46)

Effective civic education could have demonstrated that the Republican corporate Right and its neo-conservative allies have increasingly dominated U.S. politics by focusing on cultural wars rather than looking at who has power in a class-stratified country. In the wake of the contemporary gales, the perpetrators seek to convince "ordinary" people that we have only god(s) on our side. Those who are afflicted by these "gales" are led to believe that the "resources of rationality" are neither helpful nor even existent. The cultural conservative allies of capitalism, as well as the advertisers who shill for their masters, understand that logical, factual, concrete arguments are unnecessary because symbolism dominates the media world today. The Republican Party has learned more from the media about the effectiveness of symbols over logical arguments than its opponents. This is not to claim that given its deep roots within the moneyed interests, the Democratic Party has been the party of the people. It has been and remains the second party of capitalism and empire—unless pushed from below by bona fide democratic forces—which has rarely happened. Capitalist power does not allow political parties and movements to arise that have the potential successfully to oppose its hegemony and sometime more direct control. However, the absence of organized labor, workers' parties, and other movements from below that base their rational politics on concrete economic positions is what authentic democracy depends on. The manipulation of irrational symbols must never be the politics of the best of the Left(s). It must also be remembered that democracy has always been the project of the people—those who labor and have, in most cases, only their wages to depend on. Frank sums up what has been presented in the paragraphs above with this observation. The day after the 2004 election

> Bush set out his legislative objectives of his second term. Making America a more moral country was not one of them. Instead, his goals were mainly

economic and they had ... little to do with helping out the working-class people who had stood by ... [him]: he would privatize Social Security once and for all and "reform" the federal tax code. ... Businessmen everywhere celebrated the election results as a thumbs-up on outsourcing and continued deregulation. (2005, 49–50)

So much for the working poor, underemployed and unemployed people in the U.S.!

Character-Types and Democracy

As agents of the ruling elites seek to solve the accumulation crises in their own inter-ests, the powerful "gales" of capitalism help form people's characters in many intended and unintended ways. Christopher Lasch helps us understand better, through his many books and other publications, that one of the important conse-quences of these "gales" may be the weakening of the democratic psyche, namely, self-reliance, autonomy and a "self-directed" character-type. Obviously, one must take into consideration diversity within this concept, in terms of race, ethnicity, gen-der, sexual orientation, age and social class. The following is a synthesis of what I learned from Lasch and observed on my own. Perhaps it is an extreme picture—beyond what he intended? All too many "super culture" people in the United States exhibit these patterns of behavior: diffuse dissatisfactions; depression; a somewhat camouflaged sense of futility; extreme ups and downs with regard to self-esteem; impulse drivenness; inner rage that often explodes; inner emptiness (although not verbally admitted); chronic boredom manifested by being "busy" most of the time; teeter-totter rides between feelings of impotence and omnipotence; barely controlled need of admiration; insatiable cravings; hunger for having "experiences"—ones that can be reported back to others via voice and pictures; searches for instant intimacy; pursuit of pseudo-quick-fix self-insight; deep fear of aging; fascination with celebri-ties; fear of real competition and criticism; and rushing to judgment without study and contemplation. This historical character-type is not one who would likely believe there could exist a rational order of things and some rational tools to understand it. Perhaps this character-type has difficulty believing in the stability of anything, except with the aid of various forms of magic tales. These people may have difficulty believ-ing that the "resources of rationality," imperfect though they are, could be useful in pragmatic ways in order to "diminish arithmetically" (as the French writer Albert Camus has said) injustices, oppression and suffering in the world.

Lasch's conception of the "minimal self" is related to the description above. The beleaguered self faces powerful, giant forces in a nuclear and "terrorist" world, although, in these times, varied definitions of terror and terrorists, as well as the causes responsible for such actions and persons, must be taken into consideration. Lasch also uses the term "narcissist," but it is the weakness of self-concept, rather than egoism, that distinguishes the plight of the postmodern Narcissus. The replacement of natural and durable objects by a world of flickering images makes it increasingly difficult to distinguish reality from fantasy; thus it should not be surprising that the American people have twice elected an actor to the presidency.

The prefabricated world of ersatz is alienating in part because most of us have not had a role in planning and executing it. This ersatz world features a sense of simultaneity—despite the "new and improved innovation" claims—making it difficult to conceive of a society and world within which somewhat logical linear progression is possible or even worthwhile. The minimal/beleaguered/narcissist character-type views the world as disconnected, with seemingly isolated events, making it difficult to engage in theory-driven collective action. This character posture and attitude could be described, in part, by the ubiquitous constant use of the word "whatever." Another related unfortunate result might be that all too many people may fail to recognize regression from past progressive achievements.

The stimulation of infantile cravings by the advertising industry requires us to be perpetually dissatisfied. Immersed in a world of gigantic consumer sites within which to convert craving into purchase, we may not find it surprising that there is little room for thinking about politics, economics, systems theories, and how the elites really run the world. Institutions of cultural transmission, such as schools, places of worship, families, and communities that might have been expected to counter what is described above have all too often been shaped by these forces during this latest phase of capitalist "gales." For example, as Lasch argues, parents seek to make the family a "haven in a heartless world"; however, the techniques used to accomplish this goal are often derived from industrial sociology, personnel management and child psychology. These resemble the apparatus of social control itself. The French philosopher Michel Foucault might agree.

The central aim of those who lead and dominate our country is to profit from buying and selling commodities. Furthermore, through their agents, they want to export or force this model on the world. The corollary is to produce buyers—and business people who do the selling. As Neil Postman claimed, this may be the first curriculum in the U.S.: consumption as a way of life—especially revealed through television and, more recently, the internet. Persons define themselves by what they wear, drive, eat and drink, and other marks of consumer choice and power. This is different from earlier identifications, mainly through one's work. The latter is more suitable for organizing around class membership and connecting issues. Will the present, seeming, loss of support for neo-conservative and neo-liberal thinking and polices help to reverse all the damage they have done? It has been argued herein that "self" or "character" is subject to the conditions of one's society, its economic underpinnings, political systems, schools and other human-constructed institutions and practices. Therefore it may take a long time to repair and return to the point we were at before the rightist onslaught began in the last part of the 20th century. Sennett writes about accidents of time and the fragments of history. He provides a mixed picture of how things are and how they cannot be supported by the working masses under the neo-liberal order. The problem of character under this order is the lack of shared narratives about experienced difficulties—if not fate. The brutal fact of the capitalist system's disregard of persons' need to work results in the devastating question: "Who needs me?" Sennett "knows" that a "regime that provides human beings no deep reasons to care about one another cannot long preserve its legitimacy" (Sennett 1998, 147–8).

During the last years of his life Lasch weighed in on the lack of legitimacy when he warned us the American "dream"—based on the corporate, liberal, upwardly mobile (for some, if not all) model that guaranteed happiness for all who at least tried—was losing credibilty. He died in 1994. He should see us now! Writers, some in the mainstream media, now acknowledge what progressives and radicals who kept watch over the economy have been arguing since the end (circa the late 1960s) of capitalism's "Golden Age." For example, one can read in most big city newspapers, and in *Time Magazine* and its clones, that the income and wealth gaps have widened among Americans from the top to the bottom—especially since 1980 when the Reagan conservatives came to power. For those who want their analysis more poignant, an editorial in *The Nation* (April 23, 2007) informs us that the inequitable income/wealth distribution continues to grow worse. The top 1 percent of Americans now enjoy the biggest share of the national income since 1928. The top 10 percent garner a hefty 48.5 percent. The editors claim that the numbers are from the Internal Revenue Service, but some analysts maintain these figures understate the disparities.

A State of Suspended Disintegration

There are obvious consequences from such undemocratic economic realities, in the U.S. and elsewhere. Even "middle-class" families find it difficult to provide a secure environment; moreover, people who work hard and "play by the rules" express fear that they will not be able to pass on social capital—let alone capital wealth—to their children. Most people reject being pushed into being self-oriented and/or selfish. We strive to construct and hang on to solid life narratives—ones that include our ancestors and progeny. In spite of accusations made by pundits, talk radio hosts, and their allied politicians, most people want to be good at their jobs and after-work projects. Sennett and others realize that this phase of capitalism, based importantly on deskilling and sending jobs overseas to low wage and benefits, makes it very difficult to achieve these goals.

Instead of figuring out the reasons for this state of affairs, all too many just try to stay ahead of those worse off than themselves. One representative slogan is: Keep the "unqualified" immigrants—and especially "illegal" border crossers—out of the U.S. K–12 teachers have a harder time claiming that schooling provides upward mobility. Degrees have been cheapened: for example, a bachelor's degree is mostly a hunting license for a job. These facts should cause educators to look carefully at the philosophical assumptions concerning what education means, and is for, ultimately. The belief in equal opportunity is mostly trumpeted by those who lay blame on victims mired in concrete structural restraints. These obstacles are not constructed by the working class and poor themselves. The fear of downward mobility has moved up the stratified class system in the U.S. The massive industrial, technological and communication upheavals that have been unleashed—not by inclusive democratic decision-making—often serve to demoralize many persons who perhaps might be better altruistic citizens were they aware of the stakes, and be allowed to participate in the decisions that are central to our lives. I argue that only authentic, inclusive and deep democracy—one that intrudes into fundamental economic decisions—can effectively address the contradictions and crises experienced during this episode of historical capitalism. This assertion is included as a heuristic device, one that readers may question and perhaps learn from.

There are many reasons why the kind of democracy I favor is difficult to achieve. Michael Steinberg addresses some very important ones. He calls the predicament we face a state of "suspended disintegration." The present world order does not insist on any particular lifestyle; moreover, the people in charge care little about various cultures.

> It is enough that whatever ties there were among people have weakened to the point of breaking. This social space becomes the necessary and sufficient foundation for the separation imposed by the capitalist order. This is the reason that liberal capitalism is at home everywhere. It does not reestablish community on other ... contentious bases but simply stabilizes whatever process of dissolution is already underway. (Steinberg 2005, 159)

Steinberg argues further that the solid fragments of prior life are turned into mere additions to the flood of discourse and images. He is provocatively correct to state that capitalism is open to remnants, "new and improved," and what is coming next—as long as these are reduced to private interests (ibid.). Preceding Steinberg's work, Guy Debord's *The Society of the Spectacle* (1995) features the thesis that the spectacle signals the historical time when the commodity colonizes most, if not all, of social life.

Steinberg focuses on what is most crucial about the spectacle: it causes an illusion that private individuals stand in opposition to an alien outside reality. This divide makes it difficult for lonely crowd members to have an effect on the society, the economic system and the world. One can only view with continued attention the steady parade of spectacle—in the aisles of the retail stores and of course in print and electronic media. It is difficult to find a place where culture, in the best sense, has not been corroded by the market system. Marx provided a preface to this condition when he explained how workers were alienated from what they produced. As Marshall Berman (1982) and others have articulated, capitalism is an arena wherein one usually offers the self up as an individual, hoping there is a need for what one can deliver. Today's capitalism is touted as just one more arena where one has choice—if, of course, one has prepared and packaged oneself properly. Another choice opportunity is to go into the voting booth alone and choose among candidates, none of whom will or can be outside of the dominant system(s)—for example, global capitalism and the institutional schools that usually support it. One choice that is not offered is to bridge the gap between the individual and the social.

Perhaps we must relearn to say "we" with some intention of solidarity? The celebrated right to one's own thoughts and feelings may be good in itself; however, if these cannot be joined with others in the social, economic and political arenas they are very limited in terms of impact. As Steinberg points out, the antagonistic and fragmented character of life in capitalist societies cannot easily be contested. Even the critics who complain about not attending to "social needs" come up short because most of them are also committed to a view of social and community that is limited to how much the individual will benefit! The so-called liberal right to one's own castle has been a reality for the minuscule few. In these times of crises, sophisticated surveillance weapons can and do penetrate even one's private places.

Steinberg summarizes his chapter called "A State of Suspended Disintegration" as follows:

> The vaunted pluralism of the modern capitalist world neither stigmatizes social expression nor allows it to be effective. It tolerates and makes use of political and social conflict, transgressive art, sexual and transsexual variety [not everywhere], and every manner of specious diversity. All of these can be merchandised, but their usefulness goes well beyond their market value. They contribute to the thick texture of discourse in which we confine ourselves. Political and social debates are endless by their very nature; they function not to resolve anything but to reinforce the unspoken supposition shared by both [U.S.] parties. Their starting point is the separation among people and they do nothing but reproduce that separation. (2005, 165)

Caution: Given the Facts on the Ground

At this point I will address more specifically the original invitation to contribute to this book. It included a reminder that this present time is full of uncertainty, crises and opportunity. The editor, Professor Shapiro, invited us to provide our views with regard to reshaping the public language of education. He is correct in thinking that crises provide opportunities to help shape the resolution that certain actors favor, in this case, members of the inclusive democratic Left(s). However, I am compelled to express caution with regard to what really can be achieved in this country when one considers what I have presented thus far. It can be argued that George W. Bush's two administrations have caused great damage to the coalition he claims to represent, and the nakedness of his actions may make it difficult for a protégé to become president in the near future. Unfortunately, the problem is not just with the neo-conservative–neo-liberal alliance. Democratic presidents and members of Congress have also embraced this neo-liberal chapter of capitalism. Noam Chomsky has reminded us that there are precedents for the policies and illegal practices of this flagrantly destructive administration.

> The selection of issues that should rank high on the agenda of concern for human welfare and rights is … a subjective matter. But there are a few choices that seem unavoidable…. Among them are at least these three: nuclear war, environmental disaster, and the fact that the government of the world's leading power is acting in ways that increase the likelihood of these catastrophes…. That brings up a fourth issue that should deeply concern Americans, and the world: the sharp divide between public opinion and public policy, one of the reasons for the fear … [is] that "the American 'system' as a whole is in real trouble – that it is heading in a direction that spells the end of its historic values of equality, liberty, and meaningful democracy." (Chomsky 2007, 1)

The main players in the 2008 contest for the presidency do not seriously address the structural realities of capitalism and empire.

Chomsky and many other critics, for example, Michael Parenti, have figured out that the threats are deep and historical when trying to preserve the modicum of democracy we have enjoyed in this country—albeit one that was and is thin. They help us understand the connections between the democratic experiment and its original sins, for example, slavery, imperialism, predatory capitalism, lack of inclusion for those who have been characterized as the "other," and the public school leaders who have historically answered to the capitalist imperative more than to its democratic adversary. Parenti is especially informative about how the status quos are dangerously free of systematic critical examinations.

Before I provide a sketch of the possible, there is one more caution to be offered. "Notes from the Editors" of the *Monthly Review* of June 2007 provide the specifics of the larger context within which we can think about education and students. The editors comment on the British Ministry of Defence report *Global Strategic Trends, 2007–2036*. This work presents the many perceived dangers faced by the "prevailing order" in the near future. One worry is that growing global inequality may lead to anti-capitalist ideologies, populism, and even a bit of Marxism. This military report's main focus is on the structural contradictions of the global economy and how these must be confronted. The continuing decline of U.S. hegemony is mentioned, as is the rise of non-Western powers. It is feared that the U.S. and continental Europe may drift apart, importantly because of the unilateral power used by the U.S. as its hegemony declines. Perhaps of more interest, and surprise, is the reporters' concern about the so-called middle class becoming revolutionary, as its members become stuck and even downwardly mobile. This is based on the realization that many middle-class persons have the skills to make serious trouble for the global elites. The former may succeed in the task that Marx placed upon the earlier blue-collar proletariat. What is so telling about the report is that the authors urge the British military (and other allied gendarmes) to target the population at home and abroad who comprise the overwhelming "mass" of the world population. Certainly, if the *demos* consists of the working masses, and if democracy means rule by the people (producers), the powers that be are those without clothes—without a shred of legitimacy. If the ruling elites actually do see most of the world's people as the enemy, then we must keep this in mind as we theorize, strategize and act in ways that respond to this menacing possibility. I suggest that a first step might include attempting to focus on the fact that members of the global *demos* could organize around their historical position as workers.

New Story and Moral Economy

I have chosen media commentator and public intellectual Bill Moyers as a spokesperson for what can possibly be done now that neo-liberalism and neo-conservatism have been discredited in the opinions of many people. Moyers has a significantly large audience. His liberalism, in the older New Deal and Great Society sense, incorporates a recognition that the global capitalist system is not easily kept in check by interventionist government. Franklin Roosevelt and Lyndon Johnson believed that the federal government could achieve this necessary task, and there is evidence that they were correct. However, the years of conservative dominance have demonstrated that government can be used to intervene mostly in the interests of the rich and powerful. Moyers's television work and writings speak to those who still think that the American system can work for the *demos*. He also challenges the rightist claim that pursuit of private interests is magically transformed into the public good; in fact, it usually results in greater class disparities among the population.

Moyers's "A New Story for America" (2007) is an example of insight, lucidity and language usage that almost every interested person can understand. It provides a reform prelude that may spark enactment—actions that may possibly lead to more necessary radical (to the roots) changes in our politics, governance, economics, society, cultures and schooling. His presentation in *The Nation* interprets the mid-term 2006 election as a result of voter decision to stop "right-wing radicalism." The manifestations of this way of governance are many: from Iraq to New Orleans; corporate scandals; failure to abide by U.S. laws, the Constitution, and international laws—and many more examples. Perhaps the growing recognition that the capitalist economy under Bush Jr. and the Republican Party was becoming grossly "immoral" proved decisive in the election outcome. Moyers speaks of a "to do" list for the Democratic majority in Congress, but he insists that we must go further—namely, constructing a new and profoundly different story.

> Here is the real political story ... the reality of the anonymous, disquieting daily struggle of ordinary people, including the most marginalized and vulnerable Americans but also young workers and elders and parents, families and communities, searching for dignity and fairness against the long odds in a cruel market world. Everywhere you turn you'll find people who believe they have been written out of the story. Everywhere you turn there's a sense of insecurity grounded in a gnawing fear that freedom in America has come to mean the freedom of the rich to get even richer even as millions of Americans are dumped from the Dream. So let me say up front: the leaders and thinkers and activists who honestly tell that story and speak passionately of the moral and religious values it puts in play will be the first political generation since the New Deal to win power back for the people. (Moyers 2007, 12)

It is very important to clarify what one means by "religious." Morals and ethics can be, and are, secular in many instances. Moreover, there are vast differences among religious values, for example between fundamentalist Americans who support the Republican Party and the progressive liberation theology movements that began in Latin America.

Bill Moyers's easily understood article is liberal in the best sense and includes radical potential. When reforms are seen as necessary but not sufficient their promoters often intend to push further, until many reforms add up to radical change. The situation in the U.S. presently is so bad for many persons that it is possible to convince those who read and listen to consider seriously what can be done, but radical deep injuries require more than aspirins and band-aids. The use of the term "moral economy" addresses this issue and has been useful for those who have realized that an economy must be constructed and used to help people. Economists should not present it as a refined mathematical model that has little, or no, connections to our needs and wants. The ancient Greek conception of economy is "household management." It is a concrete phenomenon within which we all must live; therefore political economy must prevail—however, not within the tradition of Adam Smith's version. In fact, when agricultural capitalism was being developed in England, those who opposed it claimed that the earlier "moral economy" was best for the primary producers who worked the land—some of which was called the commons. Private ownership destroyed this older "moral economy." Smith's version represented the early capitalists' takeover of the British economy that was made possible by ideology, political power and violence. The economy must never be considered as a separate entity. It is answerable and even driven by political power, as well as the dominant social ideas and practices.

Envisioning a moral economy does not require any heroic assumptions about human nature; it does not assume that people are always cooperative and kind. On the contrary, it starts from the idea that the pursuit of self-interest has to be controlled or it will turn destructive. Market fundamentalists are the utopians; they imagine that the market magically transforms everyone into angels who can be trusted to do the right thing. The moral economy narrative recognizes that there is no easy way to produce the desired combination of prosperity, order and justice. Rather, it is through the continuous exercise of deep and broad democratic self-governance that we can reform our institutions to make both the economy and government work better to achieve our shared objectives.

Historian and political economist Gar Alperovitz reminds us that, historically, political-economic systems come and go. The present American system is not the "end of history," contrary to what writers such as Francis Fukuyama have claimed. This should help us understand that it is possible, and even necessary, to imagine possibilities that can improve what may have become dysfunctional. Alperovitz argues that, below the surface of pundit America and its regressive federal government, many people have already been thinking and experimenting on local and state levels. According to Alperovitz, these welcome rumblings must become coherent and linked to one another in many ways. He writes, and I agree, that: "Systemic change above all involves questions of how property is owned and controlled—the locus of real power in most [if not all] political economies" (Alperovitz 2005, 5).

Focus on Education within the Conditions We Face

Professor Shapiro has provided a model that speaks to this section title. In spite of the conservative backlash against earlier progressive school and societal achievements, some important ones survived and were pushed even further. However, this situation has deteriorated during the Bush Jr. administrations, resulting in an acute crisis. Part of what is being fought over can be called, in Shapiro's term, the "welfare educational state." It is best to read how Shapiro explains this term.

Receiving its impetus from progressive notions of the "whole child," the assertion that the ability to learn is inseparable from the satisfaction of an individual's physical and emotional needs has permeated the popular consciousness. Successful schooling is understood as necessarily linked to the provision of a much broader set of social services: adequate health care and access to preventive treatment; the availability of adequate food and nutritional resources; the opportunity to alleviate emotional and mental distress; and the provision of an adequate home and physical environment. In short, [public] school has become a major focus of, and the ideology of education of the whole child a major justification for, the extension of social rights and the provisions of the welfare state. (Shapiro 1990, 143–4)

Shapiro's logic takes us even beyond: the educational rights described above can and are used to demand adequate jobs and income for the student's parents. He understands that this democratic project is capable of pressuring the capitalist state (central and subsidiary governments) because the state and its schools are situated between the imperatives of capitalism and democracy.

The capitalist imperative has dominated with a vengeance during the recent Bush Jr. administrations. The mixture of aggressive capitalism, with a mostly carte blanche from the executive branch and Congress, and the unprecedented power and influence of evangelical Christians, has resulted in very difficult times for progressive and inclusive democrats. The extremely authoritarian Bush Jr. administrations and their equally authoritarian religious allies have succeeded in assaulting Shapiro's hope for the welfare educational state. Not only have the public schools been attacked under legislation such as No Child Left Behind, the private schools have grown dramatically since the early 1990s. These actions have served to thwart what has been proposed in this chapter as necessary in order to prevent neo-liberal and neo-conservative capitalism and its allies from dominating civil society, their cultures and, of course, the schools.

In response to the crisis, *Harper's Magazine* editors featured a forum in June 2007 called "Undoing Bush: How to Repair Eight Years of Sabotage, Bungling, and Neglect."

George W. Bush has done more to transform the nation than any American president since Franklin D. Roosevelt. Indeed, he may well be the perfect anti-Roosevelt. He has taken a prosperous [for some] nation and mired it in war, replaced our national composure [not for everyone] with terror, and left behind him a legacy of damage so profound that repairing it will likely be the work of generations. Before the next administration can return to solving the already considerable problems the nation faced in 2000, it must begin to correct the misdeeds and missteps of the current one. … The road back from perdition cannot be found without a good map. To that end, *Harper's Magazine* has assembled a group of journalists and thinkers to survey the damage, to determine what may (or may not) be remedied, and to find our way forward. (2007, 43)

In keeping with this chapter's focus on civil society and cultures, *Harper's* forum contributors address the following: the Constitution, the courts, the civil service, the environment, science, the economy, the marketplace of ideas, intelligence (for example the CIA and FBI), the military, diplomacy and the national character. Earl Shorris wrote the piece on character, in which he argues that the historical undoing of American character goes back to the Hiroshima and Nagasaki slaughter. These bombings resulted in fearfulness among Americans, for many reasons. This fear, caused by what was done to Japanese civilians by the U.S. government, led to the awareness that weapons of mass destruction could also be visited upon the U.S. Shorris believes that the 9/11 attack on the World Trade Center rekindled American fear and helped allow the first Bush Jr. administration, and many members Congress, to go along with the fabricated case about Iraq's role in that attack. Shorris advises us that we must come to understand and resolve this fear. One could conclude from his work that Americans must insist that our government does not—ever again—try to dominate other people. This of course would require a different kind of foreign policy—one that would not be geared to protecting U.S.-led global capitalism. How can educators address this problem?

I offer a brief suggestion that is neither new nor surprising. What can/may/ should be done must be understood in context of what I presented in this chapter. My view is that we cannot be overly optimistic about the quick decline of the U.S. Empire, because the roots are deep in our history and there are so many supporters and believers. Bush Jr. has helped many understand how bad things can become if we follow the neo-liberal/neo-conservative agendas; however, this is hardly a springboard for profound and systemic change.

However, progressive, pro-democratic and even radical educational theorists and practitioners have deepened and broadened our perceptions of problems and possibilities that we now confront. Within the space and time realities that formal schooling/education occurs, it is necessary that teachers act sensitively and kindly with students. Many of us do just that, and some accomplish this against great odds. Fortunately we have a literature and activist tradition that describe and celebrate teachers as democratic, egalitarian, smart, wise, sensitive, caring, and committed to helping bring about good things for our students. Teachers must also value the intellectual life, as well the actions that are consequences of such interests and mastery. As I have written elsewhere:

> When one looks at the literature consisting of education for: democratic empowerment, pedagogy committed to allowing heuristics to be the main student activity, respect for the individual student, recognition of multiple and varied learning styles, awareness of social class, racial, gender, ethnic, and other inequities, it is possible to construct a useful explicit model to help teachers forward the democratic imperative within our schools. Good colleges and programs of teacher education already help their teacher candidates to become these kinds of future professionals. (Brosio 1994, 537)

My hidden injuries of social class experiences, as well as attempts to understand the context in order to overcome them, cause me to end this writing with: We have not yet won; however, we shall keep trying.

Note

John Marciano and Rebecca Martusewicz provided valuable comradely assistance as I wrote this chapter. *Grazie!*

References

Alperovitz, Gar (2005) *America beyond Capitalism: Reclaiming our Wealth, our Liberty, and our Democracy.* Hoboken, NJ: Wiley.

Bell, Daniel (1976) *The Cultural Contradictions of Capitalism.* New York: Basic Books.

Berman, Marshall (1982) *All that Is Solid Melts into Air.* New York: Penguin Books.

Brosio, Richard A. (1972) *The Relationship of Dewey's Pedagogy to his Concept of Community.* Ann Arbor: University of Michigan School of Education.

Brosio, Richard A. (1994) *A Radical Democratic Critique of Capitalist Education.* New York: Peter Lang.

Brosio, Richard A. (2004) Civil Society: Concepts and Critique, from a Radical Democratic Perspective. *Notes & Abstracts in American and International Education, 98,* 1–22 [this article can also be accessed online in *Journal for Critical Education Policy Studies* and in *Cultural Logic*].

Chomsky, Noam (2007) *Failed States: The Abuse of Power and the Assault on Democracy.* New York: Metropolitan/Owl.

Debord, Guy (1995) *The Society of the Spectacle.* New York: Zone Books.

Frank, Thomas (2004) *What's the Matter with Kansas? How Conservatives Won the Heart of America.* New York: Metropolitan Books.

Frank, Thomas (2005) What's the Matter with Liberals? *New York Review of Books, 52,* 46–51.

Friedman, Thomas L. (2005) *The World is Flat: A Brief History of the Twenty-First Century.* New York: Farrar, Straus & Giroux.

Goodman, Paul (1970) *New Reformation: Notes of a Neolithic Conservative.* New York: Random House.

Greider, William (2006) Friedman's Cruel Legacy. *The Nation, 283* (December 11), 6 and 8.

Lasch, Christopher (1977) *Haven in a Heartless World.* New York: Basic Books.

Lasch, Christopher (1978) *The Culture of Narcissism.* New York: W. W. Norton.

Moyers, Bill (2007) A New Story for America. *The Nation, 284* (January 22), 11–17.

Nisbet, Robert A. (1953) *The Quest for Community.* New York: Oxford University Press.

"Notes from the Editors" (2007) *Monthly Review,* 59 (June 27).

Parenti, Michael (1995) *Against Empire.* San Francisco: City Lights Books.

Postman, Neil (1979) *Teaching as a Conserving Activity.* New York: Delacorte Press.

Seligman, Adam B. (1992) *The Idea of Civil Society.* New York: Free Press.

Sennett, Richard (1998) *The Corrosion of Character: The Personal Consequences of Work in the New Capitalism.* New York: W. W. Norton.

Sennett, Richard (2006) *The Culture of the New Capitalism.* New Haven, CT: Yale University Press.

Shapiro, Svi (1990) *Between Capitalism and Democracy: Educational Policy and the Crisis of the Welfare State.* New York: Bergin & Garvey.

Steinberg, Michael (2005) *The Fiction of a Thinkable World: Body, Meaning, and the Culture of Capitalism.* New York: Monthly Review Press.

"Time to Act on Inequality" (2007) *The Nation, 284* (April 23), 3.

Toffler, Alvin (1970) *Future Shock.* New York: Random House.

"Undoing Bush" (2007) *Harper's Magazine,* 314 (June), 43–61.

9

Education After the Empire

RON MILLER

We are living in a fragmented and troubled world at a precarious moment of history. The technocracy that rules modern civilization may be entering its final, desperate phase, its "endgame," as Derrick Jensen (2006) calls it. The industrial, political and cultural practices of modernity, he argues, are not sustainable, indeed are on the verge of chaotic collapse. Along with Jensen, various prophetic observers, including David Korten (2006), Charles Eisenstein (2007) and Joanna Macy (2006), among others, have recently declared the approaching end of technocracy, the end of empire (Bennett 2007), perhaps even the end of America (Wolf 2007). Indeed, various authors, such as Thomas Berry (1999), Richard Tarnas (2007) and Malcolm Hollick (2006), have asserted that we are experiencing one of those rare historical moments when an underlying world-view, the very basis for defining civilization, collapses and gives way to a new historical era.

The core problem with modernity, according to these observers, is that we have alienated human experience from the rhythms and processes of nature in order to assert self-serving control over the earth and its biosphere for short-term gains. Not only does this alienation render us psychologically, existentially and spiritually bereft—confused, lonely, depressed and afraid—but it unleashes the monstrous violence of colonialism, imperialism and resource wars. Furthermore, the desire for control over nature is ultimately *futile* because the earth's resources are *finite*, and we cannot indefinitely consume them and convert them into waste. We face a crisis now, in the opening decade of the 21st century, because the most important resource enabling our drive for domination—cheap energy derived from fossil fuels—is dangerously altering the planet's climate and, at the same time, beginning to run out. Industrial culture and all that it implies—urbanization, mechanization, globalization—*cannot be sustained*. If we do not thoughtfully design and start to build a new civilization better attuned to the patterns and limitations of nature, then the old one will collapse into an ugly, destructive mess, of which post-Katrina New Orleans was a modest preview.

If there is any truth to these claims, then it is terribly insufficient to tinker with existing educational practices and policies to try to make our current schools more effective or even a little more humane. If this historical moment is so critical, then no educational agenda is fully responsive to the conditions of our time unless it radically questions the foundational assumptions that produced, and continue to prop up, the educational arm of the technocracy—the corporate state institution of mass schooling. While acknowledging our responsibility to the millions of young people who attend public schools today, I argue that we need to envision an entirely new educational culture that will replace an obsolete industrial-age system with a pedagogy that embraces the emerging postmodern world-view.

In this essay, then, I am not looking for ways to fund public education more equitably, or to fine tune the curriculum so that we might teach young people to be a bit more environmentally conscious or tolerant of diversity—although in the near term both of these goals need to be pursued and achieved. I will not even condemn the travesty of No Child Left Behind, though it surely needs to be repealed for the sake of meaningful, engaged learning, for it is merely a symptom of our age, a logical result of deeper cultural assumptions, and it is these that must concern us.

The perspective that I bring to this volume is from the counter-cultural tradition of "holistic" education (Miller 1997)—the disparate assortment of radical educational alternatives that includes free schools and other independent progressive schools, Montessori and Waldorf education and other approaches rooted in spiritual philosophies, and that side of the homeschooling movement inspired by the democratic decentralism of Ivan Illich and John Holt. This counter-cultural stream was first evident in the responses that the New England Transcendentalists—Emerson, Alcott and Thoreau—made to Horace Mann's common school agenda in the 1840s. From the point of view of their holistic cosmology, they recognized immediately that mass schooling represented an industrialized, mechanized, standardized pedagogy, a technique for shaping a homogenized culture and compliant workforce rather than an organic nurturing of the human spirit. At the time, and for most of the 160 years since, the triumphant industrial culture has considered this critique to be merely "romantic" or "child-centered." But as this culture now begins to show signs of imminent collapse, I believe the time has come to take their prophetic vision seriously.

The tradition of alternative/counter-cultural pedagogy seeks to replace a mechanistic and technocratic system of schooling—education for empire—with approaches that are more organic (attuned to the rhythms and processes of nature), personalist (respectful of the uniqueness and inner depth of each individual), and authentically democratic (responsive to local communities). Holistic education espouses a cultural and educational agenda grounded in several essential principles:

1. a holistic or integral perspective;
2. respect for every person, including children (human rights);
3. decentralization of authority (human-scale democracy);
4. non-interference between political, economic and cultural spheres of society;
5. balance (openness rather than fixed ideology).

Despite the philosophical and methodological differences among the various alternative movements—a Waldorf educator and a radical unschooler, for example, would argue over numerous issues—I am convinced that these core principles are widely shared by the dissident educational approaches that have arisen in response to industrial-age schooling. I believe that they represent the post-industrial, postmodern world-view that is seen emerging across many domains of culture, from holistic medicine to organic, local agriculture to "green capitalism" and beyond. Holistic pedagogy is an attempt not to fix the public school system as we know it, but to fashion a radically new system from a radically different cultural foundation. By considering the principles that constitute this foundation, the possible shape of a "radically new system" starts to emerge.

A Holistic Perspective

This alternative pedagogy is firmly rooted in a coherent philosophical rationale—a clearly articulated holistic world-view (Miller 2000). Over the past thirty years, a serious yet still largely obscure literature has been emerging from various intellectual perspectives, including science, philosophy, cultural history and religious studies, that challenges the basic epistemological assumptions of modernism, particularly its reductionism and materialism. The thinkers responsible assert that reality is more expansive and dynamic, and human consciousness more nimble and subtle, than technocratic culture allows. They propose that there is an organic relationship between humans and the natural world, that we are intimately involved in its rhythms and processes in ways we cannot recognize when we analyze nature into discrete components and blind forces. Some deeper dimension of existence—physicist David Bohm called it the "implicate order"—gives structure, meaning, and perhaps even purpose to the processes of nature. Biologists such as Francisco Varela and Humberto Maturana describe the phenomenon of self-organization or self-emergence in living organisms, evidence that nature does not work merely through blind chance or purely physical cause and effect. Consciousness or intelligence of some sort appears to play an active role in shaping the world, and, according to holistic thinkers, we may gain access to this dimension of reality through ways of knowing that modernism and its pedagogy have abandoned, such as insight, intuition, imagination and con-templative practice (Sloan 1983; Palmer 1993).

Although many of these authors specifically describe their approach as "holistic," another term is frequently used in the literature, influenced by the prolific work of Ken Wilber, who calls his approach "integral." Since his first book, *The Spectrum of Consciousness*, was published in 1977, Wilber has established himself as the pre-eminent theorist of this postmodern world-view. Based upon extensive research across numerous disciplines as well as his own contemplative practice, Wilber's work provides sophisticated intellectual substance to a movement that the domi-nant culture is prone to dismiss as too romantic or mystical to take seriously. Among other authors who have provided the philosophical foundation of a holistic/integral world-view are Anna Lemkow (1990), Ervin Laszlo (1993), William Bloom (2004) and Malcolm Hollick (2006).

This emerging world-view is concerned with connection and relationship, with finding meaning through larger contexts. It recognizes that the incessant evolution of the cosmos continually changes these contexts. Meanings are not fixed; they are open-ended, dynamic, contingent. Therefore all of life is engaged in an ongoing process of transformation. No single way of knowing (or "single vision," as the poet

William Blake called reductionistic science) can adequately encompass the dynamic complexity of the world. When we define any phenomenon without considering the multiple, shifting contexts that give it meaning, we are what Wilber in his more recent work calls a "flatland"—a partial, distorted picture of reality. In his recent book Hollick explains that a holistic science

> welcomes and values perspectives and insights from all sources of knowledge. … We begin to see that the marvelously diverse images from science, the humanities and the arts, and from the religions and cultures of the world are all partial representations of the true Reality. We begin to see that each reflects a different fact of the wondrous, jeweled whole. (2006, 53, 57)

If this is how the world is constructed, if this is how reality actually works, then an education adequate to our existence needs to respond with dynamic open-endedness also; it needs to foster renewal and transformation, not mindless obedience to fixed standards or ideas. The holistic world-view challenges any educational approach that enshrines a selected body of "facts" into a fixed curriculum. In an information-saturated culture, no such curriculum can give students a complete picture of reality. Any educator's or technocrat's list of "what every third grader should know" represents a partial view of the world, based on one particular, necessarily biased and limited, point of view. It utterly loses a vision of "the wondrous, jeweled whole." From a holistic perspective, the primary goal of education is not to transmit portions of knowledge but to help students experience a sense of wonder and passionate interest in the world, along with habits of open-ended inquiry and critical reflection.

Respect for the Person

By shifting the focus from the transmission of culturally sanctioned knowledge to the self-organizing intelligence of every learner, the new education holds deep respect and even reverence for the human being. The individual is not defined primarily in terms of their socially constructed role as a citizen or worker, but as an end in themselves, possessing inherent worth. Holistic pedagogy is concerned, as Scott Forbes (2003) puts it, with "ultimacy"—that is, the highest and noblest qualities of our existence, such as our aspirations towards truth, goodness, wisdom, compassion and love. These ultimate expressions of our humanity are inherent in our nature; they emanate from within the person, not from the authority of society. As human beings, we carry the seeds of our highest aspirations and potential evolution within our own hearts.

The visionary educator Maria Montessori saw each child as the builder of a unique human personality, driven by a creative force from within to engage the world inquisitively and purposefully. Each person possesses both the capacity and the spiritual imperative to fashion a personality, an individuality, that will experience and live in the world in ways that no other does, and we require autonomy and security in order fully to achieve this potential. Because this individuality begins in childhood, young people are entitled to the educational and existential freedom necessary for them to accomplish their task of building a mature individual. They should not be subjected to a mechanistic pedagogy that treats all "fourth graders" as a homogenous mass, or to a standardized curriculum established and enforced by distant, elite policy-makers. Emerson gave the most eloquent statement of this position in his 1863 essay on education.

> I believe that our own experience instructs us that the secret of Education lies in respecting the pupil. It is not for you to choose what he shall know, what he shall do. It is chosen and foreordained, and he only holds the key to his own secret. By your tampering and thwarting and too much governing, he may be hindered from his end and kept out of his own. Respect the child. Wait and see the new product of Nature. Nature loves analogies, but not repetitions. (1965, 430)

A pedagogy that reflects a world-view more attuned to organic processes, and less interested in controlling them, would "wait and see the new product of nature" in the emerging life of every young person. Our entire educational structure of approved curriculum and textbooks, hierarchical management of school systems and buildings, tightly scheduled time periods, clever instructional methods, testing and grading, would be seen as "tampering and thwarting and too much governing," and we would do away with it.

Generations of holistic educators have confirmed that young people do not need to be herded and controlled in order to learn, that they achieve healthy, productive maturity by interacting freely, actively and purposefully with their world, engaging their senses, feelings and desires as well as their minds. Developmental psychologists and researchers in neuroscience have provided a rich and complex picture of how children grow and learn, and we now know, just as we know that the earth isn't flat, that the process of human development is holistic, creative and spontaneous. The mechanical management of a child's learning may serve the ends of a society's authorities, but it does not support the fullest, healthiest development of that child's potential intelligence or character.

The principle of respect for the individual child's developmental process places the notion of *human rights* at the center of holistic pedagogy. The Declaration of Independence inspired modern democratic thought with its assertion that every person is endowed by the Creator with unalienable rights. The human being possesses inherent worth and dignity, a vital spiritual core generated by God, nature or the cosmos—not something contingently granted by any faction of society. American history tells the story of a gradual cultural awakening to the power of this vision, the gradual acknowledgement that *every* person, not only property-owning white males, possesses inherent rights. Educational liberation movements insist that young people possess them as well. If democracy represents trust in each person's ability and right to manage their own life, and if we were to discover that in the proper settings young people, even at quite tender ages, exhibit this ability to a significant degree, then are children not entitled to greater autonomy in the unfolding of their personalities?

Decentralization of Authority

A commitment to personal rights and autonomy raises the question of cultural and therefore educational authority. The holistic perspective generally embraces a decentralist view of power and authority, because living systems are too complex and dynamic to be governed distantly, or from above. In the tradition of Jefferson, Dewey, and the student rebellion of the 1960s, this view envisions a grassroots, participatory democracy (Miller 2002). Authority should be close to people, not held by distant, impersonal institutions or governing elites. Individuals, including young people in their education, should be actively engaged in the affairs of their communities, in the decisions that affect their surroundings and their lives. Authority wielded for its own sake, to maintain "order" or "standards" as these are defined by ruling elites, should not be trusted because it is removed from the fluid existential realities of life.

Perhaps the counter-cultural tradition invites the epithet "romantic child-centered" because its resistance to such authority appears individualistic to the point of solipsism. There is, in fact, a distinct anarchist/libertarian element in the tradition, exemplified in the early 20th century by the Modern School movement launched in Barcelona by Francisco Ferrer and later in the century by free schools (such as Summerhill) and vigorous advocates of "unschooling." Nevertheless, it is a mistake to paint the entire spectrum of holistic alternatives with that brush. I see the libertarian element as an ideological reaction to the overbearing authority of established educational practices. In practice, virtually all alternative educators recognize, indeed honor, the importance of community in a young person's learning and development, and all recognize teachers and other adults as wise mentors in students' lives. Decentralized authority, as it is understood here, is not an atomistic individualism, not some Ayn Rand-style celebration of the self-centered, self-satisfied ego.

The anarchist thinker Paul Goodman and his younger colleague George Dennison laid out the case for decentralized authority in the 1960s, cultivating ideas they found in Dewey and then bequeathed to the New Left and the free school movement. Goodman argued that

> living functions, biological, psychosociological, or social, have very little to do with abstract, preconceived "power" that manages and coerces from outside the specific functions themselves. … Normal activities do not need extrinsic motivations, they have their own intrinsic energies and ends-in-view. (1968, 180)

Given this premise, it follows that "free choice is not random but responsive to real situations; both youth and adults live in a nature of things, a polity, an ongoing society, and it is these, in fact, that attract interest and channel need" (Goodman 1969, 99). Dennison, in his inspiring account of the inner-city alternative school he ran in the early 1960s, similarly claimed that

> the educational function does not rest upon our ability to control, or our will to instruct, but upon our human nature and the nature of experience.… [including] the life principles which have in fact structured all the

well-structured elements of our existence, such principles as our inherent sociability, our inherent rationality, our inherent freedom of thought, our inherent curiosity ... What this means is that we must rescue the individuals from their present obscurity in the bureaucratic heap. (1969, 253)

Goodman and Dennison, then, were describing an organic relationship between individual and community, student and teacher, based on an understanding that the human being possesses an intrinsic striving for growth and that our experiences are therefore inherently meaningful. Authority, when it is abstract, distant, overbearing—as it surely is in most aspects of public school policy and practice—does not support organic growth but thwarts it. A contemporary feminist theorist, Riane Eisler (2000), makes much the same point in distinguishing between "hierarchies of domination" and "hierarchies of actualization"; there are organic structures in human communities and institutions, but the authority they embody can be used either to control people through fear and powerlessness (as in high-stakes testing) or to bring out everyone's highest potentials through empowerment. Eisler uses the term "partnership education" to describe a holistic pedagogy that embraces the latter.

Radical educators argue that the curriculum itself tends to become an agent of impersonal authority. If education is to be an organic relationship between the learner and the world, then curriculum must be allowed to emerge through meaningful inquiry and interaction. Standards imposed by policy-makers reflect a judgment by certain elites that in a diverse and dynamic society there is one set of information and skills that all students need to learn. In the modern technocracy, most of us have come to accept standardized curriculum and homogenized knowledge as a given, but, from a holistic perspective, this is a deviation from the ceaselessly self-renewing democratic culture that Thomas Jefferson envisioned for America. In a 1789 letter to James Madison, Jefferson said that the question of "whether one generation of men has a right to bind another" is a "fundamental" question of government; he thought that "no society can make a perpetual constitution, or even a perpetual law," and then pronounced his famous statement that "the earth belongs always to the living generation." While Jefferson probably did not have schoolchildren in mind (indeed, his own pedagogical theory, lacking the insights of constructivism or multiple intelligence theory, was rooted in the classics), I believe his democratic sensibility would be horrified by the extent to which relentless curriculum standards imposed by government authorities thwart students' ability to practice thoughtful, critical engagement with their world. Holistic educators consider young people to be a "living generation," and their insistence on students' fully engaged participation in learning surely reflects the spirit of Jefferson's dynamic, self-renewing democratic vision.

Non-interference between Political, Economic and Cultural Spheres of Society

While we are on the subject of the founding fathers, we might consider what is perhaps the most essential feature of the American Constitution—the principle of the separation of powers. The founders addressed the potential concentration of state authority with a specific strategy—delineating boundaries between the power that each branch of government could wield. In the early 20th century, a remarkable Austrian philosopher named Rudolf Steiner (the founder of Waldorf education, among other initiatives) proposed a model of the "threefold" society that similarly divides its functions and aims to limit the concentration of authority in any one institution or sphere. Although Steiner justified his model according to his esoteric spiritual cosmology (which I, for one, find incomprehensible), I have found that the "threefold" idea stands on its own as an insightful conceptual tool for analyzing and critiquing the politics of modern schooling.

To summarize briefly, Steiner asserted that the three basic functions of social life are the economic, political and cultural. The economic sphere, he said, is concerned with the production and distribution of commodities, or more broadly with the relationship between human society and the material world. The political sphere is the domain of justice and human rights, or the proper relationships between people. The cultural sphere involves the spontaneous creative activity of the human mind; the arts and sciences and the practice of education (which Steiner saw as an art) are expressions of this free flow of spiritual energy. Economic activity, which involves differential and fluctuating material values, should not influence political judgment, which must be based on absolute equality of legal rights, and neither of these modes of social endeavor should interfere with the creative freedom of the artist, scholar or educator. As Steiner saw nearly a century ago, in modern society economic enterprise has spilled over its proper boundaries, and the result is that every aspect of our lives, including education, has become a commodity—something with a market value rather than an intrinsic value.

In other words, trying to apply economic or political criteria to creative or intellectual expression can only reduce or distort it. Economic and political endeavors use categories and criteria that are adequate and appropriate for dealing with the material world and social relations, respectively, but they cannot fathom the deeper, spontaneous sources of our ideas, or the disinterested pursuit of truth or wisdom. This is why the principle of academic freedom on university campuses has been held sacred, and it is why education at all levels should be independent of the state—especially the corporate state that fuses economic and political authority.

The invasion of the educational process by economic forces is clearly evident in the standards-and-testing movement. The corporate state provides the funding for education, considering it an economic investment and expecting a good return. Young people are considered to be intellectual capital, their learning a product with a certain value to the economy. Knowledge is packaged and delivered, increasingly through textbooks and other materials produced by corporations with political connections. Students and teachers are accountable to these investors, and must demonstrate their success in mastering the authorized body of knowledge. There is little recognition of the student as a unique individual, motivated by a spiritual yearning to reach out to the world for purposeful understanding. There is little recognition of teaching as an art form, requiring a carefully honed sensitivity and thoughtful responsiveness, because teachers increasingly become technicians tending to the authorized lessons and administering the prescribed tests. In Steiner's terms, education has been uprooted from the cultural sphere, where it belongs, and engulfed by the economic sphere, which turns it into a commodity, a soulless object to be bought and sold.

There are many dedicated teachers in the public schools, many schools with healthy roots in their communities, and many idealistic reformers who believe that a public system is the only equitable and democratic way to provide learning opportunities to all. But this system has become increasingly dominated by forces that are not truly educational, and it has become more and more difficult to realize the public school ideal in a technocratic empire. The principle of non-interference between the distinct functions of society warns us that the corporate state is not the proper provider of a truly nourishing education. School and state need to be separated, just as church and state were separated, to preserve the autonomy of each, to allow each to exercise its proper function without distorting interference.

Holistic education seeks to return teaching and learning to the sphere of intellectual freedom and creativity. The educators, parents, and young people who have left public schooling for independent alternative schools or homeschooling are not simply out to privatize the educational system, for this is still to treat learning as a commodity in the marketplace. Rather, they are intuitively (or sometimes quite deliberately) responding to the awareness that Steiner articulated a century ago, that genuine learning is an organic, spontaneous and deeply meaningful encounter between person and world that requires autonomy from the political and economic forces that have taken over public schooling.

Balance

Holistic pedagogy shares the view that John Dewey (1960) expressed in his critique of the "quest for certainty": human existence is complex, fluid and contingent, and our experience can give us only partial and tentative truths. It is natural to want certainty and security, which we attempt to find through dogmatic belief and self-assured ideology, but this expectation limits our ability to adapt intelligently to an ever-changing world. An educational system rooted in a more holistic world-view would recognize the endless diversity of students' learning styles and temperaments, personal goals and interests, as well as the diversity of their multiple social/cultural identities. It would no longer be the purpose of schooling to mold human energies into some model of intellectual and cultural conformity, to find the one best curriculum, instructional method or school management scheme.

The underlying principle here is not simply diversity, though, but *balance*. Recognizing that human existence contains endless possibilities does not mean giving free rein to every impulse; it is not a prescription for the moral relativism that conservatives so quickly associate with any whiff of progressive pedagogy. Finding balance in education means that freedom exists in relationship to structure, individual in relationship to community, rational intellect in relationship to our complicated emotional lives. This breakdown of either/or dualisms is just what Dewey insisted on throughout his work. There is, he argued, a dynamic tension between opposites, and it requires intelligent judgment to determine where, along any continuum of choices, to find the most appropriate (reasonable, pragmatic *and* moral) response to a given situation.

An educational policy striving for balance would no longer be devoted so exclusively to standards, accountability and the authorized curriculum; there would be room for individuality, local autonomy and experimentation. Above all, balance would mean that a public system of education does not, and should not, represent a coercive monoculture sanctioned by the power of the state; the system itself would seek balance by providing diverse alternatives representing various philosophical and cultural possibilities. Parents and communities could choose more rigorous academic environments or more child-centered schools, spiritually influenced or more rationalist approaches to curriculum and teaching, programs that lean towards social renewal and critical pedagogy or those that emphasize respect for tradition. All these options would be available and supported by society, giving parents and communities the responsibility to acknowledge the tension between their competing claims and make intelligent, informed decisions.

I want to emphasize that, under a system inspired by these five foundational principles, I do not see this diverse offering of educational alternatives as an educational free market that invites competition, entrepreneurial ambition or gross inequality. This is not "school choice" as the typical conservative agenda promotes it. Rather, it is a societal commitment to the best, most appropriate and relevant learning experiences that can be provided to every child. Our political culture will need to evolve beyond its technocratic fixation on standardization and narrowly measured accountability, and be willing to underwrite, as do several European nations, diverse educational options as communities and families desire them. There would not only be publicly funded "alternative schools" for the discouraged or rebellious students who would otherwise drop out, but flexible and responsive learning environments for all students, so that far fewer would become discouraged or rebellious in the first place. The proposal here is for *all* education to be what we now euphemistically call "special" education. Pedagogy would not be tailored to some bell curve that defines a mass of normal students flanked by special learners on one end and "gifted" youths on the other; every young person would be treated as both special and gifted, each in their own way.

This is an educational agenda that transcends the usual conservative and progressive framing of school policy. It was Montessori, again, who envisioned a postmodern understanding of schooling in society, many decades in advance of the culture, when she declared that society could set aside its divisiveness by focusing on the inherent developmental needs of the child and honoring each child's task of constructing a unique human personality. When we drop the modern agenda of shaping children to cultural expectations (more specifically, to the contested expectations of dominant elements within the culture), we are free to offer diverse and flexible alternatives, and to achieve a dynamic cultural *balance* in place of a static pedagogical monoculture.

The principle of balance applies to education at the classroom level as well. It enjoins the teacher to approach each learner with sensitivity and flexibility, not with ideology and method. A school may have a specific philosophical orientation but it does not need to be completely limited by this perspective. Even a school or homeschooler committed to children's freedom will face situations where the healthiest and most authentic response is to exercise the authority, expertise or wisdom that adults possess; to refrain from expressing themselves in these moments is to turn freedom into an obsessive ideology rather than a condition for growth. Similarly, even the most imaginative and carefully conceived curriculum (at the Waldorf schools, for example) loses its magic when it is applied indiscriminately to all learners in all situations at all times. Clearly, we will need a new attitude towards teacher education; it would not be so focused on methods, but would strive to cultivate personal qualities of self-understanding, sensitivity, presence and responsiveness. Holistic education theorists such as Jack Miller, Rachael Kessler and Parker Palmer have all emphasized that such qualities are essential for teaching in this way.

Conclusion

Despite the hope of many educational visionaries over the past two centuries, it seems quite clear that pedagogy does not so much shape culture as reflect it. Teaching schoolchildren about our chosen causes—democracy or ecology, social justice or religious pluralism—does not seem capable of significantly altering the political or intellectual life of society if the essential culture, embodied in powerful economic and political institutions, mass media, and the constructed landscape that surrounds young people, embraces other values. The radical educator John Holt gave up on school reform (and turned towards Ivan Illich's notion of "deschooling") when he realized that social change is a political task, the responsibility of engaged adult citizens. He wrote to George Dennison in 1976 that "to suppose that someone who is really concerned about poverty and injustice in this country can best oppose it [sic] by talking against them in public schools seems to me so nonsensical that I can hardly think about it" (1990, 195). Trying to change a culture through schooling is futile if the culture is not otherwise prepared to change.

Indeed, the influence works the other way around: the constellation of values, beliefs and epistemological assumptions that define a culture effectively determines what purposes schools will be called upon to serve, and what will actually take place in the daily life of most classrooms. When a culture is under stress, as ours is today, its dominant elements become more determined, even desperate, to defend its continued existence. Hence, we have seen ever tighter authoritarian control over public schools since the cultural earthquakes of the 1960s. From Nixon's educational policies to A Nation at Risk to No Child Left Behind, the conservative restoration has sought to ensure that schooling reinforces rather than threatens established cultural beliefs, reaffirms rather than questions the technocratic worldview. If we deconstruct the meaning of "standards" in education, we will find that this is ultimately what they are about.

The alternative ideas and practices of holistic education have remained on the "romantic" fringes of modern culture. Significantly, they began to gain more widespread recognition after the cultural upheavals of the 1960s, and I believe they will become the mainstream of educational thought if and when the emerging postmodern culture becomes established. A truly open, flexible, democratic system for educating the young and promoting lifelong learning throughout society will emerge as the culture of technocracy and empire collapses and makes room for a more organic, local, human-scale and life-affirming culture. We are not there yet, but, in many parts of the world, thousands of NGOs, grassroots networks, and visionary individuals are establishing promising new approaches in all fields of endeavor. Wherever this transformational movement has addressed the challenges of education, it has seized upon ideas and practices pioneered by the holistic tradition, or introduced exciting new ones fully aligned with that tradition. The days of standardized learning are as numbered as the days of cheap fossil fuel.

References

Bennett, Tim (2007) *What a Way to Go: Life at the End of Empire* (film). Pittsboro, NC: VisionQuest Pictures.

Berry, Thomas (1999) *The Great Work: Our Way into the Future.* New York: Bell Tower.

Bloom, William (2004) *SOULution: The Holistic Manifesto.* London: Hay House.

Dennison, George (1969) *The Lives of Children: The story of the First Street School.* New York: Random House.

Dewey, John (1960) *The Quest for Certainty: A Study of the Relation of Knowledge and Action.* New York: Capricorn Books/Putnam.

Eisenstein, Charles (2007) *The Ascent of Humanity.* Harrisburg, PA: Panenthea Press.

Eisler, Riane (2000) *Tomorrow's Children: Partnership Education for the Twenty-First Century.* Boulder, CO: Westview Press.

Emerson, Ralph Waldo (1965) Education. In *Selected Writings of Ralph Waldo Emerson,* ed. William H. Gilman. New York: New American Library.

Forbes, Scott H. (2003) *Holistic Education: An Analysis of its Ideas and Nature.* Brandon, VT: Foundation for Educational Renewal.

Goodman, Paul (1968) *People or Personnel: Decentralizing and the Mix & Systems; and Like a Conquered Province: The Moral Ambiguity of America.* New York: Vintage Books.

Goodman, Paul (1969) No Processing Whatever. In Ronald and Beatrice Gross (Eds.), *Radical School Reform.* New York: Simon & Schuster.

Hollick, Malcolm (2006) *The Science of Oneness: A Worldview for the Twenty-First Century.* New York: O Books.

Holt, John (1990) *A Life Worth Living: Selected Letters of John Holt,* ed. Susannah Sheffer. Columbus: Ohio State University Press.

Jensen, Derrick (2006) *Endgame* Volume 1: *The Problem of Civilization.* New York: Seven Stories Press.

Korten, David (2006) *The Great Turning: From Empire to Earth Community.* San Francisco: Berrett-Koehler/Kumarian Press.

Laszlo, Ervin (1993) *The Creative Cosmos: A Unified Science of Matter, Life and Mind.* Edinburgh: Floris Books.

Lemkow, Anna F. (1990) *The Wholeness Principle: Dynamics of Unity within Science, Religion & Society.* Wheaton, IL: Quest Books.

Macy, Joanna (2006) The Great Turning as Compass and Lens. *Yes! Magazine,* 38 (Summer).

Miller, Ron (1997) *What Are Schools For? Holistic Education in American Culture* (3rd ed.). Brandon, VT: Holistic Education Press.

Miller, Ron (2000) Holism and Meaning: Foundations for a Coherent Holistic Theory. In *Caring for New Life: Essays on Holistic Education*. Brandon, VT: Foundation for Educational Renewal.

Miller, Ron (2002) *Free Schools, Free People: Education and Democracy after the 1960s*. Albany: State University of New York Press.

Palmer, Parker (1993) *To Know as We Are Known: Education as a Spiritual Journey*. San Francisco: Harper.

Sloan, Douglas (1983) *Insight-Imagination: The Emancipation of Thought and the Modern World*. Westport, CT: Greenwood Press.

Tarnas, Richard (2007) *Cosmos and Psyche: Intimations of New World View*. New York: Plume.

Wilber, Ken (1977) *The Spectrum of Consciousness*. Wheaton, IL: Theosophical Publishing House.

Wolf, Naomi (2007) *The End of America: Letter of Warning to a Young Patriot*. White River Junction, VT: Chelsea Green Press.

10

Education for a Partnership World
Building Cultures of Peace[1]

RIANE EISLER

What will the world be like for our children and grandchildren? The answer largely depends on our vision for education and our commitment to putting our vision into action.

For over two centuries, educational reformers such as Johann Pestalozzi, Maria Montessori, John Dewey and Paolo Freire have called for an education that prepares young people for democracy rather than authoritarianism, peace rather than war, caring rather than cruelty.[2] Our task, and it is an urgent task, is to take their work further.

In recognition of the gravity of our situation in this age of nuclear and biological weaponry, environmental degradation, widening gaps between haves and have-nots, terrorism, ethnic warfare, and the rise of both Eastern and Western "religious fundamentalism," with its goal of top-down rule in the family and the state, the United Nations declared the years 2001 to 2010 the International Decade for a Culture of Peace and Non-Violence for the Children of the World.[3] Even before this, peace researchers and educators recognized that a fundamental cultural shift is urgently needed.[4] Thousands of non-governmental organizations working for a more peaceful and equitable world also reflect the growing consciousness that we stand at an evolutionary turning point. Some schools have introduced non-violent conflict resolution programs. Some universities offer peace studies. A few programs enlist families, schools and community agencies in violence prevention and peace promotion strategies.[5] On a more global level is UNESCO's "Declaration on a Culture of Peace" and its "Education for a Culture of Peace" program.[6]

These are all encouraging developments. But, at the same time, violence and the terrible suffering it wreaks continue to afflict our globe. And rather than countering this violence, both informal and formal education often exacerbate it. The mass media unleash a daily barrage of violent "entertainment." The news highlights violence, and boys are still systematically taught violent habits through toys, games, and stories of "manly" violence. In some world regions, children are taught that killing, even deliberately killing civilians, will be rewarded by God. And almost everywhere, the educational canon—from grammar school to graduate school—still idealizes "heroic" violence.

Why is this? And what can we do to change it?

These are some of the questions that led to the development of what I call *partnership education*. Partnership education builds on the work of earlier educational thinkers, adds new elements, and places education in the larger context of a new way of looking at society. It proposes that underneath conventional categories such as religious vs. secular, right vs. left, capitalist vs. socialist, Eastern vs. Western, and so forth, are two underlying social possibilities: the *partnership model* and the *domination model*. It proposes that education is very different for societies orienting to each of these models (it is always a matter of degree), and that, as we leave behind conventional categories and understand the configurations of each of these models, we can develop the integrated approach to education needed to build a more equitable, caring and peaceful world.

The Partnership Model and the Domination Model

We are taught to classify cultures as technologically developed or undeveloped, Eastern or Western, religious or secular, rightist or leftist, capitalist or communist. But these categories only describe particular features of a social system. They do not tell us how key institutions such as the family and education are structured. They do not even consider the construction of the relations where people first learn what is normal or abnormal, moral or immoral: the foundational relations between parents and children and between women and men. Nor do they address the key question for our future: What kinds of relations—from intimate to international—do social institutions and beliefs support? Are they relations based on mutual respect, or on domination and submission? Do they tend to inhibit the human capacity for violence or do they encourage its expression?

Based on a multidisciplinary study of human societies over the long span of human history and prehistory, the *partnership* model and the *domination* model address this crucial question.[7]

On the surface, cultures orienting to the domination model may seem completely different. But they all share the same core configuration. The first component of this configuration is rigid top-down physical, emotional and economic control in both the family and the state or tribe. The second core component is the ranking of the male half of humanity over the female half. The third is institutionalized, socially idealized violence.

We find this core configuration in societies that are from the perspective of conventional social classifications completely different: Nazi Germany, Khomeini's Iran, the Taliban of Afghanistan, Stalin's Soviet Union, the Masai of pre-colonial Africa, and the Samurai of feudal Japan. In other words, we can see the dominator configuration in both religious and secular societies, in Eastern and Western ones, in leftist and rightist ones.

In the same way, societies orienting primarily to the partnership model can be very different from one another. For example, this orientation is found today in some tribal and agrarian societies (for example, the Minangkabau of East Sumatra), as well as in industrialized Nordic nations, such as Sweden, Norway and Finland. We also see this orientation in some Western and Eastern prehistoric societies, as described in my work and in the work of scholars at the Chinese Academy of Social Sciences.[8] Most important, there is grassroots movement in all world regions towards family and social structures that are closer to the partnership than the domination model.

The core configuration of the partnership model is a democratic and egalitarian family and social structure, partnership between women and men, and no institutionalization or idealization of violence.

For example, Nordic countries such as Sweden, Norway and Finland have created societies with both political and economic democracy. These nations have a mix of free enterprise and central planning that did not result in another domination system, as happened in the former Soviet Union. They were the first nations to move towards industrial democracy, pioneering teamwork by self-directed groups to replace assembly lines where workers are cogs in the industrial machine. And while these are not ideal societies, they succeeded in creating a generally good living standard for all. In contrast to cultures orienting to the domination model, where women are rigidly controlled by men, here women's and men's status is more equal. In Sweden, Norway, Finland and Iceland, women have held the highest political offices, and a larger proportion of legislators (35 to 40 percent) are female than anywhere else in the world. As the status of women rose, so did the status of traits and activities, such as non-violence and caregiving, that are in domination-oriented cultures unacceptable in men because they are stereotypically associated with "inferior" femininity. It is therefore not coincidental that these more partnership-oriented nations pioneered such caregiving social policies as government-supported childcare, universal health care, and paid parental leave. And it was these more "feminine" social policies that, as Hilkka Pietila documents, helped make Nordic nations, which had earlier suffered from terrible famines, prosperous.[9] Neither is it coincidental that laws prohibiting violence against children in families were pioneered by Nordic nations. Or that they have a strong men's movement against male violence towards women[10] and pioneered non-violent conflict resolution, establishing the first peace studies programs, and that their students regularly rank high in educational tests.

These are not random, unconnected developments. They are all connected with the fact that the Nordic world orients more to the partnership than to the domination model.

I want to emphasize that, when we talk of gender stereotypes, we are talking not about anything inherent in women or men but about views of "masculinity" and "femininity" we inherited from more rigid dominator times. I also want to emphasize that cultures and subcultures that orient closely to the partnership model are not completely violence-free. But the difference—and it is a critical difference—is that violence does not have to be institutionalized and idealized to impose and/or maintain rigid rankings of domination.

Dominator and Partnership Education

In cultures or subcultures that orient closely to the domination system, be they Western or Eastern, tribal or industrialized, child-rearing is heavily based on the use of fear and force by both mothers and fathers. Teachers often use physical punishments, such as the canings common in European schools just a few decades ago, and still lawful in some U.S. states today.

Dominator child-rearing and education habituate children to the psychological and often physical abuse required to function in the rigid hierarchies of domination they are taught is "reality." Children chronically subjected to threats and aggression tend to become more vigilant and defensive/aggressive, and to numb themselves so as to not feel their pain. In addition, as happened to their caretakers, these children are also taught to suppress or at least compartmentalize feelings of empathy for others.

All these are ways of surviving in a hostile environment, and could thus be said to be adaptive in rigid dominator contexts. Fortunately, not everyone adapts this way. But those who do then tend unconsciously to replicate, from generation to generation, precisely the kinds of behaviors that make us feel bad, hold back our development, and perpetuate uncaring, unempathic and violent behaviors across the board. Moreover, people with this kind of background often find it extremely hard to believe there is an alternative to either dominating or being dominated.[11]

By contrast, as we already glimpsed in developments in the Nordic world, violence is not part of partnership child-rearing. For example, anthropologist Peggy Reeves Sanday, who has studied Minangkabau culture for many years, writes:

> Childcare is not authoritarian or punitive. I have never seen any child hit or even slapped … The socialization techniques fit what one would expect from the peacefulness of Minangkabau interpersonal relations: children aren't hit, I never heard mothers screaming at their children, children get their way frequently and no one seems to mind much. The idea is that they will learn sooner or later to behave as proper Minangkabau. Shunning of naughty children may be practiced—all kids know when they have taken things beyond local expectations. Sooner or later they conform.[12]

In the same way, partnership education models, and through its curricula illustrates, that mutually respectful and caring relations are possible in all spheres of life. Indeed, one of its central themes is that diversity—beginning with the fundamental difference between female and male—is not equivalent to superiority or inferiority, dominating or being dominated, being served or serving.

In domination systems, a male-superior, female-inferior division of our species is constantly reiterated through both family and cultural models of "proper" masculine roles of control and feminine roles of submission. And this division of humans into those who control and those who are to be controlled is then easily, often unconsciously, generalized to other people who are different: people of other races, religions and ethnicities.

In cultures such as those of fundamentalist Iran and the Taliban that still orient closely to the domination model, students are explicitly taught that women are not only inferior but dangerous—and hence must be rigidly and, if "necessary," violently controlled by men. Not coincidentally, in these cultures violence against different religions, and even different sects of the same religion, is endemic, as is support for terrorism against other "evil" out-groups. But even in societies that have been moving towards the partnership model, this basic education for in-group vs. out-group thinking persists. The fact that most of us see nothing strange about calling any issue that affects no less than half of humanity "just a women's issue"—even though we would think it peculiar to call issues that affect the male half of humanity "just a men's issue"—indicates how profoundly we have all been influenced by this type of socialization.

Of course, even though it is foundational, the male-superior/dominant and female-inferior/subordinate view of our species is not the only basic lesson of dominator education. Partnership curricula reveal how dominator relations are still presented as normal, and even desirable, in much of the conventional curriculum (for example, the emphasis in history books on wars and violent revolutions). They point to the structural changes needed to create partnership institutions, from more democratic families to more truly democratic political structures.

In addition to being gender-balanced, partnership curricula integrate materials on peoples of all races and many cultures. They also give visibility to people who are "different" in other respects, including people who are blind, deaf, or otherwise physically or developmentally challenged. And, by giving value and visibility to women and traits and activities such as non-violence and caregiving stereotypically associated with femininity, partnership curricula help young people acquire values in which essential activities, such as caring for children and maintaining a clean and healthy environment, that are still stereotypically associated with women are accorded the importance they merit. As Nel Noddings writes,

> All children must learn to care for other human beings, and all must find an ultimate concern in some center of care: care for self, for intimate others, for associates and acquaintances, for distant others, for animals, for plants, and the physical environment, for objects and instruments, and for ideas.[13]

The Three Components of Partnership Education

Partnership education consists of three core interconnected components: partnership *process*, partnership *structure* and partnership *content*.[14]

Partnership process is about *how* we learn and teach. It applies the guiding template of the partnership model to educational *methods* and *techniques*. Are young people treated with caring and respect? Do teachers act primarily as lesson-dispensers and controllers, or more as mentors and facilitators? Are young people learning to work together or must they continual compete with each other? Are they offered the opportunity for self-directed learning? In short, is education merely a matter of teachers inserting "information" into young people's minds, or are students and teachers partners in a meaningful adventure of exploration and learning?

Partnership structure is about *where* learning and teaching take place: what kind of *learning environment* we construct if we follow the partnership model. Is the structure of a school, classroom, and/or home school one of top-down authoritarian rankings, or is it a more democratic one? Do students, teachers, and other staff participate in school decision-making and rule-setting? Diagramed on an organizational chart, would decisions flow only from the top down and accountability only from the bottom up, or would there be interactive feedback loops? In short, is the learning environment organized in terms of hierarchies of domination ultimately backed up by fear, or is it a combination of horizontal linkings and hierarchies of actualization where authority is used not to disempower others but rather to empower them?

Partnership content is *what* we learn and teach. It is the *educational curriculum.* Does the curriculum effectively teach students not only basic academic and vocational skills but also the life-skills they need to be competent and caring citizens, workers, parents and community members? Are we telling young people to be responsible, kind and non-violent at the same time that the curriculum content still celebrates male violence and conveys environmentally unsustainable and socially irresponsible messages? Does it present science in holistic, relevant ways? Does what is taught as important knowledge and truth include—not just as an add-on, but as integral to what is learned—both the female and the male halves of humanity as well as children of various races and ethnicites? Does it teach young people the difference between the partnership and dominator models as two basic human possibilities and the feasibility of creating a partnership way of life? Or, both overtly and covertly, is this presented as unrealistic in "the real world"? In short, what kind of view of ourselves, our world, and our roles and responsibilities in it are young people taking away from their schooling?

Much of "progressive education" has focused primarily on process, and to some degree on structure. But partnership education is not only a matter of more self-directed learning, peer teaching, cooperative learning, more individualized assessment tools, and other partnership pedagogies. Nor is it only a matter of the kind of structure that schools have. It emphasizes the importance of narratives, and very specifically what kinds of behaviors and values are presented as valuable in curriculum narratives.

One of the tenets of progressive education is to give young people more choices. But much in the curriculum, even in progressive schools, does not give young people real choices because it does not offer alternative narratives. At best it does so in bits and pieces, mostly as an add-on to conventional narratives that we have inherited from earlier, more dominator-oriented times. For this reason alternative partnership narratives are a major component of partnership education.

This is particularly important in our time of dominator regression when so much in the mass media, and hence of what young people worldwide learn, still communicates the message that dominator relations are not only normal but fun. On all sides they see and hear stories that portray us as bad, cruel, violent and selfish. Video games and action adventure movies and TV shows present violence as the way to solve problems. Situation comedies make insensitivity, rudeness and cruelty seem funny. Cartoons present violence as exciting, funny, and without real consequences. As in the journalistic motto of "if it bleeds, it leads," even the stories that make top headlines focus on the infliction and/or suffering of pain as the most significant and newsworthy human events.

Rather than correcting this false image of what it means to be human, much of what children still learn in schools reinforces it. Not only do history curricula still emphasize battles and wars, but classics such as Homer's *Iliad* and Shakespeare's kings trilogy romanticize "heroic violence." Scientific stories tell children that we are the puppets of "selfish genes," ruthlessly competing on the evolutionary stage.

If we are inherently violent, bad and selfish, we have to be strictly controlled. This is why stories that claim this is "human nature" are central to an education for a dominator system of relations. They are, however, inappropriate if young people are to learn to live in a democratic, peaceful, equitable, and Earth-honoring way. If they are to participate actively in political and civic processes, young people need to learn much more about non-violently achieved social and economic reforms—from the struggle for workplace safety standards and laws prohibiting child labor to the struggle for family planning and the ongoing struggle for the rights of women and children. They also need the opportunity to experience democracy in action through more partnership-oriented school structures.

They need all this not only for themselves but also for their children. Indeed, one of the most urgent challenges today's children face relates to how they will nurture and educate tomorrow's children. Therein lies the real hope for our world.

Parenting Education

I passionately believe that, if we give a substantial number of today's children the nurturance and education that enables them to live and work in the equitable, non-violent, gender-fair, environmentally conscious, caring and creative ways that characterize partnership rather than dominator relations, they will be able to make enough changes in beliefs and institutions to support this way of relating in all spheres of life. They will also be able to give their children the nurturance and education that we are today learning makes the difference between realizing, or stunting, our great human potentials.

People who insist that the best way to teach is to punish are usually replicating their own experiences in dominator families and other cultural contexts. This is why early childhood education is so important and why partnership education includes education for partnership childcare.

Psychologists have long told us that early childhood education is critical. But now this information comes to us with lightning-bolt force from neuroscience. When a baby is born, the brain continues to develop and grow. In the process, it produces trillions of synapses or connections between neurons. But then the brain strengthens those connections or synapses that are used and eliminates those that are seldom or never used. We now know that the kinds of emotional and cognitive patterns that are established through this process are radically different depending on how supportive and nurturing or deprived and abusive the child's human and physical environment is. In other words, these patterns are shaped very differently depending on whether childcare and education orient primarily to the partnership or the domination model.

Ironically, the people who today are pushing us back to more rigid dominator pedagogies, such as the constant testing, and hence ranking into superiors and inferiors, of children and teachers and schools, argue that this is necessary for the post-industrial economy. But actually the opposite is true. To develop the qualities needed for the post-industrial economy requires partnership rather than dominator pedagogies. Whether or not we are venturesome and creative, whether we can work with peers or only take orders from above, and whether or not we are able to resolve conflicts non-violently are matters of key importance for the post-industrial information economy. And dominator pedagogies, beginning in early childhood, produce exactly the wrong results.

By contrast, partnership childcare and education prepares young people for the new information and service-oriented post-industrial economy. Here, as organizational development and management consultants emphasize, inquisitiveness and innovativeness, flexibility and creativity, team work, and more stereotypically "feminine" nurturant or facilitative management styles get the best results.[15] Whether they reside in women or men, these are all qualities and behaviors appropriate for partnership rather than dominator relations.

Human development is of course first and foremost a matter of access to adequate food and other material resources and good health care. But it is also a matter of the kind of care and education a child receives.

Positive childhood care that relies heavily on praise, caring touch, affection, and lack of violence or threats releases the chemicals dopamine and serotonin into particular areas of the brain, promoting emotional stability and mental health. By contrast, if children are subjected to negative, uncaring, fear, shame, and threat-based treatment or other aversive experiences, such as violence or sexual violation, they develop neurochemical responses appropriate for this kind of dominator environment, becoming tyrannical to themselves or others, abusive and aggressive or withdrawn and chronically depressed, defensive, hypervigilant, and numb to their own pain as well as, often, to that of others.

Children who are dependent on abusive adults tend to replicate these behaviors with their own children, having been taught to associate love with coercion and abuse. And often they learn to use psychological defense mechanisms of denial and to deflect repressed pain and anger in violence against those perceived as weak. They learn to bully and scapegoat. They later express their pain and rage in pogroms, ethnic cleansings, and terrorism against defenseless civilians.

Neuroscientists have found that regions of the brain's cortex and its limbic system (responsible for emotions, including attachment) are sometimes 20 to 30 percent smaller in abused children than in normal children. Hence these children often lack the capacity for aggressive impulse control. They also often lack the capacity for long-term planning. And children exposed to chronic and unpredictable stress suffer deficits in their ability to learn.[16]

Hence the pivotal importance of teaching partnership childcare and parenting, based on praise, caring touch, rewards, and lack of threat, through education worldwide. For optimal results, in addition to parenting classes for adults, the teaching of partnership parenting and childcare should start early in our schools, as it would in a partnership curriculum. This will ensure that people learn about it while they are still young and more receptive.

A New View of our Past and Future

But it is all of education, not only early childhood education and education for parenting, that has to be reexamined and reframed to provide children, teenagers and later adults the mental and emotional wherewithal to live good lives and create a good society. For example, partnership education offers empirical evidence that our human strivings for love, beauty and justice are just as rooted in our biology as our capacity for violence and aggression. Young people learn how, by the grace of evolution, biochemicals called neuropeptides reward our species with sensations of pleasure, not only when we are cared for, but also when we care for others.

The study of evolution from this perspective does not leave young people with the sense that life is devoid of meaning or that humans are inherently violent and selfish—in which case, why bother trying to change anything? Much of the hopelessness of young people today stems from the belief that the progressive modern movements have failed and that the only possibility is either to dominate or be dominated.

There are many factors contributing to this distorted view of possible futures. But a major reason is that education has not shown young people that—despite enormous resistance and periodic regressions—the movements towards a more just and peaceful world have in fact made great gains.

Partnership education offers young people a broader understanding of history. It shows that the struggle for our future is not between capitalism vs. communism, right vs. left, or religion vs. secularism, but between a mounting movement towards partnership relations and strong dominator systems resistance and periodic regressions.

By using the analytical lens of the partnership/dominator continuum, young people can see that along with the massive technological upheavals of the last three hundred years has come a growing questioning of entrenched patterns of domination. The 18th-century rights of man movement challenged the supposedly divinely ordained right of kings to rule, ushering in a shift from authoritarian monarchies to more democratic republics. The 18th- and 19th-century feminist movement challenged men's supposedly divinely ordained right to rule women and children. The movement against slavery, culminating during both the 19th and 20th centuries in worldwide movements to shift from the colonization and exploitation of indigenous peoples to their independence from foreign rule, as well as global movements challenging economic exploitation and injustice, the rise of organized labor, and a gradual shift from unregulated robber-baron capitalism to government regulations (for example, anti-monopoly laws and economic safety nets such as Social Security and unemployment insurance), also challenged entrenched patterns of domination. The 20th-century civil rights and women's liberation and women's rights movements were part of this continuing challenge. So were the 19th-century pacifist movement and the 20th-century peace movement, expressing the first fully organized challenge to the violence of war as a means of resolving international conflicts. The 20th-century family planning movement has been a key to women's emancipation as well as to the alleviation of poverty and greater opportunities for children worldwide. And the 20th-century environmental movement has frontally challenged the once hallowed "conquest of nature" that many young people today recognize as a threat to their survival.

But history is not a linear forward movement. Precisely because of the strong thrust towards partnership, there has been massive dominator systems resistance.

We also have over the last 300 years seen resurgences of authoritarianism, racism, and religious persecutions. In the United States, we saw laws providing economic safety nets, renewed opposition to reproductive rights for women, and periodic violence against those seeking greater rights. In Africa and Asia, even after Western colonial regimes were overthrown, we saw authoritarian dictatorships by local elites over their own people. And, worldwide, we saw a "fundamentalist" movement to push women back into their traditional subservient roles, a recentralization of economic power, and increased violence to maintain or impose rankings of domination.

These regressions raise the question of what lies behind them—and what we can do to prevent them. Once again, there are many factors, as there always are in complex systems. But a major factor is the need fully to integrate challenges to domination and violence in the so-called public spheres of politics and economics and in the so-called private spheres of parent–child and man–woman relations. Indeed, unless we address, and change, traditions of domination and violence in the formative gender and childhood relations, we will not have the foundations for a more equitable and peaceful world.

In Europe, for example, a rallying cry of the Nazis was the return of women to their "traditional" place. In Stalin's Soviet Union, earlier feeble efforts to equalize relations between women and men in the family were abandoned. When Khomeini came to power, one of his first acts was to repeal family laws granting women a modicum of rights. And the brutally authoritarian and violent Taliban, and Osama bin Ladin's al-Qaida terrorist network, have made the total domination of women a centerpiece of their agenda.

This emphasis on gender relations based on domination and submission was not coincidental. Dominator systems will continue to rebuild themselves unless we change the base on which they rest: domination and violence in the foundational human relations between parents and children and men and women.

The reason, simply put, it that how we structure relations between parents and children and women and men is foundational to how we perceive what is normal in human relations. It is in these intimate relations that we first learn and continually practice either partnership or domination, either respect for human rights or acceptance of human rights violations, as "just the way things are."

Young people need to understand these generally ignored social dynamics. With an understanding of the connections between partnership or domination in the so-called private and public spheres, young people will be better equipped to create the future they want and deserve.

The Challenge and Opportunity

I have seen how inspired both teachers and students become once they see that partnership relations—be they intimate or international—are all of one cloth. I have seen how they move from apathy to action once they fully understand that there is a viable alternative to the uncaring and violent relations that have for so long distorted the human spirit.

I know from both my life and my research that making fundamental changes is not easy. But I also know it can be done. Indeed, it has been done, or we would all still be living in a world where every woman and most men knew "their place" in rigid hierarchies of domination, a world where slavery was legal, extreme poverty was considered normal, and advocating "women's rights" and "children's rights" would have been condemned as immoral, indeed insane.

Cultures are human creations. They can be, and have been, changed. Fundamental changes will not happen overnight. There will continue to be resistance. Shifting to partnership cultures will take ingenuity, courage and persistence. But, working together, we can create cultures that support rather than inhibit the realization of our highest human potentials: our great capacities for caring, empathy and creativity.[17] We can all help build these cultures through partnership education.

Notes

1. Parts of this article are adapted from Riane Eisler, *Tomorrow's Children: A Blueprint for Partnership Education in the 21st Century*. Boulder, CO: Westview Press, 2000.

2. Johann Pestalozzi, *Leonard and Gertrude*. New York: Gordon Press, 1976 (originally published in 1781); John Dewey, *Democracy and Education*. New York: Free Press, 1966 (original 1916); Paolo Freire, *Pedagogy of the Oppressed*. New York: Seabury Press, 1973; Maria Montessori, *The Montessori Method*. New York: Schocken Books, 1964 (original 1912).

3. See http://www.unesco.org/cpp/uk/declarations/2000.htm; http://www.culture-of-peace.info/.

4. See, e.g., Eva Nordland, Betty A. Reardon and Robert Zuber (Eds.), *Learning Peace: The Promise of Ecological and Cooperative Education*. Albany: State University of New York Press, 1994; Linda Lantieri and Janet Patti (Eds.), *Waging Peace in our Schools*. Boston: Beacon Press, 1996. See also http://www.peaceed.org/what/whatbr.htm and Ingeborg Breines, Dorota Gierycz and Betty Reardon (Eds.), *Towards a Women's Agenda for a Culture of Peace*. New York: UNESCO, 1999.

5. An example is the Chicago-based Violence Prevention Peace Promotion Strategy (http://www.vppps.org).

6. See http://www.unesco.org/education/ecp/index.htm. The 1998 UNESCO "World Education Report" and the 1995 UNESCO "Our Creative Diversity Report" also pave the way for a broader report on education in terms of support for a culture of peace.

7. See, e.g., Riane Eisler, *The Chalice and the Blade: Our History, Our Future*. San Francisco: Harper & Row, 1987.

8. See ibid., and *The Chalice and the Blade in Chinese Culture*. Beijing: China Social Sciences Publishing House, 1995.

9. Hilkka Pietila, "Nordic Welfare Society—A Strategy to Eradicate Poverty and Build Up Equality: Finland as a Case Study," *Journal Cooperation South*, 2 (2001), 79–96.

10. As two Nordic men, Jorgen Lorentzen and Per Are Lokke, wrote:

   > Many men have come to believe that violence against a woman, child, or another man is an acceptable way to control another person. By remaining silent about the violence, we allow other men to poison our environments. We also allow the picture of men as dangerous to stay alive … Domestic violence is a problem within existing masculinity and it is we, as men, who have to stop it. ("Men's Violence against Women: The Need to Take Responsibility," presented at the international seminar "Promoting Equality: A Common Issue for Men and Women," Palais de l'Europe, Strasbourg, France, June 17–18, 1997, p. 4).

11. See Riane Eisler, *The Power of Partnership*. Novato, CA: New World Library, 2002; Riane Eisler, *Sacred Pleasure: Sex, Myth, and the Politics of the Body*. San Francisco: HarperCollins, 1995; Riane Eisler and Dan Levine, "Nurture, Nature, and Caring: We Are Not Prisoners of our Genes," *Brain and Mind, 3*, 1 (2002), 9–52.

12. Private communication from Peggy Reeves Sanday, January 30, 2002.

13. Nel Noddings, "A Morally Defensible Mission for Schools in the 21st Century," *Phi Delta Kappan*, January 1995, 366.

14. See Riane Eisler, *Tomorrow's Children: A Blueprint for Partnership Education in the 21st Century*. Boulder, CO: Westview Press, 2000.

15. See Riane Eisler, "From Domination to Partnership: The Hidden Subtext for Sustainable Change," *Journal of Organizational Change Management, 7*, 4 (1994), 32–46, and Riane Eisler, "Women, Men, and Management: Redesigning our Future," *Futures, 23*, 1 (1991), 3–18, for an overview of some of this literature.

16. B. D. Perry, R. A. Pollard, T. L. Blakley, W. L. Baker and D. Vigilante, "Childhood Trauma, the Neurobiology of Adaptation, and 'Use Dependent' Development of the Brain: How 'States' Become 'Traits'," *Infant Mental Health Journal, 16* (1996), 271–91.

17. For a collection of articles on this issue, see David Loye (Ed.), *The Evolutionary Outrider: The Impact of the Human Agent on Evolution*. Twickenham, England: Adamantine Press; Westport, CT: Praeger, 1998. See also Riane Eisler, "Building a Just and Caring World: Four Cornerstones," *Tikkun, 13*, 3 (1998).

Additional Resources

Tomorrow's Children: A Blueprint for Partnership Education in the 21st Century by Riane Eisler (Boulder: CO: Westview Press, 2000). With a foreword by Stanford Professor Emerita Nel Noddings, this books describes partnership education and includes practical illustrations of how to apply it in primary and secondary education.

The DVD *Tomorrow's Children: Partnership Education in Action* (Media Education Foundation, 2001). This video, by prize-winning videographer Sut Jhally, combines an interview with Riane Eisler on partnership education with lively classroom scenes of how it works in practice.

Master's degree in Transformative Leadership with a concentration in Partnership Studies at the California Institute of Integral Studies (CIIS). This on-line program offers a unique opportunity for educators who want to be agents of cultural transformation. For information, go to www.rianeeisler.com/articles/ciis.pdf.

The Montessori Foundation's Center for Partnership Education. Since 2004, the Montessori Foundation's Center for Partnership Education has co-sponsored an annual conference on integrating partnership studies and Montessori education. For information, go to www.partnership way.org/html/subpages/articles/thirdannualmonte.htm or www.montessori.org.

Partnership Education in Action: A Companion to Tomorrow's Children, edited by Dee Buccarelli and Sarah Pirtle (Center for Partnership Studies/ Foundation for Educational Renewal, 2001). More practical ideas and activities for use in the classroom.

The Partnership Way: New Tools for Living and Learning (New Revised Edition) by Riane Eisler and David Loye (Holistic Education Press, 1998). Used in settings ranging from high schools and colleges to churches and self-help groups, this is a resource for teachers and others who want to learn about and experience the Partnership Model.

Culture, Difference & Power by Christine Sleeter (New York: Teachers College Press, 2001). An innovative multimedia e-book that highlights the importance of partnership pedagogy.

Linking Up! Using Music, Movement, and Language Arts to Promote Caring, Cooperation, and Communication: Pre K-Grade 3 by Sarah Pirtle (Educators for Social Responsibility, 1998). A creative partnership book plus a CD of forty-six songs featured in the book, twenty in Spanish.

The Real Wealth of Nations: Creating a Caring Economics by Riane Eisler (San Francisco: Berrett-Koehler, 2008). This book is Eisler's roadmap for long-term, not just short-term finger-in-the-dyke, economic change. It moves us from unbridled consumption and accumulation of "stuff" to produce what really counts for us humans: health, relationships, meaning, creativity, service. It takes us beyond the old, dying economic systems—and the old capitalist vs. socialist thinking—to a new partnerist economic paradigm. For more information, visit www.partnershipway.org.

11
Critical Thinking in Religious Education

Nel Noddings

Many people today—including the outspoken atheist Richard Dawkins—recommend teaching Bible literacy in our schools. The primary reason for doing this is to familiarize students with the many biblical allusions found in literature. Some advocates of biblical literacy also want to promote inter-faith understanding, and they suggest adding portions of the Koran to the readings. Indeed, courses in world religions have become relatively common, but few advocates of inter-faith understanding encourage the critical study of religion, and students may complete a course in world religions with greater tolerance for other faiths but no understanding whatever of deism, agnosticism, atheism or secular humanism. They may not even be aware of the debates and theological uncertainties in their own religions. In standard courses in history, religious topics may be almost completely avoided. Students retain false notions about the religious orientation of major public figures, and they may be given no opportunity to consider the effects of religion on women.

The basic questions to be explored here are these: Can schools promote critical thinking on religious topics? How might we approach this task?

Bible Literacy

In the United States, teaching *about* religion in public schools is permissible under the Constitution, and there are good, secular reasons for doing so. Asked about our purpose in teaching the Bible, for example, we can make a sound secular claim for teaching the Bible as literature. The King James version has long been regarded as a literary masterpiece. In addition to its own status as literature, the Bible contains stories, expressions, phrases and proverbs that often appear in other literary works. Richard Dawkins, confessed atheist, lists almost three pages of biblical phrases found in literature, and he points out that "We can give up belief in God while not losing touch with a treasured heritage" (2006, 344).

The Bible Literacy Project has produced an aesthetically appealing book, *The Bible and its Influence* (Schippe & Stetson 2006), designed to introduce high-school students to the best-known stories and personages of the Bible. In addition to stories and passages from the Bible itself, the book includes reproductions of artistic works and discussion of great musical works based on biblical themes. It is carefully constructed to be acceptable to a wide range of Christian and Jewish groups.

It is this very acceptability that raises some questions from a critical perspective. The text avoids sections of the Bible that cast doubt on God's moral goodness— much of Leviticus, Numbers and Deuteronomy. Many of the omitted stories are horror stories and raise the possibility of an evil God. Martin Gardner, a philosophical theist, mentions some references to God as evil. In Thomas Hardy's poem "Nature's Questioning," for example, God is referred to as the Vast Imbecility. Gardner comments: "The God of Moses is not an idiot, but he is pictured in the Bible as capable of such extreme cruelty that anyone who believes these accounts to be accurate comes very close to believing in an evil God" (1983, 248). How is this conclusion to be avoided? One strategy is to do as the Bible Literacy Project does—omit most of the passages that might lead to such a conclusion. But, then, how would students respond intelligently to this paragraph from Richard Dawkins?

> The God of the Old Testament is arguably the most unpleasant character in all fiction: jealous and proud of it; a petty, unjust, unforgiving control-freak; a vindictive, bloodthirsty ethnic cleanser; a misogynistic, homophobic, racist, infanticidal, genocidal, filicidal, pestilential, megalomaniacal, sado-masochistic, capriciously malevolent bully. (2006, 31)

A critical study of the Bible should enable students to point to stories and passages that Dawkins might use to support his devastating criticism of God. Although most of biblical criticism is beyond the scope of what can or should be taught in high school, students could be made aware of how these difficulties are met by responsible biblical scholars. For example, James Kugel (2007) advises us to read the Bible as a work produced by people writing at a particular time in a particular place. This way of reading the Bible sees the accounts that horrify Dawkins as products of human story-telling, not as indictments of God. Kugel's criticisms are, if anything, even more scathing than those of Dawkins because they are so well informed by biblical scholarship. However, Kugel has remained an Orthodox Jew, and it is important for students to know that critical study of the Bible does not always culminate in a rejection of faith.

I am not suggesting that critical study of religion at the high-school level should concentrate on the stories that portray God in a bad light. Adolescents (and their teachers) are not ready for the sophisticated study required to make sense of this side of the Bible. However, the stories should not be entirely omitted. It may be especially important, given the rise of self-righteous fundamentalism, to discuss events such as the Passover. *The Bible and its Influence* provides a paragraph on the Passover and its celebrations but does not discuss God's killing of all the firstborn of Egypt. In a margin, the text advises students to "look it up." Students who do so may be shocked, however, to learn that "the Lord smote all the firstborn in the land of Egypt, from the firstborn of Pharaoh that sat on his throne unto the firstborn of the captive that was in the dungeon; and all the firstborn of cattle" (Ex. 12: 29). Does this help to explain Dawkins's claim that the Old Testament God is "infanticidal"? Can the destruction of innocents ever be justified?

Some Bible stories have been captured in romantic literature and music. The story of Ruth and her devotion to her mother-in-law is a case in point. "Whither thou goest, I will go" has been set to music that is often used at weddings. Ruth, a Moabite and daughter-in-law of Naomi, decided to accompany Naomi back to Judah when both were left widowed. It is a beautiful story of devotion between two women. But an important question arises: If a man behaved as Ruth did—giving up her country and native gods—would his devotion be so admired, or would he be considered a traitor and an apostate?

Kugel's recommendation that we read the Bible as we do other historical literature makes good sense. We then attend to the time of writing, the place, and the customs of the day. This also helps to explain apparent contradictions in the text. The "same" story has been told and retold by different people in different contexts.

The Historical Record

Not only should a sense of history guide reading of the Bible, but the historical record on religious topics as taught in our schools should be corrected. Surveys have shown that a majority of American citizens believe that the U.S. Constitution was founded on Christian principles. They believe this even though George Washington said explicitly that the nation was "not, in any sense, founded on the Christian religion" (quoted in Dawkins 2006, 40). Similarly, most Americans believe that the founders were believing Christians, despite strong evidence to the contrary. From their letters and private papers—and sometimes from their public statements—we know that Washington, Jefferson, Franklin and Paine (and probably Adams and Madison, too) are rightly classified as deists.

American history textbooks use the same strategy as that used by the Bible Literacy Project—avoidance. There is very little discussion of religion in our school history texts. Most mention freedom of religion as a reason for early immigration to America, and many provide a page or two on the Scopes trial, but the beliefs of the founders are ignored. Similarly, although students hear something of Elizabeth Cady Stanton's work for women's suffrage, they do not hear that she wrote *The Woman's Bible* and expressed strong objections to the male domination of religion.

Today most schools in the United States espouse critical thinking as one of their aims, and yet they avoid topics that invite such thinking. Students graduate from high school believing that the motto "In God We Trust" has always been on U.S. coins. They do not hear that it first appeared on a 2 cent coin in 1864, a time of great national trouble and pain. They rarely hear about the addition of "under God" to the pledge of allegiance in 1954—a time (the Cold War) when Americans were anxious to differentiate themselves from the "godless" Soviets. Indeed, they do not learn that the pledge itself was written by a Christian socialist, Francis Bellamy, in part to inspire student solidarity at the opening of the Chicago World's Fair in 1892. In a nation committed to the separation of state and religion, should expressions of belief in God appear in government-sponsored documents and currency? The question invites critical thinking.

In setting the historical record straight, the treatment of Thomas Paine should be discussed. Revered as a hero of the Revolution for his pamphlet *Common Sense*, he was reviled for his book *The Age of Reason*. Surely students should learn that Paine, like many of the founders, was greatly influenced by Enlightenment thought. He was not alone in his agnosticism, but he was more outspoken than others. Many years later, President Theodore Roosevelt referred to Paine as a "filthy little atheist." He might more accurately be described as a deist or agnostic, but students should be encouraged to ask questions about political attitudes towards unbelievers. Are all atheists bad persons? Could a confessed atheist be elected president of the United States? What do you think of Paine's motto "My country is the world, my religion is to do good"? In posing such questions, we gain opportunities to discuss both religion and nationalism.

Even the claim that the first colonists came to America for religious freedom should be subject to critical thinking. Many people did indeed come to America so that they could practice their own religion freely. However, the new immigrants were rarely eager to grant others the religious freedom they sought for themselves. The Puritans were especially severe with those who disagreed with them on religious doctrine—prescribing banishment or death for Jesuits and Quakers (Gunn 2004; Marty 1984). Even after the republic was established and the First Amendment in force, the nation experienced widespread discrimination against Catholics, Jehovah's Witnesses, Mormons, Mennonites, and other religious groups. Indeed, Jeremy Gunn (2004) refers to religious freedom as "an American founding myth." We are perhaps closer today to making that myth a reality than we ever were before—certainly closer than people were in the days of the founders.

When we speak of freedom of religion as a founding myth, we are not simply condemning it as a falsehood. A myth is a powerful story—one that can be told and retold over a great period of time. It provides inspiration and a sense of community solidarity. It may also act as an ideal, a story we want to make a reality. Critical thinkers make an important contribution when they point to the facts and remind us that we have not lived up to the ideal. Freedom of religion is what might be called a healthy myth. There are other myths, however, that have done incalculable harm. We turn to one of those next.

Women and Religion

Religion has contributed to the subordination of women. The myth of Adam and Eve, for example, has caused much harm, and students should be encouraged to think critically about it. In the first chapter of Genesis, there is a simple creation story: "So God created man in his own image, in the image of God created he him; male and female created he them" (Gen. 1: 27). Why, then, was this followed in chapter 2 with the story of Adam and the creation of Eve from Adam's rib?

Most biblical scholars now believe that the stories were written at different times by different authors, writers with different concerns. Kugel suggests that the first writer had priestly interests and was concerned mainly with observation of the Sabbath. The second writing, Kugel comments, came when human beings began to engage in agriculture and when they had discovered the cause of pregnancy. The Adam and Eve story, from this perspective, is designed to explain why farming is such hard work and why women suffer pain in childbirth.

But why would later writers and interpreters put such emphasis on Adam, Eve and the Fall? (It should also be noted that there is no mention of the Fall in Genesis, and the concept of "Original Sin" was invented much later by Augustine.) A reason suggested by feminists cannot be entirely discounted; the story has served to maintain the idea of women's moral inferiority and natural subordination (Noddings 1989). Elizabeth Cady Stanton, in *The Woman's Bible*, wrote:

[The Bible] teaches that woman brought sin and death into the world, that she precipitated the fall of the race, that she was arraigned before the judgment seat of Heaven, tried, condemned and sentenced. Marriage for her was to be a condition of bondage, maternity a period of suffering and anguish, and in silence and subjection, she was to play the role of a dependent on man's bounty for all her material wants, and for all the information she might desire on the vital questions of the hour, she was commanded to ask her husband at home. Here is the Bible position on woman all summed up. (Quoted in Ward & Burns 1999, 200)

The Woman's Bible enraged clergymen of the time, and even the women's suffrage groups that Stanton had led for so long separated themselves from it. They were afraid of losing support for the cause of suffrage. The story is an old one, but it might be argued that women even today are complicit in their own oppression— continuing to support the three great monotheisms and meekly accepting their domination by men on earth and a male God in heaven. Mary Daly (1974) has written eloquently on this topic.

Public school teachers face a host of problems in trying to address this. First, before discussion even gets started, some students may object to calling the Adam and Eve story a myth. I experienced this reaction in working with a group of seniors at an elite liberal arts college. Before venturing further, we had to spend time discussing the nature of myths. A myth, I explained, is not merely a falsehood, a product of superstition and ignorance, although it may be in part described that way. More to the point, as noted in the previous section, a myth is an enormously powerful story that lives on through seemingly endless variations (Noddings 1993). It is not an insult to call a story a myth. Indeed, the label recognizes the enormous power of such stories.

From the perspective of women, the myth of Eve and her role in the Fall is deplorable, and it still has effects on our culture. J. Anthony Phillips remarks:

It remains deeply imbedded in both male and female ideas about the nature and destiny of women, and the attitudes it has engendered are embodied in the psychology, laws, religious life, and social structures of the Western world—not to mention the most intimate of human activities. Eve is very much alive, and every member of Western society is affected by her story. (1984, 172)

Students who are interested in the myth of Eve and its effects should be encouraged to read more and to explore possibilities for moving beyond it. Can feminism be reconciled with traditional religion (Groenhout & Bower 2003)? Is a return to goddess religion feasible? What does the "death of God" movement contribute to women's liberation? This last question leads naturally to a crucial issue in contemporary religious education—the place of intelligent unbelief.

Unbelief

Many items of religious dogma strain belief. Students should become aware of attempts to prove (or disprove) the existence of God through logic, and they should learn about the many epistemological reasons people have given for rejecting religion. Staunch believers can acknowledge these reasons and admit that their own beliefs are anchored in faith, not in evidence.

It is more difficult, however, to put aside moral objections to God and religion, and people who reject religion for moral reasons are unlikely to be brought back to the fold. From the late 1800s to the present day, many thoughtful people have rejected religion because they have come to believe that the God revealed in nature and described in the Bible is *not* morally good. James Turner writes:

> Declarations of unbelief often sounded more like acts of moral will than intellectual judgments. [Robert] Ingersoll said that "I cannot worship a being" whose "cruelty is shoreless." Darwin was so appalled by the harshness of natural selection that he could no longer bring himself to believe in God: better that this horror should have sprung from blind chance. (1985, 309)

In the same vein, Bertrand Russell once wrote, "The world in which we live can be understood as a result of muddle and accident, but if it is the outcome of a deliberate purpose, the purpose must have been that of a fiend" (quoted in Miles 1995, 309).

Such writers cannot reconcile the pain and suffering they see in this world with the existence of an all-good God. Nor do they see religion as in any way necessary for human morality. Robert Ingersoll, sounding very like Thomas Paine, said:

> While I am opposed to all orthodox creeds, I have a creed myself; and my creed is this. Happiness is the only good. The time to be happy is now. The place to be happy is here. The way to be happy is to make others so. (Quoted in Jacoby 2004, 169)

This material should not be taught in such a way that students might feel compelled to reject religion. No religious point of view should be favored or taught dogmatically in public schools but, if a critical perspective is taken, some material is likely to be troubling for some students. A careful balance is required. Many believers agree with those unbelievers who see a world full of suffering and yet retain their faith. How do they explain their commitment? Alister McGrath comments:

> For some, the existence of God is called into question by suffering; for others, however, the presence of God is a consolation and support in suffering. For these, the existence of a God who suffers alongside humanity is a lifeline, without which they would sink into despair. (2004, 184)

Unbelievers are not persuaded by such expressions of faith. Indeed they argue that religion has not relieved suffering; it has more often increased it (Hitchens 2007).

Interested students may want to read more on how various religions look at suffering. Some regard suffering as a means of soul-making. Some actually glorify suffering and grant special blessings on those who accept it willingly or even inflict it on themselves. Some argue that, without suffering, our lives lose meaning.

I have myself argued strongly against views that glorify suffering or see inherent meaning in it. Heroic and compassionate people have *constructed* meaning from their suffering, but this does not mean that suffering is somehow necessary to bring meaning to human life. Suffering should be eliminated or reduced wherever possible:

> Young people should learn about the ways in which others have looked at suffering. They should hear heroic tales of noble responses to suffering, but they should also hear about unrelieved suffering and make a commitment to compassion. They should hear about ways to capture small joys, to escape melancholy without damaging the possibility of future happiness, to avoid extremes of seeking perfect happiness on the one hand and of glorifying suffering on the other. Perhaps most important of all, they should learn to feel some social responsibility to reduce suffering. (Noddings 2003, 43)

Suffering is a huge topic, and adequate discussion of it is well beyond the scope of this short chapter. However, its mention as part of religious education suggests an alternative to the usual organization of courses on world religions. Instead of arranging courses around the names of major religions—Christianity, Judaism, Islam, Buddhism—we might structure them around centrally important topics such as immortality, suffering, the role of women, significant myths, morality, the nature of gods, the importance of community, and perspectives on human nature. Such organization would be superior in that it addresses existential questions and invites critical thinking from the start.

The main point here, in this brief discussion of suffering, is to ensure that students gain some understanding of unbelief as well as greater tolerance for other religious belief systems. It is important for them to dissociate atheism from communism, for example, and to learn that many atheists are good people. It is important for them to develop an adequate vocabulary of unbelief and to understand that the terms *atheism*, *agnosticism*, and *deism* point to different perspectives on God and religion. It is also important that they begin to ask why (and whether) religion plays such a significant role in American political life. Why must a candidate for high office in the United States believe in God? And what exactly must he or she believe?

Finally, a good course on world religions will make it clear that religious belief is not necessary for morality. Impressive moral theories and ethical codes have been developed without recourse to God and religion. We can live morally without God as policeman and all sorts of threats for misbehavior. Daniel Dennett expresses doubts about religion as enforcer of moral behavior:

> Without the divine carrot and stick, goes this reasoning, people would loll about aimlessly or indulge their basest desires, break their promises, cheat on their spouses, neglect their duties, and so on. There are two well-known problems with this reasoning: (1) it doesn't seem to be true, which is good news, since (2) it is a demeaning view of human nature. (2006, 279)

Modes of Communication

The need for balance and breadth is obvious if we are to attempt the critical study of religion in schools. It may be impossible to do this, given the passion with which so many people hold their own beliefs. It is discouraging, however, to admit that we must leave a huge portion of human thought and history out of school studies. In the face of continued, subsidized ignorance, how can we claim to *educate*?

At every level of society—not just in schools—we need to seek modes of communication that might make it possible for us to connect with one another across the chasm of belief and unbelief. Discussion should be open, honest and generous, not censored, deceptive or condescending. We need not respect the views or beliefs of others, but we must care enough for these others to refrain from ridicule and cruelty.

Dawkins opens his chapter on the roots of morality with quotes from some of the nastiest letters he has received in opposition to his outspoken atheism. It is hard to believe that people who describe themselves as Christians could write such awful things to another human being. What motivates such vicious anger?

But only a few believers use intemperate, hurtful language, and some of today's atheistic writers also use questionable language. They do not threaten violence, scream obscenities, or wish their opponent an eternity in hell, but their language often ridicules belief. Dawkins, Hitchens and Harris all use language that is unlikely to invite intelligent debate. Hitchens claims that religion poisons everything, and Harris refers to theology as "ignorance with wings" (2004, 173). In another place, Harris comments:

> Nonbelievers like myself stand beside you, dumbstruck by the Muslim hordes who chant death to whole nations of the living. But we stand dumbstruck by *you* as well—by your denial of tangible reality, by the suffering you create in service to your religious myths, and by your attachment to an imaginary God. (2006, 91)

These last comments by Harris appear in a short book titled *Letter to a Christian Nation*, but his "letter" does not credit its receivers with intelligent commitment.

On the contrary, he strongly suggests that there is something wrong with them. His approach contrasts sharply with that of E. O. Wilson, who has cast his book *The Creation* in the form of a letter to a Southern Baptist pastor. At the outset, Wilson describes himself as a secular humanist and draws a sharp contrast between the pastor's religious beliefs and his own unbelief. He goes on to say that he is "heartened" by the increasing interest among evangelicals in global conservation. The purpose of his book (letter) is twofold: to tell the scientific story of creation and to invite participation in saving that creation:

> You will not agree with all that I say about the origins of life—science and religion do not easily mix in such matters—but I like to think that in this one life-and-death issue we have a common purpose. (Wilson 2006, 8)

This seems to me the right approach. It helps to build a bridge across the chasm. Daniel Dennett (2006), too, expresses both sympathy for believers and appreciation for the incomparable aesthetic legacy of religion. When we disagree with others on some vital issue, it is best to start discussion by talking about something else—something we may have in common. John Dewey once advised that we should start political discussions not with political issues but, instead, with matters on which we might agree. We may or may not attain a meeting of minds on the deep questions that divide us but, as we develop a caring relation, we will resolve not to inflict harm on one another, and we may accomplish other goals that matter to both of us. We may even reach some understanding on the issue that divides us. Critical thinking should not foreclose commitment, nor should it stand in the way of caring.

References

Daly, M. (1974) *Beyond God the father*. Boston: Beacon Press.

Dawkins, R. (2006) *The God delusion*. Boston: Houghton Mifflin.

Dennett, D. C. (2006) *Breaking the spell*. New York: Viking.

Gardner, M. (1983) *The whys of a philosophical scrivener*. New York: Quill.

Groenhout, R. E., & Bower, M. (Eds.) (2003) *Philosophy, feminism, and faith*. Bloomington: Indiana University Press.

Gunn, J. (2004) Religious freedom and laicite: A comparison of the United States and France. *Brigham Young University Law Review*, summer, 419–506.

Harris, S. (2004) *The end of faith: Religion, terror, and the future of reason*. New York: W. W. Norton.

Harris, S. (2006) *Letter to a Christian nation*. New York: Alfred A. Knopf.

Hitchens, C. (2007) *God is not great: How religion poisons everything*. New York: Twelve (Warner Books).

Jacoby, S. (2004) *Freethinkers*. New York: Metropolitan Books.

Kugel, J. L. (2007) *How to read the Bible*. New York: Free Press.

Marty, M. E. (1984) *Pilgrims in their own land: 500 years of religion in America*. Boston: Little, Brown.

McGrath, A. (2004) *The twilight of atheism*. New York: Doubleday.

Miles, J. (1995) *God: A biography*. New York: Alfred A. Knopf.

Noddings, N. (1989) *Women and evil*. Berkeley: University of California Press.

Noddings, N. (1993) *Educating for intelligent belief or unbelief*. New York: Teachers College Press.

Noddings, N. (2003) *Happiness and education*. Cambridge: Cambridge University Press.

Phillips, J. A. (1984) *Eve: The history of an idea*. San Francisco: Harper & Row.

Schippe, C., & Stetson, C. (Eds.) (2006) *The Bible and its influence*. New York: Bible Literacy Project.

Turner, J. (1985) *Without God, without creed*. Baltimore, MD: Johns Hopkins University Press.

Ward, G. C., & Burns, K. (1999) *Not for ourselves alone: The story of Elizabeth Cady Stanton and Susan B. Anthony*. New York: Alfred A. Knopf.

Wilson, E. O. (2006) *The creation: An appeal to save life on earth*. New York: W. W. Norton.

12

The Cultivation of Children's Bodies Toward Intricate Thinking and Sensitive Behavior

Don Hanlon Johnson

New visions always require radical, root-like thinking redirected towards origins—in the case at hand, to the sources that give rise to the complexity of pedagogies, curricula, instructional plans, institutional designs, and methods of assessment. In order to gain access to those primal sources of inspiration, we have to hold in abeyance all the assumptions that have led to the current situation, research conclusions, the received opinions about what must be done, the political hard lines. Bracketing all that we think we know, we need to return to fundamental questions of what we want from these institutions for our children, our communities and the world.

Here are two fundamental questions:

1. How can schools better help our children develop the kind of intricate and sinuous intelligence needed to meet the many personal and social challenges they will have to confront as adults?
2. How can schools better cultivate in children the humane qualities that make communal life and a truly democratic society possible: kindness, compassion, humor, integrity, reliability, the capacity to deal comfortably with an ambiguous world?

Favela Rising is a movement and a film about one of the Rio de Janeiro *favelas* that was the heart of the drug trade, run by the gangs, with high levels of violence. A group of people in the community made the decision to transform it through channeling the intense energies of the youth into vigorous dance, singing and music-making, away from violence, depression, incarceration or death. It is similar to Rennie Harris's hip hop movement in Philadelphia, and many other movements in depressed urban areas of the United States, where people are engaging the vibrant bodily energies of youth in danger to transform communities of violence into vibrant islands of hope. The body is the key—its capacities either for wanton destruction of self and others, or for ecstatic creativity and communion with others. These instances of working successfully with young people on the outer reaches of possible destruction illuminate how we might envision dealing with the less dramatic widespread loss of young people of all economic and social classes to addictions, depression, and a loss of dreams.

How do I dare propose this essay? Teachers, administrators and educational policy-makers are flooded with advice from politicians, educational theorists, parents, corporate executives and law enforcement officials. Since we've all spent many years in schools, and since many of us continue to have children and grandchildren in school, we all correctly think we have a stake in how they work. Smothered by a barrage of advice are poorly paid, overworked teachers who have to put up with often raucous and uncooperative children, as well as administrators who are constantly having to prove to some agency or other and aggressive PTAs, at the cost of their jobs, that their charges are being adequately prepared to deal with the jobs they might take in ten years, that they are protected from sexual predators on the internet, kept from the early stages of substance addictions, and well on their way to being well-behaved citizens. What justifies adding to this bewildering flow of advice? In struggling to answer this question, I have found what makes it possible for me to go ahead with this is not to try to add something new, but to bring to focus with radical simplicity a healthy trend that has been building for a few decades, with the hope that such a focus might inspire a few people to intensify and bring to greater fruition what is already going on.

I speak of the sea change in attitudes about the role of the human body in learning, both in the culture at large and in schools themselves.

The cultural turn to the body has taken place in two regions. One is the public realm of everyday attitudes towards the body and body practices. Since the mid-20th century, there has been a steadily increasing awareness that the cultivation of our bodily energies through such things as exercise, diet and massage therapy is part and parcel of becoming a successful adult. Not unlike medieval monks, the workforce now marks the day three times, with the morning, noon and evening runs, bikes, weight-trainings. As in the parks of China and American Chinatowns, you now see city parks all over the country filled with people stretching, doing martial arts, yoga, jogging, biking. The ubiquitous corner markets of earlier years are now rented out by exercise and yoga studios.

As in China, many have the sense that these intense daily activities are not thought to be exclusively about physical health and longevity. Even though there is not the body of communal textual reflection on these matters which has been going on for centuries in Asia, there are many indications that they are thought to be a factor in becoming a more intelligent and sensitive human being, more capable of creative activity in the world, more sensitive to the needs of one's intimates and co-workers.

This sea change is not only in the popular mind. One of the most stunning scientific movements of the past century has been the proliferation of sciences of the body: genomics, robotics, cognitive sciences, evolutionary and cellular biology, etc. In this realm of the sciences a new consensus is developing about a model of "mind" or "intelligence" that stands in juxtaposition to the older Cartesian and Platonic models. "Mind" is viewed within the context of attributes which "emerge" from the embryonic organism in its process of development. Just as the sweet random movements of the newborn, or its gurgles and grunts, will develop into intelligently communicative gestures and sentences, so, too, its early musings and wonderings will slowly develop into adult mindfulness.

These cultural changes are reflected in schools. When I left kindergarten for grade school in the early 1940s, I found myself forced into a silent Procrustean bed for the long years of school stretching before me—desks fixed in geometric rows facing forward, no chatting among us, no moving around the classroom, speaking only when spoken to, even bathroom visits so restricted that there were always "accidents" appearing on the floors. Now there is easy movement in the classroom, with tables and chairs arranged in a less military or monastic manner. You always see children moving around, getting supplies, sharpening pencils, chatting with the teacher or work partners as they go about their assigned tasks.

The national panic over obesity is a sign, though distorted, of this change. Both educational programs in the schools and new rules for the kinds of food and drink promoted by the schools reflect a broadly shared realization that a healthy body is crucial to being a thoughtful and productive adult, even perhaps more important than learning the multiplication tables, since here the stakes are illness and death. And yet there is a confusion here about the nature of the real issue. On the one hand, there is an old and demeaning identification of various forms of plumpness and big bellies with unattractiveness in comparison to the anorectic models of popular beauty. This is different from an often inarticulate intuition that growing instances of obesity among young children reflect a combination of a lack of care about our material reality: spending hours supine in front of a monitor, eating junk foods, not caring any more for the flesh than for our endangered forests and waters.

It is this intuition, and similar intuitions about the importance of children's bodies in the educational process, to which I want to speak in this chapter, with the hope that, by condensing into simple principles the variety of insights that have motivated this vast turn towards the body during the past half-century, the people who actually have to live day-to-day within the schools might find some help in thinking through making them more effective.

In the call for papers for this collection, Svi Shapiro writes:

> The severity and complexity of human problems will demand from us, and especially our children, inclinations, dispositions, and knowledge quite different from those which have shaped, and continue to shape, our social identities and ideological outlooks, moral preferences and attitudinal priorities.

The vocabulary of this call evokes the human organism: inclinations, dispositions, shaping and attitudes. These are not ideas but sensibilities earned by educational practices that are not primarily cognitive. They imply a different kind of cognition, not dissociated from experience in formulas and sentences but emergent from the human organism; not detached from, but deeply intertwined with the suffering and yearning world of everyday life.

The word "inclinations," for example, captures the experience we have of leaning this way or that, inclining towards the couch or the jungle gym, towards this person, away from that one, towards playing the guitar or riding a snowboard. "Inclinations" are the heart of effective pedagogy; when responded to by teachers, they mobilize the student's interest to learn what is at hand; when ignored, they fester in frustration and boredom.

"Dispositions" is a term that takes central place in the late Pierre Bourdieu's analysis of the various ways in which bodily comportments form the basis for the social order, including the conduct of teaching in academic institutions.[1] No matter what one thinks or imagines, the weight of bodily habituations, shaped over time, sweeps one in predictable ways, some of which are simply annoying in their seeming repetitiveness, others of which are tragic in their seemingly inevitable slide towards depression or violence. Only with great effort of sustained thoughtful practice can one dispose oneself towards a different direction. Young children are in the process of crafting these habituations, some useful, some problematic. The results of ignoring these habituations becomes painfully obvious in adult struggles to overcome one's dysfunctional dispositions—chronic hostility, lassitude, fear, self-doubt. On a larger scale, failure to deal with these habituations undercuts the creation of the kinds of flexible, resilient and open-minded thinking required in a diverse democratic society.

Shaping "social identities and ideological outlooks, moral preferences and attitudinal priorities" requires addressing these very bodily currents. But this "shaping" is often etherealized in educational theory to the point where its original references to bodily activities of hand and sweat are reduced to abstract rules and theories. A widely shared mistake in the development of Western notions of the mind is that this shaping takes place primarily through language, rules, punishment and reward. Ideas and rules are not sufficient to craft an ethical and thoughtful adult. This is the major problem of pedagogy in the modern Western world with its Cartesian heritage: ideas and rules by themselves are helpless if they are disconnected from the organic foundations of our being. Insisting that young, protean, highly mobile children sit still in desks, that they be punished for giggling and squirming, sets up an atmosphere of resentment and hatred of school as an institution of dissociated discipline, not of vibrant evolution of sensitive intelligence and imaginative craft.

Wilhelm Reich's analysis of fascism, derived from his intimate first-hand living through the horrors of Hitler and Stalin with his brilliant psychoanalytic eyes, is unique in appreciating that the roots of the fanaticisms which continue to sweep the world are to be found not primarily in ideas but in the mobilization of bodily energies, for either good or ill. Resistance and liberation are in his view not primarily matters of reason but of a more profound return to the sensibilities of our bodies.[2] The battles are between the uniforms, flags, and military choreographies of the Nuremberg rallies filmed by Leni Riefenstahl and the half-naked Gandhi, with his hand-woven dhoti and staff marching to the sea.

> To dissociate himself from the animal kingdom, the human animal denied and finally ceased to perceive the sensations of his organs: in the process he became biologically rigid. It is still a dogma of mechanistic natural science that the autonomous functions are not experienced and that the autonomous nerves of life are rigid. This is the case, notwithstanding the fact that

every three-year-old child knows very well that pleasure, fear, anger, yearning, etc., take place in the belly. This is the case, notwithstanding the fact that the experience of oneself is nothing but the total experience of one's organs. By losing the sensation of his organs, man lost not only the intelligence of the animal and ability to react naturally, but he ruined his own chances of overcoming his life problems. … Man's body sensations did indeed become rigid and mechanical.[3]

Children's Developmental Trajectories

Grades K–8 are dealing with children who are engaged in a complex transitional realm of human development. At the early stages, the child is still principally occupied in making the journey from the pre-linguistic and pre-formal-movement phases of development. Every parent knows that the infant spends many months playing with intricate plant- and animal-like protean movements long before they sit or walk in anything resembling the formal geometries of adulthood. They play with a complexity of polyphonic sounds that only slowly get shaped into articulate words, and eventually sentences. The success of later development is proportionate to the degree in which those earlier stages are integrated and consolidated in activities of syntactical speaking, reading, writing and mathematical reasoning. Without an adequate sense of continuity with the earlier stages, emphasis on the formal activities of syntax and calculation begin to leave a child with a sense of alienation. The developmental psychologist Daniel N. Stern argues that this bridge between the non-verbal world of infant experience and the linguistic world is crucial in forming a healthy personality:

> Infants' initial interpersonal knowledge is mainly unshareable, amodal, instance-specific, and attuned to nonverbal behaviors in which no one channel of communication has privileged status with regard to accountability or ownership. Language changes all that. With its emergence, infants become estranged from direct contact with their own personal experience. Language forces a space between interpersonal experience as lived and as represented. And it is exactly across this space that the connections and associations that constitute neurotic behavior may form.[4]

If the child has had good enough nurturance in the first five years, not abused or subject to the disabling displacements of war and poverty or disease, they arrive at school a vibrant, buzzing, alert organism, speaking with newly discovered words, almost poetically, wildly inquisitive, but lacking the various orderly skills of grammar and logic that characterize adulthood. The process of making the primal journey from the non-verbal into language and organized gestures is well along the way, but far from any kind of natural proclivity for the extremely formalized activities of grammar and number. The impact of the early grades school can be dramatic, for good or ill, on the delicacy of this newly forming world of syntactical communication and numerical calculation, depending on how carefully the child is helped to preserve felt links between the already highly developed movements and soundings and the dawning and tentative worlds of discourse and calculation. If the vocal exuberance and complexity of infant sounding is too rapidly squeezed into syntactical order, you have the dampened language of everyday life and adults alienated from the intricate expression feelingly connected to our interlocutors necessary to deal with the problems that face us as communities. When the constant exploratory reaches, jumps, leaps and twists are trimmed to fit the Procrustean bed of postural order, you have the beginnings of the rigid character structures that plague us as adults, making it difficult to maintain the flexibility needed to deal with our ever-changing life challenges. At the same time, it creates a distance between the child's own source of personal decision-making, leaving them more susceptible to the public winds and the emotions of the moment, not to speak of chronic back pain and headaches.

It is the unique challenge of years K–8 to give as much attention to the cultivation of this bodily substrate of adult development as to the formalities of reason and good citizenship, sending off middle-school graduates to high school and college where they will be able to take on the demands of increasingly abstract studies without losing their birthrights of vitality and open-heartedness. Is it possible for the design of these nine years to make use of this now widespread recognition of the importance of body movement, sounding and feeling as the generative matrix for the evolution of mature thinking and decision-making? Can pedagogies take seriously into account how to incorporate the fleshy liveliness of the organism—its movements, urges, fascinations, boredoms, hostilities—into the disciplines of syntactical language, mathematical reasoning, and the many other formalisms of intellectual expansion. The problem is that, even though dualism is no longer in fashion among thinking people, its residues are left unquestioned in many areas, such as school priorities. Although the popular culture and the cognitive sciences have developed a new model of reason, an older model, dating back to Descartes and Galileo, remains embedded in our institutions of education, medicine and religion, where the development of reason is thought to be relatively independent of the development of its organic foundations.

Reason

The Argentine social scientist Julia Carozzi goes to the heart of the problem which faces teachers and educational policy-makers in her analysis of the model of thinking that dominates Western academic discourse as cut off from the bodily processes that provide the matrix for the emergence of thinking: the acts of moving, reading, writing, wondering, speaking, puzzling.[5] The vibrant mobile exploratory young child enters the school, where the rich panoply of bodily streams of development are squeezed into what are thought to be the abstract forms supportive of rational development. Sitting still in geometrically designed rooms mirrors the abstractions of the alphabet and numbers. Susan Leigh Foster describes what it is like to be a scholar whose training begins in kindergarten:

> Sitting in this chair, squirming away from the glitches, aches, low-grade tensions reverberating in neck and hip. Staring unfocused at some space between

here and the nearest objects, shifting again, listening to my stomach growl, to the clock ticking, shifting, stretching, settling, turning—I am a body writing. I am a bodily writing. We used to pretend the body was uninvolved, that it remained mute and still while the mind thought. We even imagined that thought, once conceived, transferred itself effortlessly onto the page via a body whose natural role as instrument facilitated the pen. Now we know that the caffeine we imbibe mutates into the acid of thought which the body then excretes, thereby etching ideas across the page. Now we know that the body cannot be taken for granted.[6]

The cultivation of intelligence is directly addressed by the emphasis on curriculum, books, tests, and standardized educational outcomes. Are these emphases out of balance? Do they embody certain problematic assumptions about the nature of intelligence and its development?

Our schools can seem like Descartes writ large. When he was a young adolescent in a Jesuit prep school, he was troubled by the fact that most of his teachers were in disagreement about many matters of importance. While the rest engaged in constant debate, only the mathematicians could find grounds for agreement. He based his entire philosophical career on this typical adolescent unwillingness to accept the inherent messiness of life, arguing that all that was worth knowing were those matters that could be put into the absolute certainties of mathematical logic. Only this realm of our being, he argued, deserved the name Mind (*res cogitans*, the thinking thing). Our perceptions, feelings, longings, complex experiences of life are personal matters of taste and belief, not shared matters of communal reason; they belong to religion, art and physical education: the realm of Body (*res extensa*, the extended thing).

We do indeed need this Cartesian mind for counting out money at the supermarket and adding up our assets; it is what we need for executing basic jobs available in the workplace. But this kind of mind fails even within the realm of reason itself. Cognitive scientists have done groundbreaking research on the difference between our innate neural capacities for the recognition of number and simple combinations of numbers, and the difference between the basic organic substrate and the complex linguistic abilities needed for multiplication, division, and higher operations. In their view, even here the body must be taken seriously as the precondition for the successful development of mathematical reason: children need to be given the opportunity to cultivate their organic sense of number before being pushed into higher developmental realms at a speed where there is a danger of disconnecting from this neural foundation. When we approach the actual practices of good science, the Cartesian model reveals even greater flaws. Successful scientists have developed the intricate capacity to observe careful details, engage in inventive speculation, devise clever means for bypassing our preconceived opinions, the tenacity to keep to their inquiry even in the face of seeming defeat. Often, as in the case of Darwin, botanists and the early geologists, they need to have the capacity to engage in physically demanding explorations in difficult terrains, their senses keen to the unexpected just lurking out of sight.

Values

The most glaring failure of the Cartesian mind occurs when one is faced with questions about the role of schools in preparing children to meet the typical challenges of becoming an adult.

- How to negotiate questions related to choosing and succeeding in a profession that will make for a satisfying work life.
- How to care for one's health and emotional wellbeing over the long haul.
- How to work effectively with other people.
- How to negotiate the ever-challenging questions of crafting successful relationships with one's intimates.
- How to be an effective parent.
- How to satisfy one's spiritual and emotional longings.

Not only does this adolescent Cartesian fantasy create a radical separation between reason and the body, it also divorces reason from value, leaving that for religion, aesthetics or sheer power. The rapid spread of Christian, Muslim and Hindu militant fundamentalisms is partly due to the failure of the Cartesian model to deal with these crucial life questions related to the meaning of being human, leaving its graduates adrift in a virtual world of reason detached from substance. The resulting nihilism married to the growing wealth and power of the dominant scientific culture creates a formidable enemy to the traditional values of older cultures that see themselves as helpless against the technological and military might of modernity.

The uses of punishment in schools form one telling indicator of how children are being educated towards certain values. It is significant that the standard pattern for punishing bad behavior is to withhold body-based activities—recess, dance class, outdoor activities—precisely because they are so desirable. Punishment typically means sitting still and quiet indoors. It also means the curtailment of vibrant and successful learning in favor of keeping the kids in line, revealing the often hidden prioritization of conformity over the development of intelligence. This is not to romanticize out-of-control young people; they clearly need boundaries. The question I raise is about the extent and content of the means used to create boundaries, particularly tendencies to disembody learning.

The emergence of grade-school children into the playground for recess or after school is like the popping of the cork off a warm bottle of champagne—wild yelling, running, leaping, sometimes edging into aggression. Keeping children from having recess is a first-line punishment for bad behavior because, of all the day's activities, this is the most, if not the only one that is, loved.

The local middle school has for four years been attempting to establish what in California is called an "academy," an alternative learning center within the school itself which emphasizes project-based integrative learning. Last year's version had scheduled each Friday a trip to the local climbing gym. There, with the assistance of climbing instructors in addition to the school teachers, the students got to learn a variety of things in the context of the physical challenges of climbing simulated cliffs: coping with fear, the necessity of collaborating with others demanded when at the edge of severe harm, the nature and capacities of their bodies, issues around metabolism, breathing, and a host of other insights that students would share and reflect upon after the weekly event. After a few weeks during which the students expressed great enthusiasm for the weekly trip, the program was halted as a punishment for the fact that the students were behaving too wildly in the school classroom itself.

A couple of months later, another popular course in the alternative curriculum was eliminated as a punishment for bad behavior. In this project, one day a week had been devoted to students working outside on a nearby small watershed, bounded by hills and meadows. They did hard work clearing the pollutants and invasive plants. At the same time they were studying ecological science, learning about the indigenous flora and fauna, and how those indigenous plants were affected by waste products and invasive species. The students I knew were completely absorbed in these projects, relishing the outdoor labor and excited by their finds of insects and special plants, as well as by learning how everything was interrelated. As with the climbing wall, this day was eliminated as a punishment for the students being too rowdy in the classroom.

By the end of the year, the alternative nature of the academy had literally been disembodied, with project-learning still an operative concept, but the projects, like projects in regular classes, were more traditionally academic (writing a diary pretending you are Lewis or Clark, studying the physics of surfing by research on the internet, etc.). At the same time, one of the students whom I asked about this program said the best part of it was that he could go to the bathroom when he wanted to without a big deal of getting a pass, and that if he got restless he could go outside and run around for a while.

I bring up these instances as illustrations of a widely practiced pedagogy of moral training that widens the experiential gap between Mind and Body. The typical punishments meant to shore up rules of behavior are disembodiments; the pedagogical emphasis on rules of behavior is disembodied. This emphasis on abstract rules and their implementation through punishment and reward is peculiar given that we adults know all too well that enforced rules have only secondary importance in our attempts to be good; our experientially embodied tendencies of anger, envy, greed, weariness, despair and addictions naggingly keep us from following what we know is right, derailing our intent to be kind, blurring our knowledge of how to act humanely in this particular situation.

The earliest creators of our educational systems understood these issues. Classical Greek notions of education put emphasis on developing harmony in the body through gymnastics, music, dance and the arts. In Plato's plan for an ideal education, by the time the young man came to study the nature of the Good, he would be surprised to find her to be an old friend, having already gotten a feel in his body for the virtues. Similarly, in the mystical schools of East and West, virtue has always been cultivated through practice: meditation, silence, the concentration on certain kinds of focused behaviors.

Vestiges of the classical methods of developing virtue remain in military education.[7] It is no accident that difficult young men are typically consigned to the military, or military-based schools. It is clear to everyone that cocky young men cannot be trained to be completely obedient to the commands of their superior by giving them rules and orders. They must reshape their feelings and tendencies so that they learn to react instantly to commands, and to the enemy as someone who is to be eliminated by whatever means is necessary. The training is radically of the body, with rules directly related to bodily training: the drills, pushing physical endurance to its absolute limits, humiliation, uniformity, pornographic and drunken shaping of community feeling.

In a related manner, the many programs of rigorous outdoor training of youth— Outward Bound, NOLS and others—have been developed on this fundamental understanding of how values and intense physical development are intimately linked. Similarly with the various programs in the inner cities, where youth are inducted into groups where they organize themselves for success based on intense forms of bodily movement, voice and music.

Looking to these successes of embodied virtue-training, what insights might be found about how educators might better cultivate children's bodies to evoke curiosity, open-mindedness and intricate thinking? How might they shape social identities and moral preferences in the directions of justice, sensitivity and compassion? how might the bodies of children be more seamlessly woven into the heart of intellectual discipline?

"Cultivation" is a gardener's term, earth-centered, evoking care for the delicate nature of new growth and, yet, respectful of the inner wisdom of seeds and sprouts, knowing that they have their own paths to follow and need only the right conditions of nurturance, climate, and protection from external damage. But, like "education," this is no longer an innocuous term to be taken at face value. Cultivation practiced by the gargantuan agribusinesses bears little resemblance in technology or mentality to that practiced by a traditional small farmer or the backyard lover of plants.

A residue of the classical Greek and Roman notions of cultivation remains in schools' devotion to children's health.[8] There is a vibrant discourse about proper diet, exercise and rest. At the same time, there is little evidence that educators and politicians consider these activities as having any intrinsic relationships to the development of a child's intelligence and moral integrity. "Health" is structurally separate from the disciplines that are considered to be the essential core of school (and are the first to disappear when the budget becomes squeezed).

The Japanese philosopher Yasuo Yuasa presents a very different notion of cultivation in his book *The Body: Toward an Eastern Mind–Body Theory*. He writes that "personal cultivation in the East takes on the meaning of a practical project aiming at the enhancement of the personality and the training of the spirit by means of the body."[9] In his extensive analyses of this notion, it is very clear that the activities of attending to breathing, moving, sensing, imagining, and other bodily activities constitute the path towards the development of intelligence and spiritual values. He sees this as a profound difference between dominant notions of intelligence in Japan and the West:

> One of the characteristics of Eastern body–mind theories is the priority given to the questions, "How does the relationship between the mind and the body come to be through cultivation)?" or "What does it become?" The

traditional issue in Western philosophy, on the other hand, is "What is the relationship between the mind–body?" In other words, in the East one starts from the experiential assumption that the mind–body modality changes through the training of the mind and body by means of cultivation or training. Only after assuming this experiential ground does one ask what the mind–body relation is. That is, the mind–body issue is not simply a theoretical speculation but it is originally a practical, lived experience, involving the mustering of one's whole mind and body. The theoretical is only a reflection on this lived experience.[10]

In this Asian model of cultivation, the uses of the body in school are not only matters of health, but of educators thinking through how to enlist the enormous stores of raw bodily wisdom in the processes of higher learning.

These ideas are by no means original, nor is their implementation far from our noses. John Dewey, Rudolf Steiner and Maria Montessori are among the strong voices that have advocated a more intense focus on body movement, project learning, dance, art and music in the early years. Their followers have long advocated slowing the pace at which young children are inducted into reading, syntactical writing, advanced mathematical operations, and abstract social studies. The many schools in which their ideas are being practiced are easy-to-hand models of what might happen more effectively at a larger level: much less emphasis on formal academic learning in the earlier grades, and more emphasis on thoughtful activities aimed at cultivating the sensitive neurological matrix for more abstract learning. Perhaps their heirs, and the vast community of creative pre-school educators, might be enlisted in learning how we might better serve the yearning and mobile students in their early grades.

Notes

1. *Academic Discourse: Linguistic Misunderstanding and Professorial Power*, with Jean-Claude Passeron and Monique de St. Martin, trans. Richard Teese (Stanford, CA: Stanford University Press, 1994).
2. Wilhelm Reich, *The Mass Psychology of Fascism*, trans. Vincent R. Carafagno (New York: Farrar, Straus & Giroux, 1970).
3. Ibid., p. 343.
4. Daniel N. Stern, *The Interpersonal World of the Infant: A View from Psychoanalysis and Developmental Psychology* (New York: Basic Books, 1985), p. 182.
5. María Julia Carozzi, "Talking Minds: The Scholastic Construction of Intercorporeal Discourse," *Body and Society*, *11*, 2, 25–39.
6. Susan Leigh Foster, "Choreographing History," from Susan Leigh Foster (Ed.), *Choreographing History* (Bloomington: Indiana University Press, 1995), p. 3.
7. It must be noted that "virtue" originally meant "manliness."
8. Michael Foucault, in *The Care of the Self*, trans. Robert Hurley (New York: Pantheon, 1986), p. 43, analyzes the classic origins of the dominant model of cultivation in Western culture.
9. Trans. N. Shigenori & T. P. Kasulis (Albany: State University of New York Press, 1987), p. 85.
10. Ibid., p. 18.

13
To Touch and Be Touched
The Missing Discourse of Bodies in Education

Mara Sapon-Shevin

"Sit on your own carpet square and keep your hands to yourself."

"Be careful that you never touch the children."

"No recess this month; we have to get ready for the State-Wide Assessment tests."

This chapter is about the many ways in which schools try to eliminate bodies, the bodies of children and the bodies of teachers. I am speaking here not of homicide, but rather of the failure to recognize the bodies of the students we teach and those of us who teach them. It is about how schools make bodies unwelcome, unable to see them as potential sources of information or education, much less the sites of pleasure and connection. It is about what happens when we separate "minds" and "bodies" so completely that we virtually ask both students and teachers to "leave their bodies at the schoolhouse door and pick them up again at 3:30." It is about the dehumanization of schools by the enforcement of curriculum, pedagogy, management and policies that see only brains and treat bodies as irrelevant or dangerous. But this is also a chapter about hope—about what schools can (and sometimes do) look like when students and teachers teach, learn and interact from an embodied place.

The children in our schools have become the victims of educational systems that privilege academic performance above social interaction, high-stakes standardized testing over personal growth, and conformity and obedience over community and solidarity. Under the constraints of No Child Left Behind and other rigid policies, many teachers are leaving the profession, unwilling to interact with their students in dehumanizing and disconnected ways.

Shapiro says that "An excision of the flesh from educational discourse and practice means an excision of student experiences, emotions, passions, compassion and meaning-making from the ground of reason" (2002b, 9). What happens to the students forced to participate in schools and classrooms that do not recognize them as human beings at all, when schools eliminate recess, art, music and physical education in order to spend more time on subjects tested on the "official" rubric? How do these policies and practices collude with no-touch policies and other fears of bodies and physical intimacy? Although detachment and disaffiliation can be linked directly to increases in school violence and negative interpersonal behavior, there is little time or attention given to the importance of allowing students to interact lovingly.

In many schools, violence is the norm. Physical and verbal assaults are everyday occurrences. Teasing, bullying, harassment, name-calling, and social exclusion are typical. We have lost our willingness and ability to help kids to learn to be in touch with their own bodies and to interact gently with the bodies of others. Why? Is it a fear of the touch itself—that we will be sued for sexual harassment or inappropriate touch? Is it fear of being accused of promoting an "Eastern religion" if we allow meditation, deep breathing and massage, a challenge to the Christian hegemony of the school?

I have come to recognize that I live in a country in which giving children drugs for their hyperactivity is normal, but that teaching them to slow their breath through meditation is suspect. I see countless anti-bullying programs, many of which focus on the need to keep one's hands to oneself, but rarely do I see programs designed to teach children to touch one another gently and appropriately.

Our pedagogy itself is often disembodied; it is an out of body experience. In many schools, a proposal to teach body relaxation, yoga or peer massage would never be seriously entertained (unless, perhaps, it could be linked to improvements in test scores).

What would it mean to connect with our bodies while we are teaching, and to allow students to connect with their own and others' bodies as well? As hooks (1994) asserts, we must be whole as humans in the classrooms if we are allow others to be wholehearted as well. Moreover, as Shapiro (2002) has argued, a critical pedagogy of the body acknowledges that it is in and through our bodies that particular life experiences shape how we perceive others and ourselves. This chapter will present the argument that, if we are to create a society in which people see themselves as interconnected and mutually responsible, this vision must begin with school experiences that allow the intimacy and trust of touching. We must relearn how to touch and be touched. School experiences that leave students disembodied and disconnected from themselves and others cannot produce citizens who are fully present to their own lives and the lives of others.

Shapiro asks us to consider what kind of education results from schooling that separates "objective knowing from subjective experience, mind from body, the rational from the emotional—a philosophical separation between thinking and being" (2002a, 145). What kind of education and what kinds of children and teachers?

There are multiple and interconnected levels to this issue; each is complex, and even more so in their interactions and layering. I will describe what it looks like when children are not allowed to be in their bodies and when teachers are also required to be disembodied, and explore some of the consequences of these policies and standards. Lastly, I will explore what schools might look like—and how we might all benefit—if we were somehow able to reach a higher level of comfort and clarity about the importance of bodies in education.

Don't Touch

You Can't Be in your Body at School

Schools are typically structured so that bodies are unwelcome, viewed in the learning process as superfluous at best and dangerous at worst. Many schools have eliminated the most embodied parts of the school day, particularly free play and recess. In my local elementary school, recess was eliminated for the entire year in 4th grade because of the pressure of state-wide assessments. This ban on "play" has also extended to eliminating other activities during the school day that are seen as unrelated to achievement and high-stakes testing success, including music, art and physical education.

What beliefs undergird such policies and decisions? First, there is the belief that the mind and body are actually separable, two distinct entities. As my Yoga Dance teacher Megha Nancy Buttenheim would say, "The body is treated as transportation for the brain." This concept of separate entities posits that the site of learning is in the brain, and that learning does not occur and is not retained in the physical body. This flies in the face of all that is known about the ways in which the brain is part of the body, and the power of kinesthetic memory and learning.

A secondary belief positions the body as somehow a distraction to learning, even dangerous. Discussions of those "pesky hormones" which interfere with adolescent learning, or ways in which children who are very active are pathologized, labeled and medicated to reduce their body activity, are examples of a view of the body as something that gets in the way of learning. Because bodies are undesirable, and possibly dangerous, they must be subjected to surveillance and control at all times. Foucault describes the notion of the panopticon, a mechanism for being able to see everything that goes on in an institution (be that prison or school), evidence of the perceived importance of constant observation of the child's behavior. This control of bodies relates directly to methods of school discipline which succeed in making children's bodies the object of highly complex systems of manipulation and conditioning (Foucault 1977, 125).

In an article entitled "The Missing Discourse of Pleasure and Desire," Tobin writes of early childhood education:

> Children enter day care as infants and toddlers, all uncivilized bodies and unregulated desire, fluids pouring out of orifices insufficiently closed to the world. By the time they reach kindergarten, children are to be moved from sensory-motor engagement with the world to abstract thinking, from unbridled expressions of bodily desire to socially sanctioned forms of play, from excessive pleasure to good clean fun. (1997, 19)

What are the Effects on Children of the Failure to Allow them to Have Bodies, Be in their Bodies or even Talk about their Bodies?

Children are the essence of embodiment. They are "in" their bodies and they learn through their bodies. Leavitt and Power state that "The body is not only the source of unending and ever-changing feelings and emotions but is also the criterion by which we evaluate our experiences in the world, experiences that may either threaten the self or open the way to fulfillment" (1997, 43). When children are not permitted to be embodied or to learn in embodied ways, they learn not to connect with their own bodies. In many schools, children are not even allowed to urinate when they need to, their bodies so tightly controlled by others. Leavitt and Power explain that "A child who fails to learn appropriate body management incorporates this stigma into his or her self-identity" (ibid., 43). Shapiro says that "what has been missing is a way of viewing the body as something that can provide self and social understanding; liberation through critical and sensual understanding, human connection, a sensed community, and human agency through conscious ethical action" (2002b, 15).

Lack of embodiment also keeps students from learning language about their bodies, ways of describing what they are feeling, the sensations they experience. The sanctions on boys who are emotive are even harsher and directly link to homophobia; we punish boys for crying and later lament the ways in which men are "out of touch with their feelings." How could it be otherwise?

Children also learn that seeking bodily pleasure is wrong and dangerous. The little girl who leans into a classmate while seated on the rug for story time is generally told to move away from her neighbor. Fine has written eloquently of another silence discourse, that of sexual pleasure or desire, particularly for adolescent girls. She says: "The naming of desire, pleasure, or sexual entitlement, particularly for females, barely exists in the formal agenda of public schooling on sexuality" (2003, 300). Little boys who touch little girls are apt to be labeled as sexual aggressors or predators, even at an incredibly young age, and little boys who touch each other are particularly alarming. Typically, schools are more comfortable talking about the negative consequences of early sexuality (or any sexuality for that matter) than they are with helping students to explore and understand respectful, thoughtful touch, sensuality and sexuality.

Children's Bodies Shouldn't Touch Each Other

If children are not allowed to be in their own bodies, they are certainly not supposed to interact with other children's bodies either.

A colleague's five-year-old came home from kindergarten and reported that he had been admonished for hugging a friend who was crying, and told that touch was not allowed in school. His mother, certain that the child had misunderstood the real intention of the teacher's rule, engaged him in a discussion. "I'm pretty sure she didn't mean that you couldn't touch each other; she must have meant that you couldn't hit each other or hurt each other. I think you should try again." Two days later the child came home from school and reported: "Mom, you were wrong. Matthew was crying and I went to hug him and the teacher yelled at me again. She said, 'You know the rule: We don't touch other children in this classroom. Keep your hands to yourself.'" The parent—an education professor—was wrong; the five-year-old was right. He had not misunderstood. Touch, even a hug for an unhappy friend, was unacceptable.

Schools across the country have enacted "no-touch policies." At Kilmer Middle School in Vienna, Virginia, a student was suspended for giving his girlfriend a quick hug in the cafeteria. The principal explained that the no-touching rule was meant to ensure that all students are comfortable and that crowded hallways and lunchrooms stay safe.

Not surprisingly, young people themselves have pushed back. A student developed and circulated a petition which acknowledged the need for safety and order, but said, of the ban on touching:

> This is extremely detrimental to normal psychological development. In addition, it is avoidance of common adolescence problems, and is miseducating the students on what is appropriate. Help convince the school officials to find a better way to educate and support their students! (http://tribes.tribe.net/freehuggingtheworld/thread/)

On a website responding to this news story, one woman who moved frequently as a child wrote:

> In the second grade, the teacher gave me a big hug goodbye. She seemed genuinely sorry to see me leave. This is the only hug I ever remember receiving from an adult that was not sexual in nature. It meant the world to me then and still means a lot to me now. ... I will never forget how that felt to be hugged in a safe way.

In an article entitled "A Thousand Ways to Disconnect, and Now a Hugging Ban, Too," Leonard Pitts (2007) described schools across the United States that have banned hugging or even holding hands. He says that some schools attribute these bans to the problem of congestion in the hallways, while others say that PDAs (Public Displays of Affection) are a gateway to sexual harassment. Pitts lamented the dehumanization of the schools:

> We already watch television in separate rooms. Eat dinner in shifts and on the run. Go about cocooned by iPod tunes. Now we have hugging bans. As if there were not already enough in life to make you feel disconnected, disaffected, alienated. ... We're not talking about kids groping and making out. We are talking about "hugs." To hug is to reach across. It is to reaffirm common humanity. That is a powerful instinct. Now the hug joins that long list of banned things. I guess kids who need consolation, kids primed for celebration, kids who just want to know that they are not alone will henceforth have to write text messages instead.

After Pitts's article was posted on www.commondreams.org, the flurry of responses was extremely illuminating. Although some respondents echoed Pitts's lament, there were others who attacked him, and a "debate" of sorts ensued between several of the respondents. One person wrote:

> The kids are not adults and do not have adult motives. The main reason they want to hug is almost certainly sexual (unless there is something in the water up there), and living in one of the most oversexed societies in human history, and knowing that children that age are far from being able to handle sex responsibly, and knowing what the consequences are for children behaving irresponsibly with regard to sex, I have to ask you Mr. Pitts, have you lost your friggin mind?!?

A teacher who works in what she describes as an "economically depressed high school" responded:

> Three times this week alone, I have received a hug from a young black football player for my help in his English class last year (I am a white middle-aged woman). The boundaries that are erased when this lovely child lets me know how much my help means to him are a priceless treasure. There is no "sex" implied nor is this irresponsible behavior.

This writer then challenged the previous writer to examine his own fears about sexuality, implied that he had experienced negative touching in his own life, and urged him to seek counseling. She concluded: "Don't let our collective fears deny us our need for physical affection."

The ensuing dialogue became increasingly more visceral, with some respondents weighing in on the side of the importance of physical contact and others talking about confusion between touch and sex. Some wrote about the increasing isolationism of our society and ways in which other cultures are more comfortable with physical touch. Several young people wrote, describing that they hugged throughout high school and that such physical connection had been vital to their mental health.

The dialogue raises many of the key issues relative to student-to-student touch, including discomfort with touching in general, the confusion of touch with sex, and general fear of sexuality. In addition to this, same-sex touching is viewed suspiciously within a heteronormative framework, and is even more alarming to some than touching between members of the so-called opposite sexes. How can students learn to form relationships, learn ways of connecting and interacting, if they are prohibited from engaging in the most human of activities—touch? The sense of separation and isolation among students is highly problematic, not only because positive touch is not allowed, but because bodies become sites of struggle and competition, not sources of support and connection.

This fear of student–student touch becomes so pervasive that it begins to distort the teaching and perspectives of the teachers as well.

Vignette: Touching in Kindergarten

I was working in a classroom with two wonderful kindergarten teachers. There had been a recent incident in the classroom in which one little boy had grabbed the behind of a little girl. There was much upset, and the situation quickly escalated to talk of "sexual harassment" and abuse; the teachers were alarmed and tried to take charge of the situation. They gathered the students on the rug and spoke to them: "There's something very important we have to talk about. It's not okay to touch one another. You can't touch each other in this classroom. Does everyone understand?"

> The children looked puzzled about what was being said. While they were being lectured about not touching, they were sitting in close proximity to one another, some of them touching and cuddling close to each other. Moreover, this didn't sound like their teachers—both of whom I had seen hug many children throughout the day.
>
> After this conversation, I approached these teachers: "I'm wondering about what you just said to the kids," I said. "Is that really what you mean? That they shouldn't touch each other?" As we continued the conversation, they articulated quite clearly that it wasn't about touch, obviously, but about certain kinds of touch that were negative—hitting, pushing, or inappropriately intrusive (grabbing underwear). I suggested spending some time engaging in activities with the children in which they get to touch one another—in ways that are appropriate—so that we could talk to them about appropriate and inappropriate touch.
>
> We gathered the kids and went out on the playground. We played two cooperative games: "People to People," during which students touched one another in silly ways, shaking hands, elbows and knees, and "Touch Blue," a form of human twister. There was lots of giggling and silliness. We ended by doing a singing/dancing game, in which children danced with partners and then changed partners after each round. The discussion which followed was quite different. We discussed all the wonderful ways we could touch one another and the ones that were problematic.

How do we protect our children from inappropriate touch? From invasions of their bodies and their space? We can either make rules about no touching, no hugging and no interaction, or we can give children many opportunities to touch one another appropriately, to learn language about touch and feelings, and to articulate: "I don't like that" or "That makes me nervous."

It's Dangerous for Teachers to Have Bodies or Touch Children's Bodies

At the same time that children's bodies and desires must be brought under control, the teacher's own bodies and desires must be tightly regulated as well. Phelan describes the ways in which teachers' bodies become intimately connected with notions of control and classroom management. She states: "Teachers are expected to distance themselves from their students, to exercise self-control, to honor a static notion of autonomy that eliminates the possibility of intimacy with children, and to maintain a serious attitude in the classroom" (1997, 87). Leavitt and Power describe how teachers "touch children primarily to control and manipulate their bodies, to exercise their power, and much less often to express affection, tenderness, comfort, or intimacy" (1997, 65).

What is it like to teach in a setting in which one's behavior is carefully observed to make sure that there is compliance with no-touch policies? How is it possible to teach from an embodied position if one must control physical contact so carefully? Such policies instill fear, promote lack of authenticity and feel dehumanizing, driving teachers—loving, caring, affectionate humans—away from the classroom. Furthermore, curricular and pedagogical choices are constrained; practices of differentiated instruction using multiple intelligences demand that we be in our bodies.

Michael, a middle-school guidance counselor in the western United States, says, "Not being able to touch kids is the most frustrating part of my job. ... It makes me feel not authentic with them." He says that the unwritten rule of the school is that female counselors can touch students, but male counselors cannot. He attributes this to "part homophobia, and part fear of pedophilia." Michael says, "I am careful to place my hand in the center of their back. If a female student approached me, I will hug them, but not male students, for fear of repercussions." He adds, "I am more conscious of it—as a gay man."

A deaf teacher who teaches at a school for the deaf relates that she is not allowed to touch students at all—ever—in any context. If she wants to get a child's attention (critical with students who cannot be called verbally to attention), she must ask another child to touch the child in question to get his/her attention.

Concerns about sexual impropriety have produced a flurry of attempts to monitor and regulate the ways in which teachers touch their students. The fear for teachers, particularly male teachers, is palpable. They are asked never to be alone with a child, to make sure someone else is present if they have to touch a child to clean them up or assist them with toileting. A male teacher reports:

> In the school where I work I have been told by female teachers that I often appear to be cold and uncaring towards students, but with all the court appearances, who can blame me? I do show some verbal emotion towards students, but only if there is another teacher or student in the room. I avoid body contact. (Johnson 1997, 102–3)

Johnson describes the proliferation of no-touch policies as a "moral panic." He explains how schools and organizations move quickly to implement policies to safeguard their teachers and schools, often with little regard as to how these policies will affect students and teachers.

> The director of a day care center explains the center's no touch policy: The picking-up thing, I just—I don't allow it, because that's one of those issues where you have, you know, the direct physical contact, body to body, that could be misconstrued, so I—I stop it there. ... I'll say "No. No holding." Or if it's one of the little kids, I might say, "OK, Steven, now you know you need to get down," and then I will privately remind the [caregiver]. "Remember, now, we don't do that. I know you're just enjoying this child. However it could be misconstrued. It could be a problem for you." (Johnson 1997, 109)

It is mind-boggling to imagine how one could care for young children all day without touching them, but, in many settings, that is the goal and the regulation. Johnson concluded that, "As much as we try to reduce and dismiss the moral panic, ... we have, in fact, let it define our moral behavior and distort our understandings of children" (ibid., 111).

But what about children? Research on the relationship between attachment and aggression shows that children with "insecure attachment," a product of lack of loving, nurturing touch, display increased aggression and rage, decreased self-control, low self-esteem, lack of empathy or remorse, and an inability to develop and maintain friendships (Carlson & Nelson 2006). Children in the United States are touched far less than their counterparts around the world, and, although positive touch is absent in many children's lives, negative or punitive touch is easily available.

We have created a vicious circle; we are so nervous about inappropriate touch that we fail to touch children, and this lack of touch leads to ever-increasing aggressive and antisocial behavior which is responded to punitively and sometimes even with physical punishment. Although the research shows that 90 percent of reported cases of child abuse and neglect occur in the home, it is schools and teachers that have become tightly regulated (Finkelhor & Ormrod 2000).

Children who feel their teachers distancing themselves, or cold and aloof, can also be confused and troubled, particularly if this behavior represents a change from a previous relationship. Songwriter Peter Alsop captures this experience brilliantly in his song "Letter to Mr. Brown."

> Dear Mr. Brown, from the kids in Room 2
> We're writing you a letter like you taught us to do.
> [...]
> 'Cause lately you've been different and we don't know why
> Did we do something wrong? We're sorry and we'll try
> To act a little better, if we've been bad.
> We all think that you're the best teacher we've had.

They then detail all the (very) appropriate ways in which he used to touch them:

> You used to hold our hands when we walked across the street.
> You used to help us wash them just before we went to eat.
> You used to kneel down and help Jose tie up his shoes,
> And sometimes you would thumb-wrestle, usually you'd lose!
>
> You used to boost up Ray and Alice on the monkey bars.
> You used to put your arm around us when we got our stars.
> Whenever we played "tag," you were "it" the most,
> 'N' you'd even help Tyrone when he'd forget to blow his nose!
> [...]
> Tell us why you're mad at us, and honest, we will change!
> You still help us learn to read and add, but now you're acting strange.
> You never made us nervous or kept us after school.
> You never touched us anywhere that was against the rules.

(Alsop 1986)

While the need to protect children is certainly valid, there must be other ways to do this than by making blanket no-touch policies. Teaching Tolerance (teachingtolerance.org) has issued a statement on the "ABC's of Sexual Misconduct" in which they lay out rules for physical touch that both protect children and honor their need for closeness and connection. It includes suggestions for how to engage in age-appropriate "non-sexual" touching, respect physical boundaries, teach students about appropriate and inappropriate contact and discuss touch issues with students.

We can best keep children and teachers safe by making discussions about touching frequent, easy and fluid, by empowering students to make decisions about their own bodies, and by opening, rather than closing, channels of communication.

An Embodied World is Possible: What Would it Look Like if it Were Different?

What Might it Be Like for Students Themselves?

If bodies were fully integrated, accepted and valued in education, then students would be taught the language of bodies. They would be encouraged to move their bodies during the day in a variety of settings. They would be taught to talk about their feelings, paying careful attention to what was happening for them internally and externally as well. Bodies would be respected as an important source of information and knowledge. "Trust your gut" would be seen as important pedagogy.

Vignette: Seymour School

Seventeen children are sitting in a circle on little (half-size) yoga mats with their eyes closed. Their teacher, Midge, sounds a chime, and when the sound stops, they open their eyes.

They take five breaths together, while holding out their hands, fingers splayed; they "blow out" their fingers, one at a time. "Why are we doing this?" asks their teacher. "To calm ourselves," they reply. Then they take quick bunny breaths, for energy, grab the sunshine with their hands and pull it in.

In chorus, they recite their yoga pledge, each line accompanied by a different yoga pose; their pledge includes naming all the ways yoga makes them feel: energized and powerful, balanced and centered, strong and flexible, calm and focused, peaceful and loving, and all connected. They end by pointing to one another: "Your heart and my heart are one. Namaste."

Today's lesson is about birds and perseverance. The children squat down on their mats, pretending they are birds, and then they are the eggs. They come out of their shells, stretching, wet and tired. They cheep. Midge walks around and feeds them worms as they fly across the room to different mats. Then they are eagles, diving down to eat a chipmunk, then they are flamingos on one foot, then storks, with one leg raised as they balance on the other.

The children freeze and flow, dancing on their mats to music and then freezing in various yoga positions that the teacher calls out: down dog, eagle, flamingo, stork, cat, cow, bear, trees and butterfly.

They hear a story and act out the different animals. Finally, after about half an hour, it is time for calming down, for meditation. The children lie on their backs, breathing quietly. Midge walks around and places a Beanie Baby on each child's stomach, so that the animal moves up and down as the child breathes. The room is quiet and the little bodies are still. The focus is on breathing. As they close, a song is played: "Namaste." The children sing along with enthusiasm:

"I am part of all I see
I see the light in me
The light in me sees the light in you."

Midge puts a little lavender oil on each child's forehead. She gives each child an affirmation and tells each student she loves them.

She says to them: "Imagine your body getting lighter and lighter. Send your house and your family some love." She talks to them about their good bodies and the love in their hearts. Each child is asked to name something they have worked hard on. One little girl answers, "I've worked really hard on being myself."

Teacher Midge Regier, who holds a master's degree in urban education and a CAS in reading, is trained in a method called YogaKids, which is growing quickly in the U.S. The promotional materials describe the program as follows:

YogaKids is a unique approach to integrative learning using yoga as a pathway. Reading, storytelling, music, creative arts and earthcare blend seamlessly with yoga movement to educate the "whole" child. The YogaKids curriculum provides children with an exciting new way to explore and appreciate their academic and creative potential. (www.yogakids.com)

The program draws on Howard Gardner's theories of multiple intelligences and tries to integrate body awareness with academic learning. Preliminary research on the effectiveness of the method is encouraging. A study by California State University researchers of students in kindergarten through 8th grade in an inner-city school found a correlation between yoga and increased academic performance, fewer discipline referrals, and increases in attendance and self-esteem. Midge's school fits the bill: Seymour School is an elementary school in Syracuse, New York. It is a dual-language school (Spanish and English), and lies within one of the poorest census districts in the country: 98 percent of the children receive free lunch and 60 percent are considered "at risk," ESL or Special Education students. The population is predominantly Hispanic with a small group of African American students.

Midge explains:

The two biggest things that have happened has been that my teaching YogaKids has given me back the ability to take the curriculum back and be creative. It's made it fun again, and it accelerates their comprehension and also gives them ways to express themselves. The goal is for them to love themselves, love each other and to love their world. The biggest thing is that when I started teaching reading that way, their comprehension and their ability to retell what happened in a story accelerated how fast they learned all those things. These kids don't read at home. When they're doing it through their bodies, it's exponential. You're giving them what those suburban kids get all the time.

Midge reports: "I have parents come in and tell me that when they get upset, their children tell them to do the take five breaths." She says that her colleagues want it in their rooms, but they don't have time. They aren't allowed to "play" in the upper grades. Last week she had a workshop at her home and many teachers came. She says:

We're shifting the city. You're taking your power back—you know it's not right and you get to do it differently. You can teach better by integrating the brain with movement. So much is happening in their brains when they're doing this. We're changing them inside out. We don't even begin to understand what we're doing. It's monumental.

What Might it Be Like for How Students Interact with One Another?

Another body-friendly approach is called Peaceful Touch. Begun by Hans Axelson in Stockholm in the early 1990s, the Peaceful Touch program is based on three fundamentals, including that (1) touch is necessary for human growth and development; (2) the calming hormone oxytocin is activated through touch; and (3) a permission process supports healthy touch and helps establish good boundaries (www.peacefultouch.net).

More than 300,000 students in Europe have been recipients of Peaceful Touch, in which children learn to give one another massage and to touch each other gently and respectfully, and it is institutionalized in Swedish pre-schools. The developers report: "Healthy touch, which is what we'll call it here, helps foster attachment; decrease aggression, depression and anxiety; and helps children identify healthy touch so they are less vulnerable to abuse, and less likely to be prematurely sexually active" (LaPlante 2007, 76). LaPlante's article quotes Frances M. Carlson, author of *Essential Touch: Meeting the Needs of Young Children*, who says, "What I think we don't understand in this culture is that withholding touch from children from fear is as physically and emotionally harmful to children as harmful touch is." Patrick Clow, the director of a center in Newington, Connecticut, says that the Peaceful Touch training was like visiting Mars: "In my [traditional American] education, we never had any kind of coursework discussing touch, the quality of touch and the importance of touch." He describes the dramatic effects on a child with frequent temper tantrums and the ways in which other children now respond to him by saying: "Gee, you look like you could use some Peaceful Touch."

Despite stunning results, however, LaPlante reports that the last research program was over in 2004. Although many schools are interested, teachers say they can't implement it because: "We're not allowed to touch."

Vignette: Latchmere Primary School

I have just come from a school on the outskirts of London, known for its creation of a "caring school." The fifth graders all learn peer mediation, and the "Friendship Squad" circulates during recess, alert to anyone who is friendless or alone and seeking connection. Classes begin with circle time, children checking in about their moods and their feelings both in words and through photos.

I follow a group of fourth graders and their teacher up a flight of stairs to the "Blue Room." Leaving our shoes in the corridor outside, we climb the carpeted steps, past a banner that reads, "You are perfectly fine. Remember that success on the outside begins with success on the inside."

The room has walls painted blue and a bank of sofas covered with pillows at one end. The floor is carpeted, soft music is playing, and an aromatherapy machine emits a gentle scent. A bubble machine makes a peaceful sound. I watch as the children visibly change, their shoulders softening, their breath changing, their voices lowering.

They sit on the floor and their teacher asks them to explain to me why they meditate. One young boy explains that meditating helps you calm down and deal better with hard things that happen. A girl reports using meditation to go to sleep at night when there are too many things rattling around in her head. Another girl shares that she taught some of the breathing skills to her father who was stressed, and that he was really grateful.

The teacher demonstrates the principle of meditation by shaking a bottle full of water and mud, creating a murky mixture. He explains: "Through meditation, we can learn to clear our minds just like we clear the jar's water by letting it settle." The students find places on the rug and the teacher leads them through a series of breathing and relaxation exercises. There is quiet in the room, and the wiggling stops. Thirty young people breathe quietly together; the hush is palpable.

After about ten minutes, the teacher asks a volunteer to show me how they do peer massage. The boy receiving the massage lies down on the carpet and the demonstrator explains how you start with smooth and gentle strokes over the head, removing the negative energy. He explains the cupping technique he uses on the boy's back, showing how you must be careful to avoid hitting the spine or shoulder blades. He checks periodically with the boy he is massaging, "Is this okay? Too hard? Too soft?" After five minutes, he concludes the massage by gently sweeping away anything negative left in the body.

All of the children find their partners (which sometimes cross gender lines) and arrange themselves around the room. Several sit on the bank of sofas as their partners sit in front of them. Some are lying completely flat on the carpeted floor. They check in with one another: "Do you want this massage? Do you have any sore or tender areas?"

The room is filled with the gentle energy of twenty pairs giving one another massages. I am struck by the quiet and respectful ways they talk to and touch each other. Half-way through, they are reminded to switch so that both people get a massage. After they are finished, the peacefulness in the room is overwhelming. I have never seen thirty nine-year-olds this quiet or relaxed.

For the last ten minutes, the teacher leads them through a guided meditation. The room is quiet.

I am struck by what I have seen. No hitting, no pushing, no name-calling, no exclusion, no meanness. I have seen children touching each other gently, speaking in respectful ways, and being peaceful together. I have seen two boys gently rub each other's back and shoulders. How can this happen? Or, perhaps, more to the point, why doesn't this happen all the time?

What Might it Be Like for Teachers?

What would it be like to teach from an embodied place, to bring our own bodies to our role as teacher, to be able to acknowledge our students' bodies in the learning process? What might be learned and what would be different?

After years of teaching students' brains, I spent a sabbatical learning to teach dance and movement. Through a program at Kripalu Yoga and Meditation Center, I became certified in a form of movement known as Yoga Dance. Led by a brilliant teacher, Megha Nancy Buttenheim, the other members of my tribe and I learned to design and lead movement classes based on energy chakras in the body, moving students through dances and movement connected to each chakra.

Following that experience, I began to bring movement activities into all my teaching, particularly into my teaching of social justice issues. Calling what I do "Peace Movement," I have led workshops and sessions for people of all ages, often for groups that include people with significant disabilities. I have learned that, while I am very practiced in talking about social justice issues (oppression, solidarity, resistance, voice, visibility, marginality and inclusion), I have been able to teach these ideas far better through the body. This teaching has shifted my students' learning but also has altered my relationships with my students. By my being an embodied teacher, they have become embodied students. Through the connection of our bodies, we have transcended academic spaces.

Vignette: A Lesson on Exclusion and Inclusion

I am leading a session on teaching for social justice through the body, and I have asked each participant to think of a time in their life that he/she felt excluded. Every person shares his/her story in a group of three or four. I see people really listening intently; there are nods of recognition, and in some groups there are tears.

I invite each group to choose one of the stories and to create two tableaus—I call them "snapshots." The first snapshot is to show what exclusion looked like; the second what inclusion would have looked like. The groups work together to design their snapshots. The room buzzes; laughter, deep concentration, touching.

One group at a time, they get up and form their bodies into scenes showing what happened. In one scene, three people are huddled together closely, laughing and pointing at the fourth person, who stands apart, looking stricken and sad. In another scene, little bits of paper are dumped on the head of one of the group members by another member while the others look on passively.

The second set of snapshots, showing inclusion, are also powerful: an arm reaches over and embraces the excluded person, the group shifts to make room for one more, bodies move closer together and the chasm is breached. They perform their snapshots by starting with the exclusion scene and then morphing it slowly into one of inclusion. The room is quiet; the pain of the first snapshot and the relief and spaciousness of the second are profound.

In the discussion which follows, one woman says, "That was my story the group did. I think I had made resolution with it in my head, but never in my body. Not until just now." A man comments, "Watching someone else play me—helped me to see how bad it really was. No wonder it hurt so much. I can see now that I wasn't crazy for having it affect me the way it did."

That the students are visibly moved by the experience is clear, but my own body feels different also. I notice my own healing myself as I watch their connection. When the session is over, no one leaves. We have shared an embodied lesson, and our bodies are different. There is a softening in the room and a gentleness in the air.

Describing a similar teaching experience, Shapiro states: "Our challenge as educators must be to transcend the traditional ways of educating the mind to envelop the wisdom of the body. It is in that wisdom where we find glimmers of compassionate connection, discernment of concrete existence, and the desire to live in a humane world" (2002b, 20).

The struggle to claim or reclaim bodies will not be an easy one. But, always, I come back to these questions: What would schools be like if every child gave and received loving touch every day? What if we connected what we know and feel about our own bodies and the bodies of those we love with all the other bodies in the world, knowing that the nations being bombed far away were populated by real people with real bodies, a lot like ours? Although the forces of repression, control, fear and standardization all militate against teaching and learning from an embodied position, every vision of such teaching is a beacon of hope. Every child who is touched lovingly, kindly, safely and respectfully carries that memory in her body. Every teacher who is allowed to teach from an embodied position brings that sensation to his future teaching as well. And every classroom in which children and teachers are allowed to be fully and completely human—embodied—allowed to cry, hug, dance, move, touch and connect, brings us closer to a world in which all humans are connected and peaceful as well. Let's keep moving our bodies in that direction.

References

Alsop, P. (1986) Dear Mr. Brown. Moose School Music (BMI). www.peteralsop.com.

Carlson, F. M., & Nelson, B. G. (2006) Reducing aggression with touch. *Dimensions, 34*, 3, 9–15.

Fine, M. (2003) Sexuality, schooling, and adolescent females: The missing discourse of desire. In A. Darder, M. Baltodano & R. D. Torres (Eds.), *The critical pedagogy reader* (pp. 296–321). New York: RoutledgeFalmer.

Finkelhor, D., & Ormrod, R. (2000) Characteristics of crimes against juveniles. *Bulletin.* Washington, DC: U.S. Department of Justice, Office of Justice Programs, Office of Juvenile Justice and Delinquency Prevention; www.ncjrs.gov/pdffiles/ojjdp/179034.pdf.

Foucault, M. (1977) Power/knowledge: Selected interviews and other writings, *1972–1977*, ed. C. Gordon. New York: Pantheon Books.

hooks, b. (1994) *Teaching to transgress: Education as the practice of freedom.* New York: Routledge.

Johnson, R. (1997) The "no touch" policy. In J. Tobin (Ed.), *Making a place for pleasure in early childhood education* (pp. 101–18). New Haven, CT: Yale University Press.

LaPlante, C. (2007) The kids are all right. *Massage Therapy Journal, 46*, 3, 74–81.

Leavitt, R. L., & Power, M. B. (1997) Civilizing bodies: Children in day care. In J. Tobin (Ed.), *Making a place for pleasure in early childhood education* (pp. 39–75). New Haven, CT: Yale University Press.

Phelan, A. M. (1997) Classroom management and the erasure of teacher desire. In J. Tobin (Ed.), *Making a place for pleasure in early childhood education* (pp. 76–100). New Haven, CT: Yale University Press.

Pitts, L. (2007) A thousand ways to disconnect, and now a hugging ban, too. www.commondreams.org/archive/2007/10/04/4313.

Shapiro, S. (2002). Toward a critical pedagogy of peace education. In G. Salomon & B. Nevo (Eds.), *Peace Education* (pp. 63–71). Mahwah, NJ: Lawrence Erlbaum Associates.

Shapiro, S. B. (2002a). The commonality of the body: Pedagogy and peace culture. In G. Salomon & B. Nevo (Eds.), *Peace Education* (pp. 143–54). Mahwah, NJ: Lawrence Erlbaum Associates.

Shapiro, S. B. (2002b). The body: The site of common humanity. In S. Shapiro, and S. Shapiro (Eds.), *Body movements: Pedagogy, politics, and social change* (p. 351). Creskill, NJ: Hampton Press.

Tobin, J. (1997) The missing discourse of pleasure and desire. In J. Tobin (Ed.), *Making a place for pleasure in early childhood education* (pp. 1–37). New Haven, CT: Yale University Press.

14
Worlds of Change
A Vision for Global Aesthetics

SHERRY B. SHAPIRO

Introduction

> The body knows and remembers even in the silences of our lives. In dance the familiar can become strange ... more than movement, it is the act of transformational possibility.

Globalization is not a new topic for discussion. Many of us have become aware of the changes in our societies and across the world that have come as direct or indirect responses to globalization. Current themes, whether concerning the economy, culture, transnational families or the environment, have become part of our global discussions. We cannot ignore the effects of globalization and how it challenges our notion of stable identities, unchanging traditions, or the processes that effect these changes. Fluidity and flux have come to be significant metaphors for the way we define our cultures and our world.

Because the arts, dance in particular, are a product of culture we tend to not "see the forest for the trees." My reference here speaks to assumptions we have about dance and its ability to speak across cultures using movement as a common language. Housed in this assumption is the notion that, *when dance is experienced as a cross-cultural event, we have created some form of positive partnership between differing peoples.* This is a nice romantic idea and one which I myself have shared. As I have had the opportunity to observe children from different countries and cultures, of different socio-economic backgrounds, and of a different race, or ethnicity, sex or physical ability, sharing dance experiences, I too can sometimes see a vision of *all* becoming equal as they transcend the barriers of difference. In these kinds of cross-cultural experiences, dance is understood as an avenue for providing a *common* language, as if this somehow transcends and obliterates all other differences. I do not wish to posit that this isn't a significant and valuable experience for children in and of itself but, rather, that we can ask more of the arts/dance than this. What is encouraged here is to enter into an examination of what dance can offer a global society. Perhaps going beyond sharing our cultural diversities in a communal space, learning each other's dances, or adding "world" or African dance to our curriculum, we might, in addition, consider how dance is being shaped through globalization. Even more importantly, how might we shape the effects of globalization through dance?

Dance, it is well understood, offers a unique and powerful form of human expression. It has the capacity to speak in a language that is visceral and far less mediated by our thoughts and abstract conceptualizations. It provides, at times, a raw embodied way of capturing human experience. Dance, too, allows free rein to the sensual and the sentient—things that elsewhere are often circumscribed by custom and convention. It also manifests that form of playfulness which is so delightfully found in young children and then often erased from adult life. Dance, like other forms of art, provides a space in which human beings can touch the transcendent—experiencing new or alternative possibilities that are outside of our "taken for granted" life practices; it is a space that encourages and nurtures the ability to imagine different ways of feeling and being in the world. And it is the human body which makes dance concrete. To think of dance in a way which makes the global leap, without an appropriation of the other's experiences assuming a hierarchical stance of cultural superiority or arrogance, calls for a sense of *global aesthetics*. Here, the question of course must be asked "What is a global aesthetics?"

I wish to draw upon the work of postmodern and feminist scholars who have written on the effects of globalization as a way to reconceptualize what it means for the arts to engage in human change in general, and, in particular, how the body, grounded in memory and experience, provides a potentially powerful resource for change. And I will discuss how the coexisting forces of self and other constitute the universal relationship in which the body becomes the concrete place where questions of human compassion *and* human barbarism are simultaneously engendered.

Writing from the "global North," and as a white female middle-class dance educator from the United States, I cannot dismiss the context of my perspectives and my privileged position. Acknowledging this position with sensitivity leads me to recognize my own limitations and perspectives. I seek only to be part of the larger discussion, recognizing my voice as important, but not as the voice of Truth.

Dominating Aesthetics

A global view of aesthetics recognizes diversity and acknowledges that there are multiple meanings in regards to "what is dance," or "what is good dance"—each responsive to the needs of different cultures in different social contexts, regions, societies and nations. Though we have begun to acknowledge the rich presence of diversity, have respect for a more multicultural approach to dance, and have developed our sense of honoring the "particular," we must also examine the underlying assumptions and dispositions we continue to hold as part of our embodied ideology of the aesthetic. What I mean by this is the way in which we continue to see particular dance forms as superior while giving other forms less value. This is an important first step as we seek to encounter seriously the meaning of the arts within the context of a global society.

Superior dance forms have typically been identified as Western European and historically situated within a structure dominated by men or a masculine paradigm. Though this is a fairly simple reductionist view of a complicated system, what I want to problematize is the very way in which dance has capitalized on the power of the global North to devalue and subsume the global South. While, to a certain extent, with our increased multicultural sensitivity we, in the global North, have given more "space, time and effort" in our classrooms and studios to the dances of the global South, this effort has been overshadowed by the powerful ability of the global market to erase differences and impose a homogenous cultural space. While we are encouraging learning in our classroom, about "other" cultures' dance, food, dress or songs, mass media such as music videos, MTV, and movies are pumping out dance, dress and music "24/7" to places across the globe. Whether it is hip-hop, Starbucks, or MacDonald's fast food, the customs of the global North have become the desired forms of expression and pleasure.

In a parallel way Western forms of dance are portrayed as the epitome of artistic expression. Recognizing this, I want to add my voice to the suspicion of any form of dance, such as ballet, that has universal pretensions or assumptions. There must be a balance between respecting cultural diversity without allowing claims for the privileged value of a particular culture or dance form over another. This proves to be no simple task. Respecting diversity while children across the globe seek to imitate the fashion, music and dances of the West seems of little consequence. The global media have far more power and control of what children and young people are exposed to in terms of dance than the "official" dance world.

Recognizing the power of the global media and market, we must also recognize the struggle against globalization as a force that homogenizes culture, that erases the particular, the local and the indigenous. It has only been in our recent history that we have begun to attempt to respect cultural diversity and sought to avoid ethnocentrism. Burn (2005, 8) talks about the need both to celebrate differences and to emphasize our commonalities in reference to the cross-cultural study of women. The goal of this sort of multiculturalism, or interculturalism, is in "helping people to understand, accept, and value cultural differences between groups, with the ultimate goal of reaping the benefits of diversity" (Ferdman 1995). The goal is both to celebrate differences and to emphasize the dimensions of commonality or inclusion that supersede these differences (Devine 1996).

A multicultural approach goes against what some regard as our natural human tendencies to reject people and cultures that are different than our own. We like to believe "our way of doing things" is the "right" way. Our discomfort with "those" who are different from "us" provides a challenge to dance within the complexity of achieving diversity within unity. The task is in finding ways which accept both the particular while, at the same time, managing to transcend the differences. What isn't answered is: Why is this important to dance? What is the goal?

Erasure at a Price

Critics of globalization have given much attention to the erasure of local traditions under the impact of transnational capitalism. They have made us far more mindful of the terrible losses that the erasure of these local traditions represent. Local customs, dialects, religious practices, crafts, artistic expression, foods and, of course, dance represent the accumulation of human wisdom, ingenuity and sensibility over the course of countless generations. Their mere existence enriches the cultural treasure of life on earth. They provide evidence of the almost infinite ways in which human beings have learned to adapt and negotiate their existence within their natural and social habitats.

The study of dance has in part included understanding that cultural traditions have been passed down through dance. We have learned to read dance as a text and have come to value how this reading can provide insights into a specific, and often "Other," culture's values, attitudes and beliefs. Whether looking at issues of gender, patriarchy, sexual orientation, relationships, or other representations of human identity, dance has provided us with an important avenue for making sense of, and understanding, the global culture. Understanding the power of dance to document this kind of historical, geographic and specific information about culture must lead us to think carefully about the erasure, homogenization or commodification of such forms of knowledge.

Conflicting Identities

Yet, another threat to indigenous traditions exists. Not only must we concern ourselves with the migratory circuit of Western influences of the global North into the global South, we also have what is termed "glocalizaton." Glocalization refers to a process where the local affects the global and the global or transnational influences the local. An example of this is *Riverdance,* which was developed explicitly as a hybrid Irish national dance reflecting some of the Irish dance traditions but also some of the more global styles emphasizing sensual energy, pulsating rhythms and romanticized imagery. *Riverdance* was created to appeal to an international audience so as to inject Ireland into the global scene. In the post-*Riverdance* era, Venable states there has been a global growth of Irish dance which continues to invent tradition. Indeed, she says "One of the most ironic aspects of Irish dance is the continual redefinition of the word 'traditional,' especially where movement is concerned" (1999, 286). Small, wee girls with their long curly wigs, tiaras, bejeweled costumes and laced shoes take their turn performing steps learned directly from the videos of *Riverdance.* They dance in the pubs for their family and friends, imaging the dream of unsurpassed beauty and becoming the "chosen" partner of one such as Michael Flatley.

What is the "real" dance becomes a common question in dance practices which are "borrowed," "infused," or considered a "hybrid" form of traditional dance. Though, of course, this phenomenon is not new in dance. Dance has always borrowed or taken from other cultures and expressive forms. What is different is the speed and ease with which the dance traditions are being influenced and changed, and often without acknowledgement or choice.

Not only do we question what is "real" dance because of its steps or form, but in the global market we are now challenged to answer the question whether dance is authentic if it is taught "out of culture." African dance provides us with an example of this situation. In a conversation with an African dance teacher at the University of Cape Town I asked the question, "Is it still considered African dance if it is taught by someone who is not African?" Of course, we must recognize first that there is no single African dance, and that insinuated in my question was also the question "What makes it African dance?" His answer did not surprise me. He said, "African dance is about a people's history, their stories, their life; one cannot simply take the steps and then be dancing African dance." Though others may not agree with his definition, his point cannot be dismissed. African dance, he argues, is a story of a people. It is not a series of steps to be learned as a dance style. As with other traditional dance forms, there are specific movements or gestures which represent particular ideas, expressions or emotions, though it is not the dance vocabulary which is important. What is significant is the story of the people.

Looking in my own backyard of dance in the United States, we find that seeking "diversity within unity" has been not been easy, nor have we found simple solutions. A good example of this can be found in Carol Paris's article "*Defining the African American Presence in Postmodern Dance from the Judson Church Era to the 1980.*" Here Paris lays out some of the difficult choices of African American choreographers during the early postmodern dance movement. With the aesthetic changes of the avant-garde artists where they "saw the body merely as the material for a movement for movement-sake approach; not the interpreter of emotions, linear narratives, musical melodies, or explosive rhythmic structures" (2001, 235), a conflict was presented to black choreographers. This change of aesthetics in dance in the United States happened at the same time as the civil rights movement, anti-war protest, and political assassinations. It was a historic time where some black choreographers wanted to continue to use the body and dance as a way of examining the social political world, and not simply as an exploration of dance or the process of making dance itself. The "black body" during the 1950s and 1960s in the United States could not be severed from its cultural identity, nor did many of the African American choreographers of the time want to strip this representative "black body" of its power to evoke the passionate narrative of oppression and desire for freedom. To give up this particular form of embodied expression also meant to silence a country's history, a people's story, and the chance to learn from our past.

Universalism as an Ideal

Yet, in the struggle against the erasure of differences or identities and the fight against homogenization, I do not argue to rid ourselves of universality. Indeed, my argument is more nuanced in regard to universal claims. My assertion is that there is a universality which must be attended to along with the particular. The danger is in saying we are all the same—and we are not; or in saying that one culture's forms and ideas are better than another's. My argument here is that, because dance and the body are one-in-the-same (dance does not exist without the body), dance has a unique possibility to advance what Burn defines as "*universalism—the idea that all humans share the same inalienable rights*" (2005, 313). To make such a giant leap from globalization to dance, the body and a universal human ideal creates a definite challenge to our cultural and ethical imaginations.

Taking care not to diminish the importance of difference, I nonetheless want to draw attention to how we might understand human existence through our commonalities. Perhaps it is seeing the fear, suspicion and hate that is so rampant in the world today that makes me want to search for, and affirm, our *common* human attributes. It is, I believe, the commonalities of our bodies that offer ways of valuing those *shared* biological, emotional and expressive human characteristics necessary for a more humane world. To address the importance of a common humanity is to understand that the struggle for *human* rights and *human* liberation is indispensable in a globalized world.

There is a compelling need to see the commonalities of human life—the shared and universal quality of human life (indeed of *all* life)—as central to our quest for purpose and meaning. More than anything, I believe, the body, *our bodies*, is what grounds our commonalities. To address the importance of a common humanity grounded in universality is to understand that the struggle for human rights and human liberation is necessary even while recognizing the danger of the term *human* as a vehicle for imposing a particular concept of who we are. It is hard to see how one can make the case for greater freedom, for greater justice, for the end to violence, for greater human rights, without an appeal to the notion of a common humanity.

The universal is not some abstract idea or ideal. Rather, it is to acknowledge someone as a subject, granting them the same status as oneself, to recognize their sacred otherness. Ethical practices occur in specific situations. Practices in and of themselves may or may not be ethical. Rather, the "rightness" of the action, as it affects the lives and experiences of those it is directed towards, determines ethical behavior. The "rightness" of an action is not reducible to a response to the other. It includes a responsiveness to their values, beliefs and principles, their aesthetic and religious sensibilities—the values and meanings of their worlds (Farley 1985). This is what we might call compassion or the ability to "suffer with" others.

Carved by the social order, designated as a representation of one's culture, the body has come to be understood as the aesthetic realm where meaning is made, life is experienced, and truth is understood as partial and relational. Accepting the body as the aesthetic realm, aesthetics necessarily becomes concerned with issues of power, justice, and the ethics of relationships. "The human drama," writes Morris Berman, "is first and foremost a somatic one" (1989, 108), or, as Emily Martin might suggest for understanding human history, one must dwell "at the level of the social whole, at the level of 'person,' and at the level of body" (1989, 15).

Transcending Limitations and Boundaries

Today we live in a global society where cultural globalization, the transnational migration of people, information, and consumer culture, is prevalent. Our ability to experience a virtual world, even as we physically might stay in one place, has changed our sense of boundaries, our sense of location, even our sense of time. Coming to recognize the imaginary or constructed nature of our boundaries—the narratives of country, race or ethnicity—even gender—has spurred us to deconstruct what was referred to earlier as "real" or "traditional." Within this context it is significant to understand that it is not dance that creates us, but we who create dance. And it is here, through this text written by the human body, that we can begin to engage in the process of recognizing and transcending the limitations and boundaries that up to now have closed off new possibilities. We can discover new ways to live, expand our sense of being, and establish new relationships with those who share our world (Shapiro & Shapiro 2002). The process calls us towards another kind of aesthetic or meaning-making process.

Meaning-making as an aesthetic act looks towards the rational *and* the sensual, the mind and the body, the individual and the society, the particular and the shared, an aesthetics "born of the recognition that the world of perception and experience cannot simply be derived from abstract universal laws, but demands its own appropriate discourse and displays its own inner, if inferior, logic" (Eagleton 1990, 16). Or, put more succinctly by Eagleton: "The aesthetic, then, is simply the name given to that hybrid form of cognition which can clarify the raw stuff of perception and historical practice, disclosing the inner structure of the concrete" (ibid.). A global aesthetics, then, moves beyond the individual or the self to connect to the other, recognizing the concreteness of an ethical existence in a shared world.

Human suffering extends *through and beyond* the boundaries of nationality, race, ethnicity, gender, social class, and sexual or religious preference—all the ways of marking ourselves off from others. *Here, in our shared physical suffering, in the commonality of the body, is a place of deeper and mutual understanding, and thus of transcendent possibility.*

The Suffering Body Questions the Integrity of Globalization

Media images transmitted globally, albeit used to support or deter particular political interests, have already proven their power of evoking an empathetic understanding and compassion for the other. Etched into our memories are images of Iraqi children who have been victims of improvised explosive devices; child soldiers forced into acts of brutality; images of women trying to escape from possible rape or disfigurement; faces of those to be, or having just been, executed; those subjected to the fear and shame of interrogation and torture; thousands of tent cities in Darfur and other regions where emaciated and starving refugees have been forced to flee acts of genocide; and the children of famine lying listlessly at their mother's breast where their life milk has dried up. *These global images are experienced not as abstractions but as the way we come face to face with our own humanity.* The suffering body transcends the particularity of human existence and becomes a potent means of generating a sense of shared humanity. Ana Maria Araújo Freire (1994) wrote passionately about the impact of the denial or prohibition on the body in her epilogue to Paulo Freire's book *Pedagogy of Hope.*

I am fed up with bans and prohibitions: bans on the body, which produce, generation after generation, not only Brazilian illiteracy (according to the thesis I maintain), but an *ideology* of ban on the body, which gives us our "street children," our misery and hunger, our unemployment and prostitution, and, under military dictatorship, the exile and death of countless Brazilians (Freire 1994, 204).

To blind ourselves to what the body experiences, what it feels and what we might experience through our empathy towards shared pain is dangerous, as it keeps us in the rational world where one can explain, without any necessary compassion or ethical sensibility, the problems of our world. But the body refuses to be understood as an abstract object. It is not other. It is real. It is the presence of all that we know, albeit housed in narratives of meaning.

To engage in *a global aesthetics with a universal ethics as its goal* would require from us a different kind of dance education. Pedagogically we begin with the body—the body understood as the concrete material inscribed by cultural values, local and global, and the vehicle for transcending our limited social identities. A pedagogy of the body may direct us towards the recognition of a universal humanity, the still radical idea that all humans share the same inalienable rights.

Pedagogic practices that draw upon the body, and aesthetic processes which provide ways of understanding the world and ourselves intellectually, sensually, mentally and emotionally are all but non-existent in traditional educational texts, teacher education programs, classroom practices or dance studios. This absence is troubling at a time when the body has become so central to theory and cultural practice—troubling because it is the body where the global influences of the West shape our images of physical beauty, success and desire. Laurie McDade (1987) writes that knowing in the mind does not lie dormant, separate from the knowing of the heart and of the body.

> Everyday moments of teaching at school in communities, then, are personal, pedagogical, and political acts incorporating mind and bodies of subjects, as knowers and as learners. When we are at our best as teachers we are capable of speaking to each of these ways of knowing ourselves and our students. And we may override precedents in the educational project that value the knowing mind and deny the knowing of the heart and body. Students, the partners in this enterprise of knowing, are whole people with ideas, with emotions, and with sensations. If we, as teachers, are to arouse passions now and then (Greene 1986, 441) the project must not be confined to a knowing only of the mind. It must also address and interrogate what we think we know of the heart and of the body. (McDade 1987, 58–9)

Some of the reasons for the dismal construction of pedagogic practices that exclude embodied knowledge and aesthetic processes are the lack of prior educational experiences of teachers, the lack of understanding of how body knowledge can contribute to a broader social critique, the inability to turn it into an EOG (end of grade) test, or perhaps the need to be able to order and control knowledge which is defied by a curriculum in which students genuinely seek their own meaning.

In the following I want to share an example of how one might draw upon embodied knowledge and connect it to social and ethical critique. This act of educating for a kind of global aesthetics cuts across cultures and unites the arts/dance in the struggle for connection, healing (that is, overcoming fragmentation and making whole) and compassion. Each of these speaks to the need for us to see ourselves, and experience ourselves, as part of a larger community in which the quality of our lives is inextricably connected to the wellbeing of others. Though I will be describing a process I have created for dance, it is by no means only for dance, or only for the arts.

By the Virtue of Being Human

As Twyla Tharp said, "Modern dance is more, not less." I would add, "Teaching dance is more, not less." Only those who haven't been teachers hold the old adage "Those who can't dance teach." What we as educators come to know is that teaching demands us to know something about "what is" and "what is possible" of our students and of our discipline. Some important questions that confront us as dance educators are: What should we teach? How should we teach? Who should we teach? What is the role of the teacher? and, most importantly, For what are we teaching?

Asking the question "What is?" brings us to question dance. Is it a discipline? Is it an art form? Is it a way of learning about other disciplines? Is it something to learn in itself? Can it tell us something about our cultures and ourselves? Is it a way of knowing the world, or something to know? Can it tell us about the human condition? These are questions about visions that compel us to examine dance in the broader context of education. They ask of us to name what it is we care about, what concerns us, and, further, what our vision for humanity is and how education gives shape to this articulated vision. These questions take us beyond dance, recognizing the moral and political connections that accompany any act of education. It is an act of transcendence reminding us that education, any education, must engage the life-world of our students in all of their different narratives that are shaped by ethnicity, harnessed by social class and textured by culture. To know ourselves is to understand the way our thoughts, ideas and desires are always bound up with the way of being that comes from the lives that emerge out of both our local situations and the matrix of global influences. Such a pedagogy engaged in ideological critique inevitably raises moral concerns. It exposes questions of social injustice, inequality, asymmetrical power, and the lack of human rights or dignity.

Over the past fifteen years I have worked in the field of dance education, teaching at a small liberal arts college for women in the southern United States. In this position I have had the opportunity to evolve in my own thinking about dance education: from the most primitive ways of teaching, of having students reproduce the steps they have been given; progressing on to creative movement, where students learn to create from a movement vocabulary; and finally arriving at a philosophy for education/arts/dance which has as it focus the development of a critical global aesthetic process, which takes students through questions of identity and otherness, and towards compassionate and ethically responsible behavior. I will share one example of this pedagogic philosophy in my choreographic work; it is this philosophy or vision through which all the courses I teach are filtered.

This particular choreographic example centers on the biblical story of the relationship between Hagar and Sarah. I selected this story as it lends itself to raising issues of power, jealousy, domination of the stranger, compassion, and the value of women in society (the value of women as determined by their ability to bear children). For students in a women's college in North Carolina (considered to be part of the 'Bible belt' in the U.S.) this narrative takes on special significance, as Christianity has played an important role in their development as ethical human beings and in providing meaning to their own lives. This story offered them a powerful and resonant narrative from which they could critically examine issues in their own lives. I read parts of the chapters in Genesis, asking that they discuss their interpretations of this story. Specifically, I asked them to write a reflection about an experience they had had, in their own lives, that made them feel as other. Each student wrote about ones they remembered. There was little hesitation in naming such experiences. I asked them to reflect upon their memories and to return to their felt experiences. They shared with each other times they had been shunned, unable to become part of groups they so desperately wanted to "be in," of times families separated, and of times they didn't possess the "right" characteristics to be socially acceptable. From their embodied memories they created movements that expressed their life stories, reflecting their pain, humiliation and sorrow.

Next, I asked them to reflect upon times they had made others to feel as the stranger. At first they said they didn't remember any times they had done this. Blocked by their inability to accept their own behavior, which might have been experienced as hurtful or cruel by others, they were saved from, or avoided, a sense of responsibility. Also, at times, their level of understanding did not allow them to see the larger structures in which they participate in the everyday world, whether in their religious beliefs, choice of roommates, fear of black men, or, more significantly, ignorance of the larger social structures in which they are able to enter a place of privilege as white middle-class women. Yet, they did remember. They had to acknowledge their own participation, whether through action or non-action; to acknowledge experiences in which they had ignored, distanced themselves from, and even allowed themselves to believe that the plight of the less fortunate is simply because they are either too lazy to do better or that they just don't care or fail to make the effort. As one student noted: "They [the poor] don't deserve what I have or they would have it." (Let me say that these women I work with would describe themselves as "Christians"—concerned, caring and compassionate—and see themselves as women who are generous, who have "big hearts".) Again, after writing their own stories, sharing with others and discussing their experiences within the larger questions about who deserves to live well, they re-created their stories through movement.

I need to say here that for the students to enter into their feelings requires more than to talk about them. I use the modality of movement and the body as both the critical and the creative tool to form the connections between what they know but have yet to name. *Talking is not enough to address people's feelings.* Here the arts can offer a powerful pedagogy. Too often the arts are thought about only in ways that relate to performance or technical virtuosity, or as something beautiful in the traditional sense of the aesthetic. Using movement as a pedagogic method, as I do, allows students to focus on their bodies, not as objects to be trained, but rather as subjects of their world. They come to know their bodies as possible actors in history, as well as repositories of history. Indeed, without this sense of agency there can be no talk of emancipation and possibility. Education, for the most part, continues to disavow the aesthetic process as something that can tell us the "what is" of their lives and "what might be." At the least for aesthetic processes, the expectation is that students will gain skills in perceiving, interpreting, selecting, shaping and synthesizing meaning so as to create coherence and clarity in how they see the world. They learn to attend to their existential projects, their feelings and their beliefs, thinking creatively and imaginatively. But, most significantly, they learn how to name the world as they experience it. To move into a global aesthetics would mean to transcend art itself and connect this meaning-making process to self and world. In transferring these aesthetic ways of knowing and directing them towards critical, ethical and embodied social analysis, students begin to engage in a radical pedagogy, and possibly in a sense of universal connections and responsibilities. Engaged in such a pedagogy, they come to understand the relational and therefore moral aspect of life. Or, as Zygmunt Bauman suggests, they can reach a place where they may "grasp hold of the self and ... awaken it as an active moral agent disposed to care for the other; a self that experiences a sense of obligation even before it grasps the Other's existence" (Smith, 1999, 181).

The final question I asked, in the process described here, referred the students back to a time in the story when Sarah hears God speaking to Abraham about her forthcoming pregnancy. I asked them to reflect upon a time when they were surprised by something, which they thought could not happen, actually did happen to them, as it did to Sarah. My expectation was that they would name joyous memories. Instead, each and every one told stories of pain and sorrow: a father's suicide, a mother's mental illness and family breakdown, a rape by a teacher, an affair that led to the end of a marriage and the beginning of another. They cried, they mourned, they told things that shamed them. *They did what they are not allowed to do in schools.* They shared the things that make them most human, their erotic selves. *They integrated themselves into the world of feeling, and of common humanity, capturing the transformative possibility of education.* As mentioned earlier, what is of concern here is not so much the methodology but the vision and the philosophy. Guided by a purpose of education concerned with social justice and moral agency, the methodology, I argue, must elicit possibilities for students to examine the social construction of their reality, reflect upon and experience themselves as rational and sensual beings, and be brought to question the significance and meaning of their own lives. I use a pedagogic form of movement, as well as reflective writing, discussion, poetry, reading, video viewing, eating together, performing together—all those ways of connecting the personal and the political, ourselves to one another, and each to a sense of responsible choices. It is to this place that any education concerned with an ethical humanity must be brought. This is not an approach that should be viewed as either affective *or* cognitive, *or* moral, but one that transcends those differences, remembering that, as Martin Heidegger argued, "Reason is the perception of what is, which always means also what can be and ought to be" (1968, 41). It is this understanding of reason that concerns itself with possibility grounded in sensate-lived experience and made sense of through critical understanding and global ethical responsibility. Through this process of *sensual-reasoning* one can become actively engaged in re-fusing the mind and body, the particular and the universal, the self and the stranger (Shapiro 1999).

The dance which results from this process of reflection and connection takes form through imaging the joys and struggles of the dancers' lives. It speaks a language of common humanity to the audience, as it represents memories of self and other. Through this critical/aesthetic process, the students named their own oppressions and ways in which they oppressed others. They recognized that their bodies hold knowledge of their world, and they learned the meaning of their bodies as the materiality of existence. Coming to know themselves as body/subjects, they explored, examined and created connections between inner sensibilities (local) and outer context (global). The body memories that have been central to my pedagogy are, at least in part, records of the *felt world* of self and other in all of its sensuous and relational qualities. It is surely the latter that grounds the desire for a different kind of world—one of compassion, love and justice. Remembering in this sense becomes the act of identifying the self in all of its creative, critical and ethical dimensions; it becomes the process of finding a home in this torn and afflicted world (Shapiro 1999).

The overfocus on the cognitive in education has left us with people who can build smart bombs, has provided means of efficient interrogation, and has supplied us with obedient soldiers. But let us not forget the moral challenge posed by the solitary individual when confronted by the stranger. What responsibility do I feel for the other? As Bauman (1998) argues, this feeling, this moral urge, is inherent in the human context. It is rooted in the autonomy of the I and its need for relationship. Where moral rules have disintegrated with the postmodern, there remain only moral standards—standards that demand interpretation and choice. Our challenge as educators must be to transcend the traditional ways of educating the mind to envelop the wisdom of the body. It is in that wisdom that we find glimmers of compassionate connection, discernment of concrete existence, and the desire to live in a humane world.

Conclusion

Like nothing else in the education of our children, art offers ways to transcend a consciousness that fixes our world as if it is something that is unchangeable—to see the "what is" of our world and to imagine "what might be." And, as it nurtures the imagination of children and attends to their perceptions, it helps to develop them that they are able to reimagine and reshape their world. Here is where art lays the groundwork for addressing the challenges of globalization. This includes challenging the limited capabilities and powers of our democratic and civic institutions towards new transnational reality. "The results," as Falk notes, "have not been pretty: frequent warfare, many incidents of ethnic cleansing and genocide, catastrophic risks of environmental collapse, massive poverty, a disregard for future generations" (2003, 188). We can begin to understand the critical responsibility of art in a world where children are taught to accept and conform to "what is" and not to question what they are taught or the nature of their own experience. Though art cannot, or should not, be a direct mirror of life, it should tell us about life in ways that, as Maxine Greene (1988) says, make the familiar strange and the strange familiar. In other words, it should help us both to see what was obscured or hidden before and to imagine that which was unimaginable. Arts education, then, becomes revolutionary as it shows us reality in ways that heighten our perceptions, and presents images to us of what might be possible or preferable.

As dance educators we can assist children in learning how to give voice to their life stories through dance. Not only is moving their own stories pedagogically valuable, as seen in the previous example, as a way in which to deepen their understanding of who they are, but also moving them for others provides a place for students to share their stories. In voicing their stories a dialogue can begin. In learning how to represent the world as they experience it, they become better able to see themselves in others, and better able to develop that empathy for the life of another that a global aesthetics and universalism demands.

Such a community, unlike our present fragmented and competitive world, would be a place we can count on and be secure in, where we understand each other, where we are never an outcast or a stranger, where we trust each other, and where we are safe and our wellbeing is assured. While such a community represents the kind of world that is not yet available to us, it is, I believe, the loving and just world our children need and deserve. And it is one which we, as educators, must struggle to make possible.

References

Bauman, Z. (1998) *Globalization: The Human Consequences.* New York: Columbia University Press.

Berman, M. (1989) *Coming to Our Senses: Body and Spirit in the Hidden History of the West.* New York: Bantam Books.

Burn, S. M. (2005) *Women across Cultures: A Global Perspective* (2nd ed.). New York: McGraw-Hill.

Devine, J. (1996) *Maximum Security: The Culture of Violence in Inner-City Schools.* Chicago: University of Chicago Press.

Eagleton, T. (1990) *The Ideology of the Aesthetic.* Oxford: Blackwell.

Falk, R. (2003) *The Great Terror War.* New York: Olive Branch Press.

Farley, W. (1985) *Eros for Other: Retaining Truth in a Pluralistic World.* University Park: Pennsylvania State University Press.

Ferdman, B. M. (1995) Cultural Identity and Diversity in Organizations: Bridging the Gap between Differences and Individual Uniqueness. In M. M. Chemers, S. Oskamp & M. A. Costanzo (Eds), *Diversity in Organizations: New Perspectives for a Changing Workplace.* Thousand Oaks, CA: Sage.

Freire, P., & Araújo Freire, A. M. (1994) *Pedagogy of Hope: Reliving Pedagogy of the Oppressed.* New York: Continuum.

Greene, M. (1986) In Search of a Critical Pedagogy. *Harvard Educational Review, 56,* 427–41.

Greene, M. (1988) *The Dialectic of Freedom.* New York: Teachers College Press.

Heidegger, M. (1968) *What is Called Thinking.* trans. F. Wieck & J. Gray. New York: Harper & Row.

Martin, E. (1989) The Cultural Construction of Gendered Bodies: Biology and Metaphors of Production and Destruction. *Ethnos, 54*, 143–60.

McDade, L. (1987) Sex, Pregnancy, Schooling: Obstacles to a Critical Teaching of the Body. *Journal of Education, 169*, 3, 58–79.

Paris, C. (2001) Defining the African American Presence in Postmodern Dance from the Judson Church Era to the 1990. *CORD 2001: Transmigratory Moves: Dance in Global Circulation*, 234–43.

Shapiro, S., & Shapiro, S. (Eds.) (2002) *Body Movements: Pedagogy, Politics, and Social Change.* Creskill, NJ: Hampton Press.

Shapiro, S. B. (1999) *Pedagogy and the Politics of the Body: A Critical Praxis.* New York: Garland.

Smith, D. (1999) *Zygmunt Bauman: Prophet of Postmodernity.* Oxford: Blackwell.

Vernable, E. (1999) Inventing Tradition: Innovation and Survival. *CORD 2000: Transmigratory Moves: Dance in Global Circulation*, 281–90.

15
Teaching Like Weasels

Hephzibah Roskelly

"A weasel is wild," Annie Dillard notes, as she begins the story of her encounter with one in a field behind her suburban house. "Who knows what he thinks?" She is sitting quietly on a log, Dillard relates, when something makes her swivel around suddenly. A weasel is staring at her, and she stares back at him, transfixed by seeing one for the first time. The next moment connects them. "I tell you I've been in that weasel's brain for sixty seconds, and he was in mine. Brains are private places, muttering through unique and secret tapes—but the weasel and I both plugged into another tape simultaneously, for a sweet and shocking time" (1988, 2). The essay, full of clear observations and details about the weasel's habits and even speculations about what he thinks, is not really about weasels. "Living Like Weasels" is instead about Dillard and how the experience with the weasel challenged and changed her.

Though she doesn't learn what a weasel thinks, she does learn something of what she thinks. "I would like to learn, or remember, how to live … And I suspect that for me the way is like the weasel's: open to time and death painlessly, noticing everything, remembering nothing, choosing the given with a fierce and pointed will" (1988, 2). Dillard's sudden understanding of the need to grasp "our one true necessity" and not let go is occasioned by her experience, her recognition and sympathy with the wild animal she locks eyes with, and her willingness to reflect and be altered by what she has learned outside herself and within. Conscious of the particulars of her situation—middle-aged, white, female, naturalist—she uses them to find the larger connections that link her to the weasel and to her readers, who might learn something too from the energy, direction and tenaciousness she has witnessed.

Once you tease it out, Dillard's weasel story presents a fair definition of the word *experience* itself, and it's this word I want to focus on as I examine the challenges posed to today's educators in classrooms, where experience—whether in school or brought from home—has been increasingly squeezed out in favor of pre-packaged curricula and predetermined tests. As Dillard illustrates it, experience has to do with listening, speaking, changing, being changed. The term *experience* is fraught with difficulties and complications, however, and perhaps its ambiguities become one reason why education czars at state and national levels ignore it. But the increasing power of assessment strategists in schools, as well as the current popularity of theory that is suspicious of experience in universities, has compromised teachers' ability to use experience to teach. From both Right and Left, from efficiency experts and ideological conservatives who create education mandates that value general testing over local teaching to postfeminist and poststructuralist critics who caution that experience too easily becomes normative, schools are taught the lesson that experience is indeed far too compromised a concept to be a valid tool for learning. And, as I hope to show, teachers and students must be able to make experience the central and crucial component in their educational lives, as it is in their lives outside school.

In this essay, I'll examine the word *experience,* considering how education imperatives and poststructuralist critiques diminish and misread it. Using the pragmatic philosophy of John Dewey and the current realist postmodern approach of literary critic Satya Mohanty, I'll suggest some new definitions and some uses for the word that might restore experience as a ground for knowledge as well as for a critique of the ideological pressures that deny it.

If John Dewey had been able to read Dillard's meditation on experience and weasels, he might have been less unhappy with the characterization philosopher Ralph Perry made of experience as "a weasel word," a phrase sometimes mistakenly attributed to Dewey himself. Dewey objected to the metaphor for the association Perry intended with the weasel's supposed slipperiness, slyness and elusiveness. On the contrary, Dewey spent lots of time and several books to illustrate the ways in which experience is precisely not slippery, but grounded; not ambiguous but definable, testable and usable. He suggests that its critics dislike experience because its users both claim empiricism and reject the subjectivity inherent in empirical methods (1925, 1). This double meaning exposes the weasel-like nature of the word, and it presents a dilemma for theorists and practitioners. As Dewey suggests, the trap of experience lies in the belief in the perils of the subjective no matter how "true" the experiential moment, and the trap can only be avoided by completely rejecting experience as a ground for knowledge.

But Dewey is having none of it. Responding to the ambiguity Perry claims with his weasel metaphor, he asserts that the definition of experience is indeed empirical: "what the unsophisticated man [not the professional philosopher] calls experience, the life he has led and undergone in the world of persons and things" (1925, 6). But experience is empirical in rich ways, including mystery as well as facts, implicit assumptions and explicit evidence. Experience, he avows, is "something at least as wide and deep and full as all history on this earth" (ibid., 11), history denoting objective conditions, forces, events and also the human record and estimation of these events. "History," he says, "is always both subjective and objective, so with 'experience'" (ibid.).

The "double-barrelled fact" of experience, to use William James's term, means that, within individuals—and among them—experience is both social and socially verifiable rather than uniquely personal or private. A thinker should interpret experience "not in the sense in which he uses it when he implies that experience is momentary, private and psychical" (James 1904). Dewey answers critics of experience who, he notes, are quick to ask *Whose experience?* by suggesting that because experience is individual does not mean it is always, or indeed *ever,* merely that. "The implication is that experience is always somebody's, but that the peculiar nature of 'somebody' infects experience so pervasively that experience is *merely* somebody's and hence of nobody and nothing else" (1925, 5). Experience might always, is always, somebody's, but for Dewey it's always more than *mere* because it is always tested with other and others' experience, thus always modified and reframed, always ready to challenge systematic generalizations. His warning against supposed objective and simple generalizations might be offered to today's assessment idealists: "Empirical method warns us that systems we set out from things said to be ultimate and simple have always worked with loaded dice, their premises have been framed to yield desired conclusions" (1938, 30). Experience resists desired conclusions setting agendas.

Dewey's broad definition for experience, on the other hand, is complicated, as he admits: "Experience warns us that the tangled and complex is what we usually find; that we work from and within it" (1938, 32). It may be that the very complexity of listening to, and acting on, empirical experiential understanding works against its use in systems such as public education, increasingly designed to pare away complexity in favor of simple solutions. The "back to basics" movement, devoted to pursuing the simple—what every child should know—is one example. Back to basics instruction, teach and test methodology, objective assessment measures are all designed to be simple, and they work in direct opposition to Dewey's progressive schools concept, one that was only somewhat popular in the 1930s in some areas of this country, as it attempted to confront rather than deny the complexity presented by experience.

Dewey was formulating his pragmatic notions of the role of experience in knowledge and consequently in pedagogy at the same moment that another movement, far more widespread, was being popularized across the country. In 1898, Frederick Taylor began to examine the operations at a steel plant in Bethlehem, Pennsylvania, conducting a time–motion study of workers and their work that led him to design management principles for greatest efficiency— defined as what was quickest and least expensive—on the job. His findings revolutionized organizational management, and by the time Dewey was writing *Experience and Nature* in 1925, Taylorism had become an established method in school administration.

Taylor's aim, to show Americans how the "fundamental principles of scientific management are applicable to all kinds of human activities," was realized in powerful ways in business, in government and in the home; cooking became food management, housekeeping became home management. And, by 1907, William Bagley was writing *Classroom Management*, a textbook for teachers in training that stressed methods of efficiency and economy. Classroom management is "a problem of economy; it seeks to determine in what manner the working unit of the school plant may be made to return the largest dividend upon the material investment of time, energy, and money" (Callahan 1962, 152). The textbook went through thirty printings between 1907 and 1927.

"In the past the man has been first; in the future the system must be first," Taylor argued (Callahan 1962, 150). Putting the system first was one of Taylor's primary principles; it did away with the messiness of individual desire or exception. It allowed for objectivity: once the data were in on how quickly it should take a worker to haul ten barrels of coal, workers who hauled seven were clearly unacceptable because inefficient. It established clear standards—often written for workers on small cards—that indicated the correct procedures, which hand to pick up the bucket with, where to tip it, when to turn—that workers only had to memorize and conform to in order to be successful. Taylorism was a hit, promoting a passion for succeeding, and suggesting the simplicity of solutions to problems, including the problems ushered in by the new immigrants who brought new languages, habits and experiences to bear on their work and their education.

Raymond Callahan's insightful and sobering *Education and the Cult of Efficiency* (1962) traces the history of the efficiency movement in education and illustrates the continuing dominance of Taylorism in public education. In the more than forty years since its publication, Taylorism, under new names—Total Quality Management, accountability, teacher proof curriculum, end of course tests, No Child Left Behind—has continued to determine how students and teachers lead their school lives, and how learning and teaching take place. More than ever, it seems, the system must be first.

It is not difficult to see that Taylorism has only strengthened its hand in the earlier 21st century. The kind of education Dewey criticizes, which refuses to examine the power and purposes of those taught and trains its vision only on its own purposes and procedures—what Dewey called the "objective conditions"—has become increasingly the norm in American education. Dewey's insistence upon experience as the crucial component in human thought and in education has been trumped by a counter-insistence on efficiency: plans that supersede individuals' performance of them, tests that are standardized rather than locally created, accountability measures that are never adapted, but only adapted to.

As Linda Darling-Hammond puts it, today's school reformers, at state and federal levels, see their mission to "design controls rather than develop capacity" (1997, 6); that is, in Taylor fashion, to make the system, not the person, the primary goal. High-stakes testing at state or federal level is one stunning example of the desire to control design as a solution to the problem of schools. Test makers and school officials look for just the right test that will measure achievement— the right preparation, the right questions—as though the exact combination of data will unquestionably guarantee that learning has or has not taken place in the classroom. Tom Newkirk argues, in a critique of writing research, that Taylorism manifested by testing operates as a "conspiracy against experience" (1991, 128). Newkirk notes that the academy has always demonstrated a limited tolerance for lived experience, which it easily dismisses as "anecdotes" or "stories" in favor of "objectivity" (ibid., 129). Touching on the gendered dimensions of this conspiracy, Newkirk suggests that the attempt to discredit experience, especially in education and child-rearing, devalues the knowledge of "those most intimately involved in raising and educating children—women" (ibid., 132). Lessening the value of experience as knowing perpetuates a "patriarchal system where a separate class, largely male (planners, researchers, theorists), presumes to test, sanction or overrule that experiential knowledge (ibid.).

Whether "experience" and the category "feminine" are directly linked and thus disparaged may be arguable, but it's undeniable that test-makers and the thousands of test purchasers in schools across the country have bought into designing controls rather than developing capacity, elevating Dewey's "objective conditions" and suppressing the experience Dewey found at the center of learning. The newest of school reforms, the No Child Left Behind Act, which President George Bush signed into law on January 8, 2002, is far reaching in its insistence on the mission of schools as being to design controls rather than develop capacity. The language of NCLB is the language of the market: accountability, assessment, value received for costs incurred. Claiming to improve the education of all students, especially the poor and minority students, NCLB provisions depend upon standardized and "objective" accountability and assessment measures that demonstrate schools' effectiveness and student success. The rise in achievement testing under NCLB is dramatic: every child in every state is tested every year, from grades 3 to 8. Schools are required to post "report cards" that chart students' scores on standardized assessments. If schools don't make "adequate yearly progress," signaled by student test scores, schools become targeted for remediation; parents are allowed to move students to schools with higher performing student scores once a low test score school becomes in euphemistic phrase a "school of choice." All schools perform against a benchmark— National Association for Educational Progress, or NAEP—which determines average scores and reasonable growth for students in each grade.[1]

Chris Gallagher summarizes what appears to be the simple and logical approach of accountability through high-stakes testing measures like NCLB:

> Schools must prove to those who pay the bills—taxpayers as well as parents, who invest human capital—that they are a good investment. And they must do so by performing well in a competitive market. They must show *results*, expressed in terms of achievement scores (accountants need numbers). If they underperform, they must adopt the practices of higher performers (i.e. standardize). Complacent or incompetent workers (teachers) must be retooled or let go. Efficiency and economy must be paramount. All of these demands are leveraged by the imposition of incentives and disincentives. (2007, 7)

Michael Apple seconds this description of education under the rule of tests by suggesting the ways in which the belief in testing and accountability measures expose an even deeper belief in the neutrality of such measures:

> The ultimate arbiter of whether we have been successful at this [educating the young] is students' mean gains on achievement tests. A neutral curriculum is linked to a neutral system of accountability, which in turn is linked to a system of school finance. Supposedly, when it works well, these linkages guarantee reward for merit. "Good" students will learn "good" knowledge and will get "good" jobs. (2001, 6)

In Apple's formulation, neutral is opposed to the local or interactive or experiential. It is an "objective condition," efficient and thus immutable.

The Taylorist desire for control of design, and for assessments and measures of teaching effectiveness that escape subjectivity, is what Dewey hoped to tease out in his discussion (and dismissal) of the weasel nature of "experience." As Dewey argues, experience is truly educative "only when the objective conditions of education [teachers, books, equipment, tests] are subordinated to what goes on in individuals having experiences" (1938, 37). Not the subject, not the test, but learning and the learner.

Dewey was not just interested in the experience the learner brought with them and how it might be used, but devoted to fostering the interaction between what he called an "internal" and the objective condition—the connection between learners' experience and the developing work of the classroom, where experiences build on one another within and among the students. For him, that interaction defined education. The trouble with traditional education, as Dewey sees it, is in its ignoring of the interaction necessary for learning. It wasn't that educators shouldn't attempt to create an optimal environment for learning, he said. "The trouble was that they did not consider the other factor in creating an experience; namely the powers and purposes of those taught" (ibid., 39). If experience does not alter the objective conditions, then, according to Dewey, "the process of learning and teaching becomes *accidental*" rather than purposive (ibid., 44–5). Dewey's principle of interaction shows that a failure to adapt material to the learner causes lack of success in learning every bit as significant as when the individual fails to adapt to the material.

Yet, for many conservative education reformers, using experience highlights precisely what is wrong with education, as measures that make room for diverse experience seem directly in opposition to unified cultural and educational goals. Cameron McCarthy and Greg Dimitriadis call this reaction part of a "discourse of resentment," a reaction to the bewildering changes wrought by globalization and governmental intrusions. As the authors argue, the discourse of resentment propels conservative agendas to dismantle affirmative action programs, for example, or to affirm English-only policies in schools (2005, 332–3). These discourses also imply that solutions are near at hand because the problems result from individual lack. "These resentment discourses have a conversationalizing dimension … the new medium for rendering the difficult problems of political and social life accessible and amenable to individual agency and wish fulfillment" (ibid., 331).

Testing is another way that resentment operates, for testing makes up for and exposes the inadequacies of individual teachers, schools, students. In *Culture Wars* (1986), Ira Shor argues that testing organizations such as ETS have suggested that equality operates in competition with excellence and that school declines are the result of teacher and student inadequacy, a problem with people, not systems. NCLB's insistence on standards of progress, corrective action for poorly performing schools, and hope for national curriculum supports Shor's contention. In January, 2008, the New York City school system announced plans to measure and reward some 2,500 teachers on the basis of students' standardized test scores. Deputy chancellor of schools Chris Cerf acknowledged that, while personal circumstances and experiences may be taken into account, "This isn't about how hard we try. This is about however you got here, are your students learning?" (Medina 2008).

As Dewey continually affirmed, testing is deeply a part of experience. Using experience to test education allows education's purposes to be formed. "There is no discipline in the world so severe as the description of experience subjected to the tests of intelligent development and direction" (1938, 114). Unless investigators as well as students and teachers consider process, "how you got here," as well as products, in other words, any learning that happens is incidental and unplanned.

Because experience is always ultimately social rather than private, it is always necessarily dynamic and partial, as it is reflected on and used. Yet it is on these grounds—its partiality and its subjectivity—that experience is disclaimed in some recent poststructuralist and feminist theory. These critical approaches, used and taught by researchers and theorists in the university, inevitably become part of the training of teachers. In many ways, the poststructuralist critique of experience offers a needed warning about the dangers of normalizing experience and thus stereotyping and reifying behaviors and capabilities of learners. However, the critique also deepens the divide between *subjective* and *objective*, *local* and *general*, *experience* and *idea*, divisions that Dewey challenged. As such, the postmodern critique of experience makes the work of responding to the accountability/assessment craze in education even more difficult.

The questions poststructuralists ask about experience are the very ones that Dewey insists teachers ask of themselves and of students: *Who is speaking? Who is hearing?* and, especially, *Whose experience?* For the poststructuralist critic, rejecting the totalizing claims that experience can offer means resisting the lure of a unified notion of experience. Feminist critic Jane Flax, for example, argues that experiences often seem plausible even when they are not at all representative in great measure because they reflect "important aspects of those who dominate our social world" (1987, 626). She applauds the corrective effect postmodernists have had on considerations of experience: "Feminists like other postmodernists, have begun to suspect that all such transcendental claims [to cultural norms] reflect and reify the experience of a few persons—mostly white, Western males" (ibid., 622).

The essentialist tendencies that seem to accompany experience have made many activists and academics alike question the role of identity and the experience that makes it up as theoretically incoherent or practically pernicious. As an example of how poststructuralist critics read experience as unhelpful or even dangerous, hear Gayatri Spivak explaining why, in her essay on *Jane Eyre*, she doesn't discuss the experience or "subjectivity" of Jane in the text:

> If we read this account from an isolationist perspective in a "metropolitan" context, we see nothing there but the psychobiography of a militant female subject. In a reading such as mine, in contrast, the effort is to wrench oneself away from the mesmerizing focus of the "subject-constitution" of the female individualist. (2005, 194)

The experience of the fictional Jane, in other words, draws needed attention away from the larger social/cultural conditions that she represents. Without a refusal of her experience as a "militant female subject," the reader cannot penetrate the power relations and cultural conditions that produced Jane in the first place.

For Spivak and other influential poststructuralist critics, experience is *mere* when it is seen in isolation from its larger cultural and especially theoretical concerns. It becomes usable only with generalizing concepts that put experience into its place. Otherwise, it is both too totalizing and too slippery to be more than a hindrance to learning.

Historian Joan Scott also worries about the reification of experience and the naturalization of it when experience in any individual is expressed: "Making visible the experience of a different group," she notes, exposes the existence of repressive mechanisms, but not their inner workings or logics; we know that difference exists, but we don't understand it as relationally constituted. For that we need to attend to the historical processes that, through discourse, position subjects and produce their experiences. It is not individuals who have experience, but subjects who are constituted through experience. (1994, 369)

The passive voice is deliberate in that last sentence. People don't have experiences; they are had by them—and who "they" might be or what "them" constitutes is left ambiguous.

Feminist Marxist critic Teresa Ebert appears in her work to oppose the diminishing of experience in favor of theory, suggesting that theory and experience exist in dialectic: "Experience only seems local; it is, like all cultural and political practices, interrelated to other practices and experiences, and as such its explanation comes from its 'outside'" (1996, 19). Theory is an understanding of this outside and an explanation of experience. Ebert claims that the role of experience lies in its connection to theory. "Theory historicizes experience and displays the social relations that have enabled it to be experienced as experience. Such a knowledge prevents us from essentializing experience and makes it possible to produce new experiences by transforming the dominant social relations" (ibid., 22). Still, experience and theory are separate entities in Ebert's formulation, and the generalizing theory dominates the more immediate experience.[2]

Dewey acknowledges this desire for the generalizing tendency of theory and the consequent diminishing of experience: "The general, recurrent and extensive has been treated as the worthy and superior kind of Being," he says; "the immediate, intensive, transitory and qualitatively individualized taken to be of importance only when it is imputed to something ordinary." But he argues that universals are dependent upon local experiences: "In truth, the universal and stable are important because they are the instrumentalities, the efficacious conditions, of the occurrence of the unique, unstable and passing" (1925, 117). Theory, then, is not a separate act that governs experience in the way of NCLB or other educational reforms, in other words; it instead not only grows from experience but *enables* it.

The mistrust of experience is obvious in the claims, and prohibitions, of educational reforms such as NCLB. Unlike poststructuralist theorists, the assessment specialists and accountability experts in our schools desire, rather than resist, totalizing, which they enfranchise in standardized testing and curricula. Whether experience is discounted because it seems too local or transitory or critiqued because it is too totalizing, the result is that it becomes less and less a solution and a strategy for learning. Yet, if experience forms the groundwork for knowledge and for learning, as Dewey and so many others who have come after him have proved, then teachers and those who teach teachers must find ways of countering both the ignoring of experience that comes from educational mandates and the limiting of experience that comes from theory.

Literary critic Satya Mohanty proposes a path to counter the dismissal and suspicion of experience in his concept of "postpositivist realism." Like Dewey, Mohanty draws on the tradition of American pragmatism as well as analytical philosophy, arguing that postmodernist and essentialist positions present false and unhelpful dichotomies, and declaring instead a mediated subjectivity that claims identity and experience as potentially useful to knowledge. Mohanty reenvisions terms such as *objective*, maintaining, like the pragmatists, a contingency that rescues objectivity from its supra-human dimension. The postpositivist realism of Mohanty rejects either/or distinctions presented by a poststructuralism that would condemn experience by consigning it either to mere subjectivity or to false universalizing. Mohanty argues, in fact, that such postmodern critiques actually present a "disguised form of foundationalism," because they get caught in positivist assumptions about objectivity: "[Postmodern critique] assumes that the only kind of objective knowledge we can have is independent of socially produced and revisable theoretical presuppositions and concludes that the theory dependence of experience is evidence that is always epistemologically suspect" (2000, 36). But, Mohanty asks, What if we give up both radical perspectivism and the view from nowhere? Then we would have experience both socially and theoretically constructed and theory that is experience dependent—in other words, a conception of knowledge pragmatic in its emphasis on possibility and action.

Mohanty's postpositivist realism offers mediation among subjectivities as a better definition for objectivity than the kind of absolutism that infects educational reforms aimed both at curricular hegemonies and at poststructuralist positions that see objective knowledge as outside the reach of human subjects. "It is precisely in this mediated way," he notes, "that experience yields knowledge" (2000, 33). Experience is never universalized, never merely unique once it is shared. As John Zammito writes, in an essay that responds to Joan Scott's critique, "Experience always signifies an emergent, not an essence: it makes determinate claims even as it is constructed by and within a web of social and linguistic forces" (2000, 294). Once shared, experience always changes the one who tells and the one who hears, becoming a primary structure for learning.

If Mohanty and an increasing number of poststructuralist critics are beginning to take this more pragmatist position, and thus avoid the trap of skepticism and endless critique that has prevented real action from being taken in public schools, a number of teacher activists and practitioners for years have been putting Dewey's—and Mohanty's—principles to work in educational practice and planning. We know many of these stories from books and movies that celebrate the bravery of the teacher who stands up to an uncompromising system and forges a path for students. We've been conditioned to see these teachers as unique and the systems they fight as immutable.

But they are not. The common ground for these teachers' action is experience—tested, remade, combined and offered as evidence. Hero-teacher movies such as *Freedom Writers, Stand and Deliver, Dead Poets' Society* and *Asphalt Jungle* only popularize the far less mythical but no less inspiring stories from teacher theorists such as Mike Rose (2008), who visits classrooms across the country to report stunning stories of achievement, or Ellen Cushman (2002), who moves her literacy program in Los Angeles out of the college classroom and into the neighborhood. There are so many teachers who grasp the necessity of their conditions and use their experience with those conditions to act. The success of teachers such as these, documented again and again, is a proof of the efficacy and efficiency of experience—the use of observation, family backgrounds, local lives—for learning.

There is no space to write about all the teachers who have argued for the necessity of experience and won. But two might serve as examples to illustrate the point. Deborah Meier's study of the process of building a successful group of schools in Harlem provides proof of how experience can guide systems and lead to new, better action. And Chris Gallagher's report on the Nebraska school system's direct challenge to NCLB documents how education improves when standards are set and tested by local experience.

Deborah Meier wrote *The Power of their Ideas* (1995) to reflect on her experience as principal and founder of the Central Park East Schools in Harlem, where she made local needs and experiences paramount in redesigning institutional space, curricular agendas, and teacher and student responsibilities. Her radical project transformed a desperately poor and failing group of schools in one of the most poverty stricken districts in the U.S. into one where eventually over 90 percent of its graduates pursued higher education. Meier attributes the schools' success to its teachers' insistence on local experience to guide decisions: "Our experience suggested that a strong school culture requires that most decisions be struggled over and made by those directly responsible for implementing them, not by representative bodies handing down dictates for others to follow" (2002, 24). Taking the complicated rather than the simple path, Meier demonstrates how experience—contested and tested—can lead to better, more reliable decisions about school initiatives. "We have become better observers of our own practice, better collectors of information, documenters of practice as well as users of expertise," Meier says. "We thus have more to bring to the collective table" (ibid., 26). As she shows, experience always fosters change because experience itself is always changing.

Chris Gallagher wrote *Reclaiming Assessment* (2007) to document a strategy of resistance to the encroachments into local control of education presented by the No Child Left Behind Act. As he describes it, he wrote to "tell the story of a whole state that resisted going along with policies that undermined the very strengths of its educational system and the very basic premise of its local political ideal—that 'we the people' know best" (2007, xi). A professor of English at the University of Nebraska, Gallagher has been a leader in the public school movement called STARS (School-based Teacher-led Assessment and Reporting System). This system of local assessments uses multiple measures of student performance, tests the tests, insists on classroom-based assessments and prohibits high-stakes testing.

Gallagher points out how experience-led assessment forces continual reflection: "The value of ideas is their fruit, their consequences. We must ask: What does this idea make possible and what does it make impossible? How does it help us ameliorate or at least cope with important problems? What new problems does it generate?" (2007, 10). The problem with traditional accountability measures, Gallagher notes, is not just that they don't account for the multiple ways schools already demonstrate accountability. Rather, test-based accountability is both "beside the point and at worst a threat to the good things happening" (ibid., 34). As a more meaningful mode of assessment, the STARS group of teachers propose engagement as an assessment measure for school reform. Engagement embodies Dewey's ideas about experience: it looks at schools ability to be democratic, mutually responsible, interactive and collaborative, and to embrace complexity. Reporting on many of these schools, Gallagher ends with his hope that "we will build on this story, rewrite it, and perhaps write a new one altogether" (ibid., 127). Experience and the documenting of it becomes the guide for new action.

Those of us who teach teachers or do research in literacy and school reform must work to gather and investigate instances like these, not as a list of unique stories but as a body of data that demonstrates the reality of the principle of experience, the realization of the social roots and branches of it, and the need for it in all educational imperatives. Mohanty and the growing number of postmodern theorists who use his work, and Gallagher and the many who are standing up to misguided educational practice and winning, help rescue Dewey's hope for experience to guide progressive education and to protect against Taylorism in whatever guise it assumes. Dewey's *experience* is no weasel word but Dillard's weasel story, action that comes from observation and reflection. In Dillard's recognition of how the weasel "grasps his necessity" lies a lesson for teachers who despair of the continuing and growing threat to their own teaching lives that comes from the denial and refusal of experience as the guide to pedagogy. Like the weasel, teachers must see what is around them and be able to use it, observe students and act on those observations, understand the experience of others, enter into it and and be changed by it. We must learn to teach and act from experience, asserting its existence, denying its mere subjectivity by talking back to those who would diminish it or ignore it.

"In a genuine democracy," writes composition theorist Kurt Spellmeyer,

> all politics become local politics because the decision making that matters most occurs at the local levels. By the same token, a democratic culture will not teach us to look beyond our actual lives for the solution to our problems: it will remind us instead that solutions of some sort always lie at hand, even when our hands have been tied. The world of immediate human experience is always potentially whole and complete. (2003, 9)

What Mohanty calls realist poststructuralism, and what Dewey calls interaction, have their basis in the same democratic impulse. Democracy insists that answers to problems come not from outside ourselves, but from what's at hand, what we know and how we live.

To exercise democracy by making experience central to learning requires both willingness and courage, the willingness to share and the courage to change. It requires that we hold on to our necessity and affirm the freedom that comes from acting on it.

Notes

1. A summary of NCLB provisions and guidelines is provided, along with recent alterations to the law, at several good websites—http://www.edweek.org/ew/topics/no-child-left-behind/, among others.

2. See also bell hooks, "Essentialism and Experience" (in *Teaching to Transgress*, 1994) for another nuanced view of experience as necessary to experience, especially for racial and ethnic minorities.

References

Apple, Michael (2001) *Educating the "Right" Way.* New York: Routledge.

Callahan, Raymond (1962) *Education and the Cult of Efficiency.* Chicago: University of Chicago Press.

Cushman, Ellen (2002) "Sustainable Service Learning Programs." *College Composition and Communication, 54,* 1, 40–65.

Darling-Hammond, Linda (1997) *The Right to Learn.* San Francisco: Jossey-Bass.

Dewey, John (1925) *Experience and Nature.* Chicago: Open Court.

Dewey, John (1938) *Experience and Education.* New York: Macmillan.

Dillard, Annie (1988) "Living Like Weasels." In *Teaching a Stone to Talk.* New York: HarperCollins.

Ebert, Teresa (1996) *Ludic Feminism and After.* Ann Arbor: University of Michigan Press.

Flax, Jane (1987) "Postmodernism and Gender Relations in Feminist Theory," *Signs: Journal of Women in Culture and Society, 12,* 621–43.

Gallagher, Chris (2007) *Reclaiming Assessment.* Portsmouth, NH: Heinemann.

hooks, bell (1994) *Teaching to Transgress.* New York: Routledge.

James, William (1904) "Does Consciousness Exist?" *Journal of Philosophy, Psychology and Scientific Methods, 50,* 477–91.

McCarthy, Cameron, & Dimitriadis, Greg (2005) "Governmentality and the Sociology of Education: Media, Educational Policy, and the Politics of Resentment." In Cameron McCarthy, Warren Crichlow, Greg Dimitriadis & Nadine Dolby (Eds.), *Race, Identity and Representation in Education.* New York: Routledge.

Medina, Jennifer (2008) "New York Measuring Teachers by Test Scores," *New York Times,* January 21; http://www.nytimes.com/2008/01/21/nyregion/21teachers.html.

Meier, Deborah (1995) *The Power of their Ideas: Lessons for America from a Small School in Harlem.* Boston: Beacon Press.

Meier, Deborah (2002) *In Schools We Trust.* Boston: Beacon Press.

Mohanty, Satya (2000) "The Epistemic Status of Cultural Identity." In Paula Moya & Michael Hames-Garcia (Eds.), *Reclaiming Identity: Realist Theory and the Predicament of Postmodernism.* Berkeley: University of California Press.

Newkirk, Thomas (1991) "The Politics of Composition Research: The Conspiracy against Experience." In Richard Bullock & John Trimbur (Eds.), *The Politics of Writing Instruction.* Portsmouth, NH: Boynton-Cook.

No Child Left Behind Act (2002) Accessed at http://www.whitehouse.gov/news/reports/no-child-left-behind.html.

Rose, Mike (2008) *Possible Lives: The Promise of Public Education.* New York: Penguin.

Scott, Joan (1994) "The Evidence of Experience." In *Questions of Evidence: Proof, Practice and Persuasion across the Disciplines.* Chicago: University of Chicago Press.

Shor, Ira (1986) *Culture Wars.* Boston: Routledge.

Spellmeyer, Kurt (2003) *Arts of Living: Reinventing the Humanities for the Twenty-First Century.* Albany: State University of New York Press.

Spivak, Gayatri (2005) "Three Women's Texts and a Critique of Imperialism." In Cameron McCarthy, Warren Crichlow, Greg Dimitriadis & Nadine Dolby (Eds.), *Race, Identity and Representation in Education.* New York: Routledge.

Zammito, John (2000) "'Experience': The Debate in Intellectual History among Scott, Toews, and LaCapra." In Paula Moya & Michael Hames-Garcia (Eds.), *Reclaiming Identity: Realist Theory and the Predicament of Postmodernism.* Berkeley: University of California Press.

16

Transforming Status-Quo Stories

Shifting from "Me" to "We" Consciousness

AnaLouise Keating

> Are we just little-brained creatures who wind up with these limiting stories of real-
> ity because we can't look and are afraid to listen? Really, what changes the world is
> the power of a compelling story. But we seem to carefully limit the stories that reach
> us to those that won't push us to change.
>
> (Elana Dykewomon 2002, 454)

A few years ago, when I worked at a small college in a northern state, I was assigned
to a spacious office in a renovated mansion. Built in the early 20th century, the
mansion had a substantial heating system with old-fashioned, steam-generating
radiators in each room. My computer work station was situated next to a large
window and almost directly above the radiator. Because the mansion was located
in the center of an elegant garden, I was grateful for the opportunity to look at the
gorgeous view as I worked; however, I was also concerned about the radiator's
effect on the computer (which seemed fairly new). When the information technology representative visited my office to introduce himself and explain the network
system, I expressed my concern about the computer's location: I had been taught
that computers should not be exposed to direct heat. However, this computer is
sitting right by the radiator. Given the long, cold winters (which will I assume
require a lot of heat), shouldn't we move the computer? The young man carefully
considered my question and then dismissed my concern: "Well, it's *always* been like
this. The computer has *always* been there, so it must be okay." He spoke the words
with such finality that I knew further discussion would be pointless. I still marvel
at his certainty, his deep faith that the way things are and always have been is the
best—and only—way things can be.

   This interchange with the information technology rep stayed with me. As I sat
through several sub-zero winters, the radiator spewing hot air directly into the
computer's hard drive, I pondered the implications of his dismissal. I reflected on
similar comments I'd heard over the years: *"Don't waste your breath complaining;
that's just the way things are!" "People are always like that." "Hey: I didn't make the
rules; don't ask me to change them!" "It's life. Get used to it." "Oh, just live and let
live." "Don't rock the boat." "Like it or leave it!"* Generally spoken with great certainty, these comments reflect unthinking affirmation of the existing reality and
a stubborn, equally unthinking resistance to change. Deeply embedded in these

confident assertions are what I call *status-quo stories*: world-views and belief systems that normalize existing conditions so entirely that they deny the possibility of change.

As my term suggests, status-quo stories reaffirm and in other ways naturalize the existing social system. Status-quo stories have a numbing effect. When people organize their lives around such stories, they become paralyzed; they stop thinking. To borrow Elana Dykewomon's words from the above epigraph, status-quo stories do not "push us to change." It is, in fact, the reverse: status-quo stories push us to remain the same. Reinforcing the belief that the way things are is the way they always have been and the way they should (and must!) be, status-quo stories teach us to resist change. This belief in the status-quo's permanence becomes self-fulfilling: we do not try to make change because we believe that change is impossible to make. "It's always been that way," we tell ourselves, "so why rock the boat?" Status-quo stories limit our imaginations because they prevent us from envisioning alternate possibilities—different ways of living and arranging our lives.

Why do status-quo stories have such power? Like all forms of storytelling, like all world-views, status-quo stories contain "core beliefs" about reality—beliefs that shape our world, though we rarely (if ever) acknowledge their creative role. As Reginald Robinson explains, "A core belief flows from feelings and imaginations, and ordinary people reinforce this belief through words and deeds. From this core belief, ordinary people co-create their experiences and realities" (2004, 1370). Significantly, we generally don't recognize core beliefs *as* beliefs; we accept them as factual descriptions of the world. Take, for example, that well-known story of rugged individualism with its pull-yourself-up-by-the-bootstraps theory of success. My experiences in the classroom have convinced me that this Enlightenment-based story of the "self-made man" is one of the most damaging stories in U.S. culture.

This highly celebrated individualism is a dominant story of our time and a foundational element of Western modernity. As David Theo Goldberg notes, "[t]he philosophical commitment in the tradition of Western modernity is to radical and atomistic individualism—to rational, ... self-interested, self-maximizing, and self-providing individuals" (1993, 25). In the U.S., the commitment to atomistic individualism has taken an extremely virulent form in which each individual is free to pursue their own desires—no matter how this pursuit might impact others. The belief in a fully independent self has, to a great degree, shaped the ways we see ourselves, other people, and the world. We are trained to view human beings as entirely self-sufficient and self-directed; each of us is (or should be) fully "in charge" of and responsible for our own life. As Harlon Dalton observes, "All of us, to some degree, suffer from this peculiarly American delusion that we are individuals first and foremost, captains of our own ships, solely responsible for our own fates" (1995, 105). Mainstream education—with its emphasis on individual work, competition for grades, hierarchical rankings, and "forms of pedagogy based on the sovereign subject" (Peters 2003, 64)—reinforces this belief.

Lest I be misunderstood, let me emphasize that I am not criticizing all forms of individualism. I value and understand the importance of personal agency, integrity, relational autonomy and self-respect (Keating 1997). Nor do I posit a binary opposition between the individual and the collective. Rather, I focus specifically on an extreme type of individualism that defines the self very narrowly, in *non-relational, egocentric, possessive* terms. According to this hyper-individualism, each individual has a rigidly circumscribed core self that must be nurtured, protected, and in other ways honored at all costs. I describe this individualism as *self-enclosed* to emphasize its inflexible boundaries, absolute isolation, and intense focus on the isolated self. Each individual is entirely separate from the external world, including all other human and non-human life. To survive, the individual must focus almost entirely on themselves, evaluating all actions in egocentric terms: *"What's in it for me?" "How can I succeed?" "How will this event, this situation, affect me?" "What can you do for me?" "What can I take from you?"*

Self-enclosed individualism restricts our world-views, fostering what I call "*me*" *consciousness*: an adversarial framework that valorizes and naturalizes competition and self-aggrandizement. It's "Every Man for Himself," to borrow an old sexist adage—and the sexism is quite appropriate here. As feminist/multicultural scholars have observed, our versions of solipsistic individualism were developed by and within a very select group of human beings—property-owning men of Northern European ancestry.[1] Not surprisingly, then, me consciousness has its source in a restrictive definition of the individual that *ex*cludes far more people than it *in*cludes. Historically, and even today, many women (of all colors) and other marginalized people have been found lacking when measured by this exclusionary standard.

Self-enclosed individualism is premised on a binary model of identity formation, or what Kelly Oliver describes as a "conceptual framework in which identity is … formed and solidified through an oppositional logic that uses dualisms to justify either opposition and strife or awkward or artificial bridging mechanisms" (2001, 51). This configuration sets up a hierarchical relationship between self and other, where the individual and society occupy mutually exclusive poles. This hierarchy presumes and reinforces a model of domination, scarcity and separation in which intense competition leads to aggressiveness and fear: *my* growth requires *your* diminishment. Interactions between self and other are conflict-driven, and society is reduced to a collection of individuals motivated only by greedy, insatiable self-interest.

Me consciousness and the oppositional epistemology and ethics which it fosters prevent us from recognizing our connections with others and working together for social change. People who organize their lives according to this story of rugged individualism adopt a competitive, survival-of-the-fittest model of success. Distancing themselves from all that surrounds them, they become defensive, isolated, and alienated from the external world. They assume that success depends only on individual effort: those people who do not succeed have only themselves to blame, and their failure has absolutely no impact on anyone but themselves. This status-quo story of solipsistic individualism is deeply infused into mainstream U.S. culture and greatly inhibits social justice work. After all: if each individual is fully responsible for their own life, there is no need for collective action or systemic change. Just pull yourself up by your own bootstraps! Kelly Oliver makes a related point: "The individualism behind notions of formal equality and a color- and gender-blind society reduces social problems to personal sins on the part of whites and men and mental instability or physical defects on the part of people of color and women" (2001, 163). As Oliver's statement implies, this status-quo denies that color, economic status, gender, sexuality, and other human variables shape people's lives in different ways.[2]

This denial of difference points to an often-overlooked point: although it sounds paradoxical, given hyper-individualism's apparent elevation of the uniqueness of each individual, this status-quo story is based on a hidden assumption of sameness. As powell notes, "In a way individuality, even as it purports to take into account our distinctness, makes us all the same in fundamental ways. We are all rational, autonomous people and therefore we should all be treated the same" (2001, 9). In other words, self-enclosed individualism posits a monolithic definition of the individual. All individuals are, at the core, essentially the same. (I would argue that this premise of human sameness provides significant justification for standardized testing.)

My students have been seduced by stories of rugged, self-enclosed individualism.[3] Defining themselves as unique, fully independent and autonomous human beings, they have adopted me consciousness and try to enact its competitive model of success. Perceiving themselves and their world through hyper-individualism's solipsistic lens, they cannot recognize their interconnections with or accountability for others. Nor can they comprehend the continuing significance of gender, "race," and other socially constructed categories. Instead, they firmly believe in the status-quo stories of meritocracy, equal opportunity, and fair treatment for all. These stories have persuaded them (and of course many others as well) that the U.S. is a free democratic country where everyone is treated the same, everyone has the same obstacles, and everyone has the same opportunities to prosper. In the United States of America, anything is possible and all doors will open to those who work hard.[4] In short, status-quo stories of rugged individualism have made my students callous and judgmental: because they believe that each individual is the master of their own fate, fully responsible and accountable only to themselves, they blame the individual for their failure to succeed.

In addition to ignoring the systemic nature of social injustice, this dogma of meritocracy enables "white"-identified[5] students to deny the ways in which color and other markers of difference materially impact people's lives. As Dalton observes, "For a significant chunk [of "white"-raced people], the inability to 'get' race, and to understand why it figures so prominently in the lives of most people of color, stems from a deep affliction—the curse of rugged individualism" (1995, 105). When students view the world through self-enclosed individualism's status-quo story, they cannot recognize that what affects others—*all* others, no matter how separate we seem to be—ultimately affects them as well.

Status-quo stories of self-enclosed individualism have dominated our personal, professional and socio-economic lives for too long. These stories have not served us well, for they lead to an "increasingly privatized world" (Shapiro 2002) and are too limited to bring about radical change. We need new stories … stories with transformational power … stories inviting our students to question and expose the status quo … stories enabling us to eradicate social injustice and enact revolutionary change.

From "Me" to "We" Consciousness

> This ancient idea of relationship must be allowed to arise in our collective consciousness once again. In this perilous world of the twenty-first century, it may well be a matter of our collective survival.
>
> (Gregory Cajete 2000, 105)

We need new stories for transformation, stories that can shift students (and at times perhaps ourselves) from "me" to "we" consciousness. While I do not advocate moving backwards, I'm convinced that sometimes we find new visions for the future by returning to the past. And so, as my epigraph to this section suggests, I propose that we replace status-quo stories of self-enclosed individualism with what Gregory Cajete describes as "the ancient idea of relationship." According to this holistic world-view—a world-view shared by many indigenous peoples, as well as some others—we are radically interconnected. Or, as Ines Hernández-Ávila asserts (2002, 531), "we are related to all that lives." We are interrelated and interdependent—on multiple levels and in multiple ways, including (but not limited to) the following.

- *Ecologically* We are rooted in, sustained by, and interdependent with the external world. As Gregory Cajete notes, "humans and the world interpenetrate one another at many levels, including the air we breathe, the carbon dioxide we contribute to the food we transform, and the chemical energy we transmute at every moment of our lives from birth to death" (2000, 25). The Chagga people of Tanzania share a similar lesson, teaching that "the universe is a web of one interconnected, inter-related, and interdependent whole … Stones and mountains, rivers and lakes, clouds and rain, are all *alive* in their intrinsic meanings and in their active partnership to people and everything else" (Mosha 1999, 213). Not only are we intimately embedded within the natural world, but this world reinforces our interconnections with each other. In fact, it's been "roughly calculated that every breath of air we breathe contains a few atoms that have been breathed by every person in the history of the planet, from Socrates to Genghis Khan to Einstein to Hitler, as well as all the billions of unknowns" (Hayward 1984, 21).
- *Economically* Economic changes in one location often have a domino-like effect on local, national, and even global communities. Think here of the September 11th attacks and their aftermath, the domino-like effect on the airline industry, airport businesses and related services, travel agencies, tourism, and so forth, both in the United States and abroad (Anzaldúa 2003). For many U.S. Americans, "September 11 was a brutal and perverse lesson in the inevitability of interdependence in the modern world" (Barber 2002, 26). Or look at how the growth of multi- and transnational companies, recent developments in software, new forms of outsourcing, off-shoring, and other changes in the ways companies and individuals do business has led to the development of "a single global network" (Friedman 2005, 8).

- *Linguistically* Language itself both reflects and ensures our interconnections with others. The words we use come to us already infused with meaning and value. Although we appropriate and shape these words to fulfill our own intentions, even these intentions, no matter how personal and unique they seem, are never purely our own. As Mikhail Bakhtin suggests, we are born into consciousness through the words of others: "All that touches me comes to my consciousness—beginning with my name—from the outside world, passing through the mouths of others ... with their intonation, their affective tonality, and their values" (1981, 294).[6]
- *Socially* The social identity categories and labels we so unthinkingly use are relational: terms such as me/you, male/female, heterosexual/homosexual, parent/child, self/other, black/white come into being relationally and have meaning only in juxtaposition to each other. As john a. powell reminds us, "one's own sense of identity is inextricably entwined with, and dependent upon, the identity of 'others'" (1997, 1498).
- *Spiritually* According to both indigenous and non-indigenous teachings, there exists a cosmic, constantly changing spirit or force which embodies itself in diverse material and non-material forms.[7] For many tribal peoples, "[e]very act, element, plant, animal, and natural process is considered to have a moving spirit with which humans continually interact" (Cajete 2000, 69). Some non-tribal people have held similar beliefs. According to that well-known 19th-century public intellectual Ralph Waldo Emerson, "[n]ature is not fixed but fluid; spirit alters, molds, makes it" (1836, 48). For contemporary theorist Gloria Anzaldúa, as well, "[s]pirit exists in everything; therefore God, the divine, is in everything—in ... rapists as well as victims; it's in the tree, the swamp, the sea" (2000, 100).

My point here is not to prove that this multidimensional interconnectivity "really" exists, defining "really" in some scientistic fashion. Instead, I'm interested in using this "ancient idea of relationship" to develop new stories ... innovative frameworks for teaching and enacting social change. One of my primary goals as an educator is to awaken in my students a sense of our radical interconnectedness, for I am convinced that this awareness can play a crucial role in working towards social justice. At the very least, I offer interconnectivity and its relational worldviews, or what I call "*we*" *consciousness*, as alternatives to the highly celebrated belief in an entirely independent "American" self.

Seduced by stories of self-enclosed individualism, the majority of my students have no sense of their accountability to others; nor can they recognize that their actions have a profound effect on others, that "[w]hat affects one directly affects all indirectly" (Cone 1990, 200).[8] And so I posit interconnectivity as my theoretical and pedagogical framework and develop classroom strategies designed to challenge students' perceptions and invite them to shift from "me" to "we" consciousness. Positing interconnectivity serves a number of interrelated purposes.

First, adopting this story of interconnectedness enables me to redefine individual and communal identities as mutually *inclusive*, rather than mutually *exclusive*. By so doing, I present an alternative to me consciousness and the solipsistic individualism on which it relies, an alternative that does not deny individual identity but instead redefines it. Locating each individual within a larger, spirit-inflected context, I maintain that individual human beings are not self-enclosed. We have permeable boundaries. This definition of individualism invites students to shift perspectives and adopt a much broader—though inevitably partial—point of view. We are interconnected. As Anzaldúa explains, "[t]he self does not stop with just you, with your body ... [T]he self can penetrate other things and they penetrate you" (2000, 162). This permeable self extends outward—meeting, touching, entering into exchange with other subjects (human and non-human alike). Significantly, this outward movement is not an imperialistic appropriation, where the self-contained subject grows larger by extending its boundaries to incorporate or annihilate every object in its path. It is, rather, a mutual encounter between subjects.[9]

When I'm teaching, I use this permeable selfhood to replace the stories of solipsistic individualism with relational forms that value both personal and collective integrity and self-respect (Keating 2007). According to this relational model, self-definition and self-growth occur in the context of and in dialogue with other equally important individuals. (I define "individual" broadly to include both human and non-human life.) We are both distinct individuals and integral parts of a series of larger wholes. Living systems theorists offer a useful analogy for this both/and approach in their concept of the holon. Coined by Arthur Koestler from the Greek word *holos* (which means whole), a holon is, simultaneously, an *autonomous* system and a vital part of a *larger* system. As Joanna Macy explains (2007), "All living systems—be they organic like a cell or human body, or supra-organic like a society or ecosystem—are *holons*. That means they have a dual nature: They are both wholes in themselves and, simultaneously, integral parts of larger wholes."

We—each and every individual human being—are both self-contained and collective, both open and closed. We do have boundaries, but these boundaries are porous, allowing exchange with our external environment. The divisions between self and other, between individual and world, still exist; however, these divisions are not nearly as rigid and inflexible as that old status-quo story of rugged individualism would lead us to believe. Social activist Fran Peavey offers a useful analogy to describe this we consciousness:

> Human beings are a lot like crabgrass. Each blade of crabgrass reaches up to the sun, appearing to be a plant all by itself. But when you try to pull it up, you discover that all the blades of crabgrass in a particular piece of lawn share the same roots and the same nourishment system. Those of us brought up in the Western tradition are taught to think of ourselves as separate and distinct creatures with distinct personalities and independent nourishment systems. But I think the crabgrass image is a more accurate description of our condition. Human beings may appear to be separate, but our connections are deep; we are inseparable. Pull on any part of our human family and we all feel the strain. (2000, 13)

Second, stories of interconnectedness offer alternatives to the binary-oppositional models of identity formation fostered by self-enclosed individualism. I am especially interested in developing *inclusionary* identities that acknowledge yet go beyond social identity categories, and I believe that interconnectivity itself might offer a type of identity or a trigger for non-binary identity formation at both personal and collective levels. Anzaldúa makes a similar point, stating that we share an interconnectedness that could serve as "an unvoiced category of identity, a common factor in all life forms" (2000, 164). This "common factor" transcends—*but does not ignore*—social categories based on gender, "race," or other systems of difference; it is "wider than any social position or racial label" (2002, 508). Indeed, this shared identity is wider than *anything* in "human nature." As Anzaldúa explains, each person's identity "has roots you share with all people and other beings—spirit, feeling, and body comprise a greater identity category. The body is rooted in the earth, la tierra itself. You meet ensoulment in trees, in woods, in streams" (ibid., 560).

Positing interconnectedness as itself a shared identity trait, I replace binary systems of difference with a more expansive, relational approach to identity. Unlike hyper-individualism's hidden valorization of sameness, this approach does not ignore differences or in other ways deny the validity of each person's specific experiences, beliefs and desires. Instead, it enables me to reposition individual differences within a larger, holistic context—a context premised on the possibility of commonalities. Significantly, this repositioning does not negate individual differences, for "commonalities" and "sameness" are not synonymous. As I define the term, commonalities contain—without erasing—differences. Commonalities offer points of connection enabling us to incorporate and negotiate among sameness, similarity and difference; commonalities represent a synergistic mixture brewed from all three. I refer to this mix as *synergistic* to underscore its unpredictable, creative dimensions. Commonalities serve as pathways into complex, unexpected interactions with others. Commonalities make differences less divisive. We don't need to break the world into rigid categories and hide behind masks of sameness which demand that we define ourselves in direct opposition to others. We can trust that, despite the many differences among us, we are all interconnected.

Third, I use the recognition of our interconnectedness to fuel students' desire to work for social change. I invite students to consider this possibility: because self and other are irrevocably, utterly, *intimately* interrelated, what affects you—no matter how distant, how separate, how different (from me) you seem to be—affects me as well. I select readings and develop assignments designed to foster perceptions of radical interdependence.[10] I want students to recognize that the events and belief systems impacting our sisters and brothers across the street, across the state, across the globe, have a concrete effect on me and you. We all rise or sink together. David Loy makes a similar point:

> This world is not a collection of objects but a community of subjects, a web of interacting processes. Our "interpermeation" means [that] we cannot avoid responsibility for each other. This is true not only for the residents of lower Manhattan, many of whom worked together in response to the World Trade Center catastrophe, but for all people in the world, however hate-filled and deluded they may be … including even the terrorists who did these horrific acts, and all those who supported them. (2003, 108)

This recognition leads to new forms of empathy—the willingness to enter imaginatively other people's lives. When "I" empathize with "you," I enact we consciousness—a relational form of thinking, a back-and-forth movement. Immersing myself in your stories, I listen without judging, I listen with open heart and open mind. I travel into your emotions, desires and experiences, then return to my own. But, in the return, I am changed by my encounter with you, and I begin recognizing the commonalities we share.

Charting New Worlds ... Together

> Misbegotten American dreams have maimed us all. And one of these, especially, continues to distort and paralyze our simplest capabilities for cooperation as a species. Beloved, national myths about you and me as gloriously rugged, independent individuals pervade our consciousness.
>
> (June Jordan 1993, 15)

> [T]o a very great extent we dream our worlds into being. For better or worse, our customs and laws, our culture and society are sustained by the myths we embrace, the stories we recirculate to explain what we behold. I believe that racism's hardy persistence and immense adaptability are sustained by a habit of human imagination, defective rhetoric, and hidden license. I believe no less that an optimistic course could be charted, if only we could imagine it.
>
> (Patricia Williams 1997, 16)

As these epigraphs indicate, I insist on a holistic world-view positing a radical interrelationship between the material and immaterial dimensions of life: our dreams and visions shape the worlds we inhabit, though we rarely (if ever!) recognize their creative power. Like Jordan, I believe that some of our current dreams—or what I call *status-quo stories*—are profoundly destructive. And yet, like Patricia Williams, I too am an optimist at heart, with great faith in our ability to reshape our worlds in more positive ways. I, too, believe in the imagination's untapped power. I believe in our ability to tell new stories about our lives and, through these stories, to enact transformation, to materialize (to (literally) bring into being) the worlds we envision.

Language, belief, perception, imagination and action are intimately interrelated, shaping reality in complicated ways.[11] The stories we tell ourselves, the stories we learn from our cultures (our families, schooling, religion, friends, the media, the books we read, and so forth) influence our beliefs, our imaginations, our perceptions, and our actions. As Stuart Hall asserts, "How we 'see' ourselves and our social relations *matters*, because it enters into and informs our actions and practices" (2000, 272). What we imagine to be possible, coupled with what we believe about ourselves, other people and the world, affects our perceptions and these perceptions affect how we act; our actions move out into the world, affecting other people's beliefs, imaginations, perceptions and actions.[12] Our actions shape the stories we tell, the stories others tell about us, the ways they perceive us, the ways we perceive ourselves. It's an interlocking web with no clear-cut beginnings or endings.[13]

All too often, however, we assume that our perceptions and beliefs accurately reflect the entire truth about reality and ourselves. Like the status-quo stories I've described in these pages, this assumption narrows, limits, restricts our world-view and inhibits our actions. Lynda Myers makes a similar point: "The reality we perceive is shaped by an underlying system of beliefs often implicit, assumed, or unquestioned, which serves as a self-fulfilling, self-prophetic organizer of experience" (1993, 31). When these underlying beliefs are informed by status-quo stories, they close off imaginative possibilities and prevent us from recognizing our responsibility as co-creators.

To return to my opening anecdote, status-quo stories function in our cultural imaginary like computers on the radiator. They are so deeply embedded in the dominant-cultural stories we're exposed to every day, that we generally assume they are unchanging aspects of our world. "It's *always* been that way." Yet this automatic acceptance of the status quo severely damages us.[14] Maybe the stories we currently accept as the truth about reality *are* permanent and unchanging, but maybe they're not. I choose to believe that status-quo stories can—and must!—be changed. In my classrooms and in other areas of my life, I am forging some new (or, rather, extremely old yet too-often forgotten) stories about interrelatedness—stories that can lead to social change. By so doing, I invite my students to shift their perspectives, to move from me to we consciousness. I hope to awaken in them a compassionate understanding of the need to work together for social change.

Notes

1. As john a. powell (2001) explains,

   The ideology of individuality had its origins in the Enlightenment, which came concurrently with the emergence of Colonialism. During this germinative period, the essence of individualism was that Europeans were individuals as opposed to other people who were a "collective." The collectivity of the other served as a rationale and justification for the exploitation of the collective other. … In that sense, individuality was already racialized. (2001, 3–4).

   See also Warren (1984) and Goldberg (1993).
2. See also powell's assertion: "How does individualism operate on race and gender today? The answer from the individualist camp is that race and gender do not exist. We are all just individuals. … [A]ny marker of gender, race, or sexuality around which meaning is constructed socially is largely irrelevant" (2001, 9).
3. Perhaps not surprisingly, the majority of my graduate students in women's studies are not so naive. See also Rich & Cargile (2004).
4. For an important critique of meritocracy, equal opportunity and fair treatment, see Sue (2004).
5. By "white"-identified, I mean people who look, act and/or think in "white" ways. Generally, but not always, these people would be classified as "white" (Keating 2007).
6. Or, as Cajete states, "In its holistic and natural sense, language is animate and animating, it expresses our living spirit through sound and the emotion with which we speak. In the Native perspective, language exemplifies our communion with nature rather than our separation from it" (2000, 72).

7. Thich Naht Hahn (1998) has coined the phrase "inter-being" to describe this interconnectedness.
8. "Martin Luther King was right: We are bound together as one humanity. What affects one directly affects all indirectly. The sooner we realize the interconnectedness of our social existence, the sooner we will end our isolation from each other and begin to develop ways that we can work together toward the liberation of the poor throughout the world" (Cone 1990, 200).
9. For an illustration of this type of mutual encounter, see Anzaldúa's discussion of *nepantleras* (2002).
10. For examples, see the appendices in Keating (2007).
11. "One major finding, consistent with a substantial body of psychological research, is that the brain does not simply reproduce external reality. Instead, apparently, about 80 percent of what we perceive and think we have understood is in fact rooted in prior attitudes, information, ideas, and emotional reflexes" (Chickering 2006, 131). See also Robinson (2004).
12. "We must recognize the power of words, for words label experience and thus give form to thoughts" (Myers 1993, 26). See also Harjo (1996).
13. "Your identity is a filtering screen limiting your awareness to a fraction of your reality. What you or your cultures believe to be true is provisional and depends on a specific perspective. What your eyes, ears, and other physical senses perceive is not the whole picture but one determined by your core beliefs and prevailing societal assumptions" (Anzaldúa 2002, 542).
14. "We believe that a positive self-identity is not easily attained in a culture such as this one. This premise is supported by the pervasive number of '-isms' (racism, sexism and ageism) and their impact on those who would be defined as inferior by the dominant way of perceiving in this society. ... [T]he very nature of the conceptual system is itself inherently oppressive and that all who adhere to it will have a difficult time developing and maintaining a positive identity" (Myers et al. 1991, 55).

References

Anzaldúa, G. (2000) *Interviews/Entrevistas*, ed. A. Keating. New York: Routledge.
Anzaldúa, G. (2002) Now let us shift ... the path of conocimiento ... inner work, public acts. In G. Anzaldúa & A. Keating (Eds.), *This bridge we call home: Radical visions for transformation* (pp. 540–78). New York: Routledge.
Anzaldúa, G. (2003) Let us be the healing of the wound: The Coyolxauhqui imperative—la sombra y el sueño. In C. Lomas & C. Joysmith (Eds.), *One wound for another/Una herida por otra: Testimonios de latino/as in the U.S. through cyberspace*. Mexico City: Centro de Investigaciones Sobre América del Norte (CISAN), at the Universidad Nacional Autónoma de México (UNAM).
Bakhtin, M. (1981) *The dialogic imagination*, trans. C. Emerson & M. Holquist. Austin: University of Texas Press.
Barber, B. R. (2002) The educated student: Global citizen or global consumer? *Liberal Education*, 88, 22–8.
Cajete, G. (2000) *Native science: Natural laws of interdependence*. Santa Fe: Clear Light.
Chickering, A. W. (2006) Curricular content and powerful pedagogy. In A. W. Chickering, J. C. Dalton & L. Stamm (Eds.), *Encouraging authenticity and spirituality in higher education* (pp. 113–44). San Francisco: Jossey-Bass.
Cone, J. (1990) "Afterword." In *A black theology of liberation* (pp. 197–201) (original work published 1970). New York: Orbis.

n, H. L. (1995) *Racial healing: Confronting the fear between blacks and whites.* New
York: Doubleday.

kewomon, E. (2002) The body politic—mediations on identity. In G. Anzaldúa &
A. Keating (Eds.), *This bridge we call home: Radical visions for transformation* (pp. 450–58).
New York: Routledge.

Emerson, R. W. (1836) *Nature.* In *Emerson: Essays & poems* (pp. 7–49). New York: Library
of America.

Friedman, T. (2005) *The world is flat: A brief history of the twenty-first century.* New York:
Farrar, Strauss, & Giroux.

Goldberg, D. T. (1993) *Racist culture: Philosophy and the politics of meaning.* Oxford:
Blackwell.

Hahn, T. N. (1998) *Interbeing: Fourteen guidelines for engaged Buddhism.* Berkeley, CA:
Parallax Press.

Hall, S. (2000) Racist ideologies and the media. In P. Marris & S. Thornham (Eds.), *Media
studies* (pp. 271–82). New York: New York University Press.

Harjo, J. (1996) *The spiral of memory: Interviews,* ed. Laura Coltelli. Ann Arbor: University
of Michigan Press.

Hayward, J. (1984) *Perceiving ordinary magic: Science and intuitive wisdom.* Boston: Shambala.

Hernández-Ávila, I. (2002) In the presence of spirit(s): A meditation on the politics of solidarity and transformation. In G. Anzaldúa & A. Keating (Eds.), *This bridge we call home:
Radical visions for transformation* (pp. 530–38). New York: Routledge.

Jordan, J. (1993) *Technical difficulties: African-American notions and the state of the union.*
New York: Pantheon.

Keating, A. (1997) Transcendentalism then and now: Towards a dialogic theory and praxis
of multicultural U.S. literature. In L. Brannon & B. Greene (Eds.), *Rethinking American
literature* (pp. 50–68). Urbana, IL: NCTE.

Keating, A. (2007) *Teaching Transformation: Transcultural classroom dialogues.* New York:
Palgrave Macmillan.

Loy, D. (2003) *The great awakening: A Buddhist social theory.* Boston: Wisdom.

Macy, J. (2007) *Understanding our interconnections.* Retrieved January 22, 2008, from http://
www.joannamacy.net/html/living.html.

Mosha, R. S. (1999) The inseparable link between intellectual and spiritual formation in
indigenous knowledge and education: A case study in Tanzania? In L. M. Semali & J. L.
Kincheloe (Eds.), *What is indigenous knowledge? Voices from the academy* (pp. 209–25).
New York: Falmer Press.

Myers, L. J. (1993) *Understanding an Afrocentric world view: Introduction to an optimal
psychology.* Dubuque, IA: Kendall/Hunt.

Myers, L. J., et al. (1991) Identity development and worldview: Toward an optimal concep-
tualization. *Journal of Counseling & Development, 70,* 54–63.

Oliver, K. (2001) *Witnessing: Beyond recognition.* Minneapolis: University of Minnesota Press.

Peavey, F. (2000) *Heart politics revisited.* Annandale, NSW: Pluto Press.

Peters, M. (2003) Derrida, pedagogy, and the calculation of the subject. In P. P. Trifonas
(Ed.), *Pedagogies of difference: Rethinking education for social justice* (pp. 61–82). New
York: Routledge.

powell, j. a. (1997) The multiple self: Exploring between and beyond modernity and postmodernity. *Minnesota Law Review, 81,* 1481–521.

powell, j. a. (2001) Disrupting individualism and distributive remedies with intersubjectiv-
ity and empowerment: An approach to justice and discourse. *University of Maryland Law
Journal of Race, Religion, Gender & Class, 1,* 1–23.

Rich, M. D., & Cargile, A. C. (2004) Beyond the breach: Transforming white identities in the classroom. *Race, Ethnicity, and Education, 7*, 251–65.

Robinson, R. (2004) Human agency, subjectivity negated. *American University Law Review, 53*, 1361–420.

Shapiro, S. (2002) Education and moral values: Seeking a new bottom line. *Tikkun, 20*, 2.

Sue, D. W. (2004) Whiteness and ethnocentric monoculturalism: Making the "invisible" visible. *American Psychologist*, November, 761–69.

Warren, J. (1984) *The American narcissus: Individualism and women in nineteenth-century American fiction.* New Brunswick, NJ: Rutgers University Press.

Williams, P. (1997) *Seeing a color-blind future: The paradox of race.* New York: Farrar, Straus & Giroux.

17

Disposable Futures

Dirty Democracy and the Politics of Disposability

HENRY A. GIROUX

Neo-liberalism as a Theater of Cruelty

With the dawn of the new millennium, the Gilded Age and its updated neo-liberal "'dreamworlds' of consumption, property, and power" has returned to the United States with a vengeance.[1] The new exorbitantly rich, along with their conservative ideologues, now publicly invoke and celebrate that period in 19th-century American history when corporations ruled political, economic and social life and an allegedly heroic entrepreneurial spirit brought great wealth and prosperity to the rest of the country. Even the *New York Times* ran a story in the summer of 2007 providing not only a welcome endorsement of Gilded Age excess, but also barely contained praise for a growing class of outrageously rich chief executives, financiers and entrepreneurs, described as "having a flair for business, successfully [breaking] through the stultifying constraints that flowed from the New Deal" and using "their successes and their philanthropy [to make] government less important than it once was."[2] And while the rulers of the Gilded Age have suffered some major financial losses with the onslaught of one of the worse financial crises ever to befall the United States, they still retain a substantial amount of wealth and can hardly be viewed as victims; ironically, in some cases the traditional media have gone so far as to portray them in sympathetic terms because they have had to modify their lifestyles in light of the monetary losses they have incurred.

There is more at work here than a predatory narcissism, a zany hubris, and a neo-feudal world-view in which self-interest and the laws of the market are the only true measure of politics. There is also an attack on the social contract and the very notion of democratic politics. In this new Gilded Age, people are bound together not as citizens, but as consumers, while the values of self-interest, individual responsibility, and economic calculation now render ornamental "the basic principles of and institutions of democracy."[3] In the vocabulary of corporate-speak, the notion of the common good is coded as a pathology, and the future becomes a short-term investment defined largely by the bottom line. Markets rather than politics now give people what they want. In the second Gilded Age, massive disparities in wealth and power, along with the weakening of worker protections and the destruction of the social state, are now legitimated through self-serving historical reinvention in which politics is measured by the degree to which it evades any sense of social responsibility and public commitment. In this case, corporate sovereignty not only makes power invisible; it also excises a history of barbaric greed, unconscionable economic inequity, rapacious Robber Barons, scandal-plagued politics, resurgent monopolies, and an unapologetic racism.[4]

What is often ignored by many theorists who analyze the rise of neo-liberalism in the United States is that it is not only a system of economic power relations, but also a political project of governing and persuasion intent on producing new forms of subjectivity and particular modes of conduct.[5] In addressing the absence of what can be termed the cultural politics and public pedagogy of neo-liberalism, I want to begin with a theoretical insight provided by the British media theorist Nick Couldry, who insists that "every system of cruelty requires its own theatre," one that draws upon the rituals of everyday life in order to legitimate its norms, values, institutions and social practices.[6] Neo-liberalism represents one such system of cruelty, one that is reproduced daily through a regime of commonsense and a narrow notion of political rationality that "reaches from the soul of the citizen-subject to educational policy to practices of empire."[7] What is new about neo-liberalism in a post-9/11 world is that it has become normalized, serving as a powerful pedagogical force that shapes our lives, memories and daily experiences, while attempting to erase everything critical and emancipatory about history, justice, solidarity, freedom, and the meaning of democracy.

Within this heightened geography of insecurity, privatization, deregulation, outsourcing, and a marauding market fundamentalism, the primary political and economic forces shaping American life add up to what is unique to the current regime of neo-liberalism: its hatred of democracy and dissent. As finance capital reigns supreme over American society, bolstered by the "new and peculiar power of the information revolution in its electronic forms,"[8] democratization, along with the public spheres needed to sustain it, becomes an unsettled and increasingly fragile if not dysfunctional project. Moreover, the possibilities of democracy are now answered not with the rule of law, however illegitimate, but with the threat or actuality of violence.[9] Hence, it is not surprising that the war at home has given rise not only to a crushing attack on civil liberties—most evident in the passing of the Military Commissions Act of 2006—which conveniently allows the Bush administration to detain indefinitely anyone deemed as an enemy combatant while denying them recourse to the traditional right to challenge their detention through legal means—but also to an assault on those populations now considered disposable and redundant under the logic of a ruthless market fundamentalism.

While the United States has never been free of repression, there is a special viciousness that marks the current regime and its budding heirs. The celebration of war, a landscape of officially sanctioned violence against people of color, a predatory culture of fear, and an attack on human rights, coupled with the assault on the social state and the rise of an all-encompassing militarism, make this government stand out for its anti-democratic policies. And it doesn't end with Bush. During the 2008 Republican presidential primary, Rudolph W. Giuliani and Mitt Romney spoke unabashedly for the party in supporting interrogation techniques such as water-boarding, which has been deemed as a form of torture. Romney went so far as to argue that he would double Guantánamo, and Giuliani, no stranger to promoting the militarized politics of racial fear and moral panics, often told his audiences that "Islamic extremists 'hate you' and want to come to the U.S. to 'kill you.'"[10] John McCain, the Republican presidential nominee, who has repeatedly condemned the use of torture, compromised his position by eventually siding with Bush in opposing a further restriction of CIA interrogation techniques. In the heat of this campaign, the *New York Times* columnist Gail Collins has rightly noted that, "If the Republican presidential candidates go any farther right, they'll be opening their town meetings by biting the heads off of squirrels."[11] Under neo-liberalism, acts of translation become utterly privatized and removed from public considerations, and the consequence is not only the undoing of the social bond, but also the endless reproduction of the narrow registers of character and individual responsibility as a substitute for any analyses of wider social problems, making it easier to blame the poor, homeless, uninsured, jobless, and other disadvantaged individuals and groups for their problems while reinforcing the merging of the market state with the punishing state.

The varied populations made disposable under neo-liberalism occupy a globalized space of ruthless politics in which the categories of "citizen's rights" and "democratic representation," once integral to national politics, are no longer recognized. In the past, people who were marginalized by class and race could at least expect a modicum of support from the social state, either through an array of limited social provisions or from employers who recognized that they still had some value as part of a reserve army of unemployed labor. That is no longer true. Under the ruthless dynamics of neo-liberal ideology there has been a shift away from the possibility of getting ahead economically and living a life of dignity to the much more deadly task of struggling to stay alive. Many now argue that this new form of biopolitics is conditioned by a permanent state of class and racial exception in which, as Achille Mbembe asserts, "vast populations are subject to conditions of life conferring upon them the status of living dead."[12]

Disposable populations are less visible, relegated to the frontier zones of relative invisibility and removed from public view. Such populations are often warehoused in schools that resemble boot camps, dispersed to dank and dangerous workplaces far from the enclaves of the tourist industries, incarcerated in prisons that privilege punishment over rehabilitation, and consigned to the increasing army of the permanently unemployed. Rendered redundant as a result of the collapse of the social state, a pervasive racism, a growing disparity in income and wealth, and a take-no-prisoners neo-liberalism, an increasing number of individuals and groups are being demonized, criminalized or simply abandoned either by virtue of their status as immigrants or because they are young, poor, unemployed, disabled, homeless, or confined to low-paying jobs. What Orlando Patterson, in his discussion of slavery, called "social death" has become the fate of more and more people as the socially strangulating politics of hyper-individualism, self-interest and consumerism become the organizing principles of everyday life.[13] The human face of this process and the other who inhabits its geography is captured in a story told by Chip Ward, a thoughtful administrator at the Salt Lake City Public Library, who writes poignantly about a homeless person named Ophelia, who retreats to the library because, like many of the homeless, she has nowhere else to go to use the bath-room, secure temporary relief from bad weather, or simply be able to rest. Excluded from the American dream and treated as both expendable and a threat, Ophelia, in spite of her obvious mental illness, defines her existence in terms that offer a chilling metaphor that extends far beyond her plight. Ward describes Ophelia's presence and actions in the following way:

> Ophelia sits by the fireplace and mumbles softly, smiling and gesturing at no one in particular. She gazes out the large window through the two pairs of glasses she wears, one windshield-sized pair over a smaller set perched precari-ously on her small nose. Perhaps four lenses help her see the invisible other she is addressing. When her "nobody there" conversation disturbs the reader seated beside her, Ophelia turns, chuckles at the woman's discomfort, and explains, *"Don't mind me, I'm dead. It's okay. I've been dead for some time now." She pauses, then adds reassuringly, "It's not so bad. You get used to it."* Not at all reassured, the woman gathers her belongings and moves quickly away. Ophelia shrugs. Verbal communication is tricky. She prefers telepathy, but that's hard to do since the rest of us, she informs me, "don't know the rules." (Emphasis added)[14]

Ophelia represents just one of the 200,000 chronically homeless who now use public libraries and any other accessible public space to find shelter. Many are often sick, disoriented, high on drugs, intoxicated, or mentally disabled and close to a nervous breakdown because of the stress, insecurity and danger that they face every day. Increasingly, along with the 3.5 million human beings who experience homelessness each year in the United States, they are treated like criminals, as if punishment were the appropriate civic response to poverty, mental illness and human suffering. And while Ophelia's comments may be dismissed as the rambling of a crazy woman, they speak to something much deeper about the current state of American society and its abandonment of entire populations that are now con-sidered the human waste of a neo-liberal social order. Ward's understanding of Ophelia's plight as a public issue is instructive. He writes:

> Ophelia is not so far off after all—in a sense she is dead and has been for some time. Hers is a kind of social death from shunning. She is neglected, avoided, ignored, denied, overlooked, feared, detested, pitied, and dismissed. She exists alone in a kind of social purgatory. She waits in the library, day after day, gazing at us through multiple lenses and mumbling to her invis-ible friends. She does not expect to be rescued or redeemed. She is, as she says, "used to it." She is our shame. What do you think about a culture that abandons suffering people and expects them to fend for themselves on the street, then criminalizes them for expressing the symptoms of illnesses they cannot control? We pay lip service to this tragedy—then look away fast.[15]

A more visible register of the politics of disposability at work in American soci-ety can be found in the haunting images of New Orleans following Hurricane

Katrina—of dead bodies floating in flooded streets, and of thousands of African Americans marooned on highways, abandoned in the Louisiana Superdome, and waiting for days to be rescued from the roofs of flooded houses. Two years later, the politics of disposability returned to New Orleans with a vengeance and without apology in light of revelations that, though the Federal Emergency Management Agency (FEMA) had received multiple warnings about dangerous levels of formaldehyde in trailers they had provided for the victims of Hurricane Katrina, the government agency refused to "conduct testing of occupied trailers because testing would 'imply FEMA's ownership of this issue.'"[16] In other words, under the biopolitics of neo-liberalism conditions have been created in which moral responsibility disappears and politics offers no space for compassion, social justice, or fundamental provisions necessary for a decent life. Another signpost for the politics of disposability and greed is on display in the reported annual earnings of hedge-fund managers such as James Simons, who took home $1.7 billion in 2006, "more than 38,000 times the average income. Two other hedge fund managers also made more than $1 billion, and the top 25 combined made $14 billion."[17] Less fortunate CEOs of big companies had to settle for annual salaries ranging from $118 million a year to the paltry $1.35 million CEO Amin Khoury was paid by BE Aerospace.[18] In this scenario, freedom is transformed into its opposite, for the vast majority of the population as a small, privileged minority can purchase time, goods, services and security while the vast majority increasingly are relegated to a life without protections, benefits and support. And, yet, for those populations considered expendable, redundant and invisible by virtue of their race, class and youth, life becomes increasingly precarious. The collateral damage that reveals the consequences of this narrative of punishment and disposability becomes clear in heartbreaking stories about young people who literally die because they lack health insurance and live in extreme poverty. In one recent case, Deamonte Driver, a 7th grader in Prince George's County, Maryland, died because his mother did not have the health insurance to cover an $80 tooth extraction. Because of a lack of insurance, his mother was unable to find an oral surgeon willing to treat her son. By the time he was admitted and diagnosed in a hospital emergency room, the bacteria from the abscessed tooth had spread to his brain and, in spite of the level of high-quality intensive treatment he finally received, he eventually died. As Jean Comaroff points out in a different context, "the prevention of ... pain and death ... seems insufficient an incentive" to advocates of neo-liberal market fundamentalism "in a world in which some 'children are ... consigned to the coffins of history.'"[19]

All of these examples raise fundamental questions about not only the state of democracy in America but also what it might mean to take the social contract seriously as a political and moral referent in order to define the obligations of adults and educators to future generations of young people. For over a century, Americans have embraced as a defining feature of politics at least the idea that all levels of government would assume a large measure of responsibility for providing the resources, social provisions, and modes of education that enabled young people to prepare in the present for a better future, while expanding the meaning and depth of an inclusive democracy. This was particularly true under the set of policies inaugurated under President Lyndon Johnson's Great Society programs of the 1960s, which were designed to eliminate both poverty and racial injustice.

Taking the social contract seriously, American society exhibited at least a willingness to fight for the rights of children, enact reforms that invested in their future, and provide the educational conditions necessary for them to be critical citizens. Within such a modernist project, democracy was linked to the wellbeing of youth, while the status of how a society imagined democracy and its future was contingent on how it viewed its responsibility towards future generations. The end of that project can be seen in the new American reality under the second Bush administration. Instead of a federal budget that addresses the needs of children, the United States now enacts federal policies that weaken government social programs, provide tax cuts for millionaires and corporations, and undercut or eliminate basic social provisions for children at risk. As *New York Times* op-ed columnist Paul Krugman points out, compassion and responsibility under the Bush administration have given way to "a relentless mean-spiritedness," and "President Bush is someone who takes food from the mouths of babes and gives the proceeds to his millionaire friends." For Krugman, Bush's budgets have come to resemble a form of "top-down class warfare."[20] The mean-spiritedness of such warfare could be seen, for example, in President Bush's willingness to veto the State Children's Health Insurance Program, which provides much needed health insurance to low-income children who do not qualify for Medicaid. As a result of this veto, "nearly one million American children will lose their health insurance."[21] And, without any irony intended, Bush attempts to legitimate this disgraceful action by claiming that he is against this bill because "it opens up an avenue for people to switch from private insurance to the government."[22] Bush gives new meaning to the neo-liberal mantra to privatize or perish. The war against youth becomes clear not only in the cutting of programs that benefit young people, but also in the draining of the public treasury at the cost of $2 billion a week to fight a war in Iraq, "whose central feature is the government's consistent, disastrous denial of reality," a denial that promotes the needless maiming and killing of countless numbers of Americans and Iraqis.[23]

Future Matters

In opposition to the authoritarian politics of the Bush administration, it is crucial to remember that the category of youth does more than affirm that modernity's social contract is rooted in a conception of the future in which adult commitment is articulated as a vital public service; it also affirms those vocabularies, values and social relations that are central to a politics capable of defending vital institutions as a public good and nurturing a flourishing democracy. At stake here is the recognition that children constitute a powerful referent for addressing war, poverty, education, and a host of other important social issues. Moreover, as a symbol of the future, children provide an important moral compass to assess what Jacques Derrida calls the promises of a "democracy to come."[24] A vocabulary that focuses on children's current and future social importance has always been of particular importance to higher education, which often defined and addressed its highest ideals through the recognition that how it educated youth was connected to the democratic future it hoped for and its claim as an important public sphere.

But just as education has been separated from a viable model of democratic politics, youth have been separated both from the discourse of the social contract and from any ethical commitment to provide young people with the prospects of a decent and democratic future. Punishment and fear have replaced compassion and social responsibility as the most important modalities mediating the relationship of youth to the larger social order. Youth within the last two decades have come to be seen as a source of trouble rather than as a resource for investing in the future, and are increasingly treated as either a disposable population or cannon fodder for barbaric wars abroad, or defined as the source of most of society's problems. Hence, young people now constitute a crisis that has less to do with improving the future than with denying it. As Larry Grossberg points out,

> It has become common to think of kids as a threat to the existing social order and for kids to be blamed for the problems they experience. We slide from kids in trouble, kids have problems, and kids are threatened, to kids as trouble, kids as problems, and kids as threatening.[25]

This was exemplified when the columnist Bob Herbert reported in the *New York Times* that "parts of New York City are like a police state for young men, women and children who happen to be black or Hispanic. They are routinely stopped, searched, harassed, intimidated, humiliated and, in many cases, arrested for no good reason."[26] No longer "viewed as a privileged sign and embodiment of the future,"[27] youth are now increasingly demonized by the popular media and derided by politicians looking for quick-fix solutions to crime and other social ills. While youth, particularly those of color, are more and more associated in the media and by dominant politicians with a rising crime wave, what is really at stake in this discourse is a punishment wave, one that reveals a society that does not know how to address those social problems that undercut any viable sense of agency, possibility and future for many young people. For example, John J. Dilulio, Jr., a former Bush advisor, argued in an influential article published in the conservative *Weekly Standard* that society faced a dire threat from an emerging generation of youth between the ages of fifteen and twenty-four, whom he aptly called "super-predators."[28] Hollywood movies such as *Thirteen*, *Kids*, *Brick*, *Hard Candy* and *Alpha Dog* consistently represent youths as dangerous, utterly brainless, or simply without merit.

Under the reign of neo-liberal politics, with its hyped-up social Darwinism and theatre of cruelty, the popular demonization and "dangerousation" of the young now justifies responses to youth that were unthinkable twenty years ago, including criminalization and imprisonment, the prescription of psychotropic drugs, psychiatric confinement, and zero-tolerance policies that model schools after prisons. School has become a model for a punishing society in which children who violate a rule as minor as a dress code infraction or slightly act out in class can be handcuffed, booked, and put in a jail cell. Such was the case, for example, in Florida when the police handcuffed and arrested six-year-old Desre Watson, who was taken from her kindergarten school to the Highlander County jail, where she was fingerprinted, photographed for a mug shot, and charged with a felony and two misdemeanors. Her crime? She had thrown a tantrum in her kindergarten class.[29] Couple this type of domestic terrorism with the fact that the United States is the only country that voted against a recent United Nations resolution calling for the abolition of life imprisonment without the possibility of parole for children under the age of sixteen.[30] Moreover, it is currently the only nation that locks up child offenders for life. A report issued in 2007 by the Equal Justice Initiative claims that "there are 73 Americans serving [life] sentences for crimes they committed at 13 or 14."[31] Another instance of how youth are on the receiving edge of the punishing society can be found in the Bush administration's No Child Left Behind policy, which provides financial incentives to schools that implement zero-tolerance policies, in spite of their proven racial and class biases. Now more than ever, many schools either simply warehouse young black males or put them on the fast track to prison incarceration or a future of control under the criminal justice system. All across America, African American youth are being suspended or expelled at rates much higher than their white counterparts who commit similar behavioral infractions. For example, As Howard Witt, writing in the *Chicago Tribune*, points out,

> In the average New Jersey public school, African-American students are almost 60 times as likely as white students to be expelled for serious disciplinary infractions. In Minnesota, black students are suspended 6 times as often as whites [and] in Iowa, blacks make up just 5 percent of the statewide public school enrollment but account for 22 percent of the students who get suspended.[32]

As schools become increasing militarized, drug sniffing dogs, metal detectors and cameras have become common features in schools, and administrators appear more willing if not eager "to criminalize many school infractions, saddling tens of thousands of students with misdemeanor criminal records for offenses such as swearing ..., disrupting class," or violating a dress code. Trust and respect now give way to fear, disdain and suspicion, creating an environment in which critical pedagogical practices wither, while pedagogies of surveillance and testing flourish.[33]

The impoverishment of the American educational system reflects the literal poverty of American children. The hard currency of human suffering that impacts children is evident in some astounding statistics that suggest a profound moral and political contradiction at the heart of one of the richest democracies in the world: for example, the rate of child poverty rose in 2004 to 17.6 percent, boosting the number of poor children to 12.9 million. In fact, "[a]bout one in three severely poor people are under age 17."[34] Moreover, children make up a disproportionate share of the poor in the U.S. in that "they are 26 percent of the total population, but constitute 39 percent of the poor."[35] Just as alarmingly, 9.3 million children lack health insurance, and millions lack affordable childcare and decent early childhood education. One of the most damaging statistics revealing how low a priority children are in America can be seen in the fact that, among the industrialized nations, the United States ranks first in billionaires and in defense expenditures and yet an appalling 25th in infant mortality. As we might expect, behind these grave statistics lies a series of decisions to favor economically those already advantaged at the expense of youth. Savage cuts to education, nutritional assistance for impoverished mothers, veterans' medical care, and basic scientific research help fund tax cuts for the inordinately rich.

This inversion of the government's responsibility to protect public goods from private threats further reveals itself in the privatization of social problems and the vilification of those who fail to thrive in this vastly iniquitous social order. Too many youth within this degraded economic, political and cultural geography occupy a "dead zone" in which the spectacle of commodification exists alongside the imposing threat of massive debt, bankruptcy, the prison–industrial complex, and the elimination of basic civil liberties. Indeed, we have an entire generation of unskilled and displaced youth who have been expelled from shrinking markets, blue-collar jobs, and the limited political power granted to the middle-class consumer. Rather than investing in the public good and solving social problems, the state now punishes those who are caught in the downward spiral of its economic policies. Punishment, incarceration and surveillance represent the face of the new expanded state. Consequently, the implied contract between the state and citizens is broken, and social guarantees for youth, as well as civic obligations to the future, vanish from the agenda of public concern. As market values supplant civic values, it becomes increasingly difficult "to translate private worries into public issues and, conversely, to discern public issues in private troubles."[36] Within this utterly privatizing market discourse, alcoholism, homelessness, poverty, joblessness and illiteracy are viewed not as social issues, but rather as individual problems—that is, such problems are viewed as the result of a character flaw or a personal failing, and in too many cases they are criminalized.

Black youth are especially disadvantaged. Not only do a mere 42 percent who enter high school actually graduate, but they are increasingly jobless in an economy that does not need their labor. Bob Herbert argues that, marked as a surplus and disposable population,

> black American males inhabit a universe in which joblessness is frequently the norm [and that] over the past few years, the percentage of black male high school graduates in their 20s who were jobless has ranged from well over a third to roughly 50 percent. … For dropouts, the rates of joblessness are staggering. For black males who left high school without a diploma, the real jobless rate at various times over the past few years has ranged from 59 percent to a breathtaking 72 percent.[37]

He further argues that "These are the kinds of statistics you get during a depression."

At the current time, however, solutions involving social problems have become difficult to imagine, let alone address. For many young people and adults today, the private sphere has become the only space in which to imagine any sense of hope, pleasure or possibility. Culture as an activity in which young people actually produce the conditions of their own agency through dialogue, community participation, public stories, and political struggle is being eroded. In its place, we are increasingly surrounded by a "climate of cultural and linguistic privatization" in which culture becomes something you consume, and the only kind of speech that is acceptable is that of the fast-paced shopper. In spite of neo-conservative and neo-liberal claims that economic growth will cure social ills, the language of the market has no way of dealing with poverty, social inequality, or civil rights issues. It has no respect for non-commodified values and no vocabulary for recognizing and addressing social justice, compassion, decency, ethics or, for that matter, its own anti-democratic forms of power. It has no way of understanding that the revolutionary idea of democracy, as Bill Moyers points out, is not just about the freedom to shop, formal elections, or the two-party system, "but the means of dignifying people so they become fully free to claim their moral and political agency."[38] These are political and educational issues, not merely economic concerns.

In order to strengthen the public sphere, we must use its most widespread institutions, undo their metamorphoses into means of surveillance, commodification and control, and reclaim them as democratic spaces. Schools, colleges and universities come to mind—because of their contradictions and their democratic potential, their reality and their promise, though of course they are not the only sites of potential resistance. In what follows, I argue that youth as a political and moral category is central for engaging and reclaiming the purpose and meaning of higher education as a democratic public sphere, while at the same time recognizing those anti-democratic tendencies that threaten the very existence of subjects who can think, act, and struggle for a future that does not repeat the authoritarian present.

Higher Education and the Crisis of the Social

The powerful regime of forces that increasingly align higher education with a reactionary notion of patriotic correctness, market fundamentalism, and state-sponsored militarism presents difficult problems for educators. As the 21st century unfolds, higher education faces both a legitimation crisis and a political crisis. As a handmaiden of Pentagon and corporate interests, higher education has lost its claim to independence and critical learning. Turning its back on the public good, the academy has largely opened its doors to serving private and governmental interests, and in doing so has compromised its already fragile and problematic role as a democratic public sphere. In keeping with the progressive impoverishment of politics and public life over the past two decades, the university is increasingly being transformed into a training ground for corporate, military and right-wing patriotic correctness rather than a public sphere in which youth can become the critical citizens and democratic agents necessary to nourish a socially responsible future. Strapped for money and defined ever more in the language of a militarized and corporate culture, many universities are now part of an unholy alliance that largely serves the interests of the national security state and the policies of transnational corporations while increasingly removing academic knowledge production from democratic values and projects.[39] College presidents are now called CEOs and speak largely in the discourse of Wall Street and corporate fund managers. Venture capitalists scour colleges and universities in search of big profits to be made through licensing agreements, the control of intellectual property rights, and investments in university spinoff companies. In this new Gilded Age of money and profit, academic subjects gain stature almost exclusively through their exchange value on the market. While the vision of education is being narrowed and instrumentalized, the Bush administration attempts to wield more control over colleges and universities, cut student aid, plunder public services and push states to the brink of financial disaster. As higher education increasingly becomes a privilege rather than a right, many working-class youth either find it financially impossible to enter college or, because of increased costs, drop out.[40] Those students who have the resources to stay in school are feeling the pressure of the job market and rush to take courses and receive professional credentials in business and the biosciences as the humanities lose majors and downsize. Not surprisingly, students are now referred to as "customers," while some university presidents even argue that professors should be labeled as "academic entrepreneurs."[41] As higher education is corporatized, young people find themselves on campuses that look more like malls (one thinks of the humanities building at the University of Alberta), are progressively being taught by professors who are hired on a contractual basis, have obscene workloads, and barely make enough money to pay off their student loans. Worth noting is that "both part-time and full-timers not on a tenure-track account for nearly 70 percent of professors at colleges and universities, both public and private."[42] Tenured faculty are called upon to generate grants, establish close partnerships with corporations, and teach courses that have practical value in the marketplace. There is little in this vision of the university that imagines young people as anything other than fodder for the corporation or appendages of the national security state. What was once the hidden curriculum of many universities—the subordination of higher education to capital—has now become an open and much celebrated policy of both public and private higher education.

Higher education has also been attacked by right-wing ideologues such as David Horowitz and Lynne Cheney, who view it as the "weak link" in the war against terror.[43] Horowitz acts as the figurehead for various well-funded conservative student groups such as the Young Americans and College Republicans, which perform the ground work for his "Academic Bill of Rights" policy efforts to seek out juicy but rare instances of "political bias"—whatever that is and however it might be defined—in college classrooms. Left-oriented academics such as Ward Churchill, Norman Finklestein, and others are now being fired or denied tenure because they are critical of the American government. Faculty who offer classroom readings that challenge official versions of U.S. foreign and domestic policy have their names posted on websites, which often label them as un-American while calling upon their respective universities to fire them. In some states, laws have been passed that allow students to sue professors whose political sensibilities are unsettled or challenged. The state of Arizona has passed a bill that would fine faculty members $500 for advocating a political position in the classroom. As one legislator puts it, "You can speak about any subject you want—you just don't take a position." In Florida, a bill was passed legislating that social studies teachers could only provide students with facts and were forbidden to teach them the skills of interpretation or critical analyses. There is more at issue here than a vile form of anti-intellectualism. A more political analysis would argue that what is developing in the United States are not only the jingoistic hyper-nationalistic practices that make such a society incapable of questioning itself but also the public spaces that promote critical inquiry, dialogue and engaged citizens. What is emerging under such conditions is more than an imperial presidency and a militaristic empire; it is also a new type of authoritarianism.

Education and Resistance in Dark Times

The corporatization, militarization and dumbing down of rigorous scholarship, and the devaluing of the critical capacities of young people, mark a sharp break from a once strong educational tradition in the United States, extending from Thomas Jefferson to John Dewey to Maxine Greene, which held that freedom flourishes in the worldly space of the public realm only through the work of educated, critical citizens. Within this democratic tradition, education was not confused with training; instead, its critical function was propelled by the need to provide students with the knowledge and skills that enable a "politically interested and mobilized citizenry, one that has certain solidarities, is capable of acting on its own behalf, and anticipates a future of ever greater social equality across lines of race, gender, and class."[44]

In order for it to become a meaningful site for educating youth for a democratic future, educators and others need to reclaim higher education as an ethical and political response to the demise of democratic public life. At stake here is its role as a public sphere committed to increasing the possibilities of democratic identities, values and relations among its 17 million students. This approach suggests new models of leadership, organization, power and vision dedicated to opening higher education up to all groups, creating a critical citizenry, providing specialized work skills for jobs that really require them, democratizing relations of governance among administrators, faculty and students, and taking seriously the imperative to disseminate an intellectual and artistic culture.

Addressing education as a democratic endeavor begins with the recognition that higher education is more than an investment opportunity, citizenship is more than conspicuous consumption, learning is more than preparing students for the workplace, however important that task might be, and democracy is more than making choices at the local mall. Reclaiming higher education as a public sphere begins with the crucial project of challenging, among other things, those market fundamentalists, religious extremists, and rigid ideologues who harbor a deep disdain for critical thought and healthy scepticism, and who look with displeasure upon any form of education that teaches students to read the world critically and to hold power and authority accountable. Education is not only about issues of work and economics, but also about questions of justice, social freedom, and the capacity for democratic agency, action and change, as well as the related issues of power, exclusion and citizenship. These are educational and political issues, and they should be addressed as part of a broader effort to re-energize the global struggle for social justice and democracy.

Academics and Public Life

If higher education is to reclaim itself as a site of critical thinking, collective work and public service, educators and students will have to redefine the knowledge, skills, research and intellectual practices currently favored in the university. Central to such a challenge is the need to position intellectual practice "as part of an intricate web of morality, rigor and responsibility" that enables academics to speak with conviction, use the public sphere to address important social problems, and demonstrate alternative models for bridging the gap between higher education and the broader society. Connective practices are key: it is crucial to develop intellectual practices that are collegial rather than competitive, refuse the instrumentality and privileged isolation of the academy, link critical thought to a profound impatience with the status quo, and connect human agency to the idea of social responsibility and the politics of possibility.

Connection also means being openly and deliberately critical and worldly in one's intellectual work. Increasingly, as universities are shaped by a culture of fear in which dissent is equated with treason, the call to be objective and impartial, whatever one's intentions, can easily echo what George Orwell called the official truth or the establishment point of view. Lacking a self-consciously democratic political focus, teachers and students are often reduced to the role of a technician or functionary engaged in formalistic rituals, unconcerned with the disturbing and urgent problems that confront the larger society or the consequences of one's pedagogical practices and research undertakings. In opposition to this model, with its claims to and conceit of political neutrality, I argue that academics should combine the mutually interdependent roles of critical educator and active citizen. This requires finding ways to connect the practice of classroom teaching with the operation of power in the larger society and to provide the conditions for students to view themselves as critical agents capable of making those who exercise authority and power accountable. I think Edward Said is on target when he argues that academics who assume the role of public intellectuals must function within institutions, in part, as an exile, as someone whose "place it is publicly to raise embarrassing questions, to confront orthodoxy and dogma, to be someone who cannot easily be co-opted by governments or corporations."[45] In Said's perspective, the educator as public intellectual becomes responsible for linking the diverse experiences that produce knowledge, identities and social values in the university to the quality of moral and political life in wider society. Such an intellectual does not train students solely for jobs, but also educates them to question critically the institutions, policies and values that shape their lives, their relationships to others, and their connection to the larger world.

Education cannot be decoupled from what Jacques Derrida calls a democracy to come, that is, a democracy that must always "be open to the possibility of being contested, of contesting itself, of criticizing and indefinitely improving itself."[46] Within this project of possibility and impossibility, education must be understood as a deliberately informed and purposeful political and moral practice, as opposed to one that is either doctrinaire or instrumentalized, or both. Moreover, a critical pedagogy should be engaged at all levels of schooling. Similarly, it must gain part of its momentum in higher education among students who will go back to the schools, churches, synagogues and workplaces in order to produce new ideas, concepts, and critical ways of understanding the world in which young people and adults live. This is a notion of intellectual practice and responsibility that refuses the insular, overly pragmatic, and privileged isolation of the academy while affirming a broader vision of learning that links knowledge to the power of self-definition and to the capacities of students to expand the scope of democratic freedoms, particularly those that address the crisis of education, politics, and the social as part and parcel of the crisis of democracy itself. This is the kind of intellectual practice that Zygmunt Bauman calls "taking responsibility for our responsibility,"[47] one that is attentive to the suffering of others.

In order for pedagogy that encourages critical thought to have a real effect, it must include the message that all citizens, old and young, are equally entitled, if not equally empowered, to shape the society in which they live. If educators are to function as public intellectuals, they need to provide the opportunities for students to learn that the relationship between knowledge and power can be emancipatory, that their histories and experiences matter, and that what they say and do counts in their struggle to unlearn dominating privileges, productively reconstruct their relations with others, and transform, when necessary, the world around them. Simply put, educators need to argue for forms of pedagogy that close the gap between the university and everyday life. Their curricula need to be organized around knowledges of communities, cultures and traditions that give students a sense of history, identity and place. Said illuminates the process when he urges academics and students to accept the demands of "worldliness," which include "lifting complex ideas into the public space," recognizing human injury inside and outside of the academy, and using theory as a critical resource to change things.[48] Worldliness suggests we not be afraid of controversy, that we make connections that are otherwise hidden, deflate the claims of triumphalism, and bridge intellectual work and the operation of politics. It means combining rigor and clarity, on the one hand, and civic courage and political commitment, on the other.

A critically engaged pedagogy also necessitates that we incorporate in our classrooms those electronically mediated knowledge forms that constitute the terrain of mass and popular culture. I am referring here to the world of media texts— videos, films, the internet, podcasts, and other elements of the new electronic technologies that operate through a combination of visual and print culture. Such an approach not only challenges the traditional definition of schooling as the only site of pedagogy by widening the application and sites of education to a variety of cultural locations but also alerts students to the educational force of the culture at large, what I have called elsewhere the field of public pedagogy.

Any viable notion of critical pedagogy should affirm and enrich the meaning, language, and knowledge forms that students actually use to negotiate and inform their lives. Academics can, in part, exercise their role as public intellectuals via such approaches by giving students the opportunity to understand how power is organized through an enormous number of "popular" cultural spheres, including libraries, movie theaters, schools, and high-tech media conglomerates that circulate signs and meanings through newspapers, magazines, advertisements, new information technologies, computers, films and television programs. Needless to say, this position challenges neo-conservative Roger Kimball's claim that "Popular culture is a tradition essential to uneducated Americans."[49] By laying claim to popular, mass and alternative cultural spaces as important sites of public pedagogy, educators have the opportunity, if not responsibility, not only to raise important questions about how knowledge is produced, circulated and taken up in different pedagogical sites, but also to provide the foundation for students to become competent and critically versed in a variety of literacies (not just the literacy of print), while at the same time expanding the conditions and options for the roles they might play as cultural producers (as opposed to simply teaching them to be critical readers). At stake here is an understanding of literacy both as a set of competencies to be learned and as a crucial condition for developing ways of intervening in the world.

I have suggested that educators need to become provocateurs; they need to take a stand while refusing to be involved in either a cynical relativism or doctrinaire politics. This suggests that central to intellectual life is the pedagogical and political imperative that academics engage in rigorous social criticism while becoming a stubborn force for challenging false prophets, fighting against the imposed silence of normalized power, "refusing to allow conscience to look away or fall asleep," and critically engaging all those social relations that promote material and symbolic violence.[50] There is a lot of talk among social theorists about the death of politics brought on by a negative globalization characterized by markets without frontiers, deregulation, militarism and armed violence, which not only feed each other but produce global lawfulness and reduce politics to merely an extension of war.[51] I would hope that, of all groups, educators would vocally and tirelessly challenge this myth by making it clear that expanding the public good and promoting democratic social change is at the very heart of critical education and the precondition for global justice. The potential for a better future further increases when critical education is directed towards young people. As a result, public and higher education may be among the few spheres left in which the promise of youth can be linked to the promise of democracy. That is, given the dark times in which we live, it is worth remembering that higher education, even in its crippled state, still poses a threat to the enemies of democracy in that it holds the promise, if not the reality, of being able to offer students the knowledge and skills that enable them not only to mediate critically between democratic values and the demands of corporate power and the national security state, but also to distinguish between identities founded on democratic principles, on the one hand, and subject positions steeped in forms of competitive, unbridled individualism that celebrate self-interest, profit making, militarism and greed, on the other. Education in this instance becomes both an ethical and a political referent; it furnishes an opportunity for adults to provide the conditions for young people to become critically engaged social agents. Similarly, it points to a future in which a critical education, in part, creates the conditions for each generation of youth to struggle anew to sustain the promise of a democracy that has no endpoint, but that must be continuously expanded into a world of new possibilities and opportunities for keeping justice and hope alive.

Finally, I want to suggest that struggles over how we view, represent and treat young people should be part of a larger public dialogue about how to imagine a democratic future. The war against youth and critical education demands a new politics, a new analytic of struggle, but, most important, it demands a renewed sense of imagination, vision and hope. Making human beings superfluous is the essence of totalitarianism, and the promise of a radical democracy is the antidote in urgent need of being recovered. To do so, we need to address what it means to make the political more pedagogical, that is, a discourse that will allow us to re-vision civic engagement and social transformation while imagining a new understanding of the pedagogical conditions that enable and nurture thoughtfulness, critical agency, compassion, and democracy itself. We have entered a period in which the war against youth, especially poor youth of color, offers no apologies because it is too arrogant and ruthless to imagine any resistance. But the collective need and potential struggle for justice should never be underestimated, even in the darkest of times. To confront the bio-politics of disposability, we need to create the conditions for multiple collective and global struggles that refuse to use politics as an act of war and markets as the measure of democracy. The great abolitionist Frederick Douglas bravely argued that freedom is an empty abstraction if people fail to act, and "if there is no struggle, there is no progress." I realize this sounds a bit utopian, but we have few choices if we are going to fight for a future that enables teachers, parents, students, and others to work dili-gently and tirelessly in order, as Raymond Williams once pointed out, to make despair unconvincing and hope practical for all members of society, but especially for young people, who deserve a future that does a great deal more than endlessly repeat the present. We may live in dark times, as Hannah Arendt reminds us, but history is open and the space of the possible is larger than the one on display.

Notes

1. Mike Davis and Daniel Bertrand Monk, "Introduction," *Evil Paradises* (New York: New Press, 2007), p. ix.
2. Louis Uchitelle, "The Richest of the Rich, Proud of new Gilded Age," *New York Times* (July 15, 2007), http://www.nytimes.com/2007/07/15/business/15gilded.html?_r=1&oref=slogin.
3. Wendy Brown, *Edgework: Critical Essays on Knowledge and Politics* (Princeton, NJ: Princeton University Press, 2005), p. 52.
4. On the Gilded Age, see Alan Trachtenberg, *The Incorporation of America: Culture and Society in the Gilded Age* (Vancouver: Douglas & McIntyre, 2007); Michael McHugh, *The Second Gilded Age: The Great Reaction in the United States, 1973–2001* (Lanham, MD: University Press of America, 2006). See also the now classic Matthew Josephson, *The Robber Barons: The Great American Capitalists 1861–1901* (New York: Harcourt, 2001 [originally published 1934]).
5. Thomas Lemke, "Foucault, Governmentality, and Critique," *Rethinking Marxism, 14*, 3 (2002), 49–64.

6. Nick Couldry, "Realty TV, or The Secret Theater of Neoliberalism," *Review of Education, Pedagogy, and Cultural Studies, 30,* 1 (2008), 3–13.

7. Brown, ibid., p. 40.

8. Arjun Appadurai, *Fear of Small Numbers* (Durham, NC: Duke University Press, 2006), pp. 36–7.

9. Michael Hardt and Antonio Negri, *Multitude: War and Democracy in the Age of Empire* (New York: Penguin, 2004), p. 341.

10. Marc Santora, "3 Top Republican Candidates Take a Hard Line on the Interrogation of Detainees," *New York Times* (November 3, 2007), p. A13.

11. Gail Colllins, "Three-Card Morality Monte," *New York Times* (October 20, 2007), p. A27.

12. Achille Mbembe, "Necopolitics," trans. Libby Meintjes, *Public Culture, 15,* 1 (2003), 40.

13. Orlando Patterson, *Slavery and Social Death: A Comparative Study* (Cambridge, MA: Harvard University Press, 1982).

14. Chip Ward, "America Gone Wrong: A Slashed Safety Net Turns Libraries into Homeless Shelters," *TomDispatch.com* (April 2, 2007), http://www.alternet.org/story/50023.

15. Ibid.

16. Henry Waxman, "Committee Probes FEMA's Response to Reports of Toxic Trailers," Committee on Oversight and Government Reform, Washington, DC, July 19, 2007, http://oversight.house.gov/story.asp?ID=1420. See also Amanda Spake, "Dying for a Home: Toxic Trailers are Making Katrina Refuges Ill," *The Nation* (February 15, 2007), http://www.alternet.org/module/printversion/48004.

17. Paul Krugman, "Gilded Once More," *New York Times* (April 27, 2007), http://www.truthout.org/docs_2006/042707F.shtml.

18. Jenny Anderson and Julie Creswel, "Top Hedge Fund Managers earn over $240 million," *New York Times* (April 24, 2007), p. 1. Council on International and Public Affairs, "Too Much Executive Pay Scorecard," *Too Much Online Weekly* (May 1, 2007), http://www.cipa-apex.org/toomuch/ExecPayScoreboard.html.

19. Jean Comaroff, "Beyond Bare Life: AIDS, (Bio)Politics, and the Neoliberal Order," *Public Culture, 19,* 1 (2007), 213.

20. Paul Krugman, "Bush's Class-War Budget," *New York Times* (February 11, 2005), http://www.nytimes.com/2005/02/11/opinion/11krugman.html?ex=1265864400&en=c5baff37424e2a5d&ei=5088&.

21. Faiz Shakir, Nico Pitney, Amanda Terkel, Satyam Khanna and Matt Corley, "Bush Vetoes Kids," *Progress Report* (July 20, 2007), http://www.americanprogressaction.org/progressreport/2007/07/bush_vetoes_kids.html.

22. Ibid.

23. Ellen Willis, "Historical Analysis," *Dissent* (Winter 2005), p. 113.

24. Jacques Derrida, "The Future of the Profession or the Unconditional University," in *Derrida Down Under,* ed. Laurence Simmons and Heather Worth (Auckland, New Zealand: Dunmarra Press, 2001), p. 253.

25. Lawrence Grossberg, *Caught in the Crossfire* (Boulder, CO: Paradigm, 2005), p. 16.

26. Bob Herbert, "Arrested while Grieving," *New York Times* (May 26, 2007), p. A25.

27. Lawrence Grossberg, "Why Does Neo-Liberalism Hate Kids? The War on Youth and the Culture of Politics," *Review of Education, Pedagogy, a Cultural Studies, 23,* 2 (2001), 133.

28. For an analysis of the drop in youth crime in the 1990s, see S. D. Levitt, "Understanding why Crime Fell in the 1990s: Four Factors that Explain the Decline and Six that Do Not," *Journal of Economic Perspectives, 18,* 1 (2004), 163–90.

29. "Kindergarten Girl Handcuffed, Arrested at Fla. School," WFTV.com (March 30, 2007), http://www.wftv.com/news/11455199/detail.html.

30. Adam Liptak, "Lifers as Teenagers, Now Seeking a Second Chance," *New York Times* (October 17, 2007), p. A1.

31. Ibid.

32. Howard Witt, "School Discipline Tougher on African Americans," *Chicago Tribune* (September 25, 2007), http://www.chicagotribune.com/news/nationworld/chi-070924 discipline,0,22104.story?coll=chi_tab01_layout.

33. I have taken up a detailed critique of No Child Left Behind in Henry A. Giroux, *America on the Edge* (New York: Palgrave, 2006).

34. Tony Pugh, "US Economy Leaving Record Numbers in Severe Poverty," *McClatchy Newspapers* (February 23, 2007), http://www.commondreams.org/headlines07/0223-09.htm.

35. Cesar Chelala, "Rich Man, Poor Man: Hungry Children in America," *Seattle Times* (January 4, 2006), http://www.commondreams.org/views06/0104-24.htm.

36. Zygmunt Bauman, *In Search of Politics* (Stanford, CA: Stanford University Press, 1999), p. 2.

37. Bob Herbert, "The Danger Zone," *New York Times* (March 15, 2007), p. A25.

38. Bill Moyers, "A Time for Anger, a Call to Action," *Common Dreams* (February 7, 2007), http://www.commondreams.org/views07/0322-24.htm.

39. Doug Henwood, *After the New Economy* (New York: New Press, 2005).

40. Anya Kamenetz, *Generation Debt* (New York: Riverhead, 2006); Barbara Ehrenreich, "College Students, Welcome to a Lifetime of Debt?" *AlterNet* (September 11, 2007), http://www.alternet.org/workplace/62125/.

41. I discuss this phenomenon in Henry A. Giroux, *The University in Chains* (Boulder, CO: Paradigm, 2007).

42. Alan Finder, "Decline of the Tenure Track Raises Concerns," *New York Times* (November 20, 2007), p. A16.

43. This charge comes from a report issued by conservative group the American Council of Trustees and Alumni, founded by Lynne Cheney (spouse of Vice President Dick Cheney) and Joseph Lieberman (Democratic Senator). See Jerry L. Martin and Anne D. Neal, *Defending Civilization: How Our Universities are Failing America and What Can Be Done about It.* (February 2002), http://www.totse.com/en/politics/political_ spew162419.html. ACTA also posted on its website a list of 115 statements made by allegedly "un-American Professors."

44. Wendy Brown, *Regulating Aversion* (Princeton, NJ: Princeton University Press, 2006), p. 88.

45. Edward Said, *Representations of the Intellectual* (New York: Pantheon, 1994), p. 11.

46. Giovanna Borriadori (Ed.), "Autoimmunity: Real and Symbolic Suicides—A Dialogue with Jacques Derrida," in *Philosophy in a Time of Terror: Dialogues with Jürgen Habermas and Jacques Derrida* (Chicago: University of Chicago Press, 2004), p. 121.

47. Cited in Madeline Bunting, "Passion and Pessimism," *The Guardian* (April 5, 2003), http://books.guardian.co.uk/print/0,3858,4640858,00.html.

48. Edward Said, "Scholarship and Commitment: An Introduction," *Profession* (2000), p. 7.

49. Kimball, cited in Lawrence W. Levine, *The Opening of the American Mind* (Boston: Beacon Press, 1996), p. 19.

50. All of these ideas and the quote itself are taken from Edward Said, *Humanism and Democratic Criticism* (New York: Columbia University Press, 2004), p. 142.

51. Zygmunt Bauman, *Liquid Times: Living in an Age of Uncertainty* (Oxford: Polity, 2007), p. 8.

18

Unplaguing the Stomach

Curing the University of California Admissions Policy with an Ethic of Communal Justice and Care

JENIFER CRAWFORD, NANA GYAMFI AND PETER McLAREN[1]

> There are grave educational inequities in California's public schools.
>
> (Oakes 2005)

Underrepresented minority students—including African Americans, Latinos, Filipinos and Native Americans, as well as the states poorest students—are not achieving at the same levels as their white suburban middle- and upper-class counterparts (Darling-Hammond 2004; Orfield 1999). In order to achieve a more democratic and socially just California, unequal racial and class educational attainment outcomes must be addressed (Oakes et al. 2007). The University of California (UC) admissions policy provides an important opportunity to work towards greater access and equity for the state's children. Yet, since 1996, when the UC implemented race-neutral policies, there has been a substantial decline in the proportion of entering students who are African American, American Indian, and Latino (OPSAS 2003). The student body at the world's largest public institution of higher education does not reflect the state's racial and class composition (Diversity 2007).

We want to make clear at the outset that we are aware that questions of educational "access" to universities are not the same as questions of educational "outcome." The latter are tied to an even larger question of the role of the university in the wider social order—in this case, the larger social division of labor within capitalist society. We are restricting the scope of this essay to the question of educational access, understanding full well that greater access to universities within capitalist societies does not guarantee closing the economic gap between the rich and the poor. Educational access and outcome must be struggled for within the larger political optic of anti-capitalist struggle, conjugated with anti-racist, anti-sexist, anti-homophobic and anti-imperialist struggle.

The goal of the admissions policy for the UC system must be reformulated and grounded in an underlying ethic of communal justice and care as an important step towards the goal of achieving more equity for California's students. The communalistic ethos of traditional societies of Africa and her diaspora provides an alternative ethical framework for social justice that equitably and measurably achieves the goal of advancing the community through education. This alternative ethical framework will require an ideological shift where the ethical goal of the equal protection of individual rights is replaced with the ethical goal of doing what is best for the community, and especially those least advantaged. The ethical concern is not what the individual "deserves" but what the community "needs." Competition between distinct individuals is replaced by collaboration among interconnected community members. This chapter presents a new vision for a UC admissions policy while critiquing the underlying assumptions of both the affirmative action and non-affirmative action admissions policies of the past and present. There is a stalemate between liberal and conservative positions, and we need to break this binary apart. To achieve this end, we looked to other traditions and other ways of thinking about social justice. We found in African philosophical tradition what we believe will help us think in novel ways about social and educational inequity. Interestingly, there are elements of this tradition that hearken to traditions in American society.[2] Our purpose in this article is to insert concepts from a different tradition—one that has not been part of the conversation, and one that is so rich in implication that we can free up our thinking.

Ethics and Ideologies of UC Admissions Policies

 Mpatapom
"Knot of pacification/reconciliation"

In a country well-governed poverty is something to be ashamed of. In a country badly governed wealth is something to be ashamed of.

(Confucius)

The ethic of equal protection is a concept that was made a guiding American principle in 1866, when it was written into the Fourteenth Amendment to the United States Constitution: "No state shall … deny to any person within its jurisdiction the equal protection of the laws" (United States 2004). The Equal Protection Clause expanded the right of equal protection from the federal government to the states. Many conservatives argue that "equal protection"—regardless of the legacy of racism, capitalism and discrimination—must apply equally to all citizens (Chávez 1998; Mosley & Capaldi 1996). Liberals and progressives argue that different people must be treated differently in order to attain "equal protection" (Mosley & Capaldi 1996). Proponents of the latter view advocate advancing remedies for unequal racial outcomes based on historical and present-day *de jure* and *de facto* discrimination (Marable 1996), while the conservative interpretation advocates not using identifying markers such as race and gender in social policy.

The differences in the interpretation of equal protection are reflective of differences in attitudes about how society functions. The tenor of the UC admissions policies have historically depended upon the interpretation of the ethic of equal protection, which has been determined largely by the ideology of the policy-maker.[3] The conservative and liberal views of equal protection are rooted in two opposing ideologies and have promulgated different legal and social policy outcomes. When conservative justice is implemented into social policy, white middle- and upper-class men are the big winners. Conversely, when a liberal justice model is implemented, communities of color and poor people may benefit in certain situations.

According to those who adhere to a conservative ideology, society functions smoothly, like a Porsche, and all the pieces run together in perfect harmony. America is a nation of distinct individuals, and through their individual effort they realize the American dream grounded in the Protestant work ethic (Weber 1930). America is the land of the free where each person is free to make or break their own future. America is a meritocracy where any person, regardless of social status, can pull themselves up by their own bootstraps.[4] According to this view there is minimal conflict and "the social system is made up of the actions of individuals" who serve to maintain the society (Parsons and Shils 1951, 191).

The conservative interpretation of the equal protection clause is grounded in the belief that America is a meritocracy, where all individuals can climb up or fall down the social ladder depending on their own merit and hard work. Those who gain material wealth and positions carry prestige as the noble "natural aristocracy" that arises to look after the common good (Jefferson and Petersen 2004).

Equal protection protects the individuals with merit, who thereby deserve social and material rewards. Everyone has equal access to prove their merit. Thus, the category of merit becomes the standard upon which society decides who gets the benefit and the rights. Retired UC Regent Ward Connelly, former Supreme Court Justice Rehnquist, President G. W. Bush and Fox News media personality Bill O'Reilly—all profess to believe in universal individual merit as a guide in the implementation of social policy.

Conservatives assert that an admissions policy that paints merit against a backdrop of race, gender or class is unethical and unjust. Since all people have equal access to merit, then admissions policies should judge their worthiness of being admitted on their universal merit alone. An admissions policy that considers "outside" factors of race, socio-economic status and gender violates equal protection, since America provides all its citizens with the opportunity to prove or disprove their merit. Conservatives argue that, by positively considering the status of disadvantaged race, gender or class—in lieu of "merit"—affirmative action policies give an unjust advantage to people of color, women and the poor. Those applicants coming from the advantaged race, gender or class are unfairly penalized by such policies.

The conservative interpretation of equal protection was constituted as UC policy on July 20, 1995, when the Board of Regents adopted Regents Resolutions SP-1 and SP-2.[5] Thereafter, this notion of justice was made California law with Proposition 209, a 1996 ballot proposition amending the state constitution to prohibit public institutions from considering race, sex or ethnicity.[6] The liberal affirmative action admissions policy was repealed and the UC system adopted a policy fashioned under the conservative ideology. The result was a decrease in the enrollment of underrepresented minorities (URMs).[7] In 1995, 20 percent of the undergraduate students admitted were URMs, compared to 2005, when 17 percent were admitted.[8] Furthermore, fewer of these underrepresented students were entering graduate school and finishing. Only 7 percent of the PhDs awarded at the UC went to URM students in 2005. Under conservative admissions policy fewer URMs proportionately are being admitted, while the number of URMs in society is increasing. In 2000, they comprised 41 percent of California's and 25 percent of the nation's public high-school graduates (Diversity 2007).

According to the liberal interpretation of equal protection, people are in a great contest, and not everyone plays by the same rules.[9] People are constantly competing for limited resources and prestige in society. This contest occurs on the uneven terrain of historical and present-day racism, sexism and classism. Some get more advantages than others, and these differences are based largely on race, class and gender. The liberals think of America more as an old jalopy VW van that has been rusted out by racism and classism. They see America as sorely needing a tune-up before it can run smoothly. We reject the liberal term "classism" on the grounds that class is not an "ism" like racism or sexism. Our position is that class exploitation creates the conditions of possibility for other antagonisms to develop and that the ruling class wages war against the working class through the exploitation of human labor-power.

This liberal interpretation of the equal protection ethic is grounded in the ideology that people have power in society to realize any social status, but at the same time are differently constrained by their social identities of race, gender and class. Lyndon B. Johnson exemplified this liberal ideology in his 1965 speech "To Fulfill These Rights":

> You do not take a person who, for years, has been hobbled by chains and liberate him, bring him up to the starting line of a race and then say, "You are free to compete with all the others," and still justly believe that you have been completely fair. (Johnson 1966).

Society is racist, sexist and classist, but that can be fixed, and America has the potential to be democratic through some modest reforms. Opportunity and ability complicate the conservative idea of merit.[10] The merit of a potential applicant to the UC must take into account ability in the context of the proportion of opportunity the student has had.

This notion of ability in the context of opportunity to learn provides the foundation of the liberal model of affirmative action, which was codified as law after the *Brown v. Board of Education* Supreme Court case in 1954.[11] Imagine two potential UC applicants, Joe and John, who have the same academic ability. Joe has had less opportunity—on the basis of race, class or gender—than John. Because Joe has achieved the ability level that he has with limited opportunities available to him, he deserves admission to the university even if he has not achieved the same ability level as John who had more opportunity. This policy is shaped by the "idea of taking the proactive steps necessary to dismantle prejudice [that] has been around for more than a century" (Marable 1996, 4). Given the ethic of "equal protection" and the liberal ideology of contextualized ability, treating people differently is the only way to protect people equally.

UC Admissions Policy

Bi Nka Bi "No one should bite the other."	All animals are equal. But some animals are more Equal than others.
	(George Orwell)

White supremacy grounds the underlying conservative and liberal ideologies of the current and past UC admissions policies. Historically, the conservative ideology's level playing field and color-blind interpretation of individual rights has not led to socially just policy. While the liberal ideology certainly is better equipped to achieve social justice because it begins from an understanding of injustice—or the inequitable contexts in which people live out their lives—when crafting social policy, both liberal and conservative ideologies are fundamentally flawed. While the liberal interpretation at least acknowledges the inequities of history and the need to redress them, both ideologies—rooted in white supremacy—emerge from an individualism that at heart keeps us from achieving social justice, access and equity for California's citizens.[12]

The underlying ideology of white supremacy and the competitive individualism of capitalism create differential access to opportunities to develop abilities towards "advancing remedies for unequal racial outcomes through a system that expands the notion of merit in admissions is not enough" (Marable 1996, 14). American society is neither a Porsche nor a VW van, but rather has been sent to the junkyard with a cracked engine block. People have power to act upon their social and material conditions. Their power plays out on the canvas of a history of inequity based in white supremacy and capitalism that runs so deep that people of color and the poor are acting upon conditions not entirely of their own making.

Under the white supremacist ethos, the admission of applicants from underrepresented communities with academic qualifications that do not meet the UC system's standard is repugnant because those applicants are not perceived as a tangible financial or reputational benefit to the UC system. However, the admission of applicants from underrepresented communities directly and measurably benefits those communities, and therefore the larger community-admission policies which admit such applicants are viewed with contempt. In contrast, the legacy student and student athlete who may not have the GPA, SAT scores, or other academic requirements are not considered offensive affirmative action admittees within the white supremacist construct, because it is understood that the UC campus/system receives financial and reputational benefits from the admission of those students.

Communalism

Funtunfunefu-Denkyemfunefu "Siamese crocodiles"	Injustice anywhere is a threat to justice everywhere.
	(Martin Luther King, Jr.)

Unlike the ethical framework of white supremacy that imagines the world as a theoretical land of rugged individuals pulling themselves up by their individual bootstraps, the communalistic ethos knows the individual and the larger community as intricately intertwined. In the traditional African communalistic society, "[e]verybody felt responsible to everybody else in the community and its neighborhood. When a community member suffered, it was the community as a whole that suffered" (Fu-Kiau 2001, 50).

"The community" is defined from as narrowly as the local area around the campus to as broadly as Planet Earth, and includes past, present and future members. It includes anyone who contributes to and/or takes from the "community pot." The "community pot" is the repository of the community's resources, involving the efforts, labor, thoughts and monies of all of the community's members. Under the communalistic ethical framework, the UC system is an integral member of "the community" in that it takes and gives to the "community pot." Each community member, including the UC system, has a duty to the community at large, the smaller communities from where the members come, and the individual members themselves.

This communalistic ethos is well documented in traditional mores, customs and proverbs of Africa and her diaspora. The Akan people of Ghana, West Africa, for example, have several proverbs that describe the vital interdependence of the individual and collective members of the community. There are proverbs which remind the community that no one member can long escape any calamity befalling other members: "Ese tenten ne se kwatia didi biako (pe)" ("The tall and short teeth have but one grind between them") (Danquah 1968, 195). There are proverbs that remind community members that large important tasks cannot be accomplished by individuals standing alone: "Obiakafo na okum sono, na amansan nhina di" ("It takes one man to kill an elephant, but the universe to consume it") (ibid., 189). Other proverbs address the practical concern that the imbalance caused by individualism harms not only the community at large but the individual who receives the selfish benefit: "Obiako di'wo a, etoa ne yam" ("*If one alone eats the honey, it plagues his stomach*") (ibid.).

The traditional African communalistic ethos is evidenced in the African American community's view of the connection between the individual and the larger community.

> While affirming the worth of the individual, an African American psychology intimates that a person is a finite being, embedded in a web of social relations and institutional structures. This web buffers both the individual and the community from the suffering created by, for instance, a shifting economy. (Siddle Walker and Snarey 2004, 11)

Drawing on its African roots, African American society has long recognized that "[a]n individual Black American's life chances are improved with the advancement of the race as a whole. The Black American community's life chances are also linked to the personal achievements of individuals. Thus, the Black community celebrates individual success" (ibid.).

As a community member, the UC system is imputed a moral personhood and responsibility to the larger society. "Moral personhood is understood in terms of the practical moral virtues that one has acquired, and the ability to, in fact, act in ways that meet the responsibilities that are specified by a community, and the rights or social recognition that flow from acting morally" (Ikuenobe 2006, 103). There is a presumption that each member of society knows the moral standards of the community, and will take on the responsibilities, rights and reputation that result from adhering to those community moral standards. "Being a moral person involves one's ability to act in various ways that are consistent with the broad moral principles of a community that make peaceful and happy life possible for all" (ibid., 109).

The identification of the "broad moral principles" that "make peaceful and happy life for all" involves more than conversations among the most advantaged segments of society. The danger in such public discussions is that people who are already benefiting from the status quo are likely to declare broad moral principles which make their lives even more peaceful and happy, while restricting the peace and happiness of the least advantaged: "Nea wadidi amme se nea odidi anadwo ye obayifo" ("The one who has had enough to eat states that whoever eats in the night is a witch") (Danquah 1968, 192).

Thus the passage of Proposition 209 and the revamping of the UC admissions policy were part of a white backlash against the liberal ideology that had defined admissions policies for the last forty years. The intent of this backlash was not a peaceful and happy life for all, but a peaceful and happy life for white rich people. The voters who passed Proposition 209 were not concerned with the best interest of all community members, and any policies flowing from their vote would be void.

All individuals and entities that play an active and social role in a communalistic society are expected to do their part to contribute to "the good" as part of their moral responsibility to the community. In traditional Akan society, "the good" is described as beneficence, "the practice in society of doing good." The establishment and maintenance of "the good" is the only legitimate reason for individuals to gather and form communities (Danquah 1968, 181). Any "gathered togetherness" of individual community members which does not have the aim of perpetuating "the good" is of "no value and soon may fall apart in disharmony" (ibid., 182–3). The formation of groups and communities does not itself constitute "the good." The manifestation of "the good" requires specific types of beneficial social action on the part of the community's members.

Community members must satisfy their moral duties "in order for the community to exist, flourish, and provide the proper environment in which individuals can achieve personhood and their life plans" (Ikuenobe 2006, 118). Unlike the conservative and liberal interpretations of equal protection, the African communalistic ethical framework emphasizes the duty of the individual over individual rights.

> The African rationale for emphasizing duties as opposed to rights is that the emphasis on rights will suggest to individuals that they have right-claims to make of the community without any corresponding duties. However, the emphasis on duties and obligations implies that an individual's rights are contingent on the ability of everyone to contribute to the community as a pool of rights from which individuals can draw. (ibid., 117).

Until all of the individual members of the community have the ability to contribute to the community, the pool of rights cannot be accessed. In the context of admissions, no individual applicant has a "right" to be admitted until all of California's students have the ability to contribute to society through access to an education within the UC system.

The UC system has a duty to institute an admissions policy that is consistent with its responsibility to the larger community, especially community members of color, to achieve "the good" and "make happy and peaceful life possible for all" (Ikuenobe 2006, 103). The university already acknowledges its obligation to offer opportunity to students from all over the state, and has extended this responsibility to all the universities in the UC system. Pursuant to recent policy, UC campuses must reflect the diversity of culture, geography and socio-economic backgrounds of the state of California (UC Board of Regents 2007). Furthermore, the UC system has expressed its intent to increase the number of URMs at the university in order to achieve diversity (Kauer 2006).[13]

An Admissions Policy for the Community

Ese Ne Tekrema
"The teeth and the tongue"

And the King answering shall say to them, Verily, I say to you, Inasmuch as ye have done it to one of the least of these my brethren, ye have done it to me.
(Matthew 25: 40)

The main impediment to progress has been the reconciliation of individual rights under the various interpretations of the equal protection clause with the UC system's duty to the larger community. The consideration of the concerns of community members with divergent interests requires a balancing of interests. "According to the communalistic ethos, one must justify one's actions in terms of placing one's interest in the context of the community's interests" (Ikuenobe 2006, 109). Since "the good" is the ethical aim of the communalistic society, "the norms of morality are defined in terms of the adjustment of the interests of the individual to the interests of society, rather than the adjustment of the interests of society to those of the individual" (ibid.). There can understandably be a concern that totalitarian, white supremacist or other exclusive groups will suppress or ignore the interests of targeted community members as part of the definition of community good. Under the communalistic ethos, any policy that does not make life peaceful and happy for all is meritless. The adjustment of the interest of the individual to the interests of the society does not require a refusal to acknowledge the interest of the individual, since the "harmonization" of the individual and community interest is the means, and "securing human well-being" is the ends, of all moral endeavors. "The emphasis is on understanding the right *end* which is tied to the interest of the community and human well-being, on which the interests of the individual depend" (ibid., 119).

The right end of the UC admissions policy should be to provide community members with access to an education that will achieve "the good" by uprooting the current system of white power and white supremacy. In the communalistic society, the "educated know themselves to be an integral part of the nation and recognize the responsibility to give greater service [commensurate with] the greater opportunities they have had" (Nyerere 1967, 28). The ability of the educated to serve "the good" of the community is directly related to the type of education they have received.

Education has to liberate both the mind and the body of man. It has to make him more of a human being because he is aware of his potential as a human being, and is in positive, life-enhancing relationship with himself, his neighbor, and his environment. Education has therefore to enable a man to throw off the impediments to freedom which restrict his full physical and mental development. (Nyerere 1974, 3)[14]

Thus, the purpose of education is relational and contextual. Education has a duty to liberate where schooling is neither fair nor just and the society does not present youth with equal opportunities to learn and to form positive relationships with self, community and society as a whole. Even where the liberal interpretation of equal protection is the norm, educational institutions have not been able to attain long-lasting or far-reaching equitable outcomes. The number of URMs in the educational pipeline is increasing. Diversity among California's children is growing; it is predicted that, by the 2011–12 school year, 51 percent of public high-school graduates will be URMs. Yet, public schools have traditionally served to reproduce social inequalities (Bowles and Gintis 1976) inherent in capitalist and white supremacist societies. So, while Nyerere's comments were directed at African nations during the 1970s, they are applicable to marginalized communities in California today because both continue to be excluded from material and social resources that white groups enjoy.[15]

Justice and Care

Sankofa
"Return and get it"

Power at its best is love implementing the demands of justice. Justice at its best is love correcting everything that stands against love.
(Martin Luther King, Jr.)

The simultaneous consideration of the needs of the individual and the community in the same ethical space defines the communalistic justice and care model of achieving "the good." "[T]he delineation of self-care and community care into isolated categories fashions a false dichotomy" (Siddle Walker and Snarey 2004, 11). Morality in a communalistic society considers the inherent good of an action in itself and the duty it imposes, but "not to the exclusion of caring for others in the community or the goodness of the consequence of the action and its significance or relevance to the care for others and the communal interest of which one's interest is a part" (Ikuenobe 2006, 117). The communal justice and care model "seeks both carefulness and fairness, both hand-in-handness and even-handedness" (Siddle Walker & Snarey 2004, 131). "Any law that uplifts human personality is just. Any law that degrades human personality is unjust" (King [1963] 1986). "Any law that conveys uplift to the least advantaged among us is care-full. Any law that jeopardizes their uplift is unjust" (Siddle Walker & Snarey 2004, 137). Cycles of uplift are created through "the collective responsibility for the individual and individual responsibilities to the community" (ibid, 136–7).

The achievement of "the good" in education, then, requires the consideration of justice for the community and sympathy for the needs of individual community

250 • Jenifer Crawford, Nana Gyamfi and Peter McLaren

members. For example, African Americans seek schools that are "just" for their children in distribution of resources, facilities, and educational opportunities. Simultaneously, "they seek schools that provide caring environments for their children" and the individual advancement of students' knowledge and ability to achieve their post-secondary goals (Siddle Walker & Snarey 2004, 6). An individual personal sense of redress for their children is also what is driving parent actions and is not exclusive of parental concern for community uplift. In "Does the Negro Need Separate Schools?" W. E. B. DuBois writes that "Sympathy, Knowledge, and the Truth" are fundamental to the education of African American youth and depend upon the sympathetic touch of teachers, confidence in the intelligence of young African American students, and a human education (DuBois 1941).[16] According to DuBois, this sympathetic touch hinges on an intimate knowledge of the student's people's history, contact on the basis of social equality, and sympathy born out of familiar love. Without sympathetic touch, educators will not be able to create more equitable worlds through their work.

As part of the ethic of communal justice and care, educators and policy-makers must actively identify and confront white supremacy and its manifestation in liberal discourse—"color-blindness"—which has recently become the catch-phrase of the conservative interpretation of the equal protection clause.[17] Identifying the normative, economic and psychological metaphorical environment that sustains white supremacy provides an opportunity to pry open dominant discourses about race in social policy.[18] In these discourses, "Whiteness represents a regime of differences that produces and racializes an abject other" and a "discursive regime that enables real effects to take place" (McLaren 1998).[19] The social ontology of whiteness is grounded in the color-blind ideology where whites "avoid discussing their own social, political, economic and cultural investments in whiteness, mainly because they fail to see their complicity with white supremacy." This particular way of being among others focuses on extreme symptoms of white supremacy as to avoid the implications of one's own whiteness (Yancy 2004).

Color-blindness has no place in an admissions policy based on the ethic of communal justice and care. It is not appropriate in the context of admissions because race matters in access to opportunities to learn in America's public schools (Darling-Hammond 2000). It is an act of bad faith in the context of admissions because it continues to mask and normalize the social, material and economic aspects of white priviledge critiqued above. Social justice can

> be better attained both for the privileged and the less privileged in the context of communalism ... [T]he constant disposition to offer to everyone what belongs to him as a "right", ought to be extended in favour of the less privileged, under a favourable condition of human coexistence, closeness, and co-operation. (Ekei 2001, 143)

The ideology of communal justice and care requires acknowledgement of the ravages of white supremacy in education, and makes the greater effort to extend admission to those who have been victimized to the collective good of the community.

Admissions decisions should be made in a way that blends individual achievement with the common good. Including individual achievement in the criteria for admissions advances the common good. In order to get more students in medical school that will go back into communities of color and poor communities, the admissions policy should measure a potential applicant's basic bio-medical knowledge as well as direct contact with marginalized communities. The use of grades and test scores to determine eligibility is an individualistic and meritocratic principle. An admissions policy for the good of the community must possess a broader, richer set of criteria—in part a measure of individual achievement and knowledge and in part an ability to contribute to the good of the community.

The resultant admissions policy will be a radical departure from the current UC one, a mandate that the university system address social injustice while providing the type of education required by the community. The primary concern will be whether the admission of the applicant benefits the community that simultaneously provides benefits and is served by the UC system. The question will be whether the latter fulfills its duty to the community and the individual by admitting the applicant. Criteria for admission will address more than mere academic qualifications. An applicant's demonstrated commitment to community uplift will be considered as valuable as an applicant's demonstrated commitment to academics or sports. Their potential ability to serve as a role model for underrepresented community members will be as valuable as a potential ability to contribute to the global economy. Individual achievement comes into play in a communalistic admissions policy, but the criteria used to determine what counts as achievement must be expanded to include the community good.[20]

In short, applicants will be admitted because they assist the UC system in fulfilling its duty to increase social justice in the community. In admitting applicants such as a war refugee, an inner-city survivor of the foster-care system or the child of migrant workers, the UC system fulfills its duty to the community by exposing community members to experiences, cultures and social ills that they may not otherwise encounter.[21] Learning comes about through direct, vital and critical contact with social ills.[22] Dewey (1927, 1932) asserts that through public social inquiry community members and researchers "lay hold of the realities beneath the froth and foam" of everyday social problems (Dewey 1922). In this way can understand the social, cultural and political contexts that sustain inequality and support the ideologies of priviledge together with citizens making expert knowledge quotidian and common knowledge more expert (Oakes 2005; Oakes et al. 2006).[23]

Towards a Communal Justice and Care Admissions Policy

Nkonsonkonson
"Chain link"

Given the natural differences between human beings, equality is an ethical aspiration that cannot be realized without recourse either to despotism or to an act of fraternity.

(Octavio Paz)

An admissions policy based on the communalistic ethos of traditional societies of Africa and her diaspora provides the best opportunity to achieve social justice in UC admissions. It will create the context for students and citizens to be human, to care for community, and to be conscious of white supremacy and their advantage or disadvantage in the system. Communalism is defined by interconnectedness, inclusiveness, and a duty of making a happy and peaceful life for all, especially the less advantaged members of the community. The entire community is uplifted by the consideration of both justice and care. Justice occurs with the balancing of community and individual interests. Care is defined by love, solidarity, respect, and willingness to address and redress the wrongs of society. The communal justice and care ethos represents an ontological shift from conservative and liberal debate on social policy in that it accounts *all* members of society, balances individual with community needs, and attacks the roots of exclusive ideologies, including white supremacy. The communal justice and care ethos broadens admissions criteria in ways that allows the UC to fulfill its promise to Californians that the student body will reflect the racial and class composition of the state. A reformed admission policy will have only limited effectiveness if it is a revolving door. If the UC creates the right kinds of conditions—within university classes and in primary and secondary public schools—more students will be able to learn, and subsequently there will be many more students who are eligible for admissions to the university and more students will graduate. A communal justice and care ethic leverages schools to be sites where the good for all of society's members can be realized, and a peaceful and happy life for every person becomes possible.

Taking our argument further will require us to address the importance of challenging the social division of labor in which the UC system itself is embedded. By this we mean that we must recognize that the struggle to end discrimination on the basis of race and gender and sexual orientation will not likely reduce economic inequality in the United States until capitalism itself is replaced with a socialist alternative.

Notes

1. We would like to thank James Simmons and Mike Rose for their extensive suggestions and feedback on this work.
2. According to John Dewey, truth is found by public social inquiry, a gathering of people using the scientific method discussing, under the right conditions with equal voice, the good of society.
3. Ideology is the wide-ranging system of beliefs that gives people categories that provide the foundation of programs of political action and thought (Blackburn 1994). Ideologies always exist, sometimes dominant and other times not (Gramsci 1999). Ideologies are a rich net of ideas—both conscious and unconscious—that ground our understanding of the way the world is and the way people are in the world. Ideologies are the "air we breathe" (ibid).
4. Sociologists call this explanation for how society operates "functionalism" (Parsons 1949).
5. SP-1 prohibited the consideration of race, religion, sex, color, ethnicity and national origin in the admissions decision process. Similarly, SP-2 barred the use of the same

factors in hiring and contracting decisions. Both resolutions established that "nothing contained within these sections should be interpreted to prohibit any action strictly necessary to maintain or establish eligibility to receive federal or state funding" (OEOD 2005). Therefore, the requirements set forth under Lyndon B Johnson's Executive Order 11246 still applied to UC campuses (Marable 1996).

6. In July 2006 Regents Maria Ledesma and Fred Ruiz requested that the university "undertake a holistic study of the long-term impact of Proposition 209 on the University's ability to serve the State and fulfill its mission as the leading public university in one of the nation's most diverse states" (Diversity 2007). The central findings of the study group on university diversity included an acknowledgment that diversity is fundamental to UC's mission, quality and service to the state of California. To seek and support diversity effectively, clear, consistent and regularly produced data are necessary (Diversity 2007).

7. According to the UC, underrepresented minorities (URMs) include Chicano/Latino, African American, Filipino and Native American students.

8. These figures are for domestic students only.

9. Sociologists call this view conflict theory. Conflict theorists explain that people in society are in a state of perpetual struggle.

10. Ability is "the product of a hundred unseen forces playing upon the infant, the child and the man" and is directly related to the opportunities that the individual has to develop their ability (Johnson 1966).

11. The NAACP filed on behalf of a black student, Linda Brown, who was transported out of her white neighborhood to attend a black school in Topeka, Kansas. The Supreme Court ruled that separate educational facilities were "inherently unequal" and violated the Fourteenth Amendment. The next year the Court ordered segregated districts to integrate with "all deliberate speed" (Irons 2002). Executive Order No. 10,925, 1961, issued by President Kennedy, established the concept of affirmative action by mandating that projects financed with federal funds "take affirmative action" to ensure that hiring and employment practices are free of racial bias. In 1962, James Farmer, founder of the Congress of Racial Equality, held a meeting with then Vice President Lyndon B. Johnson. Farmer proposed that a program that he called Compensatory Preferential Treatment should be put in place in order to advance the equality of the black race. In 1965, Johnson (then president) renamed Compensatory Preferential Treatment "affirmative action" in a famous speech at Howard University, which became the national justification for moving the country beyond non-discrimination to a more vigorous effort to improve the status of black Americans. This concept of justice was also carried out at a grassroots level. One example is Operation Breadbasket in 1962, led by Martin Luther King, Jr., and Ralph Abernathy in Chicago. This operation consisted of targeting local employers and threatening boycotts unless more African Americans were hired by white businesses (Efrati 2007). The liberal version of justice was continued with No Child Left Behind, which began originally as a bi-partisan national educational policy for kindergarten through 12th grade public schools. All students are held to the same standards and ideally should receive equal educational opportunities. Even with this model of liberal justice, public schools remain terribly inequitable places. For example, for every 100 Latino 9th graders in California in 2002, 54 graduated high school four years later, and only five graduated having completed the required college preparatory coursework (Oakes 2007). An African American male is more likely to go to prison than to a four-year university (Kewal Ramani 2007). Over the last fifty years, the liberal version of justice has not produced equitable outcomes for California's K–12 students.

12. There is a difference between individualism and white supremacy. They are not isomorphic. Conversely, communitarian philosophy could be based in white supremacy. We are pointing to a different kind of care that is less missionary like, an acknowledging of the legacy of discrimination and a commitment to end all forms of white power that make it extraordinarily difficult for some people in society to achieve their highest potential in terms of ability, but also in terms of having the freedom to be human.

13. The university should educate the top one-eighth of high-school graduating seniors in California. Therefore, students need to maintain minimum eligibility requirements to function as an entitlement to guarantee a place at UC—although not necessarily the campus or the major of their choice. The demographic population of the state of California is different in comparison to other states, where questions of affirmative action focus largely on opportunities for whites versus blacks (Diversity 2007). California, on the other hand, is currently a "minority-majority state", with whites constituting slightly than less than half of the total population. Studies show that the high-school graduates that meet the UC eligibility standards are mostly whites, while one-third are Asian Americans, and the proportion of African Americans and Latinos is lower than 5 percent (OPSAS 2003). The UC's Academic Senate's Diversity Statement reads, in part, "Because the core mission of the University … is to serve the interests of the State of California, it must seek to achieve diversity among its student bodies and … its employees" (Lustig 2006).

14. *Mwalimu* Julius Nyerere, president of the Republic of Tanzania from 1965 to 1985, led a national literacy campaign that aimed to liberate Tanzanians from white supremacist ideas and to abolish unequal social and economic organizations left in the wake of colonial rule (Mulenga 2001).

15. Nyerere asserts,

> Education has to liberate the African [or African-American] from the mentality of slavery and colonialism by making him aware of himself as an equal member of the human race, with the rights and duties of his humanity. It has to liberate him from the habit of submitting to circumstances, which reduce his dignity as if they were immutable. And it has to liberate him from the shackles of technical ignorance for the development of himself and his fellow man.

With the full mental and physical development of all people in society, more positive and life-enhancing relationships can be forged, which, Nyerere argues, will ultimately lead to the greater good of society.

16. A sympathetic touch between the teacher and student includes: "knowledge on the part of the teacher, not simply of the individual taught, but of his surroundings and background and the history of his class and group; such contact between pupils, and between teacher and pupil, on the basis of perfect social equality, as will increase this sympathy and knowledge" (DuBois 1941).

17. On June 23, 2003, in the Supreme Court ruled against considering race to integrate schools in the *Grutter v. Bollinger* case. The Supreme Court (5–4) upheld the University of Michigan Law School's policy, ruling that race can be one of many factors considered by colleges when selecting their students because it furthers "a compelling interest in obtaining the educational benefits that flow from a diverse student body." The Court, however, ruled (6–3) that the more formulaic approach of the University of Michigan's undergraduate admissions program, which uses a point system that rates students and awards additional points to minorities, had to be modified. In *Parents v. Seattle* and *Meredith v. Jefferson*, on June 28, 2006, affirmative action suffered a setback when a

bitterly divided court ruled 5–4 that programs in Seattle and Louisville, Kentucky (2004), which tried to maintain diversity in schools by considering race when assigning students to schools, are unconstitutional.

18. Headley Clevis explains that the metaphorical environment of whiteness is composed of the economic, normative and psychological realms. The economic realm includes whiteness as property, a "possessive investment in whiteness" (Lipsitz 2006) and the racial contract, a social contract upholding the system of white supremacy benefiting whites at the cost of non-whites (Mills 1997). The normative metaphorical environment for whiteness is based on 1) sociological scholarship, where white is the norm for social acceptability, 2) civic consciousness, that is touted as beyond race consciousness, and 3) a legal system that advocates color-blindness (Harris 1993). The psychological dimension of the metaphorical environment conjures whiteness and denounces race. These metaphorical environments collectively constitute the normative discourse that shapes social ontology, the study of being among others.

19. Our self-creation through the choices we make is a manifestation of human freedom. A racialized consciousness occurs because this freedom is situated and exists within an ensemble of limitations. Existence is at once both transcendence and facticity. Whiteness and its privileges depend on a dichotomous polarity of arbitrary color. White humanity is then predicated falsely and illegitimately on the subhumanity of the "Other," and enlightenment is solely the property of whites (Birt 2004). This enlightened consciousness is held in bad faith. Sartre's notion of bad faith in *Being and Nothiness* is the intention to deceive coupled with self. Normalized bad faith is the collective untruth adopted by many. Racialized consciousness denotes the shaping of consciousness in relation to a racist social structure. Fomenting a new racial consciousness means knowing how race operates on self and racialized others.

20. Hence, under a communalistic admissions policy, an applicant would not gain admission to the UC system simply because their admission would benefit their family and its reputation or the coffers and reputation of the UC system. There would have to be a larger community benefit. If not, then the applicant would be denied admission in spite, for example, of the number of generations previously admitted to the school in the case of a legacy applicant. In fact, from a communal perspective, a legacy applicant whose family had previously benefited from admission and who could not demonstrate any larger community benefit would properly forfeit the "right" to admission for wasting past community investment in their ancestors.

21. Not every admittee will offer a window into another experience or a contact with the social ills, but every admittee should the qualification of assisting the UC system in fulfilling its community responsibilities. A communalistic ethic requires that the admissions policy address not only the admission of students but also the creation of practical mechanisms that will provide the type of "care" designed to produce graduates with the tools needed to assist in the achievement of "the good" of society. If admittees are not supported with a "sympathetic touch," and they subsequently leave or are forced out of school, the UC system loses the opportunity to fulfill its responsibility to the community. "Care" has been missing from prior UC admissions policies, and the result has been the system's failure to graduate many of the admittees whose admission was supposed to effect positive change in underrepresented communities.

22. Educators through economic and community literacy provide participation with these social ills. Students engage in this literacy and learn to read the current reality and write the possible future. Honestly and courageously facing social problems is the process by which students and society change.

23. However, Dewey stops short of being able to address how people construct knowledge through social inquiry (West 1993). "In what settings might public inquiry occur?" and "What processes might be transformative?" are important questions to answer if, as socio-cultural theorists have argued, citizens learn when knowledge is presented in authentic context, such as that of their community and the problems they face. Learning is a process that requires social interaction and collaboration at the intersection of community, shared practice, identity and meaning (Lave and Wenger 1991; Wenger 1998). Freire argued that public social inquiry occurs in "culture circles," which are educational groups rooted in the community, that draw upon popular culture and popular art (Freire 1970, 1985, 2005; McLaren & Leonard 1993). Freire's pedagogical-political program engages students in constructing a critical literacy through which citizens have the ability to understand the relationships texts have with power and domination and connect those power relationships within texts to broader social structures of inequity (Hull 1993; McLaren 1998).

References

Birt, Robert (2004) The bad faith of whiteness. In George Yancy (Ed.), *What white looks like: African-American philosophers on the whiteness question* (pp. 55–64). New York: Routledge.

Blackburn, Simon (1994) *The Oxford dictionary of philosophy*. Oxford: Oxford University Press.

Bowles, Samuel, and Gintis, Herbert (1976) *Schooling in capitalist America: Educational reform and the contradictions of economic life*. London: Routledge & Kegan Paul.

Chávez, Lydia (1998) *The color bind: California's battle to end affirmative action*. Berkeley: University of California Press.

Danquah, J. B. (1968) *The Akan doctrine of God: A fragment of Gold Coast ethics and religion* (2nd ed.). London: Cass.

Darling-Hammond, Linda (2000) New Standards and Old Inequalities: School Reform and the Education of African American Students. *Journal of Negro Education, 69*, 263–87.

Darling-Hammond, Linda (2004) Inequality and the Right to Learn: Access to Qualified Teachers in California's Public Schools. *Teachers College Record, 106*, 1936–66.

Dewey, John (1922) Education as Politics. *The Middle works, 1899–1924*. Carbondale: Southern Illinois University Press, *c.*1976–*c.*1983, *13*, 329–34.

Dewey, John (1927) *The public and its problems*. New York: Henry Holt.

Dewey, John (1932) The Economic Situation. *The Later works, 1925–1953*. Carbondale: Southern Illinois University Press, *c.*1981–*c.*1990, *6*, 182–89.

Diversity, Study Group on University (2007) *Study Group on University Diversity Overview Report to the Regents*. Los Angeles: University California, http://www.universityofcalifor nia.edu/news/2007/diversityreport0907.pdf.

DuBois, W. E. B. (1941) Does the Negro need separate schools? *Journal of Negro Education, 4*, 328–35.

Efrati, Amir (2007) You Say You Want a Big-Law Revolution, Take II. *Wall Street Journal,* October 10.

Ekei, J. Chukwuemeka (2001) *Justice in communalism: A foundation of ethics in African philosophy*. Lagos, Nigeria: Realm Communications.

Freire, Paulo (1970) The Adult Literacy Process as Cultural Action for Freedom. *Harvard Educational Review, 40*, 2.

Freire, Paulo (1985) *The politics of education: Culture, power, and liberation*. South Hadley, MA: Bergin & Garvey.

Freire, Paulo (2005) *Education for critical consciousness.* London: Continuum.

Fu-Kiau, Kimbwandende Kia Bunseki (2001) *African cosmology of the Bântu-Kôngo: Tying the spiritual knot: Principles of life & living* (2nd ed.). Brooklyn, NY: Athelia Henrietta Press.

Gramsci, Antonio (1999) *Selections from the prison notebooks of Antonio Gramsci,* Quintin Hoare and Geoffrey Nowell Smith, ed. New York: International.

Harris, C. I. (1993) Whiteness as property. *Harvard Law Review, 106,* 1709–91.

Headley, Clevis (2004) Delegitimizing the normativity of "whiteness": A critical African philosophical study of the metaphoricity of "whiteness." In George Yancy (Ed.), *What white looks like: African-American philosophers on the whiteness question* (pp. 87–106). New York: Routledge.

Hull, Glynda (1993) Critical Literacy and Beyond: Lessons Learned from Students and Workers in a Vocational Program and on the Job. *Anthropology and Education Quarterly, 24,* 373–96.

Ikuenobe, Polycarp (2006) *Philosophical perspectives on communalism and morality in African traditions.* Lanham, MD: Lexington Books.

Irons, Peter H. (2002) *Jim Crow's children: The broken promise of the Brown decision.* New York: Viking.

Jefferson, Thomas, and Petersen, Eric S. (2004) *Light and liberty: Reflections on the pursuit of happiness.* New York: Modern Library.

Johnson, Lyndon B. (1966) *Public papers of the presidents of the United Slates: Lyndon B. Johnson, 1965.* Washington, DC: Government Printing Office, *2,* 635–40.

Kauer, Susanne (2006) *UC's Shrinking Pipeline: A Look at Underrepresented Minorities in the UC Pipeline.* PowerPoint Presentation, UCOP Academic Advancement, March 3.

Kewal Ramani, A., Gilbertson, L., Fox, M. A., & Provasnik, S. (2007) *Status and trends in the education of racial and ethnic minorities* (No. NCES 2007-039). Washington, DC: National Center for Education Statistics, Institute of Education Sciences, US Department of Education.

King, M. L., Jr. ([1963] 1986) I Have a Dream. *Ebony,* January, 40–42.

Lave, Jean, and Wenger, Etienne (1991) *Situated learning: Legitimate peripheral participation.* New York: Cambridge University Press.

Lipsitz, George (2006) *The possessive investment in whiteness: How white people profit from identity politics* (rev. and expanded ed.). Philadelphia: Temple University Press.

Lustig, Steve (2006) The University of California diversity statement. http://www.gdnet.ucla .edu/gasaa/admissions/diversity.htm.

Marable, Manning (1996) Staying on the Path to Racial Equality. In George E. Curry (Ed.), *The affirmative action debate.* Reading, MA: Addison-Wesley.

McLaren, Peter (1998) *Life in schools: An introduction to critical pedagogy in the foundations of education* (3rd ed.). New York: Longman.

McLaren, Peter, and Leonard, Peter (1993) *Paulo Freire: A critical encounter.* London: Routledge.

Mills, Charles (1997) *The racial contract.* Ithaca, NY: Cornell University Press.

Mosley, Albert G., & Capaldi, Nicholas (1996) *Affirmative action: Social justice or unfair preference?* Lanham, MD: Rowman & Littlefield.

Mulenga, Derek C. (2001) Mwalimu Julius Nyerere: A Critical Review of his Contributions to Adult Education and Postcolonialism. *International Journal of Lifelong Education, 20,* 446–70.

Nyerere, Julius K. (1967) *Education for self-reliance.* Dar es Salaam: Government Information Services.

Nyerere, Julius K. (1974) *Education must liberate man: President Nyerere's speech to the Dag Hammarskjold Seminar on Education and Training, 1974.* Dar es Salaam: Government Information Services.

Oakes, Jeannie (2005) *Keeping track: How schools structure inequality* (2nd ed.). New Haven, CT: Yale University Press.

Oakes, Jeannie, Rogers, John, and Lipton, Martin (2006) *Learning power: Organizing for education and justice.* New York: Teachers College Press.

Oakes, Jeannie, Valladares, Siomara, Renée, Michelle, Fanelli, Sophie, Medina, David, & Rogers, John (2007) *Latino California educational opportunity report 2007.* Los Angeles: UCLA Institute for Democracy, Education, and Access.

OEOD (2005) A Brief History of Affirmative Action. http://www.eod.uci.edu/aa.html [accessed April 2008].

Orfield, Gary (1999) The Resegregation of our Nation's Schools: A troubling trend. *Civil Rights Journal,* 4, fall.

Parsons, Talcott (1949) *The structure of social action: A study in social theory with special reference to a group of recent European writers* (2nd ed.). New York: Free Press.

Parsons, Talcott, and Shils, Edward (1951) *Toward a general theory of action.* Cambridge, MA: Harvard University Press.

OPSAS (Office of the President, Student Academic Services) (2003) Undergraduate access to the University of California after the elimination of race-conscious policies. http://www.ucop.edu/sas/publish/aa-final2.pdf.

Siddle Walker, Vanessa, and Snarey, John R. (2004) *Race-ing moral formation: African American perspectives on care and justice.* New York: Teachers College Press.

UC Board of Regents (2007) *Board of Admissions and Relations with Schools response to Eligibility, and Admissions Study Group,* May 11. Los Angeles: University of California.

United States (2004) *The Constitution of the United States of America: Analysis and interpretation: Analysis of cases decided by the Supreme Court of the United States to June 28, 2002.* Washington: U.S. Government Printing Office.

Weber, Max (1930) *The Protestant ethic and the spirit of capitalism.* New York: Scribner.

Wenger, Etienne (1998) *Communities of practice: Learning, meaning, and identity.* New York: Cambridge University Press.

West, Cornel (1993) *Keeping faith: Philosophy and race in America.* New York: Routledge.

Yancy, George (2004) *What white looks like: African-American philosophers on the whiteness question.* New York: Routledge.

19

No Child Left Thinking

Democracy at Risk in American Schools and What We Need to Do about It

JOEL WESTHEIMER

Imagine you were visiting a school in a totalitarian nation governed by a single-party dictatorship. Would the educational experiences be markedly different from the ones experienced by children in your local school? I do not ask this question facetiously. It seems plausible, for example, that a good curriculum used to teach multiplication, fractions or a foreign language—perhaps with some adjustments for cultural relevance and suitability—would serve equally well in most parts of the world. But if you stepped into a school and asked to observe a lesson related to the country's political ideals about governance or civic or political participation, would you be able to tell whether you were in a totalitarian nation or a democratic one?

Most of us would like to believe that we would. While schools in North Korea, China or Iran might be teaching students blind allegiance to their nation's leaders and deference to the social and political policies those leaders enact, we would expect that schools in the United States would teach students the skills and dispositions needed to evaluate for themselves the benefits and drawbacks of particular policies and government practices. We would not be surprised to learn, for example, that North Korean children are taught to abide by an "official history" handed down by President Kim Jong-il and his single-party authoritarian regime. A school curriculum that teaches one unified, unquestioned version of "truth" is one of the hallmarks of totalitarian societies. Democratic citizens, on the other hand, are committed to the people, principles and values that underlie democracy—such as political participation, free speech, civil liberties and social equality. Schools might develop these commitments through lessons in the skills of analysis and exploration, free political expression, and independent thought. And U.S. schools often support democratic dispositions in just such ways.

But teaching and learning do not always conform to democratic goals and ideals. Tensions abound, and, in recent years, some of the very foundations of democratic engagement, such as independent thinking and critical analysis, have come under attack. If being a good democratic citizen requires thinking critically about important social assumptions, then that foundation of citizenship is at odds with recent trends in education policy.

In the past five years, hundreds of schools, districts, states, and even the federal government have enacted policies that seek to restrict critical analysis of historical and contemporary events in the school curriculum. In June 2006, the Florida

Education Omnibus Bill included language specifying that "The history of the United States shall be taught as genuine history. ... American history shall be viewed as factual, not as constructed, shall be viewed as knowable, teachable, and testable" (Florida Senate 2006, 3).

Other provisions in the bill mandate "flag education, including proper flag display" and "flag salute," and require educators to stress the importance of free enterprise to the U.S. economy. But what some find most alarming is the stated goal of the bill's designers: "to raise historical literacy" with a particular emphasis on the "teaching of facts." For example, the bill requires that only facts be taught when it comes to discussing the "period of discovery" and the early colonies. Florida is perhaps the first state to ban historical interpretation in public schools, thereby effectively outlawing critical thinking (Craig 2006).

Of course, historians almost universally regard history as exactly a matter of interpretation; indeed, the competing interpretations are what make history so interesting. Historians and educators alike have widely derided the mandated adherence to an "official story" embodied in the Florida legislation, but the impact of such mandates should not be underestimated—especially because Florida is not alone.

The drive to engage schools in reinforcing a unilateral understanding of U.S. history and policy shows no sign of abating. More and more, teachers and students are seeing their schools or entire districts and states limiting their ability to explore multiple perspectives to controversial issues. Students and a drama teacher in a Connecticut high school spent months researching, writing and rehearsing a play they wrote about the Iraq war titled "Voices in Conflict." Before the scheduled performance, the school administration banned the play on the basis that it was "inappropriate." (The students went on to perform the play in the spring of 2007 on an off-Broadway stage in New York to impressive critical review.) In Colorado, a student was suspended for posting flyers advertising a student protest. In Bay City, Michigan, wearing a T-shirt with an anti-war quotation by Albert Einstein was grounds for suspension (American Civil Liberties Union 2004).

The federal role in discouraging critical analysis of historical events has been significant as well, especially following September 11, 2001. In 2002, six months before the start of the Iraq war, the U.S. Department of Education announced a new set of history and civic education initiatives that the president said would "improve students' knowledge of American history, increase their civic involvement, and deepen their love for our great country" (Bush 2002, 1). We must, he emphasized, teach our children that "America is a force for good in the world, bringing hope and freedom to other people." Similarly, in 2004, Tennessee Senator Lamar Alexander (former U.S. secretary of education under President Ronald Reagan) warned that educators should not expose students to competing ideas in historical texts. Civics, he argued, should be put back in its "rightful place in our schools, so our children can grow up learning what it means to be an American" (Alexander 2003a). Presumably, for Alexander, what it means to be an American is more answer than question. Reaching back to a 1950s understanding of the American past and the workings of American society, Alexander and likeminded politicians suggest that

Americans, while representing diverse backgrounds and cultures, are all part of a unified American creed or a common set of beliefs, and that these beliefs are easily identifiable. Explicitly borrowing from consensus historian Richard Hofstadter, Senator Alexander believes that "it has been our fate as a nation not to have ideologies but to be one" (Hofstadter, quoted in Alexander 2003b).

As many people have observed, the high-stakes testing mandated by No Child Left Behind (NCLB) has further pushed to the margins education efforts that challenge students to grapple with tough questions about society and the world. In a recent study by the Center on Education Policy (Rentner et al. 2006), 71 percent of districts reported cutting back time for other subjects—social studies in particular—to make more space for reading and math instruction. Indeed, historian David McCullough testified before a U.S. Senate committee that, because of NCLB, "history is being put on the back burner or taken off the stove altogether in many or most schools" (Dillon 2006). An increasing number of students are getting little to no education about how government works, about the Constitution, the Bill of Rights, the evolution of social movements, and U.S. and world history. As Peter Campbell (2006), Missouri State Coordinator for FairTest, noted,

> The sociopolitical implications of poor black and Hispanic children not learning about the Civil Rights movement, not learning about women's suffrage, not learning about the U.S. Civil War, and not learning about any historical or contemporary instance of civil disobedience is more than just chilling. It smacks of an Orwellian attempt not merely to rewrite history, but to get rid of it.

The implications Campbell describes are not limited to poor black and Hispanic students. Any student being denied knowledge about historical events and social movements misses out on important opportunities to link their education to the quintessentially democratic struggles for a better society for all.

I focus on history teaching here, but the trend is not limited to social studies. In many states, virtually every subject area is under scrutiny for any deviation from one single narrative, based on knowable, testable, and purportedly uncontested facts. An English teacher, in a recent study undertaken by colleagues and myself, told us that even novel reading was now prescriptive in her state's rubric: meanings predetermined, vocabulary words preselected, and essay topics predigested. A science teacher put it this way: "The only part of the science curriculum now being critically analyzed is evolution."

Although some of the more restrictive policies were pushed through legislatures seeking to respond immediately to the September 11 attacks, recent school reform efforts do not always seem to benefit from the kind of cooler and more clear-headed thinking that we might expect would come with time. I have previously written about a Nebraska law—Bill 982—that required school boards to appoint a committee on "Americanism" and to "[arrange] its curriculum in such a way that the love of … America will be instilled in the hearts and minds of the youth of the state" (Westheimer 2007; Westheimer & Kahne 2003). As a result, Nebraska's State Board of Education issued the following mandate: "Teaching citizenship [must] include instruction in … the benefits and advantages of our government, the dangers of … communism and similar ideologies, the duties of citizenship, and appropriate patriotic exercises." But as recently as April 2008, the Arizona House of Representatives passed SB 1108, specifying that schools whose teachings "denigrate or encourage dissent" from American values, "including democracy, capitalism, pluralism, and religious toleration," would lose state funding. Furthermore, the Arizona bill continues: "[P]ublic tax dollars should not be used to promote political, religious, ideological, or cultural values as truth when such values are in conflict with the values of American citizenship and the teachings of Western civilization." Under the proposed bill, schools would be required to surrender teaching materials to the state superintendent of public instruction, who could withhold state aid from districts that broke the law. In defending the proposed legislation, Representative Andy Biggs (R-Gilbert) argued that lawmakers are entitled to regulate the use of tax dollars taken from Arizonans and "demand that our publicly funded education teach and inculcate our youth, our children with the values that make America what it is, the greatest and most free nation in the world" (*East Valley Tribune*, April 16, 2008, p. 1).

At this point, some readers might be thinking that conditions seem bad for students unlucky enough to be in the public schools, but that, on the whole, many independent schools prepare students for a democratic society by offering a broad liberal education that asks them to grapple with difficult and contested policy issues. Evidence indicates otherwise. As the goals for K–12 public education have shifted away from preparing active and engaged public citizens and towards more narrow goals of career preparation and individual economic gain, independent schools have, in many ways, led the pack. Pressures from parents and board members, and a broad cultural shift in educational priorities, have resulted in schools across the country being seen primarily as conduits for individual success, and lessons aimed at exploring democratic responsibilities have increasingly been crowded out. A steadily growing body of research in the United States now echoes what Tony Hubbard, former director of the United Kingdom's Independent Schools Inspectorate, stated most plainly after reviewing data from an extensive study of British independent schools: because of the immense pressure to achieve high academic results on exams and elevate prestigious college entrance rates, independent schools are "over-directed" so that students do not have "sufficient opportunity or incentive to think for themselves." Increasingly following formulas that "spoon-feed" students to succeed on narrow academic tests, independent schools, Hubbard warned, "teach students not to think."

Too many schools have become increasingly oriented towards pedagogical models of efficiency that discourage deeper consideration of important ideas. The relentless focus on testing and "achievement" means that time for in-depth critical analysis of ideas is diminished. Social studies scholar Stephen Thornton (2005) notes that, by "critical thinking," school officials too often mean that students should passively absorb as "truth" the critical thinking already completed by someone else. Current school reform policies and many classroom practices too often reduce teaching and learning to exactly the kind of mindless rule-following that makes students unable to take principled stands that have long been associated with American democracy. The hidden curriculum of post-NCLB classrooms is how to please authority and pass the tests, not how to develop convictions and stand up for them.

What Kind of Citizen?

All is not bleak when it comes to educating for democratic understanding and participation. Many teachers across the country conduct excellent educational activities concerned with helping students become active, effective and thinking citizens. But even when educators are expressly committed to teaching "good citizenship," there is cause for caution. My colleague Joseph Kahne and I spent the better part of a decade studying programs that aimed to develop good citizenship skills among youth and young adults. In study after study, we come to similar conclusions: the kinds of goals and practices commonly represented in curricula that hope to foster democratic citizenship usually have more to do with voluntarism, charity and obedience than with democracy. In other words, "good citizenship" to many educators means listening to authority figures, dressing neatly, being nice to neighbors, and helping out at a soup kitchen—not grappling with the kinds of social policy decisions that every citizen in a democratic society needs to learn how to do.

In our studies of dozens of programs, we identified three visions of "good" citizens that help capture the lay of the land when it comes to citizenship education in the United States: the *personally responsible citizen*; the *Participatory citizen*; and the *social-justice oriented citizen* (Westheimer & Kahne 2004). It's worth summarizing the differences here so you might better be able to situate your own programs with which you are familiar among these kinds of goals. They can serve as a helpful guide to uncovering the variety of assumptions that fall under the idea of citizenship education (see table 19.1).

Personally responsible citizens contribute to food or clothing drives when asked and volunteer to help those less fortunate, whether in a soup kitchen or a senior-citizen center. They might contribute time, money, or both to charitable causes. Both those in the character education movement and those who advocate community service would emphasize this vision of good citizenship. They seek to build character and personal responsibility by emphasizing honesty, integrity, self-discipline and hard work. Or they nurture compassion by engaging students in volunteer community service.

Other educators lean towards a vision of the *participatory citizen*. Participatory citizens actively participate in the civic affairs and the social life of the community at local, state/provincial, and national levels. Educational programs designed to support the development of participatory citizens focus on teaching students about how government and other institutions (e.g., community-based organizations, churches) work and about the importance of planning and participating in organized efforts to care for those in need, for example, or in efforts to guide school policies. While the personally responsible citizen would contribute cans of food for the homeless, the participatory citizen might organize the food drive.

A third image of a good citizen, and perhaps the perspective that is least commonly pursued, is of individuals who know how to critically assess multiple perspectives.

TABLE 19.1 Kinds of Citizens

	Personally responsible citizen	*Participatory citizen*	*Social-justice oriented citizen*
DESCRIPTION	Acts responsibly in their community Works and pays taxes Picks up litter, recycles, and gives blood Helps those in need, lends a hand during times of crisis Obeys laws	Active member of community organizations and/or improvement efforts Organizes community efforts to care for those in need, promote economic development, or clean up environment Knows how government agencies work Knows strategies for accomplishing collective tasks	Critically assesses social, political, and economic structures Explores strategies for change that address root causes of problems Knows about social movements and how to effect systemic change Seeks out and addresses areas of injustice
SAMPLE ACTION	Contributes food to a food drive	Helps to organize a food drive	Explores why people are hungry and acts to solve root causes
CORE ASSUMPTIONS	To solve social problems and improve society, citizens must have good character; they must be honest, responsible, and law-abiding members of the community	To solve social problems and improve society, citizens must actively participate and take leadership positions within established systems and community structures	To solve social problems and improve society, citizens must question and change established systems and structures when they reproduce patterns of injustice over time

Source: Westheimer & Kahne (2004).

They are able to examine social, political and economic structures and explore strategies for change that address root causes of problems. We called this kind of citizen the *social-justice oriented citizen* because the programs fostering such citizenship emphasize the need for citizens to be able to think about issues of fairness, equality of opportunity, and democratic engagement. They share with the vision of the participatory citizen an emphasis on collective work related to the life and issues of the community. But the nature of these programs gives priority to students thinking independently, looking for ways to improve society, and being thoughtfully informed about a variety of complex social issues. These programs are less likely to emphasize the need for charity and volunteerism as ends in themselves, and more likely to teach about ways to effect systemic change. If *participatory citizens* organize the food drive and *personally responsible citizens* donate food, the *social-justice oriented citizens*—our critical thinkers—ask why people are hungry, then act on what they discover.

Currently, the vast majority of school programs that take the time to teach citizenship are the kind that emphasize either good character (including the importance of volunteering and helping those in need) or technical knowledge of legislatures and how government works. Far less common are schools that teach students to think about root causes of injustice or to challenge existing social, economic and political norms as a means for strengthening democracy.

Recall my earlier question: How would you know the difference between educational experiences in two schools—one in a totalitarian nation and one in a democratic one? Both the totalitarian nation and the democratic one might engage students in volunteer activities in the community—picking up litter from a nearby park, perhaps, or helping out at a busy intersection near a school or a senior-citizen center. Government leaders in a totalitarian regime would be as delighted as leaders in a democracy if their young citizens learned the lessons put forward by many of the proponents of personally responsible citizenship: don't do drugs; show up to work on time; give blood; help others during a flood; recycle; etc. These are all desirable traits for people living in a community. But they are not about democratic citizenship. Efforts to pursue some conceptions of personal responsibility might even undermine efforts to prepare participatory and justice-oriented citizens. Obedience and loyalty (common goals of character education), for example, may work against the kind of independent thinking that effective democracy requires.

All Children Thinking

There are many varied and powerful ways to teach children and young adults to think. While a significant body of work has been written in this regard (for example, Greene 2000; Kohn 2004; Noddings 2007; Shapiro 2005), I want to focus here on a few of the challenges and possibilities for curriculum aimed in particular at teaching the kind of thinking necessary for democratic societies to flourish. For example, longtime teacher Brian Schultz's inspiring efforts with his 5th grade class in Chicago's Cabrini-Green housing project area included having his students conduct research on improving conditions in their own neighborhood, especially with regard to broken promises to build a new school. His students studied historical approaches to change and, rejecting passivity, demonstrated a deep attachment to their community and neighbors (Schultz 2008).

Bob Peterson, a one-time Wisconsin Elementary Teacher of the Year, worked with his students at La Escuela Fratney in Madison to examine the full spectrum of ideological positions that emerged following the September 11, 2001, terrorist attacks. Instead of avoiding the challenging questions his 5th grade students posed, Peterson encouraged them, placing a notebook prominently at the front of the classroom labeled "Questions That We Have." As the students discussed their questions and the unfolding current events, Peterson repeatedly asked students to consider their responsibilities to one another, to their communities, and to the world. Through poetry (Langston Hughes's "Let America Be America Again"); historical readings (the Declaration of Independence, the U.S. Constitution, the 1918 Sedition Act); and current events (photographs of September 11 memorial gatherings, protests in the United States and abroad, newspaper editorials), Peterson allowed students to explore political events surrounding the September 11 attacks and their effect on American patriotism and democracy (Peterson 2007; Westheimer 2007).

El Puente Academy in the Williamsburg neighborhood of Brooklyn, New York, ties the entire school curriculum to students' and teachers' concerns about the community. Named a New York City School of Excellence, El Puente boasts a 90 percent graduation rate in an area where schools usually see only 50 percent of their students graduate in four years. El Puente principal Héctor Calderón attributes the school's success to a curriculum that engages students in efforts to realize democratic ideals of justice and equality, reverse the cycle of poverty and violence, and work towards change in their own neighborhood. Students study environmental hazards in the area, not only because they care about the health of the natural environment, but also because these hazards directly affect the health of the community to which they are deeply committed. El Puente students learn that thinking requires research, analysis, and imaginative interpretation–qualities virtually impossible to learn from an exclusive focus on narrow tests of knowledge and skills divorced from social, political, and economic contexts.

In one unit, students surveyed the community to chart levels of asthma and identify families affected by the disease. Their report became the first by a community organization to be published in a medical journal. Students and teachers also successfully fought a 55-story incinerator that was proposed for their neighborhood (Gonzales 1995; North Central Regional Educational Laboratory 2000; Westheimer 2005).

These approaches to a "thinking curriculum" share several characteristics. First, teachers encourage students to ask questions rather than absorb pat answers—to think about their attachments and commitments to their local, national, and global communities. Second, teachers provide students with the information (including competing narratives) they need to think about subject matter in substantive ways. Third, they root instruction in local contexts, working within their own specific surroundings and circumstances because it is not possible to teach democratic forms of thinking without providing an environment to think about. This last point makes nationally standardized tests difficult to reconcile with in-depth critical thinking about issues that matter.

21st-Century Strategies for Change

In the midst of the 2008 presidential election season, the educationally vapid No Child Left Behind legislation's final automatic extension expired with little fanfare. A curious provision in the General Education Provisions Act (GEPA) provides funding under this extension to endure the 2008–9 school year, but a mix of under-funding and arrogance on the part of federal lawmakers under the Bush administration has made renewing NCLB politically impracticable, at least for now. A great deal of damage, however, has already been wrought. State and district challenges to NCLB have focused almost exclusively on the fact that federal requirements do not come with associated funding and are therefore impossible to meet. While such opposition has allowed for unified action among diverse stakeholders, the failure to attack the specifically *educational* shortcomings of the legislation have helped establish attitudes towards school reform that will not fade as quickly as the legislative initiatives that encouraged them. At least three such attitudes reflect historically recurring obstacles to teaching thinking strategies that strengthen democratic life. They also pinpoint important levers for change.

Strategy #1: Go Beyond Facts

The most common criticism of educators who seek to teach students to think and interpret information is that they have no respect for facts, rigor and standards. Somehow, critics have become convinced that those who say they want students to think for themselves do not care whether students can read, write, or perform addition or subtraction. This is nonsense. But many educators do want students to know more than facts and formulas. They want the knowledge that students acquire to be embedded in the service of something bigger. It is not enough for them to learn how to read; they also need to learn to decide what is worth reading and why. In other words, they need to learn how to think.

Proponents of "factual" history also rapidly lose interest in facts when those facts call into question the "one true story." Teaching students to think will require reclaiming common assumptions about what thinking requires. There are few educators who believe that facts are unimportant components of a proper education. But at a time when vast databases of information are at our fingertips in seconds, facts alone represent a profoundly impoverished goal for educational achievement. Furthermore, students tend to learn more "facts" through thoughtful participation in meaningful projects of concern, but engagement in such projects of democratic importance is rarely driven by the acquisition of facts only. In short, knowledge does not necessarily lead to thoughtful participation. In many programs colleagues and I have studied that emphasized teaching about the workings of democratic government, legislative procedures, elections, and so on, students gained solid factual knowledge without necessarily gaining the inclination or the conviction required to participate (Kahne & Middaugh 2008; Hess 2009; Llewellyn et al. 2007). In fact, we found that often it worked the other way around: participation led to the quest for knowledge. Once students gained experiences in the community, they tended to ask deep and substantive questions that led them to research information they knew little about and, until then, had little inclination to learn.

Strategy #2: Be Political

In a lecture on citizenship in the 21st century, Harry Boyte, co-director of the University of Minnesota's Center for Democracy and Citizenship, argued that politics is the way people with different values and from different backgrounds can "work together to solve problems and create common things of value" (2002). In this view, politics is the process by which citizens with varied interests and opinions negotiate differences and clarify places where values conflict. Politics is, as Bernard Crick observed in his classic work *In Defence of Politics,* "a great and civilizing activity." To accept the importance of politics is to strive for deliberation and a plurality of views rather than a unified perspective on history, foreign policy or domestic affairs. If we are to educate thoughtful, civically engaged students, we must reclaim the important place for politics in classrooms in schools. Being political means embracing the kind of controversy and ideological sparring that is the engine of progress in a democracy and that gives education social meaning. The idea that "bringing politics into it" (now said disdainfully) is a pedagogically questionable act is, perhaps, the biggest threat to engaging students in thoughtful discussion.

Strategy #3: Embrace Pedagogical Diversity

Educators who value deep thinking about complex social issues are also those that often make the case that this kind of thinking can only be taught through the kind of "progressive" pedagogy that engages the students in every aspect of the curriculum—deciding what should be taught, choosing the focus of inquiry, researching the issues, and presenting to peers what they have found. A great number of (self-proclaimed) progressive educators insist that *only* by modeling democracy in the classroom and school can we teach any valuable lessons about what it means to be a thoughtful democratic citizen. After visiting dozens of school programs throughout the United States, Canada and elsewhere, I am more convinced than ever that the kind of teaching for democracy pursued in schools varies at least as much as the different visions of the good citizen discussed earlier. There is no one pedagogy matched inextricably to certain kinds of educational outcomes.

Daniel Perlstein wrote a superb study of Mississippi Freedom Schools of the 1960s showing, in part, that, although their message was always deeply democratic and oriented towards social justice, their pedagogy was not (2002). Indeed, Lisa Delpit, in "The Silenced Dialogue: Power and Pedagogy in Teaching Other People's Children" (1995), argues persuasively that some black parents and teachers view progressive pedagogy as a concerted effort to keep less advantaged students from learning the "culture of power" that progressive change towards justice demands. In her eyes, some parents of African American children would prefer that their children be told *exactly* what to do, how to spell correctly, the rules of grammar, and so on, because these rules and codes of the culture of power is exactly what their children need to know to get ahead. "If you are not already a participant in the culture of power," Delpit writes, "being told explicitly the rules of that culture makes acquiring power easier" (1995, 127).

The absence of a monolithic relationship between particular teaching strategies and related educational goals works the other way as well. There have been many successful efforts throughout history in teaching profoundly non-democratic, anti-thinking, authoritarian lessons through what appeared to be democratic means. Most of us associate fascism with goose-stepping soldiers marching on order from above. But one need only examine the methods of the Hitler

Youth brigades to note how "progressive" were aspects of their pedagogy—inclusive (within their group at least), community-oriented, highly social, collective and cooperative (Sunker & Otto 1997). The medium does not always make the message.

Indeed, one of the fathers of progressive education himself—John Dewey—broke ranks with the Progressive Education Association that he had founded because of the dogmatic homage to "child-centered" pedagogy that began to grip the organization. In *Experience and Education*, he writes passionately that "an educational philosophy which professes to be based on the idea of freedom may become as dogmatic as ever was the traditional education which is reacted against" (1916).

To be sure, teaching for democratic understanding requires attention to the democratic (or non-democratic) nature of the classroom and the school in which the teaching occurs. But it is clear from examining the myriad of excellent programs that abound that educators need not limit themselves to one particular teaching strategy to achieve democratic learning goals. Rather, truly progressive educators might do better to examine the underlying beliefs and political and ideological assumptions conveyed by the content of their curriculum. Teaching for democracy and teaching democratically are not always the same. To the extent that an overemphasis on pedagogy detracts from a clear examination of the underlying content and values of the lesson, the conflation of pedagogy and content might serve to conserve rather than transform educational goals. There is no one-size-fits-all solution to teaching children how to think for themselves.

An Invitation to Action

For more than two centuries, democracy in the United States has been predicated on citizens' informed and thoughtful engagement in civic and political life, and schools have been seen as essential to support the development of such citizens. "I know of no safe depository of the ultimate powers of society but the people themselves," Thomas Jefferson famously wrote, adding that, if the people are "not enlightened enough to exercise their control with a wholesome discretion, the remedy is not to take it from them, but to inform their discretion by education" (Jefferson [1820] 1899). Belief in the fundamental importance of teaching citizens how to think about the issues that affect their lives has been long-standing. And yet these beliefs are at risk in schools today. Relentless pressures from the business community to link the goals of education to the needs of corporations, for example, jeopardize the democratic foundations of education. Educators concerned with the narrowing goals of schooling should continue to pose publicly the kinds of question former president of the American Educational Research Association Larry Cuban (2004) asks: Do schools geared to preparing workers also build thinking, literate, active, and morally sensitive citizens who carry out their democratic civic duties?

For democracy to remain vibrant, educators must convey to students that critical thinking and action are both important components of democratic civic life. Moreover, students must learn that they have important contributions to make. Democracy is not a spectator sport.

The exit of the Canadian War Museum in Ottawa (where I live), dedicated to a critical history of war, bears the following inscription:

> History is yours to make. It is not owned or written by someone else for you to learn … History is not just the story you read. It is the one you write. It is the one you remember or denounce or relate to others. It is not predetermined. Every action, every decision, however small, is relevant to its course. History is filled with horror and replete with hope. You shape the balance.

I suspect many readers of this book could imagine a lesson in democratic thinking by beginning a discussion with just such a quotation. Think about it.

References

Alexander, L. (2003a) Senator Alexander's American History and Civics Bill Passes Senate Unanimously. Press Release, Senator Alexander's office, June 20.

Alexander, L. (2003b) Remarks of Senator Lamar Alexander on the Introduction of his Bill: The American History and Civics Education Act, March 4, 2003, http://www.congresslink.org/print_expert_amhist.htm.

American Civil Liberties Union (2004) Michigan School Reverses Suspension of Student for Wearing "Anarchy" T-Shirt [Press Release], http://www.aclu.org/StudentsRights/StudentsRights.cfm?ID=15672&c=159.

Boyte, H. C. (2002) A Different Kind of Politics: John Dewey and the Meaning of Citizenship in the 21st Century. Dewey Lecture, University of Michigan, November 1.

Bush, G. W. (2002) President Introduces History and Civic Education Initiatives, http://www.whitehouse.gov/news/releases/2002/09/20020917-1.html.

Campbell, P. (2006) Ballot Initiatives, Democracy, and NCLB. Transform Education [blog], October 18, http://transformeducation.blogspot.com/2006_10_01_archive.html.

Craig, B. (2006) The Coalition Column: History Defined in Florida Legislature. *Perspectives*, 44(6), 16. Available: http://www.historians.org/Perspectives/issues/2006/0609/0609nch1.cfm.

Crick, B. (1962) *In Defence of Politics*. London: Weidenfeld & Nicolson.

Cuban, L. (2004) Making Public Schools Business-Like … Again. *PS: Political Science and Politics*, 37, 2.

Delpit, L. (1995) The Silenced Dialogue: Power and Pedagogy in Educating Other People's Children. In *Other People's Children: Cultural Conflict in the Classroom* (pp. 119–39). New York: New Press.

Dewey, J. (1916) *Experience and Education*. Carbondale: University of Southern Illinois Press.

Dillon, S. (2006) Schools Cut Back Subjects to Push Reading and Math. *New York Times*, March 26, p. A1.

Florida Senate (2006) *SB 28, 11-53-06, A Bill to Be entitled An Act relating to Public K–12 Educational Instruction …*, http://www.flsenate.gov/data/session/2006/Senate/bills/billtext/pdf/s0028.pdf.

Gonzales, D. (1995) Alternative Schools: A Bridge from Hope to Social Action. *New York Times*, May 23, p. B2.

Greene, M. (2000) *Releasing the Imagination: Essays on Education, the Arts, and Social Change*. New York: Jossey-Bass.

Hess, D. (2009) *Controversy in the Classroom: The Democratic Power of Discussion*. New York: Routledge.

Jefferson, T. ([1820] 1899) Letter to William C. Jarvis, September 28, 1820. In P. I. Ford (Ed.), *The Writings of Thomas Jefferson* (Vol. 10, p. 161). New York: G. P. Putnam Sons.

Kahne, J., & Middaugh, E. (2008) *Democracy for Some: The Civic Opportunity Gap in High School.* Working Paper #59. Washington, DC: Center for Information and Research on Civic Learning [CIRCLE].

Kohn, A. (2004) *What Does it Mean to Be Well Educated?* Boston: Beacon Press.

Llewellyn, K., Cook, S., Westheimer, J., Molina-Giron, L., & Suurtamm, K. (2007) *The State and Potential of Civic Learning in Canada.* Ottawa: Canadian Policy Research Network.

Noddings, N. (2007) *Critical Lessons: What Our Schools Should Teach.* Cambridge: Cambridge University Press.

North Central Regional Educational Laboratory (2000) *Viewpoints*, Vol. 7: *Small by Design— Resizing America's High Schools.* Naperville, IL: Learning Points Associates.

Perlstein, D. (2002) Minds Stayed on Freedom: Politics and Pedagogy in the African-American Freedom Struggle. *American Educational Research Journal, 39,* 249–77.

Peterson, B. (2007) La Escuela Fratney: A Journey Toward Democracy. In M. Apple & J. Beane (Eds.), *Democratic Schools: Lessons in Powerful Education* (pp. 30–61). Portsmouth, NH: Heinemann.

Rentner, D. S., Scott, C., Kober, N., Chudowsky, N., Chudowsky, V., Joftus, S., et al. (2006) *From the Capital to the Classroom: Year 4 of the No Child Left Behind Act.* Washington, DC: Center on Education Policy.

Schultz, B. D. (2008) *Spectacular Things Happen Along the Way: Lessons from an Urban Classroom.* New York: Teachers College Press.

Shapiro, H. S. (2005) *Losing Heart: The Moral and Spiritual Mis-Education of America's Children.* New York: Lawrence Erlbaum.

Sunker, H., & Otto, H.-U. (Eds.) (1997) *Education and Fascism: Political Identity and Social Education in Nazi Germany.* London: Taylor & Francis.

Thornton, S. (2005) Incorporating Internationalism in the Social Studies Curriculum. In N. Noddings (Ed.), *Educating Citizens for Global Awareness* (pp. 81–92). New York: Teachers College Press.

Westheimer, J. (2005) *Real World Learning: El Puente Academy and Educational Change* (Democratic Dialogue occasional paper series). Ottawa, Ontario: DemocraticDialogue.com.

Westheimer, J. (2007) Politics and Patriotism in Education. In Westheimer (Ed.), *Pledging Allegiance: The Politics of Patriotism in America's Schools* (pp. 171–88). New York: Teachers College Press.

Westheimer, J., & Kahne, J. (2003) Reconnecting Education to Democracy: Democratic Dialogues. *Phi Delta Kappan, 85,* 1, 9–14.

Westheimer, J., & Kahne, J. (2004) What Kind of Citizen? The Politics of Educating for Democracy. *American Educational Research Journal, 41,* 2, 237–69.

Index